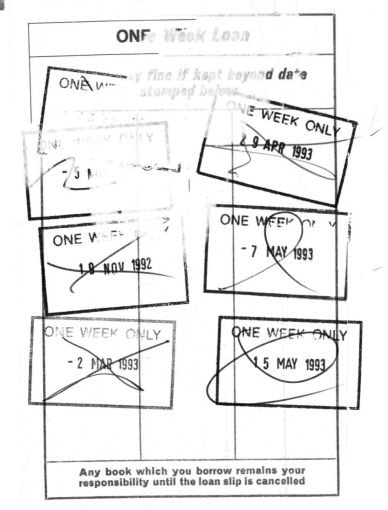

Visual Cognition

UNOTTSCI

Visual Cognition:
Computational, Experimental, and
Neuropsychological Perspectives

Glyn W. Humphreys
Cognitive Science Research Centre,
School of Psychology, University of Birmingham, U.K.

and

Vicki Bruce
Department of Psychology,
University of Nottingham, U.K.

LEA LAWRENCE ERLBAUM ASSOCIATES, PUBLISHERS LEA
Hove and London (UK)   Hillsdale (USA)

Reprinted, 1991

Lawrence Erlbaum Associates Ltd., Publishers
27 Palmeira Mansions
Church Road
Hove
East Sussex, BN3 2FA
U.K.

British Library Cataloguing in Publication Data

Humphreys, Glyn W.
 Visual cognition: computational, experimental and
 neuropsychological perspectives.
 1. Visual perception. Cognition
 I. Title II. Bruce, Vicki
 152.1'4

 ISBN 0-86377-124-6
 ISBN 0-86377-125-4 pbk

Typeset by Clear Image, London
Printed and bound by BPCC Wheatons, Exeter

For Jane and Michael (again)

For Jane and Michael again

Contents

Preface

This book was first conceived in 1981. It was to be written by Max Coltheart and Glyn Humphreys and called "Visual Information Processing". It was going to be short. The contents were going to be rather different too, with a lot on iconic memory and little on imagery. The neuropsychology was going to form a separate chapter at the end.

In the intervening years many things have changed: the authors (or at least one author), the title, much of the content and indeed the discipline itself. Only our publishers have remained constant, and patient, in the interim. Indeed, it was Michael Forster of Lawrence Erlbaum Associates who brought us together to write the book in its current form.

The text that has resulted from this collaboration is written for advanced undergraduate students in psychology and cognitive science. Our aim has been to present contemporary research in visual cognition—from early visual processing to reading and remembering—within an integrated framework. Drawing on three main research traditions (computational, experimental, and neuropsychological) we have tried to consider how converging evidence has resulted in real theoretical progress. This has meant changing the structure of the book as originally conceived, so that neuropsychological work is treated as an integral part of our analysis. However, pulling the different strands of the book together has not always been easy. The different traditions have differing aims as well as differing jargon. Although sometimes the perspectives gel, often there seem to be fundamental incompatibilities between them. We hope we have managed to conceal some of the bewilderment that we have experienced, though we have also tried not to gloss over all the difficulties and inconsistencies, particularly where we feel that these may actually stimulate future research. Certainly our efforts in jointly writing the book have led us to consider a number of future research projects. If reading the book has a similar effect on our students, then we will be more than satisfied.

Acknowledgements

The book has been considerably improved as a result of comments made by John Duncan, Rob Ellis, Jane Riddoch, and Roger Watt, and we thank them most sincerely for the care they took in reading the first draft, and for constructive suggestions that they furnished. Philip Quinlan helped to produce the final versions of the text, and Rohays Perry and Susan Wisniewska at Lawrence Erlbaum Associates took much of the last minute hassle from our own desks by organising the artwork and figure permissions where needed. Our reviewers, and the staff at LEA have had to work on these tasks at short notice and to tight deadlines because of our earlier inefficiencies, and for these we apologise. We should also like to thank Melanie Vitkovitch for preparing the Subject Index.

In these days of word processors, electronic mail, and desktop publishing, writing a book between Nottingham and London should be as easy as writing in the same department. It wasn't. Files sent from one machine to a different one at the other base would turn out to be unreadable, unprintable, too big, or too straight. We can honestly say that not a single thing that could go smoothly did. We would like to thank all the computer boffins at our respective institutions for their efforts in overcoming these difficulties which were entirely of their own making.

Finally, we must thank our families and spouses for their forebearance in these difficult final stages during which we have so comprehensively neglected both them and our domestic duties. We look forward to the Riddoch and Burton revenge text.

1

An Introduction to Methods for Studying Visual Cognition

OVERVIEW OF THE BOOK

Vision allows us to do many things. It enables us to perceive a world composed of meaningful objects and events. It enables us to track those events as they take place in front of our eyes. It enables us to read. It provides accurate spatial information for actions such as reaching for, or avoiding objects. It provides colour and texture that can help to camouflage objects against their background, and so forth. This book is concerned with understanding the processes that allow us to carry out these various visually driven behaviours.

The study of visual processing has been undertaken by psychologists for over a century. During this time a wide variety of approaches has been adopted. Psychophysical and other experimental studies have examined how perception is affected by the systematic manipulation of stimulus variables, and have provided important information about the processes of normal human vision. However, for a few unfortunate recipients of brain injury, the normal processes of vision can break down. Objects or faces may appear to lack form, or to lose their familiarity. Sometimes the world may subsequently appear in shades of black, white, and grey, whereas colours were previously seen quite normally. Neuropsychological studies of such individuals provide important converging evidence concerning the identity of various visual processes; for instance, by examining which processes survive when others are impaired we can learn about the relations between different visual processes. Recently, these psychophysical and neuropsychological studies have been supplemented to some degree by neurophysiological investigations of single cells in the visual pathway of animals, and of how these cells respond to different images.

More recently still, the study of visual perception has been enhanced by the work of cognitive scientists working on computer vision. Theories of vision may be explicitly formulated and rigorously tested using computer models, and even computer vision systems which make no attempt to model human vision, may sometimes yield insights which are important to us (for example, by demonstrating that a particular problem is soluble by certain sorts of methods).

This book provides perhaps the first attempt to integrate research from these different traditions within a single textbook. Indeed, as the late David Marr (1982) has argued forcefully, each kind of research has a particular role to play in the development of theories of vision. Computer simulation helps us determine whether a particular algorithm (a particular formal procedure) delivers the desired results. Psychophysical studies, of both normal and brain-injured subjects, can tell us whether the algorithm is that used by the human visual system or not. Neurophysiological studies can elucidate the way in which a particular algorithm may be implemented in the brain. Marr also emphasised, however, that an important level of theory involves understanding the abstract nature of the task faced by the visual system, and this level of understanding, which Marr termed "computational theory", requires analysis of the optical information presented to the visual system and the mathematical methods which could, in principle, be used to unravel this information. This study of vision at an abstract or "in principle" level will also feature in our book, particularly in Chapter 2, which deals with the area in which Marr himself made such a contribution, namely the way in which the visual system analyses stimulus dimensions.

We divide the book according to the different processing functions that vision provides. Chapter 2 begins by considering relatively "early" stages of visual processing which furnish descriptions from two-dimensional images of the three-dimensional layout of the visual world from the observer's point of view. Other processes operate on the information specified in these first stages. Chapter 3 concerns object recognition, and in particular how the viewer-centred representations of the world are transformed so that we can recognise the identities of familiar objects encountered on different occasions and seen from different points of view. Furthermore, the images of the world that fall on our retinas are constantly changing as we move relative to objects, or as objects move within a scene. We need to understand how vision enables us to see not a set of swirling, drifting, coloured patches, but people, animals, cars, etc. moving in a stable environment of surfaces and anchored objects. That is, we need to understand how vision operates dynamically. Chapter 4 is devoted to this topic. Chapters 5 to 7 are concerned with some of the other functions provided by vision. In Chapter 5 we consider the alerting function of vision, which allows us to orient our eyes and bodies in order to examine things which may prove important or threatening. In Chapter 6 we discuss the nature of visual memory and its relation to the processes involved when we perceive objects. In the final chapter, we discuss how human visual processes have been adapted to allow linguistic materials to be transcribed and read, and how the representations used for reading relate to those used in evolutionarily older activities, such as object recognition. In each chapter we try to integrate psychophysical, neuropsychological, and computational research, to provide a rich picture of the processes that make up visual cognition.

CHARACTERISTICS OF THE DIFFERENT METHODOLOGIES

Before we embark on our discussion of the visual analysis of stimulus dimensions, it is useful to contrast the emphases of the different methodological approaches we will cover, as this will provide us with a clearer idea of the goals of each approach and the way in which the approaches fit together.

Computational Studies

Attempts to implement object recognition in computers have particularly emphasised the importance of understanding real-world constraints on visual processing because it makes little sense to build a computer vision system without first understanding the nature of the information in the image that must be analysed and interpreted. Thus, a first step in computer vision requires that the "computational constraints" of the visual world are specified. The physical world has certain natural properties that are unlikely to occur accidently (e.g. when there is no object in the scene); for instance, the surfaces of objects tend to be relatively smooth, and abrupt changes in surface texture tend to occur only at the edges of the objects; also parallel or symmetrical edges tend only to occur when they are part of the same object. Because of these properties, certain "non-accidental" aspects of an image can (generally) be taken to indicate the presence of particular stimulus properties. Thus, the presence of abrupt changes in surface texture indicates an edge, and the presence of parallel edges most likely indicates the sides of an object. Indeed, by taking account of such properties of the world, problems such as finding the points of correspondence between the images in our two eyes can be solved formally (see Chapter 2).

Having formally identified these non-accidental properties, the investigator may then set about building a system capable of detecting them. The important point is that, because constraints are determined by the world and not by the particular visual system concerned (be it a computer or a person), then specifying the constraints is important for understanding human as well as computer visual systems. Many approaches to computer vision also emphasise the importance of modular processes. When writing computer programs it is often useful to divide a large program up into a number of sub-routines, which can be amended without altering the rest of the program. These sub-routines can be thought of as "modules", each specialised for handling a particular part of a task—each accepting particular inputs and delivering particular outputs to other modules in the system. The behaviour of the system can then be characterised by the pattern of interaction between the different processing modules. This idea of modularity provides us with an initial framework for thinking about vision. For instance, different modules may exist for processing different stimulus characteristics, such as the colour, or motion of a stimulus. Indeed, a case can even be made for the existence of modules specialised for the recognition of particular classes of stimuli, such as faces or words relative to other types of objects (see Chapters 3 and 7). We can thus divide up the problems of vision according to the nature of the different stimulus characteristics that must be analysed. Even if strict modularity does not hold within the human visual system (e.g. if systems interact to affect each other's outputs), the assumption of modular processes provides a good starting point for understanding the problem.

One other point to note is that work on computer vision differs according to how closely the solutions adopted match those found in human vision. In some cases, direct analogies can be made between the algorithms adopted in computer and human vision—David Marr's (1982) work being a case in point (see Chapter 2). Other solutions may differ quite radically. For instance, in Chapter 3 we discuss WISARD, a program developed for object and face recognition by Wilkie, Aleksander, and Stonham at Imperial College, London (e.g. Aleksander, 1983). WISARD essentially recognises stimuli by analysing the statistical properties of two-dimensional images—a solution to object and face recognition that is probably quite unlike that found in human vision. Nevertheless, by providing an explicit formulation of how face recognition might take place, programs such as WISARD give us a model against which we can contrast and thus learn about human vision.

Neuropsychological Studies

Neuropsychological studies of vision typically attempt to understand the visual impairments caused by lesions to specific areas of the brain. One of the basic tenets of neuropsychological research is that dissociations between processes are more informative than associated deficits. It is true that patients can suffer a range of associated deficits following brain damage; for instance, disorders of cortical colour perception typically co-occur with problems in face and object recognition (see Meadows, 1974). Indeed, such associations may even be more common than patterns of dissociation. However, associations could reflect the anatomical proximity of the processes, not their functional dependence. Brain lesions do not naturally respect boundaries between the functional components of information processing, so that it is likely that more than one process may be compromised after any given lesion. On the other hand, dissociations, and in particular double dissociations (see later), can be used to argue that two processes are functionally independent of one another.

Now, when a lesion produces a loss of one ability (a single dissociation), it could simply be that that ability was particularly difficult prior to the lesion, and so could be the first to be impaired after brain insult. This argument cannot be so readily applied when a double dissociation occurs. The term double dissociation refers to a situation where one patient (patient A) is impaired at an ability that can be shown to be intact in a second patient (patient B), even though patient A is intact on tasks where patient B is impaired. An example would be where one patient has impaired colour perception along with intact movement perception, whilst another patient has impaired perception of movement along with intact colour perception. If task difficulty was the sole cause of the problems experienced by the patients, it should not be possible for the task found difficult by one patient to be easy for the other patient, and vice versa. Rather, such double dissociations suggest that the abilities are based on separable processes so that one process can be impaired without drastically affecting the other. This argument can be refined even further. It may be that two processes normally interact, but that either could be impaired without producing equivalent impairment in the other. Two such processes could be said to be functionally separable (see Patterson & Morton, 1985). However, if the spared process can be shown to operate quite normally, it can be argued even more strongly that the two processes are not simply separable, but that they operate independently in normality—as the loss of one apparently has no effect on the other. That is, the two processes operate as separable modules. An interesting question is then whether the "modules" identified by neuropsychological studies mesh with those proposed by workers in other fields. We return to this question at various points throughout the book.

Neuropsychological studies can emphasise either the nature of the impaired processes or the location of the damage suffered by a particular patient. By identifying the precise location of the damage, investigators hope to learn about the role of specific neural mechanisms in vision. For instance, the occipital lobes at the back of the brain receive the major projections from the retina, and are conventionally thought of as the primary centre for visual processing in the brain. After initially passing to the occipital lobes, visual information is then passed forward in the brain along separate pathways to the parietal and temporal lobes (respectively at the top and side of the brain). Now, the kinds of visual processing problems experienced by patients with occipital lesions tend to differ from those experienced by patients with lesions to the parietal or temporal lobes. Crudely put, occipital lesions tend to produce deficits in "early" stages of visual processing concerned with the analysis of specific visual dimensions (such as colour or depth; see Chapter 2). Parietal lesions can affect the ability of patients to orient to visual stimuli (see Chapter 5). Temporal lesions can impair processes concerned with object recognition and naming (Chapter 3). Accordingly, one might argue that the occipital cortex is the site of early visual processing, the parietal cortex the site of visual orienting, and the temporal cortex the site of object recognition.

However, there are also problems connected with localisation arguments. One is that patients with the same functional deficits (in terms of the visual processes that are impaired) may often have lesions affecting different brain sites. In such instances it is difficult to know whether there are simply individual differences in the neural implementation of visual processes, or whether the processing function is itself distributed across a number of brain sites and so can be affected by lesions to more than one area.

The second problem connected with localisation arguments is that lesions may sometimes "disconnect" processes, rather than impairing them *per se*. In this case, it is misleading to conclude that a particular visual process is located at the lesion site, as the lesion affects the interaction between different areas in the brain. We consider this argument most explicitly when we deal with visual attention in Chapter 5; nevertheless, the argument could be raised in other places.

Because of the above problems, and because a focus on the "neuro" of neuropsychology would change our emphasis from the processes involved in visual cognition, we do not dwell on the locus or nature of the lesions suffered by different patients.

Neurophysiological Studies

Neurophysiological studies, by their very nature, concern the way in which visual processes are implemented in the brain. Because of their emphasis on neural implementation, rather than on the nature of the processes alone, our coverage of neurophysiological work is less extensive than our coverage of the other relevant areas of empirical work. Nevertheless, much of the early psychophysical work on the analysis of stimulus dimensions was strongly influenced by investigations of the properties of cells in the retina and the occipital cortex (see Chapter 2). More recently, neurophysiological work emphasising the selective responses of cells to particular stimulus properties, such as colour or motion, has influenced thinking about the modular organisation of visual processing—linking closely to studies of patients showing selective losses of the ability to perceive these different characteristics. In such instances, neurophysiological work is directly relevant to our present concern with the functional organisation of vision.

Psychophysical and Other Experimental Studies

Psychophysical studies involve detailed investigation of how different stimulus characteristics affect performance (often that of highly trained observers). To isolate the effects of stimulus characteristics, investigators often use stimuli that vary along only one dimension (such as colour, depth or motion; see Chapters 2 and 4). From such studies we learn about the "tuning" of the visual system to different properties of the image. This knowledge can then be used to guide the choice of algorithms by workers in the field of computational vision. For instance, in Chapters 2 and 4 we discuss algorithms to compute shape information using only stereo-depth and motion cues that have been developed because, at least in part, psychophysical studies have shown that stereo-depth and motion cues alone can be used to derive shape information.

Unfortunately, when stimulus characteristics are eliminated from displays we lose the opportunity to study how they influence vision when combined with the variables under study—for instance, how shape cues combine with stereo-depth cues to influence depth perception (see Chapter 2). Yet, in the real world we are faced with multiple cues, whose interaction may be important for normal functioning. Also, psychophysical studies are often concerned with measuring the limits of our perception (e.g. by determining the threshold for a given task). Outside the laboratory however, cues are presented supra-threshold, so that it can be difficult to extrapolate from the laboratory to the field.

For reasons such as these, it is useful to consider the evidence offered by other experimental approaches, such as that offered by reaction time (RT) studies. In RT studies stimuli are typically presented above threshold, and RTs to perform various tasks are measured. It is assumed that the visual processes engaged during the tasks each take a finite length of time, so that the durations of particular processes and their relations to other processes are revealed by the time subjects take to respond. RT studies are not without their own problems. For instance, such studies are often compounded by factors concerned with decision making rather than visual processing alone, making it difficult to pin-point any particular effect within the chain of processes leading to the response. Despite this, RT studies at least provide an opportunity for various visual processes to interact with one another, and thus provide an important further source of insight into visual processing.

Converging Evidence

From our brief discussion it is clear that each approach has both virtues and vices. Our understanding of vision from any single line of evidence will be subject to certain limitations. However, by considering data from each different approach, the limitations of any particular area can be lessened if not overcome. It is thus important to look for converging evidence from research within computer vision, neuropsychology, neurophysiology, psychophysics, and experimental psychology. The value of converging evidence from these differing sources will become apparent at a number of points in our book.

2 Seeing Static Forms

INTRODUCTION

In this chapter, we begin by considering relatively early stages of visual processing which furnish descriptions of the three-dimensional layout of the visual world from the observer's point of view. The input upon which these early stages operate is the retinal image.

Each eye acts to focus *images* of a viewed scene on to the light-sensitive retina. This camera-like function of the eye has encouraged psychologists, physiologists, and computer scientists to consider visual perception as resulting from the processing of a rapid succession of such retinal "snapshots". In these terms, motion becomes a complication—something which is to be added back in during the process of perception. We will adopt this position to begin with, and consider first the perception of artificially static patterns, returning to consider the analysis of motion in Chapter 4. Before discussing how the visual system processes such images, we must first consider the nature of images, the kinds of structures which might be detected within them, and the relationship between image properties and world properties. An understanding of the structures to be perceived can place important constraints on theories of how perception proceeds (cf. Garner, 1978; Marr, 1982).

WHAT IS PERCEIVED?

Properties of Intensity Distributions

Let us first consider ways of describing the structures present in a two-dimensional, static, monochrome image. An example of such an image is shown in the photograph in Fig. 2.1. As it has been explicit in most

FIG. 2.1. (a) An image made up of 256 × 256 square pixels with 256 grey levels. The same image is represented with 64^2 pixels at (b), 32^2 at (c) and with only 4 grey levels at (d). (Images processed by Ian Craw and David Tock.)

psychological and computational treatments of vision that the starting point for perception is a retinal "image" of the world, descriptions of the structures present in photographs can give us insight into the kinds of structures that the visual system might itself detect in retinal images.

Any image can be described as comprised of a finite, but huge, number of picture elements *(pixels)* each with its own particular degree of lightness or darkness *(grey level)*. Some images, such as newspaper photographs, are actually printed in this way. For others, the pixel description is an approximation of underlying continuous changes in intensity. In the example shown in Fig. 2.1a, the image is made up of 256^2 pixels each of

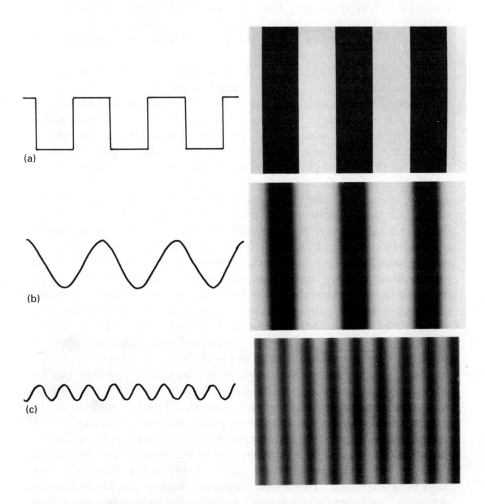

FIG. 2.2.   (a) A square wave pattern; (b) and (c) sine wave patterns. The sine wave shown in (c) has three times the frequency and a third the amplitude of that at (b). The intensity distributions of each pattern are plotted at the left.

which can take any one of 256 shades of grey. We can think of each of these pixels as replacing a discrete, square-shaped sample of the intensity from the original array of light impinging on the photograph, with the average intensity within the square. The more pixels and the more grey levels used to record an image, the finer the "grain" of the picture and the more closely it will approximate underlying continuous changes in intensity. If fewer pixels and grey levels are used, then less fine detail will be recorded, although overall shapes may still be preserved. Figure 2.1b and c show the image of Fig. 2.1a reduced to 64^2 and 32^2 pixels respectively, and Fig. 2.1d shows it reduced to only four different grey levels. Thus, the first (and most long-winded) way of describing the information content of an image would be to specify the grey level of each pixel present. The number of different shades of grey used, and the scale of the spatial sampling, would determine the degree to which the fine details of the structure are preserved in this description.

A rather different understanding of the kind of information contained in pixel descriptions of different "grains" can be gained by considering images as spatial *patterns* in which intensity varies continuously (rather than in discrete pixel samples) as a function of distance from a fixed point in the pattern. To do this it is easier, to begin with, to consider a spatial pattern which varies in only one dimension. Figure 2.2 shows three different patterns of stripes, and plots out each of these patterns as a distribution of light intensity as a function of position (from left to right across the pattern). In each case, the stripes can be described as a *waveform*. The rise and fall in the intensity of the pattern of "sharp" stripes (Fig. 2.2a) describes a square wave pattern, while the rise and fall in the gradually changing stripes (Fig. 2.2b) describes a sine wave pattern. A sine wave pattern has a *spatial frequency,* which describes how many cycles of the pattern there are per unit of distance, where a cycle describes a full excursion from the darkest point in one stripe to the darkest point in the next dark stripe. A pattern also has an *amplitude,* which describes the difference in intensity between the darkest and brightest points in the pattern. Figure 2.2c shows a sine wave pattern of three times the frequency and a third of the amplitude of that in Fig. 2.2b.

Sine wave patterns are not very common in nature, but they can be shown to be the basic mathematical elements from which all sorts of other, more natural patterns can be constructed. "Fourier analysis" is a mathematical technique for decomposing a *complex* waveform into a set of simple, *sine wave* components of appropriate frequencies and amplitudes. A square wave pattern, for example, can be decomposed into an infinite series of sine wave components of ever increasing frequency and decreasing amplitude. The lowest frequency, highest amplitude component (the "fundamental" frequency) describes the overall rise and fall in intensity of the stripes of the square wave, whereas the higher frequency, lower amplitude components contribute to the description of the sharp edges of the square wave stripes. (For the square wave, all these higher frequency components have frequencies which are simple integral multiples of the fundamental frequency: such higher frequencies are termed "harmonics".) Figure 2.3 shows how the first few sine wave components of the square wave can be added back together to yield a pattern which

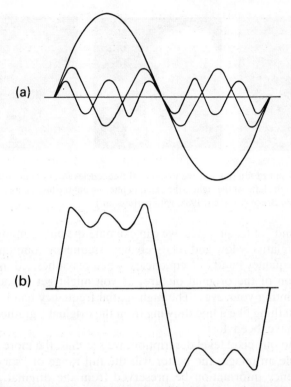

FIG. 2.3. The synthesis of a complex waveform (b) which approximates to a square wave by the addition of fundamental frequency, its third harmonic and its fifth harmonic (at one-third and one-fifth amplitude of the fundamental respectively). (Reproduced from Bruce & Green, 1985, with permission.)

approximates a square wave in shape. The more high frequency components we add back in, the better the approximation. Lower spatial frequency components thus describe the overall configuration of a pattern, while the higher spatial frequency components add in finer local details.

Thus, a rather different way of describing the information in an image is to list its underlying sine wave components. The analysis is complicated when spatial variations in two dimensions, rather than one, are considered, as the orientation of each sine wave component must also be specified, but the principles remain the same. The lower spatial frequency components describe the rough overall variations in intensity, while higher spatial frequency components add the sharp details of local components. Figure 2.4 illustrates this for a complex, two-dimensional pattern—a human face. If we decompose the picture of the face into its underlying spatial frequency components, and then resynthesise the components from just a

FIG. 2.4. The result of filtering out the low spatial frequencies from the photograph in the centre is shown at the left. At the right is the result of filtering out the high spatial frequencies. (Reproduced from Bruce & Green, 1985, with permission.)

restricted "band" of frequencies, we can examine the different information conveyed by relatively low and relatively high frequency components. The low spatial frequency band of frequencies, when resynthesised, produces a "fuzzy" version of the original picture, as you might get if you blur the image by squinting your eyes. The high spatial frequency band, however, produces something like a line drawing from the original—gradual changes in intensity have been lost.

Returning to our pixel level description, we see that, the more pixels are used to sample an image, the better will the full range or "spectrum" of spatial frequency information be preserved from the original. If a very coarse chunking of the image is used, then only the lower spatial frequencies will be preserved. Thus "coarse quantisation" (or pooling) of an image into larger sized pixels is one way of representing only the lower spatial frequencies from the original. There is a problem with using coarse quantisation to filter out the higher spatial frequencies, however. The sampling of average intensities from regularly shaped areas of the original introduces new higher spatial frequency components not present in the original image by introducing "edges" to each of the resulting pixels. The use of different kinds of averaging function can reduce this problem. For example, suppose that instead of taking the arithmetic mean intensity over a series of square patches, we took a weighted average in a circular region around each of a series of spaced points, so that the average reflected the contribution of the central part of the circle more than the outer part. By doing this, we can again blur the image, to an extent dependent upon the size of the circles, but in a much smoother way, which does not introduce high spatial frequency noise. Later in this chapter we will discuss how the human visual system seems to operate in just this kind of way.

What relevance has this discussion of pixels and spatial frequencies to our concern with human vision? The retinal image itself can be considered as an array of pixels—because there are a finite number of light-sensitive receptor cells, each responding as a function of the amount of light they receive. Thus, by its very structure, the human visual system can be thought of as encoding an initial pixel-like description. The responses of these receptor cells are pooled at the ganglion cells, via complex connections of amacrine, horizontal, and bipolar cells. Particularly in the periphery of the retina, some ganglion cells pool information from relatively large areas of the retina—they are described as having large "receptive fields", whereas ganglion cells near the fovea have smaller receptive fields. The pooling of responses across larger receptive fields can be thought of as one step on the way to achieving a very rough spatial frequency analysis of the image, it achieves a kind of coarse quantisation of the intensities in the original image. (We will discuss the receptive field organisation in much more detail later in the chapter. For the moment note that the way in which ganglion cells pool information serves also to enhance responses to intensity *changes* in the image.)

In addition to such physiological considerations, there is a considerable body of psychophysical evidence which suggests that the human visual system does indeed handle different bands of spatial frequency in different channels. The sensitivity of the human visual system to different spatial

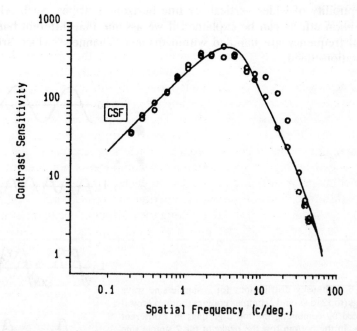

FIG. 2.5. Data (from Campbell & Robson, 1968) showing the contrast sensitivity of observers to sine wave gratings of different spatial frequencies (measured in cycles per degree of visual angle). The solid line is the theoretical prediction from MIRAGE (see p. 29) which gives a very good fit. (Adapted from Watt, 1988.)

frequencies is most often studied by measuring how much "contrast" between the dark and light stripes of a pattern is needed for the pattern to be seen as "striped" rather than uniform in intensity. The contrast is defined as (Imax − Imin)/(Imax + Imin) where Imax and Imin are the maximum and minimum intensities of the stripes. Contrast sensitivity is the reciprocal of the contrast at threshold—the value of Imax and Imin at which the subject can just discern that the test pattern is striped. When such measures are made for sine wave patterns of different spatial frequency, the contrast sensitivity function shown in Fig. 2.5 is obtained (e.g. Campbell & Robson, 1968). Human vision is very much more sensitive to intermediate spatial frequencies than to very low (broad stripes) or very high spatial frequencies (narrow stripes). The sensitivity to different frequencies can, however, be selectively affected by adaptation. In 1969, Blakemore and Campbell found that prolonged viewing of high-contrast gratings of particular spatial frequencies selectively affected the detectability of low-contrast gratings of similar spatial frequency and orientation. For example, looking at a pattern of fine vertical stripes made it more difficult to see fine vertical stripes—the threshold contrast between the dark and light stripes was elevated for a few seconds following adaptation. Adaptation to fine vertical stripes did not, however, affect the perceptibility of wider vertical, or fine horizontal stripes. Such selective adaptation effects can be explained if we assume that different bands of spatial frequency are handled within distinct "channels" which are also orientation-tuned.

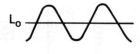

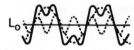

FIG. 2.6. Intensity distributions for 2 simple sine wave gratings (top 2 rows) and 2 complex gratings (bottom 2 rows) produced by combining the top 2 gratings in 2 different phases. In the bottom row the peaks of the 2 simple sine waves *add*, whereas in the row above the peaks *subtract*. Reproduced from Graham & Nachmias, 1971, with permission.)

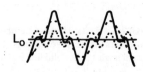

There have been numerous similar demonstrations consistent with spatial frequency tuned channels (Braddick, Campbell, & Atkinson, 1978; Woodhouse & Barlow, 1982 give reviews of this literature). We will mention just two further experiments. Graham and Nachmias (1971) argued that if there were independent channels for different bands of spatial frequency, and if these channels reached threshold independently, then the threshold for detecting a grating comprised of two sine waves should be independent of the *phase* of its sine wave components. If we make a complex waveform by adding a low frequency fundamental and higher frequency harmonic sine wave together, the second wave can be superimposed so that its peaks *add* with those of the first, or so that its peaks *subtract* (see Fig. 2.6). Now, as Fig. 2.6 illustrates, the contrast between the peaks and troughs in the combined waveforms differs according to their phase relations. If the visual system were just sensitive to "total" contrast in a single channel then we might expect different thresholds for the two complex waveforms. In particular, where the peaks add, we might expect that the complex waveform could be detectable even though the contrast of each of its components is below the threshold for its detection when presented alone. If the visual system handles spatial frequencies in multiple channels, however, then it should make no difference whether the peaks add or subtract in the complex wave—the threshold for the detection of the complex waveform would never be lower than that for the most detectable of its two component waves. Graham and Nachmias examined the detectability of such gratings and found that their data were compatible with the mutiple- rather than single-channel model. More specifically, their data led them to suggest that the visual system contains at least three, and possibly more independent channels tuned to different bands of spatial frequency.

Stromeyer and Julesz (1972) adopted a similar logic, and examined the detectability of a simple sinusoidal grating in the presence of masking "noise"—a complex pattern of stripes which contained a range of different spatial frequency components. They found that the detectability of the simple grating was unaffected by the presence of noise provided that the noise was filtered so that it contained no spectral components within two octaves of the frequency of the "target" grating. Experiments such as these suggest that the visual system handles spatial frequencies within distinct, although rather broadly tuned, channels.

Component and Configurational Properties of Patterns

So far, we have described how the raw material of visual perception—an image—may be described as an array of intensities or as a "spectrum" of spatial frequencies, and we have outlined how the visual system itself appears to use both these levels of description in the early processing of retinal images.

Describing the details of the intensity distributions of a picture is about the lowest-possible level description of the structure present. When we look at a photograph we can describe local properties such as edges and corners of different sizes and at different orientations, and moré global properties such as repetition (as in the striped patterns of Fig. 2.2a), and symmetry. We might just as legitimately describe Fig. 2.2a as a set of vertical bars, as describe it as an infinite set of sine wave components. The problem is that whereas an analytic system such as Fourier analysis is rigorous and formal, the ways in which people talk about local and global properties of patterns is informal, and inconsistent. As Garner (1978, p. 100) decries:

> Unfortunately, the language used by psychologists to describe different properties of stimuli is so poorly differentiated that it is difficult at times to avoid the feeling of chaos. One writer refers to dimensions that have levels (values to another writer), and another talks of variables and their aspects.

Garner (1974; 1978) has produced a set of formal definitions for describing pattern variations. At the level of local components, he distinguishes *features* of patterns from *dimensions* of patterns. A feature is either present or absent. Thus a line can be a feature, and its presence or absence is what distinguishes a "Q" shape from an "O" shape. A dimension, in contrast, has different levels of variation and may be continuous or discrete. Line length, orientation, brightness, or shape could be dimensions which vary continuously between patterns, whereas "number of spots" could be a dimension with discrete levels of variation. Most natural patterns have dimensional components such as size, orientation, and so forth, but some man-made patterns (including letters) may have key variations better captured in terms of features, as in the example of "Q" and "O", earlier. Often, it is quite possible to use features and dimensional descriptions interchangeably. An "E" differs from an "F" in terms of the presence or absence of an extra horizontal line (a feature), or in terms of its value on the (discrete) dimension "number of horizontal lines". Garner (1978) argues that the visual system seems to prefer "feature" descriptions in many information-processing tasks. We will consider the possible relevance of this a little later.

Whether features or dimensions, a simple description of components is not sufficient to make important distinctions about the *configurations* of these components. A configuration is a "wholistic" property of an entire pattern which is not captured by a simple list of the feature or dimensional values present, but emerges from some aspect of their spatial relationship. For example, Bruce and Morgan (1975) investigated the perceptual

FIG. 2.7.   It is easier to detect a slight violation to bilateral symmetry than to detect repetition about the vertical midline in matrix patterns such as these (Bruce & Morgan, 1975).

salience of bilateral *symmetry*. In computer-generated random matrix patterns in which the right half of each pattern bore a regular relation to the left half, observers found it easier to detect a slight violation of symmetry than of repetition about the vertical midline (see Fig. 2.7). Here the "features" of the symmetrical and repeated patterns were similar—it was their configural relations which differed.

Garner's distinctions between features, dimensions, and configurations give us some clear directions for considering the processing of two-dimensional patterns such as geometric shapes and alphanumeric characters. We must understand how the visual system derives from a distribution of intensities, or of spatial frequency components, a description of these more informative components of an image.

During the 1960s, it seemed that neurophysiological research would provide the answers to these questions, with the discovery by Hubel and Wiesel (1959; 1968) of "feature detectors" in the visual cortex of cats—so-called "simple cells" which responded strongly when stimuli such as bars or edges at particular orientations were presented within their receptive fields. It was thought that such feature detectors could be built from pooling responses from rows of ganglion cells having the centre-on or centre-off organisation which we describe later (see Lindsay & Norman, 1976, for an example). The problem is, however, that the response of a "feature" detector built in this way is inherently ambiguous (Marr, 1976). A "vertical edge detector" built in this way could not, for example, distinguish a dim vertical edge from a brighter line oriented away from the vertical. For this reason, recent years have seen a reinterpretation of the functions of cortical simple cells, and it is these more recent ideas which we will discuss later in this chapter.

An even more fundamental problem with theories of perception which stress the detection of simple components, such as features, is that the perception of images which are to be understood *only* in two dimensions, is rather rare, and probably occurs frequently only when we are reading. More often, any retinal image is interpreted as a projection of the world.

Properties of the World

In the preceding section, we mentioned some ways in which we can describe the structures in images of the world, and mentioned some of the mechanisms which might be involved in the internal construction of such descriptions by the human visual system. When these images are of simple geometric patterns, our descriptions of them can be couched simply in terms of aspects of the component and wholistic forms present. Yet, when we look at pictures like those in Fig. 2.1, we are more likely to describe the structure present in terms of the objects depicted. It is a picture of a building, some trees and a lake. And we see these objects as having distinct locations in a three-dimensional, not two-dimensional, space. The trees are at different sizes and distances, but all are nearer to us than the building. Any act of perception involves relating the 2D properties of the image to properties of the three-dimensional *objects* and *surfaces* of the world. Surfaces in the world have "intrinsic" properties such as reflectance, and have particular orientations and distances from a viewer. These are the kinds of properties that an observer needs to be able to perceive, in order to act properly.

The fundamental problem of early visual processing is that of deriving representations of *object* properties from retinal images. Unfortunately, there is no one-to-one relationship between image properties and world properties. Any image could, in principle, arise from numerous actual world scenes. We see but one of these possible worlds. This can readily be illustrated when we trick the visual system into seeing the wrong possibility, in illusions such as the "hollow face" (Gregory, 1973) or "Ames room" (Ittelson, 1952). Most traditional perceptual psychologists, and recent computational theorists, have viewed the process of perceiving as one of inferring, from ambiguous "clues" in the image, the objects which are most likely to have given rise to this image. Such inferences are possible only if some *additional* knowledge is brought to bear on the process of interpreting the pattern of intensity in the retinal image. For some psychologists, such as Gregory (e.g. 1980), the knowledge is of the properties of specific objects. Perception proceeds by the generation and testing of distinct hypotheses about particular object identities or surface layouts which are known, from experience, to be more likely than others. Thus, for example, we see the Ames room as rectangular because rectangular rooms are common in our environment. In contrast, the late David Marr and his associates (e.g. Marr, 1982) have given us a rather different way of thinking about the image interpretation process, in which it is very general knowledge about the physical world which is used in making sense of our retinal images. This kind of knowledge includes such things as the fact that surfaces are generally smooth, or that light comes from above—the kind of assumption which a visual system need not discover from experience but might have "hard-wired" (i.e. innately specified). According to Marr, in order to perceive aspects of a particular instance of the world, we make assumptions which are generally true of that world. Object-specific hypotheses are used only at relatively late stages of visual processing, or as a last resort. It is Marr's framework which we will describe here, as it provides one of the most integrated accounts to date of how the visual system gets from structure in the image to structure in the world. The details of Marr's theory are not necessarily correct (see Morgan, 1984, for a critique), and we will give pointers to alternative accounts of these details where appropriate, but the *kind* of approach exemplified by Marr's theory almost certainly is the most successful of recent approaches to vision. A framework such as Marr's allows us to make sense of the functions played by the neurophysiological machinery of vision, in terms of a more abstract description of the goals subserved by that machinery.

One of the most important features of Marr's theory, which will have implications for discussion throughout this book, is his emphasis that a number of different representations must be constructed from the information in the retinal image, and that these representations subserve different functions and goals. An early representational stage, *the primal sketch*, captures the two-dimensional structure of the retinal image. The primal sketch is a description of the edges, blobs, and bars present and their spatial arrangement in two dimensions. In order to interact with, and navigate within the world, some representation of its three-dimensional layout from the current viewpoint is required. This representation Marr terms the *2½D sketch*. The 2½D sketch describes how surfaces are oriented *with respect to a viewer*, and roughly how far away they are. Finally, in order to recognise objects irrespective of viewpoint, Marr argues that a representation of the three-dimensional shape of the object must be constructed in a view-independent coordinate system. Such descriptions are termed the *3D model representations*. We leave discussion of object recognition until Chapter 3, where we will raise some objections to the particular theory of object recognition proposed by Marr. However, the distinctions between a representation of an image, and representations of the world, and between viewer-centred and object-centred coordinate systems, are both fundamental and important. In this chapter we are concerned with the recovery from the retinal image of information intrinsic to the scene being viewed, and its representation within a viewer-centred coordinate frame. The kind of approach that we describe sees the analysis of spatial frequencies or the discovery of features as means to the end of discovering properties which are true of the world, rather than of an image.

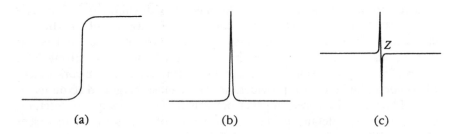

(a)   (b)   (c)

FIG. 2.8.   The intensity change shown at (a) gives rise to a peak in its first derivative (b) and a *zero-crossing*, Z in its second derivative (c). (Reproduced from Marr, 1982, with permission.)

DERIVATION OF THE PRIMAL SKETCH

From Retinal Image to Zero-crossings

Because the job of the visual system is to relate "image" and "world", the first stage is to locate structures in the image that might reflect significant aspects of the world. One such significant aspect is the boundary of an object, or the boundary between one surface region (sand) and another (sea). Such boundaries in the world will usually result in intensity discontinuities ("edges") in the image, as different kinds of surface rarely reflect light in the same way. A first stage in image analysis should thus involve edge detection, as this will be an important first step in revealing important boundaries in the world.

There are numerous different ways of finding edges in images (Ballard & Brown, 1982, review several of these). One way is to *differentiate* the function relating intensity to spatial location, in order to find the rate of change of intensity across the pattern. The edge can then be located where there is the maximum rate of change, or "peak" in the first derivative of the intensity distribution (the first derivative is the function obtained after differentiating once). Now, if we were to differentiate a function a second time (to obtain the "second derivative"), the peaks in the first derivative would become "zero-crossings" in the second derivative—locations where the function crosses zero (see Fig. 2.8). Thus, edges can be located at peaks in the first derivative or zero-crossings in the second derivative of the intensity distribution. (Whether we choose to look for peaks in the first derivative or zero-crossings in the second does not matter, it depends which may be found most conveniently, given the mathematics used.) Edge detection is not as straightforward as this implies, however. Naturally occurring edges may be very steep, or may be spatially extended. This is unfortunate because an easy way to achieve a differential operation is to compare the intensity of the light falling on each half of a "mask" (see

FIG. 2.9. A simple mask which could detect a vertical edge.

Fig. 2.9). If there is a difference, then some kind of edge must be present. However, the mask shown in Fig. 2.9 would fail to detect change of a very gradual kind, and the much larger masks needed to detect gradual changes would not be able to locate very sharp edges.

Marr and Hildreth (1980) suggested that this problem could be resolved if edges were detected simultaneously at different scales. This is achieved by "blurring" the image to different degrees, and then looking for edges independently within each of these differently blurred channels. The blurring of an image involves preferentially passing only its lower spatial frequency components. As we noted earlier, one way to achieve this is to divide the original image into small areas, and replace the original intensity array with the average intensity within each of these small areas. The problem is that such a coarse quantisation process can introduce high spatial frequency "noise" not present in the original image. Marr and Hildreth suggest that the use of a two-dimensional Gaussian-(normal)-shaped weighting function minimises such problems. This works by pooling intensity within a circular region of the image, so that intensities from the centre of the circular area are weighted more strongly than those at the periphery, according to a Gaussian function (G). The size of the circles is specified by the standard deviation (spread) of the Gaussian. The differently "blurred" channels are thus created by independently convolving the original image with Gaussian functions of different widths. To detect the intensity changes within each of these channels, Marr and Hildreth took the second derivative of the "blurred" image with a Laplacian operator (∇^2). The Laplacian operator was chosen for the differentiation because it is non-directional—it can be used to look for intensity changes simultaneously in all directions. Thus, the early stages in edge detection, according to Marr and Hildreth, involve locating zero-crossings independently at different spatial scales by convolving the image (I) with differently scaled ∇^2G operators. (This convolution is represented by ∇^2G*I.)

An important, although controversial, ingredient of Marr and Hildreth's (1980) theory is the relationship they suggest between the $\nabla^2 G * I$ operation, and known properties of retinal ganglion cells in the mammalian visual system. (Most people would agree that retinal ganglion cells are in some way involved in the early stages of locating intensity changes at different spatial scales, although not all would accept Marr and Hildreth's (1980) specific suggestion about how such cells implement this detection.) Before describing Marr and Hildreth's proposals, we must digress to outline the properties of retinal ganglion cells in more detail.

Retinal Ganglion Cells

As we noted earlier, retinal ganglion cells seem to pool responses from receptor cells lying within a particular area known as the *receptive field* of the ganglion cells. Near the fovea, ganglion cells have relatively small receptive fields, whereas further out in the periphery, receptive field sizes are larger. Ganglion cells do not merely pool light, but respond to light falling within their receptive fields in a way which will maximise responses to intensity changes and minimise responses to uniform areas of intensity. By recording from ganglion cells in the cat retina as spots of light were moved across the visual field, Kuffler (1953) showed that some receptive fields were circularly symmetric, with some cells excited by light falling within a central circular area of field and inhibited by light falling in an outer circular area ("centre-on" cells), and others inhibited by light in the central area and excited by light in the periphery ("centre-off" cells) (see Fig. 2.10). Circularly symmetric receptive field organisation has been observed in a number of species, including monkeys. Of course, we have no direct evidence that human receptive fields are organised in this way, but a number of psychophysical demonstrations are consistent with similarly organised receptive fields in the human visual system.

A simple but persuasive demonstration is shown in Fig. 2.11, where faint grey patches are seen at all intersections in the network apart from the one which you focus on. We can explain these illusory dim patches in terms of the net excitation experienced at centre-on ganglion cells whose receptive

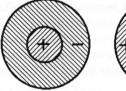

FIG. 2.10. Schematic representation of receptive field organisation in retinal ganglion cells. The cell to the left is excited by light in the centre of its receptive field and inhibited by light in the periphery. The cell to the right is inhibited by light in the centre and excited by light in the periphery of its field.

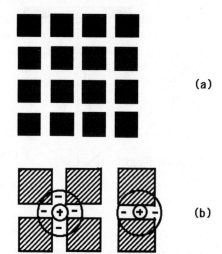

(a)

FIG. 2.11. The Hermann grid illusion (a) in which faint grey patches are seen at the network intersections can be explained in terms of the net excitation received by retinal ganglion cells. (b) The ganglion cell receptive field shown to the left will receive more inhibition from the four white "arms" of the intersection than will the ganglion cell shown at the right.

(b)

fields coincide with different parts of the pattern, as shown in Fig. 2.11. An explanation in terms of ganglion cell receptive fields is consistent with the absence of the dim spots from the intersection fixated centrally, because we know that receptive field sizes are larger in the periphery than in the fovea. (You might wonder why, on this account, the pattern of excitation at the centre-on cells is not balanced by an opposite pattern at centre-off cells: To understand this requires that we recognise the inherent asymmetry in processing produced by combining excitatory and inhibitory systems as cells can never be inhibited to respond negatively.)

Now, an on-centre circularly symmetric receptive field organisation could be achieved by superimposing a small excitatory region or dome on top of an inhibitory dome extending across the whole of the receptive field (Rodieck & Stone, 1965). Enroth-Cugell and Robson (1966) suggested that these two domes might be Gaussian in shape, and that the centre-surround receptive field organisation was thus computing the Difference Of two Gaussians, or "DOG" function (see Fig. 2.12). Now, with suitably adjusted standard deviations of these Gaussians, a DOG function is almost indistinguishable from a $\nabla^2 G$ function (see Marr, 1982), and thus the retinal ganglion cells might be seen as implementing the Marr and Hildreth edge-detection algorithm. To one side of a zero-crossing, an on-centre cell will fire maximally, and to the other side an off-centre cell will fire maximally, so that the zero-crossing could be located by examining the outputs of these two different classes of cell. The independent detection of zero-crossings in differently scaled channels could be achieved if the responses from ganglion cells with differently sized receptive fields were kept separate. As we noted earlier, there is convincing evidence that

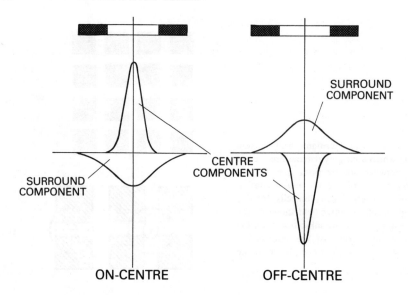

ON-CENTRE   OFF-CENTRE

FIG. 2.12.   Enroth-Cugell and Robson's (1966) model of the organisation of X-cell fields. The contribution of light intensity to the excitatory central portion and the inhibitory region which falls throughout the field is weighted by a Gaussian function. The response of the cell is thus determined by the difference between the two Gaussians. (Reproduced from Bruce & Green, 1975, with permission.)

human vision partitions its input into broadly tuned bands of spatial frequency, consistent with the suggestion that edge detection initially proceeds independently at different spatial scales.

The retinal ganglion cells described above belong to a class known as "X-cells", which give sustained responses to the onset of light falling within their receptive fields, and whose responses result from a linear combination of light falling within centre and surround. There is always a way of balancing the light falling on excitatory and inhibitory regions to produce a null response from such a cell. Enroth-Cugell and Robson (1966) distinguished X-cells from Y-cells, which give transient responses to light onset or offset only, which have generally larger receptive field sizes than the X-cells, and which do not seem to combine information from centre and surround in a simple manner. It was thought for some time that this division between the sustained and transient retinal ganglion cells reflected an early division into physiological systems which independently analysed form and movement. To a certain extent in this book, we are retaining the distinction between form and motion, although, as we see in Chapter 4, some recent computational treatments suggest that motion and form analysis may be more interlinked than this would suggest.

From Zero-crossings to Primal Sketch

The detection of zero-crossings is still an early stage in the detection of structures in the retinal image. Marr and Hildreth (1980) go on to suggest how information from all the zero-crossings found within and between the channels may be combined. Within each (G) channel, zero-crossings of similar orientations and slopes can be joined to form *zero-crossing segments,* which represent the little bits and pieces of edge present in the original image. Returning to the level of neural implementation, Marr (1982) suggests that the simple cells of the visual cortex detect zero-crossing segments by pooling responses from circularly-symmetric X-type retinal ganglion cells arranged as in Fig. 2.13. It is the alignment of the ganglion cell receptive fields in this way which could produce the orientation specificity of the spatial frequency channels. Note that the simple cells are not, on this scheme, seen as "feature detectors", but as *measuring devices* which contribute to a description of the features present in the image. Once zero-crossing segments are located in each channel (at different scales), these can then be associated with those found in other channels using the "spatial coincidence assumption". The assumption is that if zero-crossing segments of similar slope and orientation are found in adjacent $\nabla^2 G$ channels, then these segments arose from the same physical source in the world, and can be linked. The amalgamation of zero-crossings within and between the channels leads to the discovery not only of edge segments but of terminations, and little blobs and bars. The representation which results from all these amalgamation processes is known as the *raw primal sketch.*

In most natural images, shadows and other lighting effects can obscure significant boundaries and introduce false ones. Consider Fig. 2.14. Here the boundary between the teddy bear's neck and its background is almost

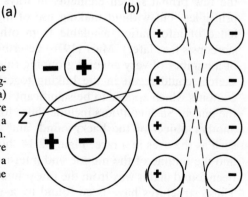

(a)   (b)

FIG. 2.13.   Marr and Hildreth's scheme for the detection of zero-crossing segments by simple cells in the cortex. At (a) the fields of an on-centre and off-centre cell overlap. If both are active, then a zero-crossing (z) must lie between them. At (b) parallel rows of on- and off-centre cells (surrounds not shown) will detect a zero-crossing segment falling between the dashed lines when both rows are active.

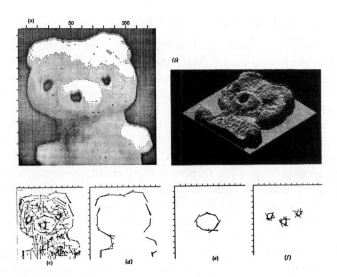

FIG. 2.14.   An image of a teddy bear (a) shown as an intensity map (b). At (c) is shown the location of small edge segments in the raw primal sketch. These have been grouped to reveal the structures shown in (d), (e), and (f). (Reproduced from Marr, 1976, with permission.)

impossible to detect from the intensity distribution alone. Lots of false boundaries are also present in this image. As well as obscure and false boundaries, natural objects have surface markings and texture which result in discontinuities in intensity, and hence will be represented in the raw primal sketch. Thus, the raw primal sketch will be a very complex and messy affair (see Fig. 2.14), which captures intensity changes at many scales and from numerous sources. From this messy description, the structures which we see so easily must still be revealed.

A certain degree of organisation can be achieved by grouping together the raw primal sketch elements in ways which obey some very general principles, but without making use of higher-level object-specific know-ledge of information available from other processing modules such as stereopsis (see later). Marr (1976) described how the recursive application of a number of very general grouping rules to elements of the raw primal sketch, could result in the linking together of edge segments to reveal contours which appear to be significant in terms of the objects depicted in the image. Such contours include those formed where one object occludes another object or the background, and the contours of internal regions such as the eyes in a face. Figure 2.14 shows how the outline of the head, and the outline of the muzzle and internal features of eyes and nose have been found in this way from the raw primal sketch of the teddy bear's head. These structures have been found by aggregating nearby small elements along lines of good curvature, and grouping together elements on the basis of their similarity to one another. Preference is given for groupings which lead to smooth or closed contours. Such grouping principles are reminiscent of the *Gestalt* "Laws of Organisation", and there is ample evidence that perceptual organisation by human vision involves principles of similarity, proximity, good continuation, and so forth (e.g. see Bruce & Green, 1985). These *Gestalt* "Laws" work, according to Marr, because they reflect sensible assumptions which can be made about the world of objects being viewed. For example, because different parts of the surface of a single object will often reflect light in the same way, similar elements in an image are quite likely to belong together; as smooth shapes are common in nature, smoothly changing contours should be preferred; as objects have closed boundaries, their contours in an image are likely to be closed, and so forth.

It is a feature of Marr's work that he stresses that we will progress more rapidly in suggesting algorithms for visual processing if we are clear about the job which these algorithms are seeking to do, and formulate any constraints which can be exploited by the computation. Algorithmic theories, the "how" of perception, and implementation theories, the "where" of perception, must be guided by theories of the computation— the "what" and the "why". Further examples of Marr's characteristic approach are given later, when we consider processes of depth and motion perception.

Marr's (1976) computer program was successful in furnishing descriptions of significant occluding contours from natural images such as that of the teddy bear. Descriptions of surface markings and texture were also made explicit in the full primal sketch. However, the program was unsuccessful on one of the images—a picture of a potted plant—where it failed to segregate the occluding contour of one leaf from that of another which it overlapped. For this image, the grouping procedures had to be supplemented with object-specific information by being "told" that these two contour segments arose from different sources. However, in human vision, other sources would have been available to disambiguate the processing of this image. The two leaves would be seen to be at different depths, through stereopsis and motion parallax, and so there would clearly be an alternative source of data-driven information available to disambiguate the image segmentation procedures. In the next section, and in Chaper 4 (where we deal with motion) we consider such processes in their own right.

Marr and Hildreth's (1980) scheme is not the only suggestion for the derivation of the primal sketch. Recently, Watt and Morgan (1985; Watt, 1988) have described a different system, "MIRAGE", which gives a rather better account of human psychophysical data and thus may provide a more plausible theory of how the human visual system solves the edge-finding problem. In the MIRAGE system, an image is again convolved with a range of $\nabla^2 G$ filters (functions which, again, could be implemented by retinal ganglion cells). However, MIRAGE then differs from Marr and Hildreth's account as there is no stage at which edges are detected from the output of each filter independently (as Marr and Hildreth achieve through finding zero-crossings from the output of each spatial filter). In MIRAGE, the outputs of all the filters are recombined, but in a way which keeps the positive and negative portions of the functions separate. Positive and

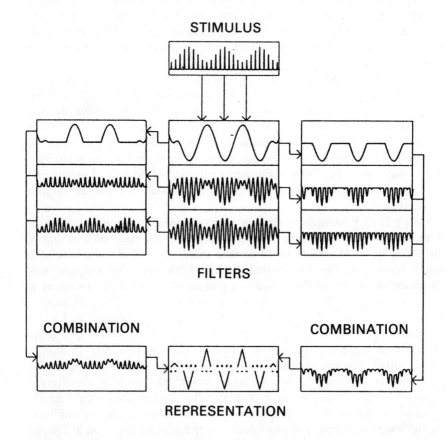

FIG. 2.15.   MIRAGE. At the top is shown a stimulus luminance profile and below it are the responses from three different $\nabla^2 G$ filters with the largest at the top. These filter responses are then split into positive and negative portions, shown to the left and right of the filter responses. The positive signals are all added together, as are the negatives, to yield the $S+$ and $S-$ "combinations" shown to the left and right at the bottom of the figure. The centroids of each zero-bounded mass in the $S+$ and $S-$ signals are used to identify the kind of intensity change present. (Reproduced from Watt, 1988, with permission.)

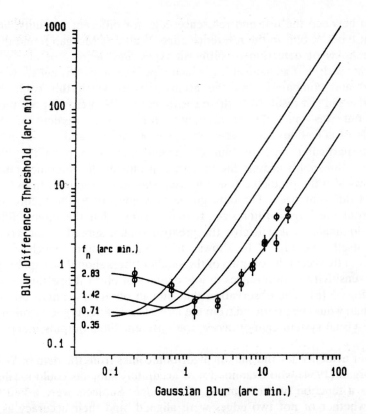

FIG. 2.16. The solid curves show the predicted variation in blur difference thresholds for 4 different $\nabla^2 G$ filter sizes, against data points from Watt and Morgan (1983). (Reproduced from Watt, 1988, with permission.)

negative filter outputs are separately *summed* to form what Watt calls the $S+$ and $S-$ signals (see Fig. 2.15). The locations of edges, bars, and luminance plateaus are then determined from measurements made on each portion of the $S+$ and $S-$ signal which departs from zero (the zero-bounded "masses"). The "centroids" of these zero-bounded masses (marked with chevrons in Fig. 2.15) play a particularly important role in identifying the nature of an intensity change, in contrast to the zero-crossings of Marr and Hildreth's scheme.

Watt (1988) presents a great deal of psychophysical evidence to suggest that the MIRAGE algorithm may provide a good account of edge detection in human vision. One example comes from an experiment by Watt and Morgan (1983) who asked subjects to discriminate differences in *blur* between two "edges" (step changes in intensity). On each trial, subjects were asked simply to say which of the two edges looked most blurred, and Watt and Morgan measured the smallest difference in blur that could be detected between the test and reference edge for different amounts, and different types of blur in the reference edge. Watt and Morgan found that the thresholds of detection of different types and degrees of blur was consistent with a mechanism in which "peaks" and "troughs" were localised and compared, and the accuracy with which this could be achieved could not result from the measurement of zero-crossings or their slopes, but was much better accounted for by measurement of the centroids of zero-bounded masses in the separate $S+$ and $S-$ signals.

For a particular type of blur (Gaussian) Fig. 2.16 plots the blur difference thresholds against the variation in blur of the reference edge, and shows also the predicted functions that should be obtained from $\nabla^2 G$ filters of different sizes. The data give a very good fit to the theoretical curve from the largest filter size. It makes sense that the largest filter should dominate as it will give the greatest spatial spread in the visual system itself. As Fig. 2.16 shows, however, a system which could independently access the outputs of the smaller filters should be capable of greater sensitivity to differences in low degrees of blur (at less than 1 arc min in Fig. 2.16). The observation that human observers cannot do any better than would be predicted from the largest scale filter is good evidence that the visual system cannot access the different filter outputs independently.

Further evidence for the MIRAGE algorithm comes from the data of Watt and Morgan (1984) who examined how accurately subjects could localise edges as a function of the contrast of the edge. Subjects were asked to decide whether or not two edges were aligned, and their accuracy as a function of contrast was compared with theoretical curves based upon the detection of peaks and zero-crossings from the second derivative, and the detection of centroids of zero-bounded masses in $S+$ and $S-$ signals. As Fig. 2.17 shows, the data are much better fit by the curve predicted by centroid measurement than by measurement of peaks or zero-crossings.

This section has shown how our understanding of the physiology of early vision, combined with principled computational theories may allow us to formulate theories of edge detection, such as that of Marr and Hildreth (1980). Careful psychophysical studies, as exemplified by the research of Watt and Morgan, may help us refine such theories and to discover which of a number of plausible schemes the visual system itself appears to adopt.

Lightness and Colour

So far we have emphasised how the visual system may be able to recover a representation of the edges, blobs and boundaries in an image—a "sketch" of the important forms present. However, when we view the world we also know that some surfaces and objects are darker than others, and when illumination is good we also see a range of different hues. Objects appear

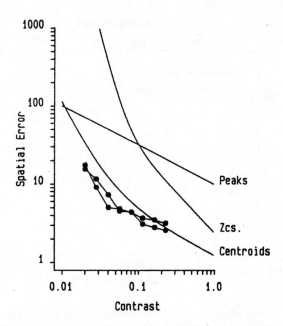

FIG. 2.17. The spatial error associated with judgements of edge location plotted as a function of edge contrast. Data points come from Watt and Morgan (1984). The solid curves are the predictions based on the detection of peaks, zero-crossings (Zcs), and centroids from the $S+$ and $S-$ signals. (Reproduced from Watt, 1988, with permission.)

to have different lightnesses and colours because their surfaces absorb and reflect light of different wavelengths in differing ways. A "black" object, such as a piece of coal, absorbs light of all wavelengths—a "white" object, such as a piece of paper, reflects light of all wavelengths. Many objects selectively absorb light of some wavelengths, and their resulting "colour" arises because of the way in which our visual system encodes the light which they reflect. The perception of an object's lightness and colour is, however, far from straightforward. We are able to see a lump of coal as black even when it is underneath a bright lamp, and a piece of paper as white even when it is in a dark corner of the same room. In such a situation, the coal may actually be reflecting much more light than the paper! Similarly, the paper appears "white" even when it is illuminated by artificial light which may contain a very restricted range of wavelengths. Somehow our visual systems are able to separate out the effects of particular illumination conditions and reveal the "real" colours and lightnesses of objects across a very wide range of conditions.

Land and McCann (1971) suggested that the visual system could recover "true" reflectances despite variations in illumination by ignoring any *gradual* changes in intensity across an image and attributing abrupt ones to

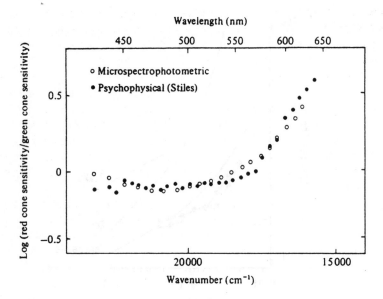

FIG. 2.18. A comparison of microspectrophotometric ○ and psychophysical ● estimates of the sensitivities of long- and middle-wavelength cones. (Reproduced with permission, from Mollon, 1982, who gives full details of the derivation of these data points.)

reflectance changes from one surface patch to another (see also Horn, 1974). Frisby (1979) gives a detailed account of how such a system for lightness computation could work, and how it could account for our perception of lightness and darkness in a range of situations. Land and McCann (1971) extended the same principles to develop a theory of colour vision. Before describing their theory, we should outline the physiological basis for colour perception. Here we can only briefly mention aspects of colour vision—the interested reader should consult Mollon (1982) for a more extended introduction.

The primate retina contains not one but two different kinds of photoreceptors—rods and cones. The cone system is responsible for high acuity central vision, and also allows us to see in colour. There are three different kinds of cone pigment which, in the human eye, maximally absorb light of wavelength 419nm, 496nm, and 559nm (Dartnell, Bowmaker, & Mollon, 1983), which correspond to relatively short, medium, and long wavelengths. These three cone types are often labelled as "blue", "green", and "red", as their peak sensitivities correspond very roughly to the "blue", "green", and "red" regions of the visible spectrum respectively. Human psychophysical experiments have provided us with extensive evidence for the "trichromatic" theory of colour vision (see Mollon, 1982, for a clear introduction), and the agreement between the sensitivities of the "green" and "red" cone systems obtained through psychophysical measures (Wyszecki & Stiles, 1967) and direct measurement using microspectrophotometry is very close (Fig. 2.18). A further, extensive source of evidence for the theory of trichromacy has come from the study of different forms of *colour blindness* which can result from the absence, or alteration, of one or more of the normal cone pigments. Such individuals are rarely colour *blind*, in the sense of seeing the world in shades of grey. More usually, their colour vision is anomalous due to defects in the cone system. Mollon (1982) again provides a succinct introduction to the varieties of colour blindness and their probable causes. Later in this section we will mention how damage at a more central level in the nervous system can also occasionally result in colour blindness.

To provide for colour vision there must be some way of comparing the outputs of the three different input cone systems. Physiological studies have revealed "colour opponent" cells in the retina and cortex of cat and monkey (e.g. de Monasterio, 1978). The "sustained" or X-type ganglion cells in the monkey retina have been found to form several different types. The two most common have concentric fields in which the centre is excited by red cones and the surround inhibited by green ones, or vice versa. The other kinds involve excitation from blue cones and inhibition from a combination of inputs from the red and green channels (i.e. "yellow"). Mollon (1982) suggests, however, that the existence of cells which are inhibited by inputs from the blue cones is questionable.

Land and McCann's "retinex" theory of colour vision (see also Land, 1986) sees the three cone systems as independently computing lightness (as we outlined earlier), with "hue" resulting from the comparison of the reflectances computed independently by each of these three systems. The theory was developed in response to some remarkable demonstrations by Land (1959). In Land's demonstrations, a complex array of coloured objects is twice photographed on to monochrome film through two different filters which selectively pass relatively short- (green) or relatively long-wave (red) light. The result is two different grey-level images, which each look slightly different as one has been photographed through a red filter and the other through a green filter. Now, if these two grey-level transparencies are each projected onto a screen and superimposed, with the "red" transparency illuminated with red light and the "green" transparency with white light, the resulting image is seen with a range of different hues—yet at each point on the projected image there should be some mixture of red light and white light only.

Clearly, the visual system is responding to something other than the wavelengths of reflected light on a point-by-point basis. Rather, it seems to be the balance of longer and shorter wavelengths across the entire visual scene which determines the hues we perceive. The retinex theory, in which reflectance maps are computed within independent channels and compared, is an attempt to explain such phenomena. However, Brainard and Wandell (1986) have recently compared the predictions of the retinex model with the actual changes in the appearance of colours seen by human observers, and found the fit was rather poor. In addition, there has been no attempt to consider how colour-opponent cells might be involved in implementing such an algorithm. It seems that we are still some way from a complete computational account of colour vision. One source of evidence to inform the future development of such a theory may come from disorders of colour perception which can result from brain injury.

One example of selective visual loss after brain damage is termed achromatopsia, the loss of ability to see colours. Like many selective visual disorders, achromatopsia is rare, and follows lesions (usually bilateral) of the prestriate visual cortex at the back of the brain. Cerebral achromatopsia can be separated from the more usual forms of congenital colour blindness due to the loss of certain pigments from cones in the retina. For instance, achromatopsics can have entirely normal colour vision prior to the lesion occurring, and they can retain the normal three cone mechanisms (for red, green, and blue) and their associated spectral sensitivities (Mollon, Newcombe, Polden, & Ratcliff, 1980). Achromatopsic patients can also be separated from patients with colour naming problems. Patients have been documented with problems in naming colours whilst at the same time being good at matching colours together (e.g. Beauvois, 1982). Achromatopsic patients are poor at colour matching as well as colour naming. Thus, the disorder seems to reflect a disturbance to the central mechanisms concerned with colour perception. For these patients, the world is perceived in shades of black, white, and grey, and their judgements are based on the brightness rather than the colour of patterns.

Although many such patients have associated losses in form recognition (e.g. Humphreys & Riddoch, 1987a; Meadows, 1974) this is not always found (Heywood, Wilson, & Cowey, 1987; Sacks & Wasserman, 1987). For example, the patient studied by Heywood et al. (1987) had some loss of acuity, but could still recognise the faces of famous people and seemed to have no major loss of form vision. Nevertheless, he performed at random on tests requiring the matching of colours whose brightness levels were equated, despite being able to match different shades of grey (using brightness alone). This patient provides strong evidence for colour processing being handled by the brain independently of other types of processing. It seems then that colour vision may be construed as a processing "module" independent of that concerned with form perception. Such modularity seems to be a feature of early visual processing, as we discuss at more length in the next section.

INFERRING SURFACE STRUCTURE FROM RETINAL IMAGES

As we have already mentioned, most psychological and computational theories of perception agree that perception involves a process of *inferring* the three-dimensional structure of a scene from features and dimensions of the two-dimensional retinal image. In the last section, we outlined two slightly different theories of edge detection, both embodying a physiologically and psychologically plausible set of processes from which two-dimensional structures may be revealed from the pattern of light intensities in the retinal image. We now consider how such processes may be supplemented by further analysis of surface structure and layout. Analysis of the contours and colours in two-dimensional images is one way in which clues to surface structure may be revealed, but there are many others. Stereoscopic depth perception, the rate of change of gradients of texture and shading, and the analysis of motion (which we discuss in Chapter 4), can all reveal aspects of three-dimensional structure.

It is interesting to note that the visual system seems to be organised, at least initially, such that the analysis of these different properties proceeds largely independently of each other. Marr himself pointed to the advantages of *modularity* in the design (cf. evolution) of any complex computational system. Independent modules can be designed, altered or damaged without too much impediment to the system as a whole. There is considerable evidence, as we will see in this chapter and later in the book, for the initial independence of visual modules for the perception of such qualities as depth, motion, form, and colour, and to a certain extent such independence has a certain logic in terms of the goals of the visual system. We wish to recognise an object irrespective of its distance, or know how fast something is moving independent of its colour, and so forth. Consistent with early modularity, Zeki (1978) has outlined how the visual cortex of the monkey seems to be organised in terms of different areas which are primarily involved in the analysis of colour, orientation, and direction of motion. The extent to which such "modules" are truly independent of each other in the early stages of vision, and the possible ways in which the outputs of such modules may subsequently be combined, are current questions in vision research—questions which we will raise at a number of points in this book.

Stereopsis

Because the goal of early vision is to describe the three-dimensional layout and structure of the viewed scene, we would expect an important role to be played by stereopsis. Stereopsis is the process of combining two slightly

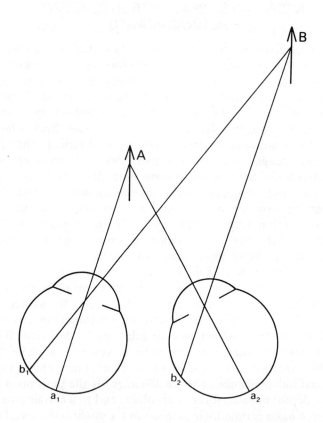

FIG. 2.19. If the eyes are focused on an object at A, with the image of A falling on corresponding retinal points (a_1 and a_2), images of nearer or more distant objects (such as B) will fall on disparate points on the two retinas (b_1 and b_2).

different retinal images of the world, received by our two eyes, to form a single view in depth. If you alternately open and close each eye you can see this shift from one eye's view to the other's. When we view a scene, a particular set of points within it will be focused on corresponding points in the two retinas, but nearer or more distant points will fall on disparate points, with the amount of disparity varying with location in depth (see Fig. 2.19).

Although a potentially powerful means (at close range) of determining relative depth, and hence detailed information about surface layout, stereoscopic fusion is computationally complex. Somehow the brain must match the correct "features" of one eye's image with features in the other eye's image. Only when this correspondence problem is solved can the disparity involved in the match be determined and hence the part be located in three dimensions. Now, the more similar the features in each image, the more ambiguous will be the matching process. Because of this problem, it used to be thought (e.g. Sherrington, 1906) that forms were independently recognised from the image in each eye, and then matching of the two eyes' views resulted. According to this theory, when viewing images like those in Fig. 2.19, the visual system does not need to decide, for example, which line segment in each eye's image matches one in the other eye's—instead it can match the "arrow" in one image with the "arrow" in the other image, for which there is no ambiguity.

This theory was finally abandoned with the invention of the random-dot stereogram (Julesz, 1965; 1971). A random-dot stereogram is shown in Fig. 2.20. Each image appears to be a uniform sheet of random texture, and no form can be seen within either image. However, if these two images are viewed with a stereoscope, so that the left-hand image is seen by the left eye and the right-hand image by the right eye, a square form will be seen floating above the background texture. Forms can be *revealed* as a *result* of "global" stereoscopic matching which were not visible in either eye's image. Random-dot stereograms provide powerful psychophysical evidence for a depth perception "module" which is not dependent on prior recognition of form.

The separability of depth perception from other aspects of form perception is also supported by neuropsychological evidence. Many of the early advances in neuropsychological testing took place during and

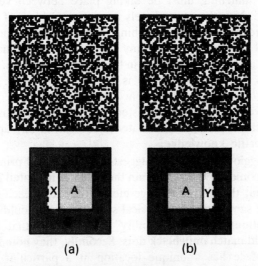

(a)   (b)

FIG. 2.20.   Top: A random-dot stereogram of the type devised by Julesz. If this pair was viewed in a stereogram, a square would be seen floating above the background. Below: (a) and (b) are the top two stereo images shown in simplified form. Both have the same surrounding texture (S) within which a central region (A) has been shifted (to the right in (a) and to the left in (b)). The gaps left have been filled in with more texture (X and Y). (Adapted from Julesz, 1965.)

immediately after World War I, when servicemen with selective missile wounds were examined. Both Holmes and Horrax (1919) and Riddoch (1917) documented patients with an apparently general loss of ability to see depth, but without any associated deficits in object recognition. For example, the patient described by Holmes and Horrax was unable to perceive the thickness in solid objects and saw a flight of stairs as "a number of straight lines on the floor". Such striking disturbances seem consequent on a primary loss of all types of depth perception, including loss of the ability to appreciate monocular depth cues as well as stereoscopic depth. In other cases, patients can suffer selective disturbances of stereoscopic depth perception alone (e.g. Danta, Hilton, & O'Boyle, 1978), and Lawler (1981) has argued that some patients may have impaired "global" stereopsis with intact "local" stereopsis (i.e. an ability to match only simple line stereograms). Such observations illustrate the potential of neuropsychological research to "pull apart" processes that might otherwise be assigned to a common mechanism, and provide converging evidence for some independence of depth perception from form recognition.

If stereopsis does not result from the matching of recognised forms in each eye's image, then on what basis is matching achieved? Julesz (1971) was able to demonstrate that random-dot stereograms could be matched even if local patterns within each image were broken up with visual noise, suggesting that matching must be taking place between very primitive elements indeed. Yet, this immediately raises the problem of ambiguity in the matching process. Suppose matching is at the level of individual dots (as Julesz, 1971, suggested), then any dot in one eye's image could in principle match any of the other dots in the other eye's image. A simplified diagram of this matching ambiguity is shown in Fig. 2.21. Despite the wealth of *possible* matches, and hence interpretations, people viewing random-dot stereograms adopt consistent solutions. Somehow the potential ambiguity can readily be eliminated, yet without any apparent help from object-specific knowledge.

Marr and Poggio (1976; 1979) suggested how general principles of the physical world could serve to constrain the matches tolerated in stereopsis. They pointed out that for two image elements (one in each eye) to have arisen from the same patch of physical surface, they should have similar physical descriptions (the "compatibility" constraint), so that, for example, black dots should match only black dots. Secondly, they noted that a given point on a surface has a unique location at a particular instant (the "uniqueness" constraint), so only one match should be tolerated for each dot in the stereogram. Finally, they argued that as the surfaces of objects are generally smooth and abrupt changes in distance are rare, being found only at the edges of objects (the "continuity" constraint), disparity should vary smoothly almost everywhere in an image.

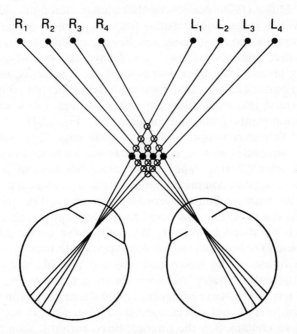

FIG. 2.21.   Two eyes viewing a simplified stereogram in which each eye sees just 4 dots. Each of the left eye's dots (L_1 to L_4) could match any of the right eye's dots (R_1 to R_4), so that the number of possible matches, shown with filled and open circles, is very large. The visual system chooses the matches which are shown with filled circles. (Adapted from Marr & Poggio, 1976, and reproduced from Bruce & Green, 1985, with permission.)

   If these *constraints* are placed on the possible matches between two random-dot stereograms, an algorithm can be devised which solves random-dot stereograms (Marr & Poggio, 1976) by applying the three matching rules simultaneously. The algorithm thereby demonstrates the power of assumptions about the natural world which can place constraints on the solving of seemingly impossible visual problems. Later in this chapter we will describe Marr and Poggio's algorithm in some detail, as it provides a particularly clear example of the kind of neural network model which is currently attracting considerable interest. As an account of human stereopsis, however, the particular algorithm proposed by Marr and Poggio is unsatisfactory, as it provides no account of a variety of psycho-physically observed phenomena in human stereo-matching. Stereopsis research provides a particularly good example of the way in which human psychophysical experiments can help elucidate which of a number of successful stereo algorithms provides the best account of the method used by human vision. Here, we will mention just three experiments whose results must be accommodated by a theory of human stereoscopic matching.

Julesz and Miller (1975) discovered that human stereo-matching could take place within independent spatial frequency tuned channels. They constructed random texture stereograms, like the random-dot stereograms illustrated earlier, but whose "dots" could have any one of a range of different grey levels. They then decomposed these patterns, using two-dimensional Fourier analysis, into their underlying spectral components, so that they could selectively filter out either the higher or lower spatial frequency components from the original (cf. Fig. 2.4). First, they demonstrated that stereoscopic fusion was quite easy when only low or high spatial frequencies were represented in the stereogram which was reconstructed after filtering. They then added masking "noise" to the stereo images. The noise comprised dots of the same size as in the original stereo pairs, but with randomly determined grey levels. Like the original stereo images, the noise patterns could themselves be filtered to contain selected bands of spatial frequency. When the noise contained spectral (spatial frequency) components which overlapped with those in the stereo images, then fusion of the stereo pair was not possible and observers experienced binocular "rivalry" between the images seen by the two eyes (they saw the left and right eye's images in rapid alternation). But when the noise was itself filtered so that it contained no frequencies closer than two octaves to those contained in the filtered stereo patterns, then binocular fusion of the two patterns was possible. Such observations led Marr and Poggio (1979) to formulate a new algorithm in which stereo-matching took place at successively finer levels of spatial scale, and between zero-crossing segments located within the independent $\nabla^2 G * I$ channels (note that it was Marr and Poggio's work on zero-crossings which was further elaborated in Marr and Hildreth's theory of edge detection which we described earlier, p.27ff.)

Although the phenomenon of random-dot stereograms demonstrates that stereopsis can occur prior to form recognition, Saye and Frisby (1975) showed that monocularly conspicuous features could aid the fusion of such stereograms. In their experiments, subjects were asked to press a button as soon as they could see the "square" in the random-dot stereogram. They measured how the latency of the button press varied according to the presence and nature of these features. When small disparity stereo pairs were shown, fusion was no faster when the outline of the square was shown, or when a cross was shown in the plane of the target square, compared with the standard condition where no such features were shown. However, when large disparity stereograms were shown, both the square and the cross reduced fusion latency, and there was no increase or decrease in this effect with experience of the task. These findings were among those which led Mayhew and Frisby (1981) to formulate a stereo-matching algorithm in which false matches were eliminated in part by a "figural continuity" constraint.

In classical studies of stereopsis it has been claimed that stereo-matching can only take place provided disparities lie within a limit known as "Panum's fusional area". However, Burt and Julesz (1980) have shown that the limit on stereo fusion lies not with absolute disparity between the to-be-matched features, but rather seems to be in terms of the *disparity gradient* which can be tolerated. The disparity gradient is the difference between the disparities of neighbouring objects divided by their separation. If this gradient exceeds 1, stereo pairs cannot be matched, even if the disparities present lie within Panum's fusional area. Pollard, Mayhew, and Frisby (1985) have recently produced a new algorithm for stereopsis which accommodates this, along with many previous empirical findings. It remains to be seen whether their "PMF" algorithm becomes the accepted theory for human stereo vision, certainly it seems one of the most comprehensive to date.

Stereopsis is only one of the ways in which three-dimensional structure is revealed. Quite a large proportion of the population (2–5% according to Braddick, 1982) manage with defective stereo vision, and all can perceive the layout of the world at distances far too great for stereopsis to operate. In the next section, we briefly mention other processes which may reveal shape and orientation from information contained within static monocular images.

Contour and Shading

From monocular images, important information about surface layout is *implicit* in the contours and textures which are represented in the primal sketch. Marr (1977; 1982) places particular emphasis on the analysis of the *occluding contour* in the derivation of a description of the three-dimensional shape of an object. Occluding contours alone can give remarkably powerful impressions of three-dimensional shape, as Marr demonstrates persuasively by showing silhouettes of objects. Two examples are shown in Fig. 2.22. It is interesting that we choose a particular interpretation of these contours, despite their potential ambiguity. Marr (1977) claims that as any silhouette could have arisen, in principle, from an infinity of shapes, but people interpret them in such consistent ways, there must be constraints on the possible range of interpretations imposed by certain assumptions made by the visual system about the silhouette shapes

FIG. 2.22.   Silhouettes show that objects can easily be recognised from their occluding contours.

FIG. 2.23.   Texture density gradients inform us about surface slant.

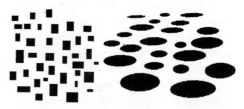

viewed. Marr (1977) showed that if a shape is a *generalised cone* then its silhouette is constrained in certain ways. Generalised cones are the shapes produced by sweeping out a cross-section of variable size but constant shape along an axis (which may itself bend). Marr suggests that we perceive such contours as though they stem from shapes whose components can be described (at least approximately) as generalised cones. In the next chapter, we will return to consider other possible theories of the interpretation of occluding contours, which clearly form important indicants of an object's three-dimensional shape. Other clues, however, are provided by different kinds of contours within the boundary defined by the occluding contour.

Gibson (1950; 1966; 1979) has argued forcefully that important information about spatial layout is contained in gradients of texture density. Consider Fig. 2.23. In the left pattern, the uniform size and spacing of the texture elements informs us that the surface is oriented at right angles to the line of sight, whereas in the right-hand pattern, the gradual decrease in size and increase in density of the texture elements gives an impression of a surface receding away from us in an orientation which is parallel to the line of sight. Gibson's own analysis of texture density gradients was largely informal, but more recently Stevens (1981; 1986) has provided a rigorous analysis of the way in which certain *surface contours* of an object may be used to discover the local slant and tilt of the surface. (Stevens did not examine the perception of foreshortening of texture, with which Gibson was concerned, but concentrated instead on how surface contours—a kind of texture—are informative about the undulations of a surface within a particular plane.) Figure 2.24 shows how a set of such contours can give a strong impression of surface layout. Stevens has made explicit those assumptions which can allow local surface slant to be computed from a pattern of contours such as these. The most important of these assumptions is that a curved line is assumed to follow the line of curvature of the

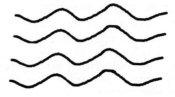

FIG. 2.24.   Surface contours give a strong impression of surface shape.

underlying surface, an assumption which Stevens argues will be true for many natural and manufactured objects.

Contours found within the image of an object or extended surface thus potentially provide a rich source of information about the layout of the surface in space. However, it is easy to gloss over difficult questions raised by such a contour interpretation process. For example, how does the visual system know that a particular piece of contour forms part of the outline, or part of the textured surface? One possibility (e.g. see Pentland, 1986b) is that information from other sources is used to help the interpretative process. For example, Pentland suggests that an analysis of local shading may help resolve whether a particular contour results from a concave or convex edge, or from a surface marking.

Pentland's suggestion reminds us that, as well as information in patterns of contour, the gradation of light intensity across part of an image (the "shading") also informs us about its shape. Make-up artists try to deceive our perception of shape by creating false shade to make a face look thinner or softer than it would otherwise appear. Again, careful analysis of the shape-from-shading problem by Horn (1975; 1977) and more recently by Pentland (1986b) has revealed assumptions that are necessary to recover the local orientation of an unknown surface from the variation of light intensity in an image.

The work on analysis of surface contours, shape-from-shading, and so forth has shown how such problems could be solved *in principle*. We still do not know how the visual system solves these problems in practice. Further work at a psychophysical and neurophysiological level will be needed to answer such questions.

THE 2½D SKETCH REPRESENTATION OF VIEWER-CENTRED INFORMATION: AN INTRODUCTION TO "CONNECTIONIST" MODELS

So far, we have emphasised how the analysis of certain properties of visual stimuli, such as edge detection and grouping, stereopsis, and shape-from-shading, operate as relatively independent processing modules. One major question in vision research is how such independently coded properties are combined to enable us to see coherent scenes. We consider this question at some length in Chapter 5. Marr (1982) argued that the processing modules for stereopsis, shape-from-shading, and so forth, independently contributed to a representation of visible surfaces of objects coded from the current viewpoint—the 2½D sketch. As conceived by Marr, the 2½D sketch is an integrated representation describing surface boundaries and the orientations and rough distances of the surfaces using a vector-like set of primitives (see Fig. 2.25). Such a representation would be useful for

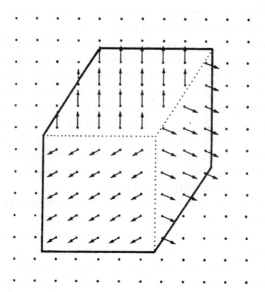

FIG. 2.25.   Marr's conception of the 2½D sketch of a cube. The surfaces are represented by a set of needle-like vector primitives. The length of each needle represents the degree of tilt of the surface, and its orientation represents the direction of surface slant. (Reproduced from Marr, 1982, with permission.)

guiding actions such as reaching out towards or grasping objects. The 2½D sketch was also held to act as a buffer store to hold the products of early visual processing from one instant to the next; and later in this book, in Chapter 6, we will describe how research on visual short-term memory provides evidence consistent with such a discrete representational stage in human vision.

Early vision can be viewed as a process of constraint satisfaction where multiple computational constraints operate to limit the range of possible solutions to visual processing problems (see our discussion of stereopsis, earlier). We end the chapter by considering one approach to solving multiple constraints by using "neural" networks of simple processing units. Such networks are often termed "connectionist" models of behaviour. Connectionist models are built from large numbers of processing units that each perform computationally simple functions, such as exciting or inhibiting other units they are connected to (hence the term "neural" when describing such networks). Complex behaviours emerge from the patterns of activation across the whole network. Connectionist models have become increasingly popular devices for conceptualising information processing in a number of fields, and we will draw upon them several times in this book. They have the merit of being computationally explicit, whilst also related directly to psychological and physiological evidence—and so become particularly appropriate given our concern to integrate work from different approaches to vision.

A clear example of a model that satisfies multiple constraints in early vision was proposed by Marr and Poggio (1976). The model specifically concerned the matching of stereoscopic images, but it provides a good example of a connectionist network and so will serve as a general model for other connectionist accounts we shall discuss. Recall that the computational theory of stereopsis specified the constraints of compatibility, uniqueness, and continuity which led to three *matching rules* for the stereo algorithm to apply. The rules were that black dots should match black dots (and white match white), only single matches should be made, and matching should keep disparity uniform as far as possible. Figure 2.26 shows a simple network of processing units which are driven by inputs from the left eye's and right eye's images of a single row of black and white dots from a random-dot stereogram. The right eye's image of the row is the same as the left eye's, apart from the disparate "strip" within the row. There is a processing unit for every possible fusion between one dot in one eye's

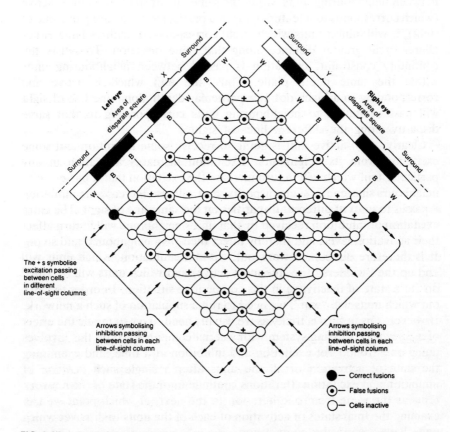

FIG. 2.26.   A portion of a neural network to solve random-dot stereograms. (Reproduced from Frisby, 1979, with permission.)

image and another dot in the other eye's image. Thus, there is a unit for every fusion that we do not make when looking at such stereograms as well as one for each fusion that we do make (cf. Fig. 2.21). Each unit thus represents a particular three-dimensional location in the world that a feature *could* have. The job of the network as a whole is to arrive at a single solution to the problem of finding the actual three-dimensional location of each feature presented in each eye's image.

This is achieved as follows. Each processing unit has a particular resting level of activation which is initially boosted when it receives input from identical features (two white dots or two black dots) in either eye's image. Thus, the active units marked in Fig. 2.26 are those which are satisfying the compatibility constraint. The next problem is to eliminate the "false" matches from those marked and retain the "correct" ones (i.e. the matches which we see when viewing such stereograms). This occurs as a result of the balance of *excitation* and *inhibition* received by each unit from its neighbouring units. To satisfy the uniqueness constraint, inhibition passes between neighbouring units within the same line of sight. If a unit is active (which corresponds to a feature lying at a particular depth along one line of sight), it will inhibit units which could correspond to features lying either nearer or at greater distance along that same direction. To satisfy the continuity constraint, excitation is passed between neighbouring units within the same depth plane. Thus, the unit which is active and corresponding to a black dot at a particular depth along one line of sight will pass excitation to neighbouring units corresponding to that same disparity along the different lines of sight.

Clearly, each active unit is going to receive some inhibition and some excitation from its neighbours. Excitation increases activation in any particular unit which will in turn increase the excitation that it passes on to neighbours sharing the same disparity, and will also increase the inhibition it passes to units at different disparities on the same line of sight. The extra excitation or inhibition received by that unit's neighbours will in turn affect their activation levels and thereby affect their own neighbours, and so on. It is therefore difficult to work out, without simulation, which units will end up the "winners" (i.e. the most active) and which units will be killed off (to a state of inactivity) in this competitive situation. In order to work out which units will "win", we need to run a simulation of such a network. However, this in turn is tricky as we usually need to try to mimic the effect of a *parallel* processing system with a serial computer. To do this involves doing one "round" of excitation and inhibition at a time, and examining the state of activation of all the units after a single such *iteration* of inhibition and excitation. Iterations continue until the state of the network remains the same from one iteration to the next, at which point we can examine the final states of activation of each of the units to discover which units have "won" the competition.

By implementing such a network Marr and Poggio (1976) were able to demonstrate that the network, set into action, converged to a state where the most active units corresponded to the depth solutions reached by human observers viewing random-dot stereograms. So, in our example in Fig. 2.26, where there is a disparate "strip" of black and white dots within the row seen by either eye, the network would end up with its most active units corresponding to two distinct depth planes, with dots in the "surround" located at one depth and those in the disparate strip located at another. Similarly, in simulations of such a network operating on two-dimensional arrays of dots (rather than the single rows shown here), a network of this type shown a random-dot stereogram with a disparate square of texture will converge to a solution in which there are two depth planes, one corresponding to the dots in the square and one corresponding to the dots in the surround. The network has thus located a "square" region of its input at a depth which is different from that of the surrounding region, just as the human visual system does.

Now, we have already noted that this particular algorithm for stereoscopic matching does not provide an account of other observations of human stereo vision. However, there seems no reason why these other findings should not be incorporated as additional matching rules within a network of this kind. For example, units could be excited or inhibited according to constraints from figural continuity or disparity gradient limits (see p.42). It is important to note that the units in the "stereopsis" module could also receive inputs from units in other early processing modules, so that the visual system could seek consistency between the solutions achieved through stereopsis, contour analysis, shape-from-shading, and so forth, even though each module can proceed independently when other inputs are absent.

In this way such a network could implement a slightly different conception of intermediate (2½D sketch) level representations that has been given by workers such as Barrow and Tenenbaum (1981) and others. These workers see the results of analyses of intrinsic properties as written into a number of topographically correspondent "intrinsic images". A set of intrinsic images might include discrete representations of the distance, reflectance, local orientation, and illumination of the surfaces being viewed. The recovery of each set of properties is seen to involve the satisfaction of constraints both within and *between* these different layers.

As we have illustrated, an attempt to satisfy a number of different constraints simultaneously lends itself most naturally to computation using a parallel network of interconnected processing units, and powerful solutions to a range of visual problems can be conveniently implemented in such parallel systems (e.g. see Ballard, Hinton, & Sejnowski, 1983, for a review). Importantly, such implementations seem to have a certain kind of biological plausibility. The early stages of the visual system are massively parallel, and excitatory and inhibitory connections between simple processing units seem to form the basic machinery of early vision. These new connectionist approaches to modelling visual processing could promote exciting theoretical developments over the next few years (see recent collections edited by McClelland & Rumelhart, 1986; Rumelhart & McClelland, 1986; and Morris, 1989, for a detailed introduction to this area) in which we may develop a clear idea of how the visual machinery of the brain achieves consistent interpretations of surface layout. As we have described them here, such connectionist models complement and enhance other theoretical accounts of vision in which the logic and procedures of visual information processing are made explicit. (However, there is a more radical camp within connectionism too—one which suggests that certain kinds of connectionist models will make other kinds of account redundant. We do not share this opinion, although we will encounter and confront it in the next chapter. See Humphreys (1989) for further discussion of this issue.)

In this chapter we have outlined how the ambiguous information in the retinal image may be interpreted by making use of additional assumptions about the visual world. Making use of such assumptions it is, in principle, possible to derive from a retinal image, a description of the layout of different surfaces from the viewer's perspective. Where appropriate, we have discussed how known physiological mechanisms seem to be involved in deriving such descriptions. In the next chapter, we consider how the surfaces and objects located by early vision may subsequently be identified as belonging to familiar categories.

3

Visual Object Recognition

INTRODUCTION

In the previous chapter we discussed the early visual processing of patterns of light intensity, and considered how the visual system constructs descriptions of image features (in the primal sketch), and surface layout (in the 2½D sketch) from these spatial patterns. These viewpoint-dependent descriptions of visual information may subserve important functions in guiding action in the world. However, an important additional goal of vision is to *recognise* the structures thus described, as belonging to familiar categories. How is this achieved?

Most computational theories of object recognition have construed the problem as one of matching a description of an object derived from an image, with one of a set of stored representations of the visual characteristics—"appearances"—of different kinds of objects. Thus, to recognise a "horse", involves matching the derived description with the representation stored for "horse", rather than "dog", "cow", or "banana". To consider how such matches may be achieved requires that we consider not only the nature of the internalised representations against which input descriptions are compared, but also the processes whereby suitable descriptions may be derived from the image. Later in this chapter we will consider these representational and matching processes in some detail. First, however, we consider how neuropsychological and experimental evidence has enabled us to develop a broad framework which describes the relationship between such visual processes and subsequent cognitive processes which are also involved in object recognition.

DIFFERENT LEVELS OF OBJECT "DESCRIPTION"

Object "recognition" is not a unitary activity but makes available a number of different visual, semantic, and verbal descriptions. Normally, when we recognise a particular instance of a familiar category, we are able to describe how the object would look if seen from a different viewpoint—we have some apparent understanding of its three-dimensional shape. On looking at a view of a horse, for example, in which one of its legs was occluded by another, we would expect to see the "invisible" leg if the horse was seen from a different viewpoint. We are also able to describe the functions or uses of a familiar object category ("a domesticated animal, previously used as a means of transport, now ridden largely for pleasure or sport") and know of other objects with which it may be associated ("cart", "hound"). Additionally, we can label a familiar object with a particular name ("horse"). Such activities reveal that we have visual knowledge of an object's shape, *semantic* knowledge of an object's function and associates, and *verbal* knowledge of object names.

Experimental evidence (much of it reviewed in detail in Humphreys & Riddoch, 1987b) suggests that there are distinct stages in the processing of objects at which perceptual classification, semantic classification, and name retrieval are achieved (e.g. Ratcliff & Newcombe, 1982; Riddoch & Humphreys, 1987a; Warren & Morton, 1982). The perceptual classification stage involves matching a given view of an object to a stored representation of the appearance of that object—it is the stage at which different views of the same object can be seen as belonging together, distinct from other object categories.

Experimental evidence for this as a distinct stage in normal subjects comes from *repetition priming* experiments. Items which have been encountered in an earlier phase of an experiment are recognised more easily than those which have not been encountered, but these effects seem to be material-specific. For example, Warren and Morton (1982) showed that subjects could identify a briefly presented picture of an object at a lower exposure duration if they had earlier named the same or a different picture of that visual object compared with a control condition where no prior exposure was given. Earlier exposure to the object's *label* however, had no effect on subsequent recognition. This material-specificity suggests that processing is facilitated at some stage not accessed by the picture's label. Assuming that object labels and pictures access the same, or similar, semantic descriptions (see later), the stage affected is one influenced by representations of an object's appearance.

The semantic classification stage is the point where the functions and associates of a given object are retrieved from a semantic memory system. Most theorists propose that the same semantic information will be accessed if an object is seen, felt, or heard (if it is a noisy object) or if its name is read or heard (e.g. Ratcliff & Newcombe, 1982; Warren & Morton, 1982). Thus, whether we see a baby, or hear one crying, or read the word "baby", we will access a common core semantic "definition" of what a baby is, although additional semantic-level descriptions may be modality-specific (we may be able to see that a baby is cute, or hear that it is hungry). Evidence for some common store of semantic associations derives in part from experiments on *semantic priming* (Sperber, McCauley, Ragain, & Weil, 1979), which we will discuss in more detail towards the end of this chapter.

The semantic classification system is distinguished from the stage of name retrieval, and available evidence suggests that the names of objects can only be accessed via this semantic stage: with normal subjects, semantic classification of pictures is much faster than decisions which require access to object labels (Potter & Faulconer, 1975). This contrasts with word recognition, where words can be named (read aloud) more quickly than they can be categorised. It is as though objects and pictures have "direct" access to meanings, perhaps reflecting the fact that the physical properties of many objects constrain their functions—animals have legs in order to walk, saws have serrated edges to facilitate cutting. In contrast to their direct access to meanings, objects may gain only indirect access to their labels, via the semantic system. Interference effects are also consistent with this proposal: irrelevant names do not interfere with the process of classifying pictures of objects or faces according to whether they belong to particular semantic categories, but irrelevant names do interfere with naming objects or with naming faces (Glaser & Dungelhoff, 1984; Smith & Magee, 1980; Young, Hay, & Ellis, 1986). However, although the stages of object recognition appear to operate in the sequence: perceptual classification—semantic classification—name retrieval, it is possible that these stages may operate in "cascade" with a later one starting before an earlier one is completed (Humphreys, Riddoch, & Quinlan, 1988).

Neuropsychological evidence is also consistent with this broad framework. Problems in recognising objects can arise through deficits within or between any of the stages, and the patterns of impairment in object recognition which have been observed in brain damaged patients are revealing about the relationship between these different stages, and the internal organisation of each.

A profound disability in object recognition can arise if descriptions constructed of an image of an object are not suitable to match the stored representations of object appearances. For example, H.J.A., who has been extensively studied by Humphreys and Riddoch (e.g. 1987a) finds it very difficult to recognise objects, faces, and places since suffering a stroke which produced bilateral brain damage. Further testing has shown that he

OBJECT DECISION TASK
a. Line drawings

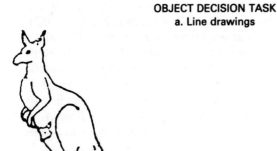

b. Silhouettes

FIG. 3.1.   Examples of novel stimuli for an "object decision" task created by transposing "parts" from different objects: (a) line drawn versions; (b) silhouette versions. (Reproduced from Humphreys & Riddoch, 1987a, with permission.)

is unable to distinguish line-drawings of real objects from those of non-objects created by interchanging parts of real objects (an "object decision" task: see Fig. 3.1). However, he is able to copy line-drawings that he cannot recognise showing that he can *see* the images he fails to recognise. He is also able to *draw* objects from memory, showing that his store of the visual appearances of objects is intact. Figure 3.2 shows some examples of H.J.A.'s drawings. Although drawing and copying are effortful tasks for H.J.A., and he occasionally omits parts of objects from his drawings, the results none the less show that he seems to have retained fairly accurate visual knowledge of the appearances of these objects.

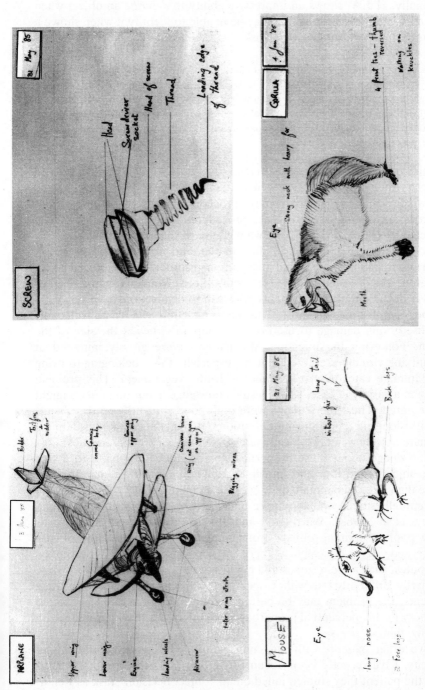

FIG. 3.2. Examples of H.J.A.'s drawings from memory, together with his notes on the salient parts of each object. (Reproduced from Humphreys & Riddoch, 1987a, with permission.)

55

Finally, H.J.A. shows an impressive ability to *describe* an object when given its label, even though he may be unable to identify it when shown a picture of it. For example, when asked to define a lettuce he replied:

> A lettuce is a quick growing, annual plant, cultivated for human consumption of its succulent crisp leaves which grow, during younger stages of the plant, tightly formed together in a general ball-shaped mass. Widely cultivated, lettuces are of many varieties and of absolutely no value as a food. They do, however, enable one to eat delicious mayonnaise when using a knife and fork in polite places.

Such observations suggest that H.J.A. has good stored knowledge about objects, their appearance as well as their functions. Such intact stored knowledge can be separated from the procedures needed to assemble input descriptions of objects. It is these procedures which seem to have been affected by H.J.A.'s stroke, and we will discuss the nature of his resultant deficit in more detail later in this chapter and in Chapter 5.

In other patients the visual recognition disorder can be traced to an apparent loss of visual knowledge about objects. Warrington and Shallice (1984) documented four patients who suffered infection from the virus herpes simplex encephalitis. This viral infection can cause relatively localised brain damage focused on the temporal lobes at the side of the brain. Following the infection, the patients were grossly impaired at identifying visually presented objects, especially those belonging to living and animate categories (e.g. animals, fruits, vegetables). This problem arose in a variety of tasks where visual knowledge about the objects might be required. Thus, the patients were both poor at identifying the objects from vision and at producing definitions of the objects. When defining animate objects we may typically refer to their perceptual properties. Loss of knowledge about these properties would impair the ability to define such objects, and it would impair the identification of animate objects more than that of inanimate ones because animate objects tend to be more perceptually similar and so require finer perceptual differentiation (Humphreys et al., 1988). Warrington and Shallice also showed that patients were poor at defining objects from inanimate categories if the objects concerned were typically defined on the basis of their perceptual attributes, such as gem stones and clothes (e.g. an emerald and a ruby are primarily differentiated with respect to their colour). Thus, for these patients, the problem may be better accounted for in terms of impaired memory for the perceptual properties of stimuli rather than a problem with "living things" *per se*.

Two other patients with the same pathology, and apparently similar deficits, have recently been documented. Job and Sartori (1988) report that the patient they studied failed on an "object decision" task as well as on tasks requiring access to semantic and name information about objects. Problems with object decision would be expected if the patient's memory for the appearance of objects was disrupted, making it difficult to decide even whether a stimulus has a familiar form. Silveri and Gainotti (1988) have further shown that the problems of such patients are more pronounced when they have to retrieve visual rather than verbal knowledge about objects. They asked their patient to name objects from definitions which stressed either the visual/perceptual or the verbal/functional properties of the objects. For example a "visual" definition of a butterfly was "an insect with broad, coloured ornate wings", whereas a "verbal" definition of a pig was "a farm animal used to obtain salami and ham". The patient was better at answering the verbal compared with the visual definitions. This result indicates that the patient has not lost general knowledge about living things; rather there is a problem in retrieving the visual appearances of objects. The particular problems with living things may occur because our knowledge of living things is focused around these characteristics, and because finer perceptual distinctions may be needed to identify living relative to inanimate objects.

Other patients reveal intact procedures for assembling input descriptions, intact stored visual representations and intact semantic knowledge and naming, but seem to have lost the ability to get from perceptual classification of an object's shape to certain kinds of semantic knowledge. J.B. (Riddoch & Humphreys, 1987b) was involved in a road traffic accident in 1981 that resulted in extensive damage to his left cerebral hemisphere. Following this he had difficulty naming many common objects from vision, despite the fact that he could often identify the same objects from touch and he was able to give the correct names when given a definition. This shows that he did not have a general problem in finding the names for objects (an "anomia"). J.B. was good at object decision tasks requiring quite fine discriminations between objects and non-objects, even though he was typically unable to identify the objects concerned. This fits with J.B. having intact access to visual knowledge about objects.

However, J.B.'s object decision performance can be contrasted with his performance on an associative matching task, where he had to decide which two of three objects placed before him were used together (e.g. a hammer, a nail, and a screw). When given the names of the objects, he found the task trivially easy. This shows both that J.B. understood the task, and that he has intact associative knowledge about the objects. Yet when the objects were presented visually he scored only just above chance (Riddoch & Humphreys, 1987b). J.B.'s case seems to suggest a dissociation between visual knowledge about objects and semantic knowledge of object associations. Such observations are thus consistent with our distinction between "perceptual" and "semantic" classification of objects.

Things are not quite as clear-cut as this, however. Although J.B. might fail to identify an object by name, he was often able to give a quite specific gesture to show how it might be used. For instance, he would make a right hand "cutting" gesture to a knife and a left hand "feeding" gesture to a fork, though he was typically unable to differentiate which was which when looking at them, and when asked to point to the knife he would often point to the fork, and vice versa. Such observations suggest that J.B. can access some "semantic" information visually, and indeed some theorists have used cases such as these to support a distinction between separate "visual" and "verbal" semantic systems (cf. Warrington & Shallice, 1984). However, the observation that J.B. cannot make associative judgements to visual objects severely restricts the notion of a separate "visual semantic" system, and we find it more parsimonious to maintain that J.B.'s difficulties result from impaired access to an amodal semantic system from the perceptual classification system. How, though, can J.B. sometimes produce specific gestures to objects? One suggestion is that, for familiar objects, direct associations may be built up between a visual memory and a motor action (e.g. between a memory of a hammer and the action of hammering). These direct associations may bypass semantic knowledge about object functions and associations. J.B.'s case is interesting because it motivates questions about the kinds of stored knowledge about objects that is used to direct immediate action as opposed to that which allows us to explain an object's uses and associations to another person. To use J.J. Gibson's terminology, a particular shape may "afford" grasping, or even cutting, but this linkage of shape to action could be achieved independently of the system that allows us to reflect upon its possible uses (see Bruce & Green, 1985, for further discussion of action-based perceptual theories such as that of the late J.J. Gibson).

Although patients such as J.B. seem to have problems accessing associative and functional knowledge from vision, in other patients the recognition problems seem more directly related to a loss of such semantic knowledge itself. The loss is found however the patient is probed, be it with objects, printed words or speech. For example, Marin (1987) reports a lady with pre-senile dementia who would turn pictures of objects into their correct orientation (presumably using stored visual knowledge) whilst being quite incapable of matching pictures of a candle with a lightbulb, a violin with a trumpet, etc. which would seem to require access to associative knowledge. Unlike J.B., this patient was unable to perform any categorisation tasks based on functional or associative knowledge about stimuli. This was true whether the stimuli were presented pictorially or spoken, and seems to reflect a central deficit affecting performance in many modalities. The most parsimonious explanation of such a central

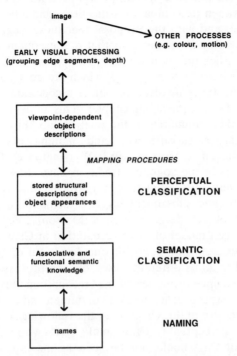

FIG. 3.3.   A simple model showing the sequential stages involved in visual object recognition and naming.

problem is in terms of a loss of semantic knowledge tapped by all input modalities.

Finally, all the above examples of impaired object recognition may be distinguished from "anomias" where the problem seems to lie in the access of labels from intact visual and semantic classification systems (e.g. Kay & Ellis, 1987). Such circumscribed deficits in naming with intact visual and semantic classification are consistent with the suggestion that naming is achieved subsequent to the access of visual and semantic representations. Additionally, if naming were contingent upon the prior access of visual and semantic representations, then patients with impaired perceptual or semantic classificiation should also be impaired at object naming, and in fact this is true of all the patients we have described. Although some cases have been reported where patients can name objects of which they fail to show *detailed* semantic knowledge (e.g. Warrington & Taylor, 1978; Chertkow, Bub, & Caplan, Reference Note 1), there are no convincing demonstrations of patients who can name objects in the absence of any semantic knowledge at all.

Thus, experimental and neuropsychological evidence is consistent with the distinction between perceptual classification, semantic classification, and name retrieval, and with the proposal that these stages act sequentially, although possibly in cascade, so that a subsequent stage can get going before an earlier one is necessarily completed. This sequence of processing stages is illustrated in Fig. 3.3, which presents a model to show how the processing stages involved in object recognition are related to those we considered in the preceding chapter. This model is rather similar to a number of earlier summaries of the relationship between perceptual classification, semantic classification, and naming of objects (e.g. Seymour, 1979; Warren & Morton, 1982; Warrington & Taylor, 1978). Several such authors in the cognitive tradition have drawn a distinction between "recognition units" ("pictogens") which house descriptions of object appearances, and subsequent levels of semantic description and verbal labelling of objects (e.g. Warren & Morton, 1982) (cf. our discussion of the logogen model of word recognition in Chapter 7). Such a framework provides a starting point for our discussion of *how* an object may be recognised in all its different views, but the processes involved in doing this are side-stepped by models of the "recognition unit" variety. It is this problem which has concerned workers in human and computer vision, and which we emphasise in this chapter. In the following sections, we will describe the task of perceptual recognition of objects within a computational framework, but this should not be seen as incompatible with the framework summarised earlier (Fig. 3.3). Our aim is to provide a more adequate and detailed account of one stage of the model—the perceptual classification stage—than can be achieved with simple "box" models.

TEMPLATES, FEATURES, AND STRUCTURAL DESCRIPTIONS

To introduce the problem of how we may be able to recognise different views of an object as equivalent, let us briefly consider problems of two-dimensional *pattern*, rather than three-dimensional *object*, recognition. A good example of an everyday pattern recognition task is the recognition of alphanumeric characters. Despite the great variety of sizes, orientations, and exemplars of each kind of letter and number, we have no difficulty categorising novel instances appropriately. It is easy to pick out letter Ms from the patterns shown in Fig. 3.4, for example. Introductory textbooks (e.g. Lindsay & Norman, 1976) generally go into some detail about the relative merits of feature-based compared with template-based models of pattern recognition. Here, we will summarise such arguments very briefly. For the moment, we will make the additional, simplifying assumption that the patterns to be recognised are always seen upright and orthogonal to the

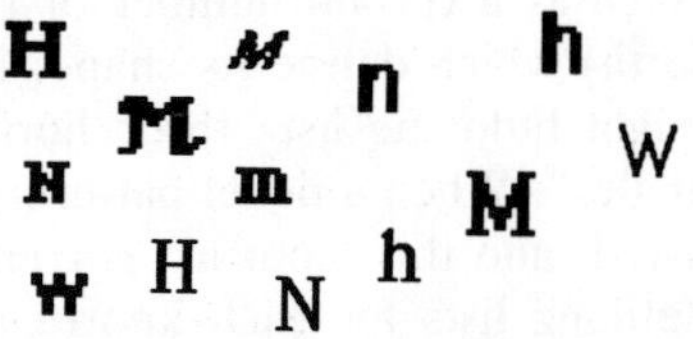

FIG. 3.4.   It is easy to pick out the letter Ms, despite the variety in their shapes and the shapes of the other background letters.

line of sight—later we will add in the complications produced by tilting the head or the pattern.

One possible means of recognising different patterns would be to compare a novel pattern against some set of stored *templates*—one for each pattern class to be distinguished. A template is a wholistic representation of a shape which you can imagine as being like a stencil for the shape. Matching an unknown pattern against a set of templates would involve seeing which known stencil overlapped the most with the unknown shape. Provided input patterns are standardised in terms of their size, each template could be successfully matched against pattern exemplars viewed at different distances, and normalisation procedures could, in principle, cope with effects of tilt, which we consider in detail shortly. More intractable problems for template models derive from the variability in basic pattern shape which can be tolerated by human recognition processes. The letter Ms in Fig. 3.4 differ in a number of ways, not just in their size and orientation. At the very least, we would have to assume that we stored multiple templates for each known pattern, and such solutions have tended to be dismissed as inelegant and unparsimonious (although compare this with the later descriptions of connectionist treatments). However, template-matching models provide an efficient practical means of recognising shapes with basic forms which do not vary. The numerals on bank cheques are recognised by machines using template matching—the form of each numeral does not vary, and has been specially designed to make each number as distinct as possible from all others.

Patterns, such as letters, seem to be defined by critical local *features* rather than global shape. The important thing which distinguishes a Q from an O seems to be the presence or absence of the bar, not the exact shape of the circular body of the letter. As we mentioned in the previous chapter, much physiological evidence obtained during the 1950s and 1960s suggested that cells in the visual cortex are selectively responsive to features such as bars or edges in particular orientations (e.g. Hubel & Wiesel, 1959; 1968), and such evidence influenced the production of a number of feature-based models of pattern recognition, the most familiar being Selfridge's "Pandemonium" account (Selfridge, 1959; see Lindsay & Norman, 1976). In the Pandemonium system, each letter or number is represented internally by a "demon" which holds a list of local features (such as a certain number of right angles, vertical lines, curves, and so forth) which define its shape. For example, the demon for the letter E might hold the list "three horizontal lines, one vertical line, four right angles". When a novel pattern is presented, its features are analysed and listed, and this input list is compared in parallel with each of the stored defining lists for each known pattern. The closer the input feature list matches one stored for a known pattern, the more "loudly" does the corresponding pattern demon "shout", and the pattern is classified as belonging to the category represented by the demon shouting the loudest. Pandemonium systems can learn to give more weight to certain features than others, and when set up as learning systems in this way they become similar to some of the connectionist schemes we describe later in the chapter. The problem with the Pandemonium system as described lies not in its basic architecture, but in the nature of the representations it encodes. The features which have been considered in the development of such models are very local parts of patterns, like bars and angles. Feature lists of this kind are not rigid enough—for something to be a letter T, the spatial arrangement of its features is important, not just the features themselves. We can tell a W from an M, where the features are identical, but their orientation differs. A Pandemonium demon which defined the letter E in the way we suggested above would respond equally strongly to each of the shapes shown in Fig. 3.5. We need a way to describe component features and their spatial arrangement, but less rigidly than can be achieved by templates.

Structural descriptions are symbolic descriptions of the features of a pattern and their spatial arrangements, which have proved useful in more recent approaches to pattern and object recognition. A structural description of a T-shape for example, might specify that one part (a vertical line) supports and bisects a second part (a horizontal line). Novel patterns can be classified by comparing derived descriptions of them with stored structural models of different object classes, in which some aspects of the description are made obligatory. For something to be a "T" there *must be* a vertical line and a horizontal line, and the former *must* support the latter at a point about midway along its length (see Fig. 3.6) (cf. Winston, 1975).

The great advantage of this kind of approach is that we can leave certain parameters unspecified in the structural model which defines a concept, whereas others are made obligatory. Within quite wide limits, the relative and absolute lengths of the vertical and horizontal bars of a T do not

FIG. 3.5. If the features which define letters were horizontal lines, vertical lines, and angles, each of these shapes could be recognised as a letter E.

matter, it is the manner of their intersection which is important. So a structural model for a T can specify that any kind of vertical line must support any kind of horizontal line, provided perhaps that the horizontal line is shorter than the vertical. As stated, structural descriptions do not constitute a theory of pattern recognition, because we would need to specify more fully how the features and their arrangements were encoded from an image, and the nature of the matching algorithm enabling recognition to occur. However, compared with templates and feature lists, only structural descriptions provide a representational medium which is sufficiently rich and flexible for the development of such a theory.

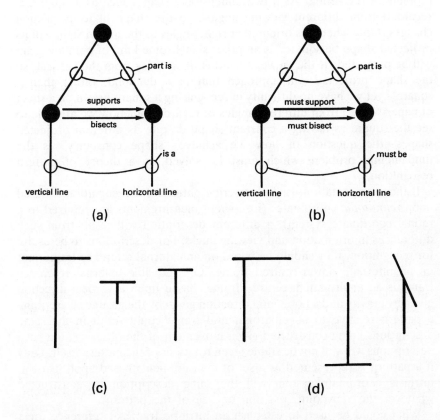

FIG. 3.6. (a) A structural description for a letter T. The description indicates that there are two parts to the letter—one part is a vertical line, the other part a horizontal line. The vertical line supports and bisects the horizontal. (b) A structural model for the letter T. This is like the description at (a), but now the essential aspects are specified. For something to be a "T" a vertical line *must* support and bisect a horizontal line, although the relative lengths of the lines are not important. Using this model, shapes at (c) would be classified as Ts whereas those at (d) would be rejected. (Figure reproduced from Bruce & Green, 1985, with permission.)

REFERENCE FRAMES

Our complete theory of pattern recognition must specify how structural descriptions suitable for recognition can be derived from retinal images and matched against stored structural models which define particular object categories. A major problem for any such theory is to account for the recognition of patterns whose orientations with respect to the retina may vary (because the pattern, or the viewer's head, has been rotated), and whose projected shapes on the retina may vary due to changes in the slant of the pattern with respect to the viewer. Imagine the shapes of letters projected on the picture plane—a way of envisaging the nature of the problem at the retina. As a two-dimensional shape, such as a square, is regarded from different viewing angles, so the shape of its projection changes. Only when it is oriented at right angles to the line of sight will its projected shape be square, at all other slants some kind of parallelogram will be projected. If the viewer's head is tilted away from the vertical, so the shape projected will approach that of a diamond, rather than a square—yet we have no difficulty in recognising a square drawn on a sheet of paper viewed from different angles of regard. Somehow we are able to see the square as having a constant shape despite its different projected shapes—the question of how we achieve "shape constancy" is the fundamental problem which must be solved by a theory of pattern recognition.

If the representation used to describe patterns for recognition is based upon *retinotopic* coordinates (i.e. where measurements are referred to a retinal coordinate system), a different description will result from such differences in orientation and viewing angle. For descriptions to be useful for recognition, they should be based on an external reference frame, not on an internal, viewer-centred frame. One possible external reference frame is an environment-centred frame, based upon a vertical direction given by gravity and a horizontal direction given by the ground. Describing a pattern relative to an environmental frame could result in the same descriptions being constructed given movement of the observer, but such descriptions will still not be stable given rotations of the pattern itself. Only if a pattern is represented as a set of measurements based upon its own, intrinsic coordinate system will the same description be constructed whatever the viewpoint, position or size of the pattern.

What could be used to establish an intrinsic frame of reference for a pattern's description? Marr and Nishihara (1978), whose theory of object recognition we consider in more detail later, have suggested that descriptions for shape recognition could be referred to a coordinate system based upon the major axis of an elongated and/or symmetrical shape. For example, to return to our structural model for the letter T, we suggested that an adequate model for recognition of this letter would specify that a vertical line must bisect and support a horizontal line. To be recognised as a T, a novel pattern's description must match this, but a tilted T will contain neither horizontal nor vertical lines if these are defined with respect to the retina or the environment. If, however, the axis of elongation of the T shape is taken as the reference frame, with this axis defining "vertical", then tilted T's would be recognised. (Things become a bit more complicated when we consider what happens if the T is rotated by 180 degrees. Although its axis of elongation would again define the vertical, whether such a pattern would satisfy the "supported by" relationship would depend upon which end of the T was seen as being its "top", and this might depend upon what else the viewer knew about the context in which this pattern was being presented. Intuitively, it seems, we might recognise an upside-down T as a "T" in the context of upside-down writing, but if presented without any orienting context, we would probably fail to recognise it as a familiar symbol at all.)

There has been extensive research in visual perception examining which kind of reference frame we make use of when viewing simple patterns such as letters, and we cannot do justice to the complexities of this literature here (see Humphreys & Quinlan, 1987; Rock, 1973, for reviews). One important finding which has emerged from such studies, however, is that under some circumstances at least, the perception of elongated shapes does seem to be based upon their intrinsic axes of elongation, consistent with Marr and Nishihara's suggestion. Humphreys (1984) asked subjects to decide as quickly as possible whether or not two presented items had the same shape. When the shapes were the same, they were either both elongated parallelograms, or scalene triangles. On "same" trials, the two shapes could be presented with the same or different overall orientations, as defined by the directions pointed by their axes of elongation, and with the same or different locations of their "top" features (see Fig. 3.7). (Where both the orientation and "top" locations were the same, the second shape was, of course, untransformed relative to the first.) Humphreys found that when subjects could not predict the precise location of the second shape, there was no advantage for untransformed items over those which preserved orientation but changed the relative location of the "top" feature (e.g. the point of the triangle), but both these conditions yielded faster matching than was obtained when the orientation changed, even if this change preserved the position of the "top" (see Fig. 3.7). Quite different results were obtained when subjects knew where the second shape would be presented, however. In this case, untransformed trials had the advantage over both the other two conditions, which did not differ. These results suggest that under conditions of spatial uncertainty (which of course characterise normal object perception), we may make use of the

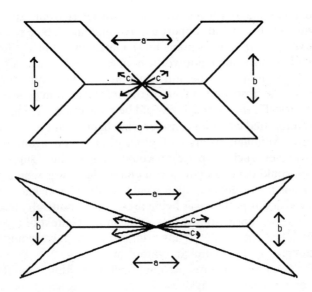

FIG. 3.7.   Diagram showing the possible transformations between two shapes (parallelo-grams—top; triangles—bottom) to be judged the "same" in Humphreys' (1984) study. (a) Transformations where the orientation of the shapes are altered but the "top" features remain in the same location; (b) transformations where the orientations are altered and the top features are relocated; and (c) transformations where the orientations are preserved but the top features are relocated.

overall axis of elongation to help compute a description of a shape which is useful for matching it with others. Such axis-based descriptions have played an important role in the development of theories of object, rather than pattern recognition, as we will see in the next section.

THEORIES OF OBJECT RECOGNITION

Our brief discussion of pattern recognition should suffice to alert you to the potential complexity of the problem of object recognition. As we noted earlier, even a simple two-dimensional shape, like a circle, regarded from different viewing angles, projects different shapes to the retina. When a complex three-dimensional shape, such as a horse, is viewed from different angles, its projection changes even more dramatically, as shown in Fig. 3.8. And the recognition of an articulated shape such as this is complicated even more by the way in which its configuration changes as the animal moves. How can we recognise each of these radically different views as being "a horse"? The problem of "object constancy" is yet more complicated than that of two-dimensional shape constancy.

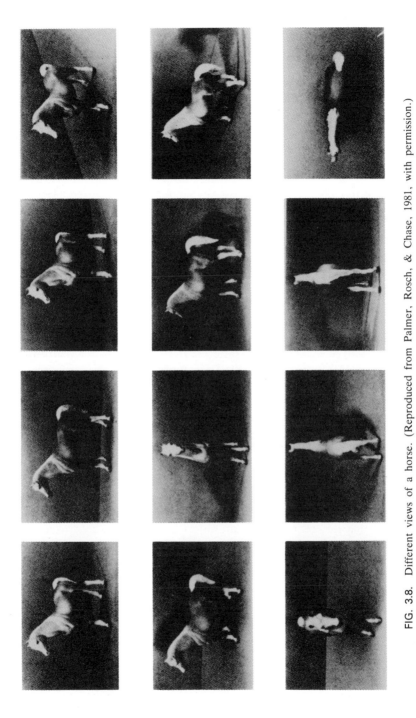

FIG. 3.8. Different views of a horse. (Reproduced from Palmer, Rosch, & Chase, 1981, with permission.)

The fundamental problem of object recognition is how we get from the features revealed by a particular view of an object to a representation specifying the object in question. Amongst simpler animals, there appear to be mechanisms of object recognition which can bypass some of these complexities by recognising an object on the basis of a single "landmark" feature which is common to all views of the object in question. For example, one male stickleback may recognise another on the basis of the patch of red which is found on the male stickleback's underbelly. Crude models of fish with a red underside are displayed to aggressively, whereas accurate models which lack this "key stimulus" are ignored (Tinbergen, 1951). Bruce and Green (1985) discuss some other examples of recognition on the basis of such key features, but point out that such mechanisms lack the flexibility and subtlety which characterise human powers of object recognition.

Some authors (e.g. Minsky, 1977) have suggested that several distinct views of a particular object are stored, to enable recognition over the range of viewpoints with which we deal. In its simplest form, the suggestion that discrete views of objects are stored and matched independently reduces the problem of object recognition to that of pattern recognition, with independent recognition of the different two-dimensional shapes projected from different views of an object. The equivalence of these different views (i.e. the fact that they are related more closely than views of different objects), would have to be attributed to the common semantic description and/or name accessed when recognition of any of the views was achieved. However, there is compelling neuropsychological evidence against such a model, as there are patients who can correctly "see" the equivalence of radically different views of objects, yet not know their uses or their names, and others who can recognise objects but only when shown from conventional views (e.g. Warrington & Taylor, 1978). Such observations (which strongly influenced Marr in the development of his theory of vision) suggest that different views of an object are somehow used to access an overall, composite description of the object's shape. Later in this chapter we will consider how such a composite description might nevertheless emerge from the storage of different viewpoints through the superposition of many different instances within a distributed memory system. First, however, we describe the more established approach to object recognition, which is to assume that it is mediated by an explicit computation of an abstract description of the object's shape.

Marr and Nishihara's Theory of Object Recognition

Marr and Nishihara (1978) argued, largely on the grounds of elegance and parsimony, that a unique, object-centred description could be stored to mediate the recognition of that object in all its many views. The

AXIS

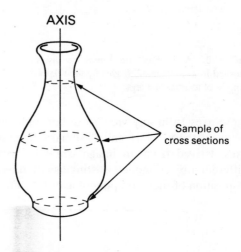

Sample of
cross sections

FIG. 3.9.   An example of a generalised cone. (Reproduced from
Bruce & Green, 1985, with permission.)

representation they proposed was based upon the axes of the overall shape
and component parts of objects, and they suggested that the lengths and
arrangements of these axes were recoverable from any (or at least most)
views of known objects. The kinds of objects discussed by Marr and
Nishihara (1978) were those comprising of one or more *generalised cone*
shapes. A generalised cone is the shape which results from sweeping a
cross-section of constant shape but variable size along an axis. A vase is a
generalised cone, with a circular cross-section which expands and contracts
along its length (see Fig. 3.9). Many other natural, elongated shapes can be
described as approximate generalised cones, and Marr (1977) suggested
that silhouettes (which show only the occluding contours of an object) were
interpreted as though comprised of such shapes. Indeed, Marr was so
impressed by our abilities to interpret silhouettes of unfamiliar shapes that
he based much of his thinking on the kind of representation which might be
derived from occluding contours alone. In what follows we will initially
follow Marr's emphasis on the information available from occluding contours, although later we will examine the importance of other routes to
recognition.

Marr and Nishihara argued that many important kinds of object could be
considered to be constructed from generalised cone components, and that
the lengths and arrangements of the axes of these components, relative to
the major axis of the object as a whole, could be used to distinguish
between different object classes. Take, for example, the difference
between a "human" and a "gorilla" shape (see Fig. 3.10). Each comprises
(approximately) a set of generalised cones corresponding to head, trunk,
arms, and legs, but the relative lengths of the axes of the cones
corresponding to arms and legs differ. A visual system which could derive

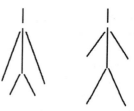

FIG. 3.10. A "gorilla" (left) may be distinguished from a "human" (right) by the relative
lengths of its arms and legs.

these axes from any view of either animal would be able to distinguish
between them. Marr and Nishihara suggested that the configuration of
axes derived from an image could be used to address a catalogue of
different object models distinguished on the basis of the number and
disposition of their component axes (see Fig. 3.11). Note that they suggest

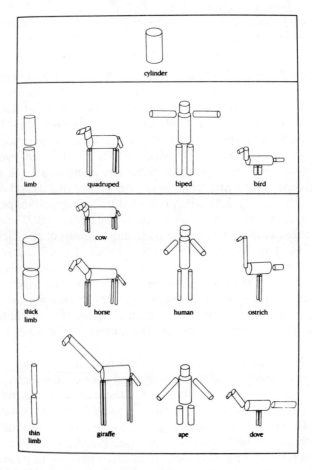

FIG. 3.11. A catalogue of 3D model descriptions at different levels of specificity. (Reproduced from Marr & Nishihara, 1978, with permission.)

a hierarchical organisation of this catalogue, in which a rather crude description would suffice to distinguish a biped from a quadruped, but more detail would be needed to tell which kind of biped (ape or human), and so forth.

There is some evidence showing that object recognition can be based on quite general descriptions of objects. For instance, Eleanor Rosch and her colleagues (e.g. Rosch et al., 1976) showed that subjects apply a "base-level" name to objects faster than they can supply their specific names. Thus, we identify a robin as a bird faster than we identify it as a robin; similarly we identify a "granny smith" apple as an apple before we identify its variety. One way of thinking about base-level representations is that they conform to the structural properties common to exemplars from a category. Note, however, that base-level representations tend only to be involved for objects that are good exemplars of their category. Objects that are poor category exemplars are identified fastest at an individual item level. Thus we identify a penguin as a penguin faster than we identify it as a bird (Jolicoeur, Gluck, & Kosslyn, 1984). The degree to which recognition is hierarchical depends on the overlap between the object and the more general stored descriptions. Indeed, the existence of such category-based representations could be used to explain why pictures are categorised so quickly, particularly where the category judgement (e.g. this is an animal) maps on to a super-ordinate structural description (e.g. a quadruped; cf. Potter & Faulconer, 1975). [This cannot be the only explanation for rapid access of semantics from pictures, however, as pictures of familiar faces can be rapidly categorised according to occupational category (e.g. politicians) even when there is no visual basis for the distinction (e.g. the non-politicians are of a similar age and appearance; Young, Ellis, & Flude, 1988). We will return to consider the particular case of face recognition later in this chapter.]

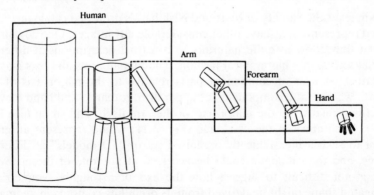

FIG. 3.12. A hierarchy of 3D models. Each box shows the major axis for the figure of interest on the left, and its component axes to the right. (Reproduced from Marr & Nishihara, 1978, with permission.)

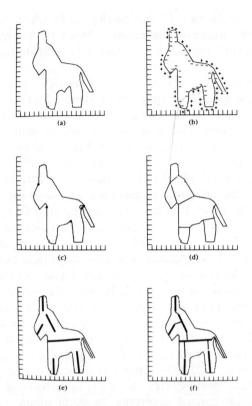

FIG. 3.13.   (a) An outline of a toy donkey. (b) Convex (+) and concave (−) sections are labelled. (c) Strong segmentation points are found. (d) The outline is divided into a set of smaller segments using the points found at (c) and rules for connecting these to other points on the contour. (e) The component axis is found for each segment. (f) The axes are related to each other (thin lines). (Reproduced from Marr & Nishihara, 1978, with permission.)

Whatever the validity of Marr and Nishihara's proposed catalogue, axis-based representations have other considerable advantages. One advantage is that they allow us quite naturally to construct descriptions at different spatial scales, in a hierarchical fashion. The human arms and legs may be described as axes of component parts relative to the major axis of the figure, whereas the components of upper arm, forearm, and hand may be described relative to the major axis of the arm itself, and so on (see Fig. 3.12). Each entry in the catalogue (Fig. 3.11) would represent an entry point to such a hierarchically organised set of "3D models" at different scales, and the catalogue could be accessed at any one of these levels.

It is not difficult to suggest how the axis of a roughly symmetrical, elongated shape might be derived from its occluding contours in an image, and we have already discussed, in Chapter 2, how occluding contours might be built up from the messy information in the raw primal sketch.

However, Marr and Nishihara's theory must explain how we get from the occluding contour of a complex shape comprised of several components, to the axis of each, and this requires that a complex contour be *segmented* into a number of distinct parts. Marr and Nishihara (1978) described a program by Vatan which segmented the contour of a silhouette of a toy donkey into distinct parts by finding concavities in the contour (see Fig. 3.13). There are now independent grounds for the proposal that humans make use of concavities of this kind to segment images, which we describe in the next section.

Segmenting Parts for Recognition

Hoffman and Richards (1984) point out that distinct parts of objects intersect in a contour of concave discontinuity of their tangent planes (the transversality regularity). At any point around the intersection, a tangent to the surface of one part forms a concave cusp with the tangent to the surface of the other part (concave means it points into the object rather than into the background, see Fig. 3.14). Now, this transversality regularity means that in an image of a complex shape, "concavities" mark the divisions between the contours of distinct parts. Concavities can be detected in contours of smooth shapes by seeking places where there is greatest negative curvature.

Hoffman and Richards provide some compelling demonstrations as evidence for the importance of these concavities in our segmentation of shapes. For example, they examine a number of classic ambiguous "reversing" figures, such as the Schröder staircase, and the "faces-goblet" (Figs 3.15 and 3.16) and show how our perceptions of their parts are predicted from the reversal of their figures. In the Schröder staircase (Fig. 3.15) for example, the Hoffman and Richards partitioning scheme says that

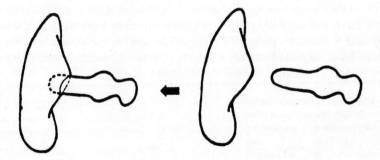

FIG. 3.14. The transversality regularity. Any two surfaces interpenetrating at random always meet in concave discontinuities. (Reproduced from Hoffman & Richards, 1984, with permission.)

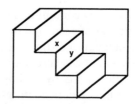

FIG. 3.15. In the Schröder staircase, part boundaries change when figure and ground reverse: x and y which appear to lie on adjacent surfaces of the same step will appear to belong to surfaces of different steps when the figure reverses. (Reproduced from Hoffman & Richards, 1984, with permission.)

a "part" of the figure must be a "step", as this is bounded by two lines of concave discontinuity. Now, when the staircase is seen in one orientation, with the plane marked "x" in Fig. 3.15 facing upwards, then the steps defined by concave discontinuities pointing into the solid body of the staircase are such that planes "x" and "y" are seen to belong together as faces of the same step. But when the figure reverses, so that plane "x" appears to face downwards, the concavities pointing into the body of the reversed figure (which now lies in the upper right of the picture) define a different set of steps: planes "x" and "y" now form faces of different, adjacent steps. With the faces-goblet figure (Fig. 3.16), when the figure is the goblet, then concavities pointing into it define its parts as the base, stem, and bowl. When the figure is either of the faces, then the concavities pointing into them define the parts as forehead, nose, chin, etc. This demonstration can help explain how the same contour can be "recognised" as two distinct objects: what matters is the way in which the contour is partitioned prior to recognition, and this in turn seems to involve a simple search for concavities relative to the centre of the region which is seen as figure.

There is thus good evidence for the possibility that human vision makes use of such local concavities to segment occluding contours prior to the derivation of the axes of each of the parts. However, the means of segmentation proposed by Hoffman and Richards is independent of the nature of the "parts" within the image. It will work if these are generalised cones, but it will work also if they are quite different kinds of shapes. Since Marr and Nishihara's theory of recognition was formulated, a number of authors have suggested extensions to their basic approach, to encompass a wider range of shapes among the component parts.

FIG. 3.16. The reversing faces-goblet. If part boundaries are defined by minima of curvature on the face, this divides the face into forehead, nose, lips, and chin. If the parts are defined by minima on the goblet, it divides into base, stem, bowl, and lip of bowl. (Reproduced from Hoffman & Richards, 1984, with permission.)

FIG. 3.17.   A scene constructed from "superquadric" components. (Reproduced from Pentland, 1986a, with permission.)

Beyond Generalised Cones

Pentland (1986a) has proposed a more flexible system of volumetric representation than can be achieved with generalised cones. Pentland suggests that most complex natural shapes are comprised of *superquadric* components. Superquadrics include basic shapes like spheres, wedges, and so forth and all kinds of deformations on these basic shapes which preserve their smoothly varying form and which do not introduce concavities. Figure 3.17 shows a scene constructed with superquadric components. Pentland's suggestion is that these might be the basic components which we recover when analysing images of natural objects. He has shown how the superquadric components present in a scene can be recovered from information about surface *tilt* at a number of distinct image locations. Tilt can be estimated by analysing gradients of shading, but additionally it is known accurately at occluding contours, which is why, Pentland suggests, contour information is so powerful in specifying an object's three-dimensional shape.

A framework which seems to provide a potential synthesis of the ideas we have discussed so far is that suggested by Biederman (1987). Like the authors whose work we have discussed earlier, Biederman stresses that objects are recognised as spatial arrangements of component parts which themselves come from a restricted set of basic shapes such as wedges and cylinders. Biederman calls these basic shape primitives "geons" (geometric ions), suggesting an analogy with spoken words which can likewise be constructed from, and decomposed into, combinations of basic primitives—phonemes. An occluding contour derived from an image of an object is segmented at regions of sharp concavity, and the resulting parts of the image are matched against representations of these primitive object shapes. The nature and arrangements of the geons found can then be matched with structural models of objects. The representation of each known object is a structural model of the components from which it is constructed, their relative sizes, orientations, place of attachment, and so forth.

The important aspect of Biederman's theory is the suggestion that geons are defined by properties which are *invariant* over different views. According to this theory, it is not necessary to make use of occluding contours to recover an axis-based three-dimensional shape description. Instead, occluding contours of the different component parts contain information which can lead to the direct access of the identities of particular components, each of which has its own "landmark" features in the two-dimensional primal sketch level representation. Biederman argues that there are a number of "non-accidental" properties of edges in images which can be used as reliable cues to related properties of edges in the world (cf. Kanade, 1981). Such properties include collinearity, curvilinearity, symmetry, parallelism, and co-termination (see Fig. 3.18). If any of

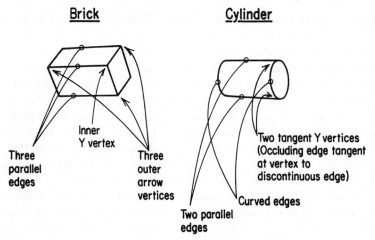

FIG. 3.18.   Differences in the non-accidental properties between a cylinder and a brick. (Reproduced from Biederman, 1987, with permission.)

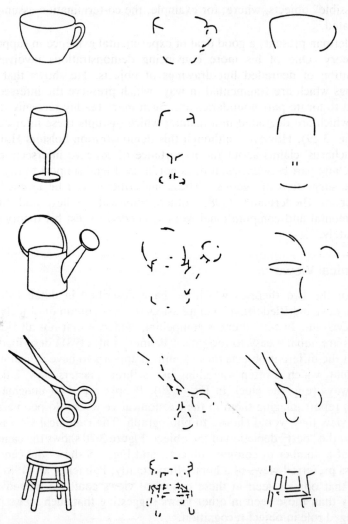

FIG. 3.19. Objects (left) are much more easy to recognise when their contours are degraded in ways which preserve their concave part intersections (centre) than when contours are deleted at regions of concavity (right). (Reproduced from Biederman, 1987), with permission.)

these properties is detected in an image, then the assumption is made that they are true of the world. Thus, parallel lines in the image signal parallel edges in the world; symmetry in the image signals symmetry in the world, and so forth. A geon is identified by a particular set of defining features (such as parallel edges) which can be accessed via these non-accidental properties. Biederman suggests that the assumption of non-accidental properties could explain a number of illusions such as the Ames chair, and "impossible" objects, where, for example, the co-termination assumption is violated.

Biederman presents a good deal of experimental evidence in support of his theory. One of his more convincing demonstrations involves the recognition of degraded line-drawings of objects. He shows that line-drawings which are fragmented in ways which preserve the intersections needed to locate part boundaries are much more readily recognised than those which are degraded in a manner which disrupts these intersections (see Fig. 3.19). However, although this demonstration bolsters Hoffman and Richards' claims about the importance of concave intersections for establishing part boundaries, it does not in itself lend support to the more specific suggestion of "geons". The same criticism can be levelled at a number of Biederman's (1987) other empirical studies, and further experimental and computational work is needed to test his theory more adequately.

Canonical Views

Each of the two theories which we have described in detail (Marr & Nishihara's, and Biederman's) emphasises the recognition of objects from any viewpoint. In fact, there is compelling evidence that not all views of objects are equally easy to recognise. Palmer et al. (1981) described how each of the different objects they examined appears to have a "canonical" viewpoint, which is often something like a three-quarters view, although not always (e.g. the clock in Fig. 3.20). People asked to imagine such objects report imaging them in their canonical views, as do people asked which view they would choose to photograph. The canonical view is also rated as the "best" depiction of the object. Figure 3.20 shows the canonical views of a number of common objects, and Fig. 3.8 shows the canonical and less preferred views of a horse. Importantly, Palmer et al. (1981) also found that objects seen in these canonical views could be named more quickly than those seen in other views suggesting that such views play a privileged role in object recognition.

Although the theories above stress the recognition of objects independent of viewpoint, each could readily accommodate such canonical view effects. Marr and Nishihara (1978) emphasise that certain viewpoints will conceal important major axes which are needed to derive a shape description. For example, a top view of a bucket conceals the axis of elongation which is probably crucial to its description. In these terms, then, canonical views should be those which are optimally revealing about the major and component axes of a figure. For Biederman, certain views may conceal the non-accidental properties which define the "geons", and other views may better reveal them. It is thus not critical for "view-independent" models of object recognition that certain aspects of the process may be view-dependent.

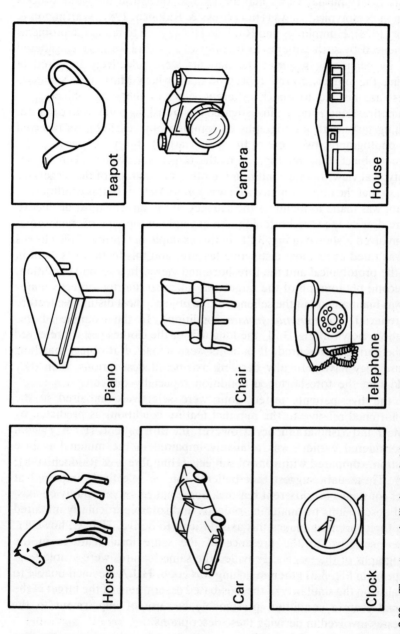

FIG. 3.20. These "canonical" views of objects were those that Palmer et al. (1981) found to be most readily imaged and most rapidly named. (Adapted from Palmer et al., 1981, with permission.)

Neuropsychological studies also support a role for "prototypical views" in object recognition. Some patients who find it difficult to recognise objects from unusual views may be able to recognise the same objects shown in prototypical views (Humphreys & Riddoch, 1984; Warrington & Taylor, 1978). Humphreys and Riddoch (1984) tried to relate the problems experienced by such patients to theories of the kind we have considered here, by examining whether the patients were selectively impaired at deriving the object-centred representations which Marr and Nishihara suggest are needed to match different views of the same object.

Humphreys and Riddoch investigated this by asking patients to carry out matching tasks with photographs of common objects. Subjects received three photographs, two were of the same (target) object and one was of a different object. One photograph of the target was always taken from a prototypical view. In one condition the other photograph of the target was taken so that the object's major axis was *foreshortened*. In this condition an attempt was made to maintain the saliency of the target's most distinctive feature despite the foreshortening. An example of the type of transformation involved is shown in Fig. 3.21. In this example the spring of the clothes peg was rated as its most distinctive feature, and this feature is salient in both the prototypical and the foreshortened views. In a second condition, the second photograph of the target was taken so that the object's major axis was maintained but the salience of the object's most distinctive feature was reduced (the *minimal feature* condition). In the example of this condition shown in Fig. 3.21, the long axis of the clothes peg is preserved but the spring is obscured. If patients were impaired at object matching because they have difficulty deriving axis-based descriptions, then they should find the foreshortened condition especially difficult.

Of the five patients tested, four were selectively impaired in the foreshortened relative to the minimal feature condition, as predicted by the Marr and Nishihara theory. However, the fifth patient, H.J.A. (whom we considered earlier) was relatively impaired in the minimal feature condition, compared with control subjects (Humphreys & Riddoch, 1984; 1985). These data suggest that patients can be selectively impaired at object constancy for different reasons. Some patients seem to rely on axis-based descriptions for matching objects, and so are particularly impaired when foreshortening makes this axis difficult to derive. H.J.A., however, seemed sensitive to the presence of the same local features in the photographs of the targets. Provided the same features were visible (e.g. the spring in Fig. 3.21) then matching was good. H.J.A. seemed unable to capitalise on the similarity of the axis-based descriptions of the target in the minimal feature condition, presumably because of impairment to the processes involved in deriving these descriptions.

This result indicates that object constancy may be achieved in more than one manner. Both axis-based and more local feature-based descriptions

 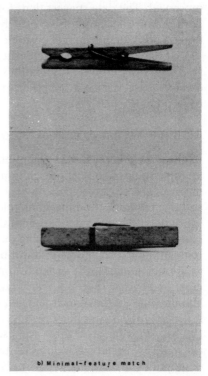

a) Foreshortened-view match   b) Minimal-feature match

FIG. 3.21.   Examples of the foreshortened view and minimal feature view transformations used by Humphreys and Riddoch (1984). (Reproduced with permission.)

may be derived in parallel. The recognition of objects in unusual yiews may be determined by whichever description provides fastest access to the stored prototypical representation of the object (Humphreys, 1987; Humphreys & Quinlan, 1987). Models in which object constancy is determined by a single process have difficulty with this result.

But do the results with the remaining four patients really support Marr and Nishihara's theory? Problems in matching foreshortened objects might arise for a number of reasons. For instance, such matches might be difficult if patients were impaired at deriving axis-based descriptions; they might also be difficult if patients were simply overly sensitive to viewpoint-dependent information, as foreshortening produces large changes to any viewpoint-dependent representation of an object. Riddoch and Humphreys (1986) investigated this last possibility with the same patients as in their earlier study. This time the patients had to match objects that were *both* minimal feature and size-transformed (to three times larger or smaller than the prototype). This joint manipulation again disrupted matching in some patients, even though the major axis of the object was now preserved. The data suggest that, following brain damage, object recognition in patients can be driven solely by viewpoint-dependent representations. Such patients manifest problems whenever objects are transformed so that their viewpoint-dependent representation differs greatly from their stored prototypical representations. As we will see in a later section, connectionist accounts of object recognition might provide a way to conceptualise such results.

Multiple Routes to Object Recognition

In the previous section we mentioned the possibility that there may be multiple routes to object recognition—either via an axis-based description, or via local features. The theories of object recognition we have considered so far emphasise the important role played by the occluding contour in specifying the three-dimensional shapes of particular types of object. However, it is worth emphasising that the occluding contour is not the only route to the recognition of the object classes we have considered.

Normal subjects, for example, find the "object decision task" that we described earlier (Fig. 3.1.) very much easier if they are shown elaborate line-drawings of the objects and non-objects than if they are shown shaded-in versions of the same line-drawings in silhouette (Humphreys and Riddoch, 1987a), showing that they are using internal features of the objects as well as occluding contours to access their catalogue of object descriptions. Interestingly, patient H.J.A. performs an object decision task more accurately from silhouettes than from line-drawings, scoring 72% correct from silhouettes compared with only 55% (approaching chance) with line-drawings. Other studies of H.J.A. (which we mention in Chapter 5) suggest that internal features can cause him to segment objects wrongly. It may be that internal details can give cues to segment objects into different parts, or even into separate "object descriptions", unless overridden by overall shape information. Clearly, this requires interplay between the visual descriptions derived from objects over different spatial scales, and segmentation might result if this interplay is disrupted. We return to consider the relationship between global form recognition and local part recognition later in this chapter and again in Chapter 5.

So far we have considered only that objects might be recognised in terms both of their global shape and of their internal features. Vaina (1983; 1987) discusses the way in which recognition might proceed in independent modules, with some based upon characteristic movements and textures of objects. Vaina (1987), for example, reminds us that some objects, such as pineapples and sheep, have characteristic surface *textures* which could allow us to recognise the object in the absence of visible distinctive features or salient axes. Vaina (1987) describes how right-hemispheric damage can lead to a selective deficit in recognising such objects from their textures.

These issues should remind us that different routes to object recognition may be more or less useful for recognising the same object in different viewpoints (which may reveal or conceal different aspects of global shape or distinctive features), or for recognising different *kinds* of object. The theories of object recognition we have considered in detail can really only be applied to certain kinds of objects whose classification depends upon fairly gross differences in overall shape. When we come to consider how we recognise different individuals from within a category (individual cars, cows or faces) then different kinds of representation may become appropriate. We consider the particular example of face recognition again later in this chapter.

So far in this chapter we have discussed theories of recognition which assume that objects are recognised via a representational level in which the essential properties of objects are stored in a quite abstract form—divorced from the details of particular instances or viewpoints seen on distinct occasions. In the next section, we turn to consider how recent connectionist models of object recognition can give a feel for how such "abstract" representations might be built up from discrete encounters with objects in different views.

CONNECTIONIST ACCOUNTS OF OBJECT RECOGNITION

We described in Chapter 2 how models of early visual processing have been built in which networks of simple processing units converge on solutions to problems which require the simultaneous satisfaction of a number of constraints. Such parallel processing models have proved important in the development of artificial intelligence (AI) techniques to solve computational problems which would be inefficient, and perhaps impossible, if implemented in other ways (e.g. optic flow computation, see Chapter 4). However, there has been a debate in recent years about whether such models simply provide convenient ways of *implementing* algorithms (e.g. Broadbent, 1985; Mayhew & Frisby, 1984), or whether such models provide an alternative way of conceptualising the algorithms themselves (e.g. Rumelhart & McClelland, 1985).

When we turn to consider connectionist approaches to object recognition, we find examples from both camps. Hinton (1981) described how a connectionist architecture could be used to implement a means of getting from a particular view of a pattern, to a viewpoint-independent description, without knowing the identity of the shape in advance. This could be achieved by setting up a network of simple units, with some, "retina-based units" responding to specific local features falling at particular locations and orientations, and other, "object-based units" responding to features oriented and located with respect to an object-centred frame (Fig. 3.22).

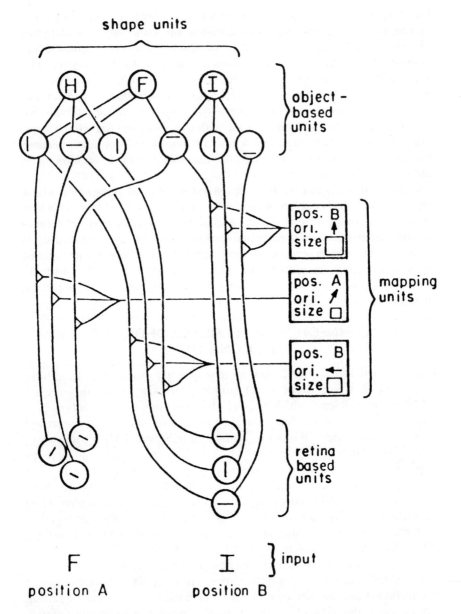

FIG. 3.22. A network for mapping from retina-based to object-based units. (Reproduced from Hinton, 1981, with permission.)

Activation within the retina-based units in turn excites the object-based units, but the degree of excitation will be modified by a separate set of "mapping units" which add in a bias towards particular frames (see also

Fig. 3.3). Hinton suggests that there might normally be a bias towards a vertical reference frame, reflecting our own bias, for example, to recognise "I" as "I" rather than "H", which has the same features. This kind of connectionist model clearly complements the kind of theories of object recognition that we considered earlier, by showing how certain kinds of computational operations might be achieved efficiently and quickly in a system of simple units with some of the properties of neurons. While complementing such conventional accounts, the connectionist implementation also adds something. Hinton's system can be extended to recognise patterns when the mapping rules are not known in advance, because of inbuilt biases from the object level which give more weight to combinations of features which define objects irrespective of orientation. Such biases can result in a letter being recognised even if oriented horizontally. Within such a scheme, an object's identity and the frame of reference for its description are recovered simultaneously through the converging pattern of activation. There is no need, once this kind of network is considered, to think of first setting up the reference frame and then recognising the object. It is possible that the difficulties experienced by Riddoch and Humphreys' (1986) patients in matching size-transformed images of objects (with distinctive features obscured in one image) could be considered to involve impairment to such mapping units, making recognition overly viewpoint-dependent.

A radically different conception of object recognition is exemplified by the kind of approach offered by Aleksander and Stonham (e.g. Aleksander, 1983; Stonham, 1986) with WISARD, a general purpose object-recognition device which is constructed to model a neural network (although it is in fact implemented rather differently). In WISARD there is no notion of "reference frame" or "features" at all. The WISARD system demonstrates how a network which stores the responses to a large number of different instances of different pattern exemplars may subsequently be able to classify novel patterns into appropriate pattern classes. For example, Stonham (1986) describes how a WISARD system which had been trained on a large number of different views of the faces of each of 15 individuals, was then able to decide which of the 15 faces was shown, without any apparent computation or description of features, reference frames, and so forth. How does the system work?

WISARD takes as its input a large array of pixels, in each of which the grey level is set at either "black" or "white". This pixel array is then sampled by selecting "n-tuples" of pixels so that the entire array is sampled. For example, if there is a 100×50 array of pixels (5000 in total), and "n" is two, then 2500 pixels pairs will need to be taken to sample the whole image. Note that each n-tuple need not sample adjacent pixels—in our example the pixels contributing to each pair can be quite widely separated in the pattern. When an n-tuple is sampled, there are 2^n possible results of sampling. When n is two, the pair of pixels may be both black, both white, the first black and the second white, and vice versa. If n were 3, the number of possible results is increased to 8. If a number of exemplars of the same pattern were sampled with the same n-tuples, some outcomes would never occur and others would often occur. For example, consider the pattern "T" shown in Fig. 3.23. If pixel triplets "a" and "b" shown in the figure were among those used to sample this pattern, then imagine what would happen to the results obtained from sampling as different example "T"'s were shown. For triplet "a", the three pixels would never all be black if a T was shown; for triplet "b" the pixels will never show more than one black. Now, if the same pixels were used instead to sample exemplars of a different pattern, the letter "O" (Fig. 3.23), a rather different pattern of outcomes would be obtained. Triplet "b" for example, could find three black pixels. WISARD learns different pattern categories by being exposed to many exemplars of each, and storing the results of the pixel sampling process on each occasion. It thereby builds up a representation of the responses obtained when sampling Ts and another of the responses obtained when sampling Os. After training, an unknown pattern may be presented and categorised (as either a T or an O), by seeing whether the response obtained from the same sampling process more closely resembles those stored for Ts or Os. Exactly the same principles are used to recognise faces as those described here for letters. The only difference is that a very large array size is used, and a very large number of instances of each face are sampled in training. At no stage are facial "features" (eyes, lips, etc.) found and measured, or configural relationships between different features determined.

The WISARD system is impressive, and lends itself to a number of applications where, say, industrial parts must be recognised for sorting purposes. In such applications it is possible to ensure that lighting conditions and background surfaces remain the same. A WISARD trained to recognise objects placed against a white background would have problems if the background at test was dark, because the "features" sampled are raw pixel values. There are a number of limitations on WISARD's powers to generalise to novel views not encountered during training, and these

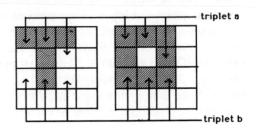

FIG. 3.23. The triplet of pixels (a) would never all be black if a T were shown, but could all be black if an O were shown. Triplet (b) will never find more than one black pixel if a T is shown but could if an O were shown.

limitations are not characteristic of human vision. WISARD is an interesting and powerful "pattern" recogniser, but it is not a good model of human object recognition processes.

Nevertheless, WISARD illustrates that much can be achieved by virtue of brute force, in the form of massive memory, but ignorance of any abstract defining characteristics of objects. In its current implementation, however, the WISARD system does not depart radically from current conceptions of memory as highly *localised,* as each category that WISARD learns is given its own portion of memory space. Within a category, however, responses to different instances are distributed across the same set of memory elements, albeit in a rather uninteresting manner.

A more radical theme, which is proving of increasing interest to psychologists, is related work on *distributed* memory networks (Hinton & Anderson, 1981; McClelland & Rumelhart, 1985, 1986; Rumelhart & McClelland, 1986). In such networks, an object category is represented by a pattern of activity across a number of elementary processing units, each of which might, for example, represent a different "feature" in the image. Successive instances of the same or different categories can be encoded over the same set of processing units. McClelland and Rumelhart (1985) for example, show how, in principle, a network exposed to patterns of features corresponding to hypothetical instances of "Lassie" and "Rover" along with the information that both were "dogs" could retain distinctions between the two different dogs' identities, while also learning the more general characteristics of "dogs" from such examples. Moreover, a network of this kind can not only extract the general characteristics of the different categories to which it is exposed ("Lassie", "Rover", "dog") it retains sensitivity to the patterns corresponding to particular recent instances.

This ability both to extract the defining characteristics of concepts, and to retain sensitivity to details of particular instances of them, is a characteristic of human recognition. For example, in recognition priming experiments (Warren & Morton, 1982; see earlier), although one view of an object will prime a quite different view, greatest priming is observed when an identical view of an object is repeated in the test phase (see also Bruce & Valentine, 1985; Ellis, Young, Flude, & Hay, 1987.) Such a sensitivity to recent instances is not obviously a property of object recognition theories such as Marr and Nishihara's, which we considered earlier in the chapter.

The "parallel distributed processing" models of object recognition clearly have some interesting properties which make them attractive as theories of human recognition processes. One weakness of such demonstrations at present is that they have not been applied to real objects. It is assumed that "Fido" is represented as a set of activities across a set of unknown encoding dimensions or features, and such assumptions beg many of the interesting questions about perception—questions which have been tackled more satisfactorily within the kind of computational framework proposed by Marr. Where distributed memory models have been tested on pictures rather than arbitrary sets of features, they have taken as their input raw pixel values (e.g. Kohonen, Oja, & Lehtio, 1981) rather than the oriented edge segments or blobs which seem to be delivered by the early stages of human vision. Another weakness is that a distributed memory system which represents two concepts with the same set of units, cannot recognise both categories at once (in our example, the network could not recognise Lassie and Rover at the same time). Because of problems such as these, completely distributed representations may not offer a satisfactory solution for many visual problems, and additionally some forms of modular representation may need to be reconsidered. To this extent, developments in this field will complement rather than challenge fundamentally such theories as Marr's, by revealing how patterns of neural activity can be seen as implementing implicitly the different representational stages of human vision.

A question which is of considerable interest in the context of our discussion of distributed memory models is the extent to which there may be separate processing "modules" dedicated to the recognition of different object classes. A particular class of objects—human faces—are most often considered to be recognised via such a specialised module. In the next section we review briefly neuropsychological and experimental evidence relevant to this issue.

SPECIFIC RECOGNITION MODULES: THE CASE FROM FACE RECOGNITION

Patients who are agnosic for objects also typically have problems recognising faces. Again, this problem tends to be confined to visual recognition. For instance, some seven years after his stroke, the agnosic patient H.J.A. (Humphreys & Riddoch, 1987a) still cannot recognise the faces of even his closest relatives by sight, yet he experiences no especial difficulties recognising people's voices. Thus, such patients do not have a general problem in person identification or in their memory for people's identities.

Bodamer (1947) coined the term prosopagnosia to refer to patients with impaired face recognition. The term implies a degree of specificity; that is, that prosopagnosic patients experience problems in face recognition over and above their problems with other objects. However, this specificity could simply reflect the high levels of visual similarity amongst faces. As we have already discussed, agnosic patients often have more difficulty identifying objects from categories with visually similar exemplars (such as living things) than those from categories with visually dissimilar exemplars (e.g. man-made objects). We should not infer that face recognition is completely independent of object recognition simply because patients can have especially severe problems with faces. Indeed, many of the "purer" prosopagnosic patients have turned out, on closer examination, to have subtle recognition problems for other objects. Damasio, Damasio, and Van Hoesen (1982) studied three prosopagnosic patients who were also unable to recognise familiar cars, articles of clothing, cooking utensils, and food ingredients, all of which required visual discrimination within their respective categories. Similarly, Bornstein (1963) reported an ornithologist who lost the ability to identify different birds as well as faces. The most convincing exception to this is the prosopagnosic patient documented by De Renzi (1986), who succeeded at many "within-category" discriminations (such as distinguishing between different types of coins, or his own possessions from those of other people). Yet even here a sceptic might argue that more detailed tests would show some residual difficulty. A way round this is to consider whether some patients can have greater problems with other objects than with faces.

Some interesting work has been done using evidence from an unusual source, namely prosopagnosia in farmers. Assal, Favre, and Anderes (1984) report the case of a prosopagnosic farmer who eventually regained the ability to identify faces whilst remaining unable to identify his own cows. This can be contrasted with the case of another farmer reported by Bruyer et al. (1983), who remained able to identify his own cows whilst having severe problems in face recognition. These contrasting deficits suggest that at least some of the processes required for face recognition are indeed separate from those for discriminating between members of other categories (such as particular cows).

We need then to ask, what processes might be specially developed to facilitate face recognition? Work with normal subjects is relevant here. Yin (1969; 1970) first showed that we are particularly poor at recognising inverted faces, when compared with inverted objects, houses, costumes, etc. Inversion seems especially hurtful to face recognition, perhaps because specialised processes are developed for face recognition that are also sensitive to orientation. Diamond and Carey (1986) confirmed this effect, but also suggested that it was not unique to faces. They found that, for people expert enough to individuate different dogs of the same breed, the effects of inversion on the recognition of different dogs were as severe as the effects on face recognition. Diamond and Carey suggest that "perceptual expertise" is based on the development of processes sensitive to what they term "second-order relations" between the features of objects. These processes are also sensitive to orientation, as they are developed for objects that have a prototypical orientation. Hence, there are strong effects of inversion. Possibly brain damage can selectively impair the processes sensitive to such relational features. A common pattern of deficits across objects will emerge if people rely on the same processes to identify different types of object, whilst some divergence may be expected if the identification procedures become tuned to the particular relational features distinguishing the objects within certain classes.

Unfortunately, few studies have examined whether prosopagnosic patients are sensitive to relational features in faces. One relevant study was conducted by Perrett et al. (1988). They had a prosopagnosic patient, R.B., perform a "face judgement" task. He was presented with faces containing their usual configuration of features or with non-faces created by jumbling features (whilst maintaining symmetry). R.B. simply had to decide whether a face or a "non-face" was presented. Normal subjects respond faster to faces than to non-faces. In contrast, R.B. responded faster to the non-faces than to faces. Perrett et al. suggest that, normally, fast responses are based on the configural properties of faces (including, presumably, second-order relational features). R. B. is insensitive to such properties, and has to check the location of each feature serially to decide whether a stimulus is a face. Because he can only respond that a face is present when he has checked all the features, faces are responded to more slowly than non-faces. Thus, at least with this patient, there are grounds for arguing that prosopagnosia can be linked to a specific deficit in using higher-order perceptual features for recognition.

However, there may be other reasons for the specificity of face recognition problems. For instance, our stored representations of faces may differ from those of other objects. To begin with, the nature of the stored information will differ (the particular local and relational features involved, the role of three-dimensional coding which may be especially important for face recognition, etc., see Bruce, 1988). Also, the face recognition system will be highly differentiated. We are capable of recognising many hundreds of faces, of family members, colleagues, famous people, etc. This is not usually true of other objects, where the differentiation is often between the object one owns and others from the same category. Thus, we can think of a model of face recognition in which there exist "face recognition units", distinct from the prototype visual representations we have proposed for object recognition (e.g. Bruce & Young, 1986; Hay & Young, 1982; see Fig. 3.24).

According to the model in Fig. 3.24, impairments to stored representations dealing selectively with faces will produce relatively "pure" cases of prosopagnosia. Indeed, prosopagnosia could result even when faces activate stored face recognition units, if there is then a failure to access semantic or other types of information. In this respect it is interesting that recent research has shown that some prosopagnosics have implicit knowledge about the faces they fail to identify. This was first shown by measuring the autonomic responses produced by patients during face recognition tasks. For instance, Tranel and Damasio (1985) found

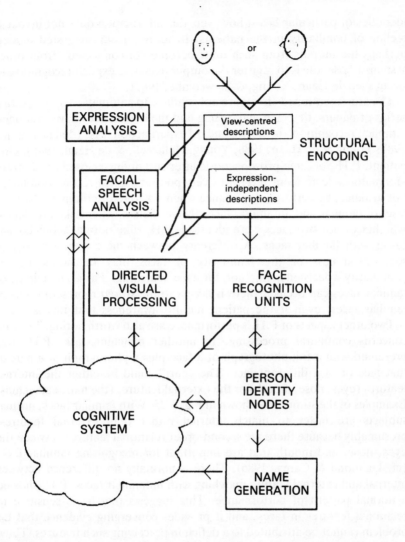

FIG. 3.24.   Bruce and Young's (1986) model of the functional components involved in face recognition, and their relationship with other components of face perception such as expression analysis.

prosopagnosics who produced more frequent and higher amplitude galvanic skin responses to familiar than to unfamiliar faces, and Bauer (1984) reported a similar result when the patient was given the correct rather than the incorrect name when presented with a familiar face. These data suggest that these patients derive appropriate information from faces, sufficient to differentiate familiar from unfamiliar faces or even the identities of particular faces; however, this information does not invoke a feeling of familiarity in the patients. In terms of our suggested model, perhaps the outputs from such units become "disconnected" from other systems whose role is to register the output to enable explicit recognition to occur (see de Haan, Young, & Newcombe, 1987).

The aforementioned effects are not confined to automatic responses. In a series of papers, de Haan and Young and their colleagues have examined "implicit recognition" in more standard experimental tasks (de Haan et al., 1987; Young & de Haan, 1988; Young, Hellawell, & de Haan, 1988). One patient, P.H., became prosopagnosic after sustaining a closed head injury in a motorcycle accident. P.H. was very poor at explicit recognition tasks. For instance, he performed at chance when asked to discriminate between a set of familiar and unfamiliar faces. Nevertheless, when asked to decide whether or not two faces were identical, P.H. (like normal subjects) was faster with familiar faces. A difference between these two tasks is that some awareness of the familiarity of faces may be necessary for "familiarity" decisions, but not for face matching. Faster matching of familiar faces can occur if there is access to the stored representations of familiar faces, even if the patient has no awareness that this is so.

Two other aspects of P.H.'s performance are also worth noting. The first concerns configural processing. In another matching task, P.H. was presented with a full photograph of a face plus a photograph of a part of that face or of a different face. The "part" could be either the internal features (eyes, nose, mouth) or the external features (the hair, ears, chin). Examples of the stimuli are shown in Fig. 3.25. With familiar faces, normal subjects are faster to match internal rather than external features, presumably because there are second-order relational features between the eyes, nose, and mouth that are important for recognising familiar faces (cf. Diamond & Carey, 1986). There is normally no difference between internal and external feature matching with unfamiliar faces. P.H. showed a normal pattern of performance. This suggests that he is sensitive to relational features in faces, and it provides converging evidence that his problem cannot be attributed to a deficit in perceiving such features. Thus, we can draw a distinction between prosopagnosics such as R.B. (Perrett et al., 1988), who seem to have an impaired input description of faces, and patients such as P.H. whose problem seems to relate more to gaining explicit access to the outputs from the face recognition system. This distinction is supported by other evidence showing that some prosopagnosics show no implicit recognition of faces (Newcombe, Young, & de Haan, 1989). Presumably the patients who show no implicit recognition do not derive sufficiently precise descriptions of faces to gain selective access to the stored representations of particular faces.

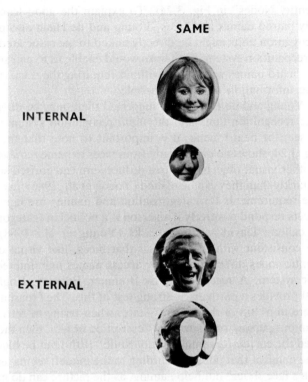

SAME

INTERNAL

EXTERNAL

FIG. 3.25.   Examples of stimuli from an internal versus external feature matching task used by de Haan et al. (1987). (Reproduced with permission.)

The second point is that, at least in P.H., there are some constraints on his implicit recognition. For instance, as well as showing good matching of familiar faces, P.H. can also learn to associate names with the appropriate face faster than he learns to associate the wrong name with a familiar face (de Haan et al., 1987). This again confirms that P.H. has implicit recognition. However, he shows no advantage for learning to associate the face of a familiar politician with the name of the appropriate political party (e.g. that Peter Walker is a Conservative), relative to when he is asked to pair a politician's face with the wrong party (that Roy Hattersley is a member of the SDP). From this it seems that access occurs to representations that allow a face to be linked to its name, but not to (semantic) representations that provide detailed information about the person's occupation, or about our prior associations with them. In terms of the model in Fig. 3.24, we can suggest that there is intact access to face recognition units along with impaired access to the semantic system (the

"Person Identity Nodes" in Fig. 3.24). To explain the good learning of appropriately paired names and faces, Young and de Haan also propose that face recognition units might be directly linked to the associated names in the word recognition system. Such links would enable us to pair seen and possibly also heard names with faces, without requiring the retrieval of all our semantic information about the people.

Although Young and de Haan have suggested there may be direct links between face recognition units and the *input* recognition system used to recognise a seen or heard name, it is important to note that the model shown in Fig. 3.24, shows no direct route from faces to name *retrieval*. Like pictures of other visual objects, pictures of faces are categorised semantically more quickly than they can be named (Young et al., 1986), even when the response requirements for categorisation and naming are equated by having subjects respond positively if a person is a politician (categorisation task) or is called "David" (naming task) (Young et al., 1988). Such findings are consistent with the proposal that faces, like visual objects, access semantic codes directly, and they access names only indirectly via the semantic system. A recent study by Brennen, Baguley, Bright, and Bruce (1990) provides a particularly strong test of this. They reasoned that if people were in a "tip-of-the-tongue" state, when trying to retrieve the name of a famous person from a written description of him, then they must have accessed the correct "Person Identity Node" (PIN) but be blocked in retrieving the name at that point. According to the model, seeing a picture of the person's face should not help naming, as the picture can do no more than access the same PIN again. Brennen et al. found, consistent with the model, though counter to our intuitions, that seeing the face when in a tip-of-the-tongue state was indeed no more helpful than hearing the same semantic description a second time. Subjects when shown the face said: "But I know what he looks like, it's his *name* I've forgotten". In contrast, seeing the initials of the missing name was helpful, leading to resolution of the tip-of-the-tongue state on about 50% of such occasions.

The observed similarity between faces and other visual objects in terms of the functional organisation of semantic access and name retrieval is important for two reasons. First, it demonstrates that the same organising principles appear to hold for the recognition of faces and other visual objects, even though there may be grounds for supposing that face recognition has a specialised "module" devoted to it. So although there may be *face-specific* processes there may not necessarily be *unique* processes involved in face perception and recognition (cf. Hay & Young, 1982). Secondly, given the similarity in functional organisation, faces provide a very important class of visual objects in which it is possible to vary physical and semantic properties independently. A person may look like a sportsman but actually be a politician. In this way, faces can provide a challenge to the idea that we raised earlier that objects access the semantic system directly simply because their meanings are specified by their shapes. The particular identity of a face cannot be known from its particular configuration, and in this respect familiar faces are more like words than other visual objects—yet they are processed more like objects than like words (see Bruce, 1983; Bruce & Young, 1986, for further discussion).

It therefore seems that face recognition is achieved within a specialised processing "module" that nevertheless is organised in a similar way to the module (or modules) used to recognise other kinds of visual object. Further similarities are revealed when we turn to consider the ways in which visual context can affect the recognition of visual objects and faces.

VISUAL CONTEXT EFFECTS IN OBJECT RECOGNITION

In much of the aforementioned, we have discussed object recognition as though it proceeded uninfluenced by other acts of recognition occurring earlier or simultaneously. Yet "context" can have powerful influences upon the ease with which objects or their component parts may be recognised. So wide-ranging are the kinds of influences which we might include under this heading, it is debatable whether the label "context" is really helpful—it has been used to include the broad environmental setting and emotional state in which an act of recognition takes place, as well as in the sense we intend here. Here, we use the more precise label, "visual context" to refer to other or earlier parts of a scene or object which may influence the interpretation of the object we are currently recognising. Even confined to this narrower sense, we will demonstrate the ubiquity of contextual influences.

Consider Fig. 3.26, a demonstration suggested by Palmer (1975a). None of the parts of this "face" is recognisable when shown in isolation, yet within the context of the entire "face" it is easy to label each part as "eye", "nose", and so forth. Parts of figures may gain meaning from their configural relations with other parts. Indeed, this meaning may even conflict with that available from the local level, as shown by another of Palmer's (1975a) examples. In the "fruit-face" (Fig. 3.27), each part has its own identity when seen in isolation, yet each part also gains a new identity

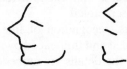

FIG. 3.26.   The parts of the face at the left are not recognisable as facial features when shown in isolation (right). (Adapted from Palmer, 1975a.)

FIG. 3.27.   A "fruit face". (Adapted from Palmer, 1975a.)

as eye, nose or mouth within the total pattern. The result is a rather bizarre perception, in which one may even feel one's interpretation flipping from fruit to face, and back again. Palmer (1975a) used these ingenious figures to demonstrate what he termed the "parsing paradox". How can we know what the whole figure is when its parts are undefined (Fig. 3.26) or inconsistent (Fig. 3.27)? In fact, we would not now view such demonstrations as paradoxical, given our better understanding of the generation and use of visual descriptions at different spatial scales. The visual system seems to scan from coarser to finer spatial scales over time (Watt, 1988), with descriptions of overall spatial structure (i.e. low spatial frequencies) probably available more quickly than those of fine detail. It is entirely consistent that recognition of the whole configuration may guide the definition of parts within it. Indeed, it has been suggested by several authors (e.g. see Humphreys & Quinlan, 1987; Sergent, 1989) that visual pattern and object recognition might rely more on descriptions available from relatively low spatial frequencies since such descriptions will remain invariant over minor perturbations of the pattern from one instance to the next.

The use of coarse-scale structural descriptions to guide the refinement of finer-scale ones may explain the "face superiority effect" reported by Homa, Haver, and Schwartz (1976). In Homa et al.'s experiments, subjects were briefly presented with schematic faces, whose features were either arranged as they would be in a real face—eyes above nose above mouth, or they were rearranged to form a jumbled face. The subject's task was to select the correct feature (the right nose from a set of different noses, for example) shown in a given face, and they found subjects were more successful when the features were arranged normally than when they were scrambled.

Thus, recognition of fine detail or individual parts may normally be preceded and influenced by recognition of the global figural context within which the details are embedded. This suggestion gains some independent support from experiments on the priority of global form descriptions in

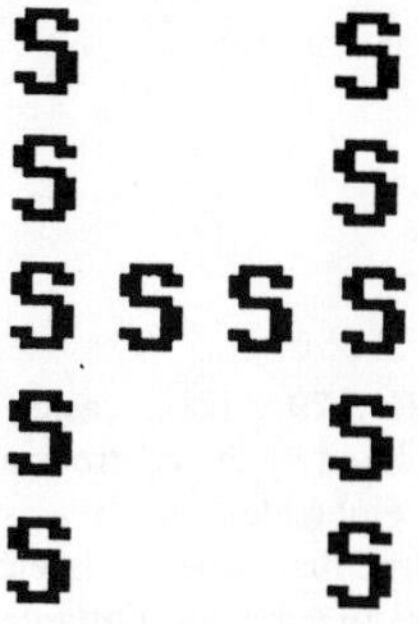

S   S
S   S
S S S S
S   S
S   S

FIG. 3.28.   A global letter H made of small letter Ss. (Adapted from Navon, 1977.)

visual attention. Navon (1977) presented subjects with shapes in which small letters were arranged to form larger letters (e.g. see Fig. 3.28). The small letters could be the same as, or conflict with, the identity of the global shape, and the subject's task was to make a decision about either the global or the local letter identities. Navon found that, where these identities conflicted, decisions about the local letters were slowed by the conflicting information from the global identity, but that the reverse was not found: the identity of the small letters had no effect upon the decisions made to the global letter. Now, such results may be interpreted within the "recognition" framework of this chapter, to suggest an order of priority for the construction of descriptions which subserve recognition. Perhaps more legitimately, however, such results lend support more generally to the notion of attentional scanning from coarse to fine spatial scales (cf. Watt, 1988). It is in this context that we will return to consider these experiments and later variants of them again in our chapter on visual attention (Chapter 5).

We will mention one final set of demonstrations of the influence of global structure upon local part perception. Palmer (1980; 1985; Palmer & Bucher, 1981) has provided a number of examples of how the global configuration may influence the interpretation of more local structures. For example (Palmer, 1980), subjects required to identify the direction pointed by a triangle were faster if the target triangle lay within a configuration whose direction (of principal axis) was consistent with the required response (see Fig. 3.29). Subjects required to identify whether a central shape was a "square" or a "diamond" were influenced by surrounding figures which could be aligned with either the "diagonal" axis of the diamond or the "parallel" axis of the square (see Fig. 3.30; Palmer, 1985).

An interesting extension to this work comes from Palmer et al. (1988) who examined whether these effects of configural orientation on shape perception operate on two-dimensional or three-dimensional representations of space. They showed that if pictorial depth cues were added to

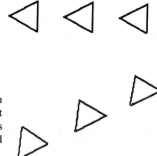

FIG. 3.29. It is easier to decide the direction pointed by the centre triangle (left or right) when it is embedded in an axis-aligned row of triangles (top) than when it is embedded in a base-aligned row of triangles. (Adapted from Palmer, 1980.)

those displays where, for example, squares were arranged such that the axis of the configuration was diagonal (see Fig. 3.30), then the effect of this configural axis was dramatically reduced, suggesting that perceptual organisation is based primarily on reference axes constructed within a three-dimensional frame of reference. Such findings are consistent with theories such as Marr and Nishihara's who see object recognition operating on representations derived from the 2½D sketch level in which the layout of surfaces in space has already been described.

Influences of global context are pervasive. Nevertheless, we would expect such influences to be relative, rather than absolute. If the global structure is too large to be resolved in a single fixation—that is, if it falls outside the bounds of a natural spatial scale, then we might expect a reversal of the effect, with the relatively more "local" parts helping to define the overall structure. It is the relationship between form and scale which is important, and this may help explain why global influences may be more reliably demonstrated when shapes are relatively small or when they are presented to the periphery of the visual field (Kinchla & Wolfe, 1979).

There is also another way in which the global context in which an item appears may affect the interpretation of local shapes. In a number of experiments, Biederman (1972; Biederman, Mezzanotte, & Rabinowitz, 1982) has shown how the context established by a coherent scene of objects may facilitate the recognition of individual objects within the scene. In an early experiment (Biederman, 1972), subjects were briefly exposed to a photograph, and asked to identify which of four alternative objects was shown at a particular, cued location within the scene. Their accuracy at this

FIG. 3.30. The effect of a diagonal axis of configuration on the identification of square shapes (left) is reduced by the addition of pictorial depth cues (right). (Adapted from Palmer et al., 1988.)

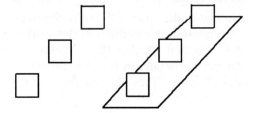

task when the scenes were intact was compared with their performance when the scenes were jumbled up by rearranging sections from the original photograph. Although the integrity of the target (cued) objects was never affected by the jumbling, subjects were more accurate at identifying the target from intact scenes even when they were given the spatial cue and the four possible alternatives *before* the scene was presented. Thus, a correctly organised scene aided the identification of its component objects even when subjects knew where to look and what to look for.

In subsequent work, Biederman and his colleagues went on to investigate the basis of this effect of scenic context by examining the perceptibility of objects whose position within scenes violated either "physical" or "semantic" relations with other scene members. Within a real-world scene, certain physical relations are obeyed—most objects must be seen to be supported by the ground or another surface, rather than to float in the air, and they should occlude their background, rather than be transparent. Semantic relations include the likelihood of certain object types at certain places. Biederman et al. (1982) found that violation of semantic relations was as disruptive to object perception as was violation of physical relations like support, which led them to conclude that the access of an object's semantic relations occurs simultaneously with access of its physical relations and with its own identification. One interpretation of such findings would be to suggest that Biederman's experiments are tapping a representational stage which is later than those considered to date, in which individual object identities are written back into a "viewer-centred" (although not retinotopic) frame of reference. Perceivers need to know more than the layout of as-yet-unidentified surfaces (the 2½D sketch level), or the identities of individual objects (the 3D model level). They must know *what* is *where* in the world in order to plan future actions accordingly (see Chapter 6, where we discuss the relation between this level of representation and short-term visual memory).

Another way in which context can influence object identification is where a particular object becomes expected given the *earlier* occurrence of another object or scene. Palmer (1975b) produced the visual equivalent of word identification experiments (e.g. Tulving & Gold, 1963; see Chapter 7), in which a target word is perceived more accurately if preceded by an appropriate compared with an inappropriate sentence context. In Palmer's experiment, subjects were required to try to identify briefly exposed pictures of objects which were preceded by scenes within which the object would be either appropriate (e.g. a picture of a loaf of bread preceded by a picture of a kitchen scene) or inappropriate (the loaf of bread preceded by a picture of a garage). Palmer found that an appropriate prior context facilitated recognition of the object, and inappropriate context impeded recognition, compared with a no-context control condition. Moreover, an inappropriate object (e.g. an American-style mailbox in a kitchen scene), which was similar in shape to an object which *would* be appropriate in that context (a mailbox resembles a loaf of bread) was recognised less well than an object which did not resemble an appropriate item. The former tended to be misidentified as the item it resembled.

The pattern of results obtained by Palmer (1975b) was consistent with the predictions which would be derived from a "recognition unit" account (see earlier), in which the appropriate context is seen as influencing the "threshold", or sensory evidence requirement, of a perceptual classification unit which contains the structural description of the object in question. Similar kinds of context effects, also compatible with a "recognition unit" framework, have been found where pictures of objects have been preceded by other pictures of semantically associated objects. Sperber et al. (1979) found that picture naming was speeded if an item was preceded by a semantically related picture, compared with a condition where there was no association between the two pictures. Kroll and Potter (1984) used an "object decision" task, in which subjects had to decide whether a presented picture was a real (familiar) object or whether it was a nonsense object, created by combining traced parts of different, real objects to form novel arrangements. Subjects were able to decide more quickly that a familiar object was real if it was preceded by an associated object, an effect which is similar to that found with words in the analogous lexical decision task (Chapter 7). Both Kroll and Potter (1984) and Sperber et al. (1979) found that such priming effects with pictures were larger than those found using words, which Sperber et al. suggested might be because pictures of semantically related objects tend also to be visually similar, which is not true of words. For example, pictures of different animals may all share such components as legs and eyes, but there is no more resemblance between words such as "cat" and "mouse" than there is between, say, "cat" and "house". This explanation is given some support by experiments on semantic priming in face recognition. For a face, there is no close link between its appearance and its identity—a face may look like a comedian, but actually be that of a politician. Thus, the faces of close associates such as Prince Charles and Princess Diana need share no more resemblance than their names. Bruce and Valentine (1986) used a face familiarity task (in which subjects responded positively if each of a series of faces was familiar), and found that familiar faces could be responded to some 100msec more quickly if they were preceded by closely associated faces (e.g. Princess Diana followed by Prince Charles) than if they were preceded by unassociated or unfamiliar faces. The size of the priming effect, although large, was no greater for faces than for names used in an analogous experiment. This suggests that, where greater priming is observed for pairs of pictures than pairs of words, it may indeed be attributed to additional priming at the level of shared visual features.

These effects of semantic priming from one item to another in speeded decision tasks may be accommodated quite comfortably within the recognition unit framework which we mentioned briefly early in the chapter. Activation of the structural description which defines one item can lead, via the semantic system, to activation spreading to associated locations, thereby facilitating the recognition of items whose descriptions are housed at those locations. Almost equivalently, we could imagine how activation at one part of a "catalogue" of object descriptions (cf. Marr & Nishihara, 1978) could facilitate the activation of other parts of the catalogue which were related visually or through association. The recognition unit metaphor copes rather less comfortably with effects of global context on the perception of local components, as recognition units have tended to be seen as all-or-none devices, rather than as a simple shorthand way of referring to a bundle of structural descriptions at different scales. The computational perspectives offered by such researchers as Marr and Nishihara have given us a means of "unpacking" the recognition unit metaphor to consider how each known object category may be represented at a number of different spatial scales. Connectionist accounts would also accommodate certain kinds of contextual effects quite naturally, particularly where, say, the perception of one part of a pattern aided the perception of a different part. However, it is rather more difficult to see how massively distributed systems (in which all visual objects were thought to be defined by patterns of activity over the same set of processing units) would cope with some of the simultaneous priming effects mentioned.

Clearly, we are some way from an entirely satisfactory theory of visual recognition which can integrate insights gained from computational modelling with all the empirical findings such as those about visual context effects. What we have done in this chapter is to introduce some of the complexity of the object recognition problem, and described some recent, and interesting attempts to provide accounts of how the human visual system solves this problem. So far in this book we have emphasised the perception of single visual scenes rather than sequences of events. In the next chapter we discuss how research on motion perception and visual masking has revealed how the visual system deals with rapidly changing visual events.

4 Dynamic Aspects of Vision

MOVEMENT PERCEPTION

Analysis of Motion

All of our discussion to this point has assumed a stationary observer viewing a frozen world. Such a situation is not just unlikely, it is impossible. Even if a comfortably seated observer views a scene containing only motionless objects, the observer's eyes will be in continuous motion. In addition to relatively large-scale eye movements—(saccades) from one fixation to the next, smooth pursuit tracking movements (when there are moving objects in the scene to pursue), and vergence movements to focus objects at different distances, the eyes constantly make little flicks, jerks, and tremors. Indeed, if the effects of such eye movements are neutralised, by artificially stabilising the image on the retina, the world "disappears" (Heckenmuller, 1965). The constant motion is essential to perception, as neurons habituate to constant stimulation, and respond maximally to change.

What are the consequences of motion in the world, or by the eyes, for the pattern of stimulation at the retina? Rather than considering the starting point for vision as a pattern of light intensities varying only across space, we must consider the input as a spatio-temporal pattern, with variation over time and space. Any movement on the part of the observer, whether of their body, head or eyes, will produce a transformation in the entire retinal image, a transformation which Gibson (1950; 1966) termed optical flow.

If, for example, the observer turns their head from left to right, there will be a lateral flow of information across the retina. If the observer moves forwards through the world, there will be an expanding pattern of optical flow, and so forth (see Gibson, 1950, 1966; or Bruce & Green, 1985, for further examples). The optical flow which results from our movement, in turn informs us of our movement. We can demonstrate this informally in situations where optical flow alone produces the (false) impression that we are moving—an example is when we think our own train is pulling out from the station when in fact it is a neighbouring train which is moving. As well as informing us about our own movements, there is evidence that human observers use expanding patterns of optical flow to inform them about the time to contact surfaces towards which they are headed, and hence to recover information about their distance from a surface (Lee, 1980; see Bruce & Green, 1985). Thus global patterns of optical flow also inform observers about the three-dimensional layout of the world through which they are moving.

In contrast to the global patterns of optical flow produced by movement of the observer, movement of an object in the world will produce a local disturbance in the pattern at the retina. These patterns of local disturbance can themselves inform us of the three-dimensional structures in motion. Perhaps the most famous example is given by our perception of human figures in Johansson's demonstrations. Johansson (1973) illuminated points on the joints (shoulders, elbows, knees, etc.) of actors and filmed them in the dark so that only these illuminated points were visible. When stationary, the pattern of points was just a meaningless jumble, but as soon as the actors moved, their human shapes could be seen, and the nature of their movements accurately described (see Fig. 4.1)

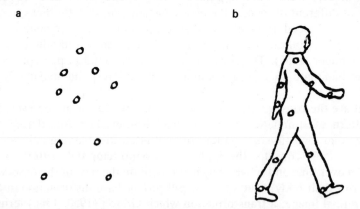

a   b

FIG. 4.1. The "moving lights" demonstration. When the subject is stationary, a random pattern of lights is seen (as in (a)). When the subject moves, observers report the vivid impression of seeing a person walking (as in (b)). (Adapted from Johansson, 1973; reproduced from Humphreys & Riddoch, 1987a, with permission.)

Runeson and Frykholm (1983) conducted a number of experiments which illustrate the subtlety of the information which observers may pick up from such point-light displays. In one experiment, films were made of two actors throwing sandbags to targets at varying distances. The bags themselves were invisible, but from the actors' motions observers could accurately decide how far the actors were intending to throw the bag on each trial.

Other examples of the perception of structure from motion come from the kinetic depth effect (Wallach & O'Connell, 1953), where the three-dimensional shape of a wire structure, the shadow of which is shown on a screen, can be seen from the expanding and contracting shadow pattern observed as the shape is rotated behind the screen. More recent examples of the perception of structure from motion are given by Ullman (1979).

The entire pattern of flow at the retina must therefore be decomposed into different components of translation and rotation, in order to inform the observer about the nature of their own movements in the world, and to reveal the residual patterns of motion attributable to events in the world external to the observer's own movement. How does the visual system sort out all these different motion components? And how is the analysis of motion related to the analysis of structures in the world? These are difficult and controversial questions.

The pervasiveness and usefulness of visual motion was one of the major influences on the development of J.J. Gibson's theory of "direct" perception, in which he denied that visual perception involved "comput-ation" or "inference" from "static" retinal snapshots at all. Instead, Gibson claimed that information to specify the structures in the world, and the nature of an observer's movement was detected "directly" from dynamic patterns of optical flow. Although the details of Gibson's theory and criticisms of it lie outside the scope of this book (see Michaels & Carello, 1981; Bruce & Green, 1985), it does seem possible to combine Gibsonian insights with a computational perspective (Bruce & Green, 1985), in which we ask not just what information is detected from optical flow patterns, but how it is detected. Recent computational approaches have begun to tackle this question, and we will give a flavour of this approach here.

Directional Selectivity

If you stare for some minutes at something like a waterfall which moves continuously in one direction, and then transfer your gaze to a motionless region, such as the river bank, you will experience a strong illusion of movement of the river bank (with no change in position) in a direction opposite to that of the waterfall. Such direction-specific motion after-effects can be explained by the selective adaptation or "fatigue" of receptors which are sensitive to movement in a particular direction. Such directionally selective cells have been observed directly in the rabbit retina (Barlow & Levick, 1965), and Barlow and Levick produced a computational scheme for their operation. Barlow and Levick suggested that directionally sensitive cells receive both excitatory and inhibitory input, according to the direction that a stimulus is moving. When the stimulus moves in the cell's preferred direction the cell first receives excitatory input followed by inhibition. However, when the stimulus moves in the opposite direction the cell first receives inhibition, blocking any subsequent excitation. Thus, the cell responds selectively to stimuli moving in a preferred direction.

More recently, Marr and Ullman (1981) suggested an algorithm for directional selectivity which is rather different from Barlow and Levick's, but nicely consistent with Marr and Hildreth's theory of static edge detection. The initial stage involves detecting motion by taking the derivative with respect to time of the $\nabla^2 G$ operations. Remember that $\nabla^2 G^* I$ is used to locate a zero-crossing (and thereby signal an "edge"). Marr and Ullman have demonstrated that at zero-crossing locations, a positive value of the time derivative of $\nabla^2 G^* I$ signals movement in one direction, and a negative value signals movement in the opposite direction (the directions themselves depending on the direction of the contrast of the edge). Moreover, Marr and Ullman argue that what is known of the mammalian Y-type ganglion cells is quite consistent with their functioning to detect the time derivative of $\nabla^2 G^* I$. Marr (1982) goes on to show how zero-crossing segment detectors can be combined with the operation of Y-type cells to produce a directionally-selective zero-crossing segment detector. In other words, a "moving edge" detector could be obtained quite easily from the right combination of inputs from retinal X- and Y-type ganglion cells.

Optic Flow Analysis

The Marr and Ullman theory of directional selectivity explains how we may be able to label the orientation of a moving edge with a rough measure of its direction of movement. To get more precise information about the nature of the motions present, and thereby to use this information in turn to reveal structure from motion, would, according to Marr, require the solution of "the correspondence problem". Just as stereopsis requires that correspondences be established between particular parts of one image and appropriate parts in another image which is displaced in space, so computational theorists have argued that motion analysis requires that a similar correspondence be computed between parts of two images displaced over time (e.g. Ullman, 1979). However, further work on the computation of motion has suggested that this "indirect" recovery of motion may not be needed to discover a number of useful pieces of information from a time-varying image. For example, Buxton and Buxton (1983) have also extended the Marr–Hildreth edge-detecting algorithm, but in a manner more suited to the demands of optical flow computation. In order to make use of information in, say, a globally expanding optical flow pattern, it is important that we can, in principle, recover the rate of retinal expansion, because important variables such as the time to contact a surface are specified by relative rates of expansion or "looming" on the retina (Lee, 1980). Buxton and Buxton replace the Marr–Hildreth $\nabla^2 G^* I$ operator with a space–time operator of the form $\Box^2 G(r,t)$, where $\Box^2$ is the "d'Alembertian ∇^2", and $G(r,t)$ is a Gaussian in space-time. (Although this is probably mathematically obscure to most readers of this chapter, the important point is that whereas Marr and Ullman elected simply to differentiate their edge-detecting operator with respect to time, in order to analyse the motion present, Buxton and Buxton have made the time dimension an integral aspect of the edge-detecting algorithm itself, by incorporating notions of temporal as well as spatial resolution.)

Using this space–time operator, Buxton and Buxton show how zero-crossings can arise in two distinct ways. The first they call a static edge, and is in effect equivalent to the Marr–Hildreth kind of zero-crossing discovered at very high temporal resolution (which in the limit approaches a static "snapshot"). The second kind of zero-crossing is called a depth zero, and is found towards the periphery of the field of view, resulting from the motion of the observer relative to an object in view. Where a static edge in the periphery coincides with a depth zero, the slope of the zero-crossing of the static edge will change sign (or "cross over") as the depth zero passes through it. Buxton and Buxton show how this cross-over effect can be used to detect time-to-contact to a surface (and hence its distance) from moving edge features in the periphery of view. This requires a longer temporal resolution integration (i.e. a longer sample of the time-varying image) than does the detection of static edges, but shows that certain information can indeed be computed from this time-varying image without requiring that the correspondence problem can be solved explicitly.

In this work, Buxton and Buxton made the simplifying assumption that only translatory components of optical flow are present (i.e. components due to translatory motion in the world). However, Longuet-Higgins and Prazdny (1980) have shown that translatory components can be distinguished from rotatory components which would be created by head and eye movements so such a scheme could probably be extended to the more natural situation.

Buxton and Buxton's research has revealed that the correspondence problem need not necessarily be solved in order for information which may be useful for the guidance of action to be recovered from optic flow patterns. Note, however, that "depth zeros" are found particularly towards the periphery of the field of vision. The kind of motion analysis conducted in peripheral vision may be particularly tailored to the guidance of motion or to orienting functions—a flashing or moving light tends to draw our eyes to it (see Chapter 5). Once fixated, however, the way in which we analyse the structure in motion may involve some quite different processes, possibly including the solution of the correspondence problem.

Different Systems for Motion Analysis

There are a number of grounds for considering motion analysis to involve at least two distinct systems subserving discrete functions. Braddick (1980) distinguished between two kinds of "apparent" motion, one of which seems to involve mechanisms implicated in directional selectivity, and the other which seems to involve more cognitive factors. Apparent motion, first investigated by the *Gestalt* psychologists (e.g. Wertheimer, 1912), is seen when two lights at different locations are switched on and off alternately. At a certain interstimulus interval between the offset of one light and the onset of the other (which will depend on the luminance, duration, and spatial separation of the lights) one light will appear to move smoothly to and fro between the locations occupied by the two lights. This kind of apparent motion can be seen between simple lights, lines or figures (such as squares or circles) at interstimulus intervals of up to 300msec (Neuhaus, 1930), it can be seen if successive stimuli are shown to different eyes (Shipley, Kenney, & King, 1945), if the lines are created by chromatic (colour), as well as by brightness contrasts (Ramachandran & Gregory, 1978), and is unaffected by whether the interstimulus interval is bright or dark.

Braddick (1980) investigated a different kind of apparent motion, using random-dot kinematograms (after Julesz, 1971). A random-dot kinemato-gram is composed of a number of frames of random texture which are shown in sequence. No form is visible in any individual frame, but in fact the dots within a central portion of each frame are displaced by a constant amount from one frame to the next, while those in the background remain the same. When the sequence of frames is viewed, the dots comprising the central region are seen to move as a whole and reveal a boundary between the central moving figure and its stationary surround. Apparent motion in random-dot kinematograms is much less robust than that in classic line or form displays. Braddick found that the interstimulus interval must be less than 100msec for a 100msec frame exposure duration for motion to be seen. Also, motion can only be seen when successive stimuli are presented to the same eye, and it is abolished if the interstimulus interval is bright, and if the edges in the kinematograms are created by chromatic rather than brightness contrasts (Ramachandran & Gregory, 1978).

Braddick (1980) concluded that apparent motion in random-dot kinematograms was a much shorter-range process than that obtained with classic
line or form stimuli, and tentatively identified this short-range process with
the response of directionally sensitive neurons in the visual pathway. He
suggested that higher-level processes were responsible for the more
"interpretative" phenomena of apparent motion which can be obtained
with lights, lines or more complex shapes. Ullman (1979) has provided one
account of how such "higher-level" processes in apparent motion could
allow us to recover three-dimensional structure from displays of points in
motion. For instance, by assuming the existence of rigid objects in space,
we can recover the three-dimensional structure of any object from a set of
elements undergoing a two-dimensional transformation. It is thus clear
that higher-level motion perception is intimately bound up with the
perception of form, although the particular form representations involved
remain controversial. For instance, long-range apparent motion can be
seen between two different shapes, such as a square and a triangle, with the
shape appearing to distort as it "moves" from one location to another
(Humphreys, 1983). This might suggest that the critical aspects of form are
edges, so that long-range apparent motion is computed from representations at the level of the primal sketch (Ullman, 1979). Nevertheless, where
the possible movements that could be seen are ambiguous, coherent
movements that maintain the perception of the shape are preferred
(Ternus, 1926). Stronger movement also tends to be seen between shapes
whose "structural description" is preserved across presentations. Humphreys (1983) reported the degree of apparent movement perceived
between either isosceles triangles or squares rotated 45 degrees within-the-
plane. Squares appear to change their structural description when so
rotated, to become diamonds, whilst the structural description of isosceles
triangles remains constant. Apparent motion was more likely to be seen
between the triangles than between the squares, across a range of
interstimulus intervals. Thus, it seems possible that both line and "shape-
based" representations mediate long-range apparent motion. In contrast,
short-range motion, linked to directionally selective motion detectors, is
probably best thought of as part of an alerting and orienting "module"
which is quite independent of that used to recover three-dimensional
shape.

DEFICITS IN MOVEMENT PERCEPTION

Whatever the different mechanisms involved in motion perception,
evidence from neuropsychology shows that defects in motion perception
dissociate from defects in colour and form recognition. Perhaps the
clearest loss of movement vision following brain damage was documented

by Zihl, von Cramon, and Mai in 1983. Their patient had suffered bilateral damage to the prestriate cortex. Following this damage, the patient's ability to see continuous movement was severely impaired. She found it difficult to cross the road because she could not judge traffic speed. She found it difficult to follow conversations because she failed to take notice of face movements. Social interactions became difficult partly because of this, and partly because, in a crowd, people would appear and disappear suddenly as they moved around. Also, when pouring tea into a cup, the tea appeared frozen "like a glacier"; she then found it difficult to judge when to stop pouring because she could not detect the rising liquid in the cup. Despite these marked difficulties in movement vision, she remained able to recognise stationary forms and their colours.

In contrast to this patient, other patients with severe deficits in recognising forms can have a relatively spared ability to see movement. The agnosic patient, H.J.A., discussed in Chapter 3, is markedly impaired at object recognition, yet he can see shape defined by movement in random-dot kinematograms. These cases illustrate that at least some aspects of form and movement perception are separable. Future work with patients needs to be more directed by the theoretical distinctions between short- and long-range motion, and between the different mechanisms of motion perception, in order to assess whether all aspects of form and motion perception doubly dissociate.

VISUAL MASKING

When either objects or observers move, the image typically changes continuously, and earlier we considered the processes that allow us to see coherent objects in motion either from transforming images or from sequences of images in apparent motion. We can also learn about dynamic aspects of vision by studying a rather different situation, in which two or more discrete images of different patterns are presented rapidly to observers. This situation is analogous to that faced by an observer each time the eyes are moved, and the current scene is replaced by a slightly different one. Rapid presentation of such discrete images in the laboratory often leads to "masking", when the responses to one stimulus (the target), are adversely affected by the presentation of a second irrelevant stimulus (the mask). Masking occurs when the visual system is given insufficient time to identify individual stimuli.

Psychologists have studied masking for various reasons. Primarily though, masking procedures allow the experimenter tight control over the relations between consecutive images—their visual and spatial relations, how quickly they follow one another, etc. Masking thus provides an experimental tool to prise open otherwise hidden aspects of dynamic vision. However, as we hope to show, the phenomena revealed by masking studies also turn out to be of considerable interest in their own right.

We consider first some experimental data on masking, in order to build a full picture of the phenomena that theorists must try to explain. We then proceed to discuss the relations between the data and underlying visual processing mechanisms.

Some Empirical Evidence

A major study of visual masking was conducted by Turvey in 1973, and we will draw heavily on the experiments reported in that paper to illustrate our arguments. We begin with an experiment that examined two major variables: The time interval between the target and the mask, and the relative "energy" (brightness) of the two stimuli. Turvey (1973, experiment XVIII) had subjects identify letters from briefly presented consonant trigrams (i.e. rows of three consonants, such as RBL—the target). Each target was followed by a mask, consisting of lines of similar length, orientation and width to those in the target (termed a "pattern" mask; see Fig. 4.2). The mask was presented so that it superimposed the location where the target letters had appeared. The target and mask were exposed for just 10msec each, and the number of letters reported from each trigram was measured, relative to the time interval between the onset of the target and the onset of the mask (the stimulus-onset asynchrony—SOA). In one condition the target was twice as bright as the mask (T:M ratio of 2:1); in another, the mask was twice as bright as the target (T:M ratio of 1:2). The results are shown in Fig. 4.3.

There were striking differences between the results with the two target: mask energy ratios. When the target has less energy than the mask (T:M= 1:2), performance was extremely poor when there was only a short interval between the stimuli. Performance then improved monotonically as the SOA increased. We will refer to this as the monotonic masking function. This masking function shows that we are better able to identify the target as the time increases between the target and the arrival of the mask. Remember that the target was presented for the same duration in all cases. Thus, it seems that identification processes continue after the offset of the brief stimulus, and they can be interfered with by a subsequent mask.

Consider now the condition where the target has more energy than the mask (T:M=2:1). At short SOAs subjects reported the target accurately. However, as the interval increased, target report actually became more

PATTERN MASK (PM)

FIG. 4.2. An example of a "pattern" mask. (Reproduced from Turvey, 1973, with permission.)

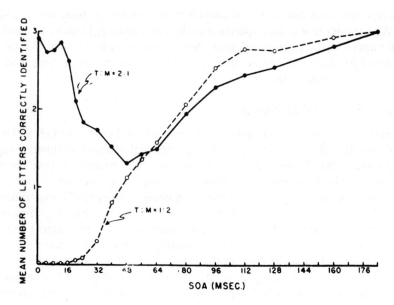

FIG. 4.3.   An example of monotonic and U-shaped masking functions. (Reproduced from Turvey, 1973, with permission.)

difficult, and only later did it improve again as the target-mask interval became even longer. That is, there was a U-shaped masking function. This result is counter-intuitive, in that performance became more difficult as more time was allowed to identify the target before the mask was presented.

We can view these two results another way. When there is a short interval between the target and the mask (roughly 48msec or less, in Fig. 4.3), performance is strongly affected by the target:mask energy ratio. When there is a longer target:mask interval (over 48msec, in Fig. 4.3), performance is not affected by this ratio, but by the target:mask interval (performance improves with an increasing interval).

The following interpretation can now be put forward. Stimuli separated by very short intervals are integrated together. This makes the target difficult to identify (i.e. it produces masking) if the target is dim and the mask bright, because the mask will be the more salient of the two within the integrated percept. Correspondingly, the target is easy to identify if it is bright and the mask dim. "Integration masking" is maximal when the interstimulus interval is zero. With longer intervals between the stimuli, the critical time over which integration operates elapses (as it must, otherwise all percepts would run together). Yet from Turvey's results it is clear that the target remains difficult to identify (and in fact the bright target becomes harder to identify as the SOA increases up to some critical point). This suggests that a second type of masking takes place at the longer intervals. For instance, at longer intervals masks may interrupt the identification processes initiated by the target. From Turvey's data (Fig. 4.3) interruption masking is greatest with an interval of about 40–50msec between the stimuli. This may be because interruption effects are greatest when the target attains a particular level of representation, which takes some time to be achieved—we return to this point when we consider "higher-order effects" in masking. Finally, as the interval between target and mask increases even further, interruption masking decreases and performance improves. The U-shaped masking function occurs for bright targets because they suffer minimal integration masking at the short SOAs followed by significant interruption masking at the longer SOAs.

From this single result of Turvey's we can propose that visual masking involves at least two "mechanisms": Integration of perceptual information from stimuli, and interruption of the identification of a first stimulus by a second stimulus. A useful analogy for "interruption masking" was put forward by Kolers in 1968, in terms of the relations between a "clerk" and a "customer":

> a customer who enters a store is usually treated as fully as the attending clerk can treat him; a second customer then entering, the clerk tends to shorten the amount of time he spends with the first. In a store whose customers enter aperiodically, the amount of treatment depends upon whether a second customer enters; if he does, treatment of the first is usually shortened.

In this analogy, the visual inputs are the "customers" and the processes required for identification to occur can be conceptualised as the "clerk". The idea is that the mask limits the time over which identification processes can operate on a target. According to this account, masking should decrease as the time available for processing the target increases. Also, if interruption reflects competition between targets and masks for common processes, then it will vary according to the similarity of the stimuli: The more similar the stimuli, the more similar their processing and the stronger any competition for common processes.

Integration masking may occur because of the poor temporal resolution of the visual system, which sums signals over time. Normally, integration is beneficial to vision, enhancing the perception of a coherent world when successive images contain the same stimuli; it is only when successive images contain different stimuli that integration becomes harmful (producing masking). When targets and masks are presented briefly and in rapid succession, they are summed together. The effect of integrating images of different stimuli will typically be to degrade the target. For instance, even if the mask is something as simple as a flash of light, it will reduce the contrast of the target when the two are integrated (see Eriksen &

Hoffman, 1963). When the mask has some form of pattern, it will tend to camouflage the target. Whether or not subjects will be able to identify the target will depend on factors such as the relative brightness of the two stimuli.

Effects of Target:Mask Similarity

Turvey (1973, experiment XII) contrasted the effects of a pattern mask (Fig. 4.2) with those of a random noise mask (see Fig. 4.4). The random noise simply comprised randomly positioned black and white squares, so there was minimal pattern based on elongated contour. Pattern-based masking should be more pronounced with the pattern than with the random noise mask. In contrast to the earlier masking experiment we discussed, Turvey varied two factors: The duration of the target, and the interval between the onset of the target and the offset of a 50msec mask (the critical interstimulus interval, ISI). Measures were based on the critical ISI needed to identify the target. Figure 4.5 illustrates the critical ISIs needed for pattern and random noise masks for various target durations.

Two basic points are apparent. One is that the noise mask interferes less with performance than the pattern mask, as the critical ISIs needed are generally lower in the former case. The second is that masking reduces as the target duration increases (again, the critical ISIs needed decrease). A more critical finding, however, is that, for the pattern mask, different relations seem to hold for brief targets and for those presented for longer durations. For brief targets, the critical ISI needed to identify the target decreases rapidly as the target is presented for longer. In fact, multiplying the target duration by the critical ISI yields a relatively constant number. For instance, for target durations of 2, 3, and 4msec, the product of the duration and the critical ISI was 180, 186, and 213msec respectively (for the random noise mask the equivalent figures were 115, 122, and 118msec respectively; Turvey, 1973). All the effects with the random noise mask conform to this multiplicative relationship. For the pattern mask a second masking function emerges as the target duration increases further. In this case, adding the target duration and the critical ISI together yields a constant number. For instance, for target durations of 24, 32, and 40msec, the sum of the duration and the critical ISI was 58, 60, and 59msec respectively (pattern mask only).

FIG. 4.4. An example of a "random noise" mask. (Reproduced from Turvey, 1973, with permission.)

RANDOM NOISE (RN)

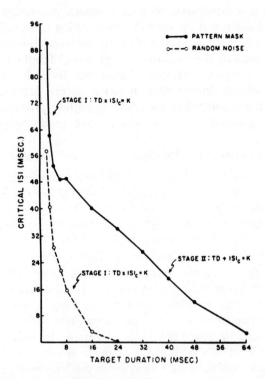

FIG. 4.5.   Multiplicative and additive masking functions to random noise and pattern masks. (Reproduced from Turvey, 1973, with permission.)

Pattern masks produce two types of masking, depending on the interval between the target and the mask. With a relatively long interval (e.g. at the longer target durations here), performance depends on the total interval between the target and the mask (i.e. the target duration plus the ISI; note that this is equivalent to the SOA). That is, performance depends on the time available to process the target. With shorter target:mask intervals (i.e. at the shorter target durations), a different, multiplicative relationship holds.

Now, when visual stimuli are briefly presented (e.g. for less than 100msec), their duration and their intensity (brightness) can be interchanged without altering the visual effect. This relationship is known as Bloch's law (see Davy, 1952), which states that duration × intensity is a constant (corresponding to stimulus energy). Essentially, the visual system is poor at resolving brief stimulus durations, and so can be "fooled" into equating the durations of a brief, bright stimulus and a longer, dim one. This trade-off is encapsulated in the multiplicative relationship. Similarly, the multiplicative relationship which holds for masking at short target:

mask intervals is symptomatic of poor temporal resolution for briefly presented visual stimuli. It fits with the "integration masking" account of the data in Fig. 4.3, when masking with short intervals between targets and masks is determined by their relative energy levels. Random noise masks seem only to generate integration masking; they do not produce interruption masking. Interruption masking seems dependent on the target and the mask competing for common pattern processing mechanisms, and so is greatest when the stimuli have similar structures.

Forward and Backward Masking

Other differences between integration and interruption masking can also be teased apart. For instance, interrupution should only occur when the mask follows the target (a procedure termed "backward masking"). Integration should take place whichever stimulus comes first, providing they come close enough together in time.

Turvey (1973, Experiment xiv) contrasted backward masking with "forward masking", when the mask precedes the target. The critical ISI needed for target report was again measured. The data are shown in Fig. 4.6. As in Fig. 4.5, backward pattern masking generated both a multiplicative and an additive relationship between target duration and the critical ISI, depending upon the target duration. In contrast, forward pattern masking generally conformed to the multiplicative relationship, and it was weaker than backward masking at the longer target durations. Forward masking by pattern (as here) is thus equivalent to backward masking by random noise (see Fig. 4.6), and both illustrate integration masking.

Summary

We have considered Turvey's experiments in some detail because they demonstrate the lawful nature of masking as revealed by systematic experimental study. The experiments demonstrate that masking is not a unitary phenomenon. At short target:mask intervals, masking can be characterised in terms of the integration of information from masks and targets. Performance is determined by the relative energy levels of the target and the mask rather than by their visual similarity or by the absolute time available for target processing, and masking occurs both when the mask precedes and when it follows the target (i.e. under both forward and backward masking conditions). At longer target:mask intervals, masks interrupt target processing. Performance is determined by the time interval between the stimuli and not by their relative energy levels; it is affected by the visual similarity of the target and the mask (occurring only with pattern masks when the targets are letters); and it occurs only under backward masking conditions.

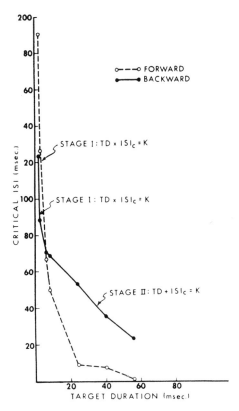

FIG. 4.6. Multiplicative and additive masking functions under forward and backward masking conditions. (Reproduced from Turvey, 1973, with permission.)

Monoptic vs Dichoptic Masking: Some Complexities

In all the experiments we have discussed so far, targets and masks were presented to the same eye; that is, masking was monocular. Dichoptic masking occurs when the target is presented to one eye and the mask to the other. Following binocular combination, targets and masks should be treated equivalently regardless of whether they are presented independently to each eye. Dichoptic masking can therefore be used as a tool to study where in the visual system any interactions take place between targets and masks, as dichoptic masking can only occur after binocular combination in the cortex.

Studies of dichoptic, backward masking on pattern recognition have generally produced quite clear results. When either uniform light flashes or random noise masks are used, there is minimal dichoptic masking (e.g. Mowbray & Durr, 1964; Schiller, 1965; Smith & Schiller, 1966; Turvey,

1973, Experiment III; although see Kinsbourne & Warrington, 1962a). When pattern masks are used, dichoptic masking occurs, and it is relatively unaffected by stimulus intensity (e.g. Boynton, 1961; Schiller, 1969; Turvey, 1973, Experiment VIII). These results confirm the distinction between interruption masking by pattern and integration masking by noise. They suggest that interruption masking is central in origin; integration masking is more peripheral.

Unfortunately, the simple dichotomy between peripheral, integration masking and central, interruption masking does not hold good. Michaels and Turvey (1979, Experiment B1), using a pattern mask, showed that some forward masking did occur under dichoptic conditions—even though only integration masking should occur with forward masks. Thus, it appears that, whilst interruption effects on pattern recognition only occur centrally, integration masking can occur both peripherally (e.g. with a light flash mask) and centrally (with a pattern mask). As we shall see, there are grounds for suggesting that the two types of integration effect reflect separate processing mechanisms.

PROCESSING MECHANISMS IN VISUAL MASKING

The processes we have labelled integration and interruption have been defined purely at an operational level, with the two types of masking producing different effects on stimulus identification. To go beyond this, we need to consider more precisely the types of processing mechanism involved, and to relate the results to processes in everyday visual tasks.

Iconic Memory

When the first detailed information processing studies of visual masking got underway in the 1960s and 1970s, the effects were typically attributed to interference to an initial stage of perception—concerned with the registration of a relatively unanalysed perceptual memory of the target. Such an unanalysed perceptual memory was termed iconic memory by Neisser in 1967. Iconic memory was conceptualised as a kind of input buffer, in which visual stimuli could be held temporarily in a literal form prior to their being matched to stored knowledge for identification or for storage in memory. This input buffer might then play an important role integrating the information we pick up as we glance around the world (although see Chapters 6 and 7).

The seminal experiments on iconic memory were conducted by Sperling in 1960. When subjects are asked to report letters from a briefly presented display consisting of, for example, three rows of four characters, they typically identify only about 40% of the characters correctly (i.e. 4 to 5). Sperling presented subjects with brief displays of this sort, and followed the displays with a cue which told the subjects only to report a particular subset of the letters present (an auditory tone, whose pitch indicated whether the top, middle or bottom row was to be reported). Sperling showed that, when the cue came immediately after the display, subjects could typically report about 75% of the letters from each row. Averaging across the display, performance was considerably better when subjects were cued (the partial-report condition) than when they had to report all the letters (the whole-report condition). In the partial-report condition, subjects did not know which row had to be reported until the display offset. It follows that, after display offset, a high percentage of letters are available for report. Sperling also showed that, as the time between the display offset and the presentation of the cue increased, partial-report performance decreased. After about a 250msec interval, partial-report performance was roughly equal to that in the whole-report condition.

From these results, it was suggested that subjects form an iconic memory of all the characters in the display, with the icon persisting for about 250msec. Providing that the cue arrives within the time the icon is available, partial report is accurate. However, whole-report is limited by the rate of identification, which is sufficiently slow to preclude more than the identification of 4 or 5 items from brief displays—presumably because iconic memory has decayed by the time this number of characters has been identified. Figure 4.7 gives a schematic description of typical partial-report experimental results.

Subsequent experiments (e.g. Averbach & Coriell, 1961; Sperling, 1963) showed that the advantage for partial-report over whole-report was lost if the displays were immediately followed by a mask. Sperling (1963) used a random noise mask similar to that of Turvey (1973), and so we may presume that masking was of the integration variety. Information from the target may be integrated with that of the mask in iconic memory, impairing the read-out of information from the icon when the partial report cue arrives. Any target information which is reported under those conditions will reflect the information read-out unselectively, prior to the partial report cue being presented. This will be equivalent to performance under whole-report conditions.

Iconic Memory and Visual Masking

There are problems with this simple alignment of masking with effects on iconic memory. For instance, the iconic account alone does not allow us to distinguish peripheral from central integration; nor does it account for the distinction between integration and interruption masking. Integration in iconic memory cannot provide a complete account of visual masking.

Also, consider the decline in the partial report advantage as the interval

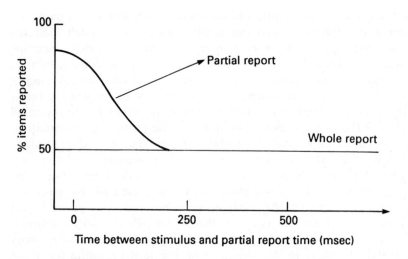

FIG. 4.7. Schematic description of results from a partial-report experiment showing the partial-report advantage, and the loss of this advantage as the stimulus-cue interval increases.

between the display and the cue lengthens. Sperling (1960) proposed that this reflected the decay of iconic memory. A number of studies have subsequently shown that the decline is brought about mainly by the tendency for subjects to make "mislocation errors" as the display-cue interval increases: that is, subjects report letters that were present in the display but were in non-cued positions (Dick, 1974; Eriksen & Rohrbaugh, 1970; Mewhort & Campbell, 1978; Mewhort et al., 1981; Townsend, 1973). The number of "intrusion errors" (i.e. the reporting of nondisplayed letters) does not change so dramatically. These data on mislocation errors indicate that the identities and the positions of the characters in the displays seem to decay at different rates. In addition, Mewhort and his co-workers (Mewhort & Campbell, 1978; Mewhort et al., 1981) have shown that mislocation errors are particularly increased when the displays are masked, and these mislocation errors vary according to the positions of the characters in the visual field. Mislocations are most likely for the letters in the central positions of an array, and least likely for the end letters. Both the differing decay rates for letter position and identity, and the effects of masking on mislocations, are difficult to reconcile with any simple loss of information in iconic memory. We return to discuss wider issues about iconic memory in Chapter 6. For now we note that masking cannot be ascribed solely to disruption of the "icon".

Masking and Interactions between Sustained and Transient Processing Channels

In Chapter 2, we discussed evidence for a distinction between two classes of cell in the visual system: X or sustained cells and Y or transient cells. These different classes of cell can be thought of as providing two different "channels" of visual input. Here we briefly elaborate on the properties of these two different classes of cell, and consider how interactions within and between the cells may provide an explanation for visual masking effects. Sustained cells respond maximally to stationary stimuli which are small or composed of high spatial-frequency patterns, they have a long response latency and they are affected by image blurring (e.g. Cleland, Levick & Sanderson, 1973; Dow, 1974; Ikeda & Wright, 1972). Transient cells are sensitive to rapid motion, they respond to large or low-frequency patterns, they are unaffected by blurring, they show a short response latency (firing can be completed within 50msec of stimulus onset), and they respond preferentially to the abrupt onset and/or offset of a pattern (e.g. Cleland et al., 1973; Dow, 1974; Enroth-Cugell & Robson, 1966; Hoffman, Stone, & Sherman, 1972; Ikeda & Wright, 1972). Sustained cells may primarily determine pattern recognition, whilst outputs from transient cells are important for the perception of flicker or motion (Breitmeyer & Ganz, 1976; Kulikowski & Tolhurst, 1973; Tolhurst, 1973)—although some pattern and motion processing may be performed by both systems (see Derrington & Henning, 1981; Green, 1984; Lovegrove & Evans, 1980). Physiological evidence has also shown that the two systems can mutually inhibit each other (Singer & Bedworth, 1973).

Earlier in this chapter we discussed how outputs from sustained and transient cells may be combined to provide information about "moving edges". In this instance, the outputs from the two channels interact co-operatively. Because of the different temporal response properties of the two channels, transient activation generated by a stimulus will become available prior to sustained activation. Co-operative interactions between the channels may depend on this temporal ordering of firing. However, consider the situation when two different stimuli are presented one after another in close temporal succession. In this case, sustained activation from the first stimulus will overlap temporarily with transient activation from the second. Under this circumstance, transient channels may inhibit concurrently active sustained channels (Breitmeyer & Ganz, 1976; Breitmeyer, 1980). It follows that masking may provide one means for studying the properties of these processing "channels" in the visual system.

Breitmeyer and Ganz (1976) argue that various interactions can occur between targets and masks, both within a processing channel or across channels. This creates different masking effects. For instance, when there are relatively short intervals between masks and targets, the transient and sustained signals activated by the two stimuli will overlap in time. Breitmeyer and Ganz argue that, at a pre-cortical (peripheral) level, there is mutual inhibition within each channel: that is, there is "transient on transient" and "sustained on sustained" inhibition. Once signals reach the cortex, however, there is a summing of activity within each channel. Integration masking occurs because of this summation process. Masking due to within-channel inhibition, and masking due to integration, should be indifferent to whether the mask precedes or follows the mask. However, some interactions will be specific to forward and to backward masking.

Consider backward masking first. When the interval between the target and the mask increases, sustained information from the target will overlap temporally with transient information from the mask. Breitmeyer and Ganz propose that transient signals from the mask inhibit sustained signals from the target. This transient-on-sustained inhibition would be maximal between channels coded for the same orientation, and so it would be affected by pattern similarity (e.g. greater masking when the stimuli have the same orientation). We may thus think of these inhibitory interactions as underlying "interruption" masking in Turvey's (1973) terms. Figure 4.8 illustrates how sustained and transient channels might be activated by targets and masks, and how transient activation from the mask could inhibit sustained activation from the target. Sustained-on-transient inhibition was also demonstrated physiologically by Singer and Bedworth (1973). Breitmeyer (1980) speculates that this might play some role in forward masking, as sustained information from the mask might then inhibit transient activity produced by the onset of the target.

In the brain, inhibition has been found between neighbouring cells with receptive fields in close but non-overlapping spatial regions (e.g. Benevento, Creutzfeldt, & Kuhnt, 1972; Hess, Negishi, & Creutzfeldt, 1975). It follows that masking due to across-channel inhibition should not be critically dependent on targets and masks appearing at the same location in the field (Breitmeyer & Ganz, 1976). This is useful, because masking effects can occur even when the stimuli appear in different (although neighbouring) spatial regions. Masking of this sort was shown in some of the original experiments on iconic memory, by Averbach and Coriell (1961).

They displayed a row of letters followed by a ring which encircled one of the letters. The ring was intended to act as a partial report cue (indicating which letter had to be reported). In fact, subjects were typically unable to

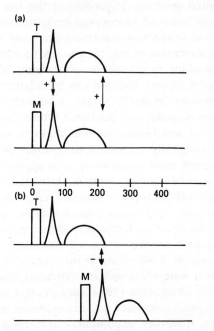

FIG. 4.8. Hypothesised time course of activation in sustained and transient channels. (a) When the target and mask are presented concurrently there is central summation of sustained and transient signals from both stimuli. (b) When the mask follows the target, transient signals from the mask inhibit sustained signals from the target. Only central interactions are shown here.

report the letter because it was masked by the ring. Masking between non-overlapping stimuli is termed paracontrast when the mask precedes the target, and metacontrast when the mask follows the target (equivalent to forward and backward masking between overlapping stimuli). Breitmeyer and Ganz's (1976) account of masking in terms of interactions between sustained and transient processing channels has strength in that it attributes masking with overlapping and non-overlapping stimuli to essentially the same processing mechanisms.

The "channel" account of masking is attractive in that it enables masking to be linked to known physiological responses of the visual system. It can also address some of the findings on iconic memory. For instance, transient channels can provide coarse location information (see Breitmeyer & Ganz, 1976; Watt, 1988). It is therefore possible for this information to be selectively disrupted (in forward masking, due to sustained-on-transient inhibition), producing the loss of position but not form information. By a similar argument it is possible for location information to be selectively preserved under masking conditions (in backward masking, due to transient-on-sustained inhibition), producing the loss of form but not position information. Selective loss of position information due to masking is the result reported in the iconic memory literature (although typically with backward not forward masking; Mewhort & Campbell, 1978). Studies of metacontrast masking have, on the other hand, shown that forced-choice detection of a target's location can be relatively unaffected even when form information from the target is strongly masked (but with backward not forward masks; e.g. Schiller & Smith, 1966).

Finally, Breitmeyer and Ganz's account provides grounds for arguing that masking is ecologically important for normal perception. We can consider this argument most easily when it is applied to a task such as reading. When we read, our eyes move through a series of saccades separated by fixations (Chapter 7). Average fixation pauses can be of the order of 200–250msec, and such pauses enable us to process the information from the pattern of printed letters and words on the page. Average saccades take place over about 6–8 characters (about 2 degrees of visual angle; Rayner & McConkie, 1976). Saccades operate to bring regions of text which were previously in peripheral vision on to the fovea for detailed analysis. Breitmeyer (1980) suggests that, after each fixation, we should expect some persistence due to continued activity in sustained processing channels. If allowed to go unimpeded, this continued sustained activity would interfere with processing on the next fixation, due to central integration (see Fig. 4.9). However, Breitmeyer also proposes that each saccade generates transient activity, which inhibits any sustained activity due to prior fixations. The resultant response is one where there is no persistence across fixations to disrupt reading (Fig. 4.10). Lovegrove, Martin, and Slaghuis (1986) have more recently applied this account to children with specific reading disorders, suggesting that such children have a deficient transient system, and so they are susceptible to masking effects as they read.

The "channel" account of masking thus has breadth of appeal. Unfortunately, however, the evidence for the account is mixed. Whereas

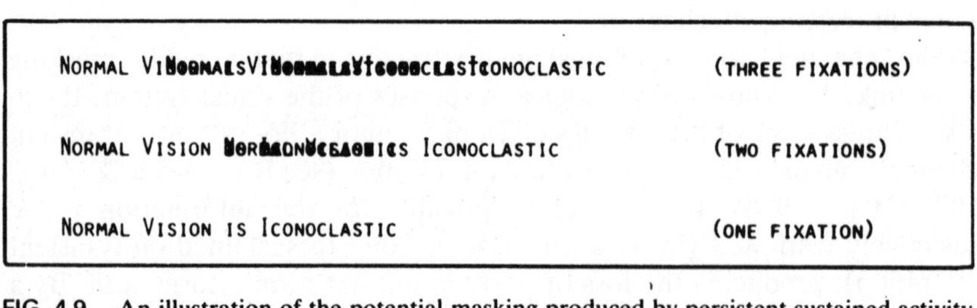

FIG. 4.9.   An illustration of the potential masking produced by persistent sustained activity being carried across fixations during reading. (Reproduced from Lovegrove et al., 1986, with permission.)

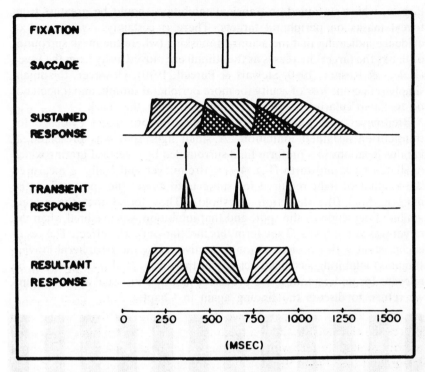

FIG. 4.10. Hypothesised response sequence of sustained and transient channels during 250msec fixation intervals followed by the two 25msec saccades. Sustained responses are thought to be modified by activation in transient channels after each saccade. (Reproduced from Lovegrove et al., 1986, with permission.)

there is evidence to link masking with activity in sustained and transient processing channels, the fine details of Breitmeyer and Ganz's proposals are not strongly supported. Also, there are grounds for arguing that interactions between "early" processing channels cannot fully explain masking (see pp.132–138). In the next section we review this evidence.

Transient-on-Sustained Inhibition

Manipulations of transient and sustained responses have typically been based on the differences between foveal and peripheral stimulus presentation. It has been proposed that sustained cells have a high proportion of the receptive fields in the fovea, and the number of sustained-cell receptive fields decreases rapidly in the periphery. The receptive fields of transient cells are sparse in the fovea but are more prevalent in the periphery (Fukuda & Stone, 1974; Hoffman et al., 1972). Consequently, transient-on-sustained inhibition should be greatest from peripheral masks on foveal targets, whilst sustained-on-transient inhibition should be greatest from foveal masks on peripheral targets. There is certainly a good deal of evidence indicating that metacontrast masking (where the mask surrounds or flanks the target) increases as the stimuli are moved away from the fovea (Kolers & Rosner, 1960; Stewart & Purcell, 1970). However, this might simply reflect the loss of acuity for more peripheral stimuli, and it need not be tied particularly to transient inhibition from the mask.

Breitmeyer and Valberg (1979) produced more direct evidence for transient-on-sustained inhibition. A small light spot was presented at various locations in a uniform field surrounded by a vertical grating which oscillated back and forth (Fig. 4.11). Breitmeyer and Valberg measured the amount of light required for subjects to detect the spot against the uniform field (the detection threshold). They found that the grating inhibited detection of the spot, and that inhibition was maximal when the target was at the fovea. They term this the "far-out jerk" effect. The result is consistent with transient channels (activated by the peripheral moving stimulus) inhibiting sustained activity at the fovea. It also turns out to be relevant for understanding the processes involved in visual attention, and we return to discuss the finding again in Chapter 5.

FIG. 4.11.   A representation of the stimulus display used to measure the "far-out jerk" effect. Fixation could be at any of the locations indicated by the X's. The target light was presented at the centre of the display. (Reproduced from Breitmeyer, 1980, with permission.)

However, Breitmeyer and Valberg's experiment requiring the detection of a light spot is some way from studies requiring form recognition (e.g. letter identification). In fact, there are remarkably few studies of masking on form recognition which have attempted to test whether masking can be generated from transient-on-sustained inhibition. One relevant study is that of Forster (1982). Forster required subjects to identify target photographs, which were followed by a random noise mask filtered to remove either its high spatial-frequency components (i.e. a low spatial-frequency mask) or its low spatial-frequency components (i.e. a high spatial-frequency mask). Forster found that the high-frequency mask produced only a monotonic masking function, whilst the low-frequency mask produced a U-shaped function (cf. Fig. 4.3). The U-shaped function with the low-frequency mask would be expected if, in addition to any early within-channel effects, there is also later acting transient-on-sustained inhibition. This inhibition should be lacking with a high-frequency mask, which produces a much reduced transient response. But this is by no means the only explanation for the result. Forster's low-frequency mask contained more form-like elements than the high-frequency mask, so that the masks resembled Turvey's (1973) pattern and random noise masks. The U-shaped function for the low-frequency/pattern mask could be given the account offered for Turvey's data, and it does not demand interpretation in terms of transient-on-sustained inhibition.

Sustained-on-Transient Inhibition

Evidence for sustained-on-transient inhibition was presented by Von Grunau (1978). Subjects were asked to judge whether they saw apparent motion between two brief light flashes. The first flash could occur either at the fovea or in the visual periphery. In one condition subjects viewed the flash through a de-focusing lens, otherwise viewing conditions were normal. The idea here was that the lens would selectively remove high-spatial frequency components from the display, and so should selectively impair the sustained response system (Ikeda & Wright, 1972). Von Grunau found that motion was more likely to be perceived and it occurred over shorter intervals between the flashes when: (1) the flashes were in the periphery; and (2) they were seen through the lens. Both results are consistent with the idea that the transient system is particularly sensitive to detecting motion with short intervals between the stimuli. That this was most apparent under de-focusing conditions also suggests that the transient system might normally be suppressed by sustained responses. Reducing the level of these sustained responses by de-focusing leads to increased sensitivity in the transient system.

Whether these inhibitory responses are important in masking is less clear. Breitmeyer (1978) examined metacontrast masking produced by flanking bars on a central pattern stimulus. Masking was reduced when the bars were themselves flanked by two other bars presented continuously throughout the display. He proposed that sustained responses produced by the continuous bars inhibited transient responses produced by the masking bars, so reducing their masking effect.

Yet alternative explanations can be offered for any of these results taken in isolation. In Breitmeyer's (1978) study the continuous bars could "mask" the masking bars because the two sets of bars compete for the same processing mechanisms, not because of sustained-on-transient inhibition. Stronger converging evidence is needed here. For instance, would masking vary with factors influencing sustained and transient responses—such as the spatial-frequency of the patterns or their spatial locations? These questions await future research. At present, however, the case for a role of across-channel interactions in masking cannot be considered conclusive.

Within-Channel Interactions

Breitmeyer and Ganz (1976) propose that peripheral masking is best conceptualised as within-channel inhibition. Peripheral masking can occur with masks containing minimal pattern, such as random noise masks (Turvey, 1973). Experiments using such masks should therefore be informative about this type of masking. The limiting case is where the mask is simply a light flash.

The first major study of masking by light was performed by Crawford in 1947. Subjects had to detect a briefly presented light spot which was flashed against a uniform field—similar to the task used by Breitmeyer and Valberg (1979). The test spot was presented before, during or after a light-flash mask (on for a relatively long 500msec). The results, given in terms of the threshold for detecting the light spot, are presented schematically in Fig. 4.12A. Masking is indicated by threshold increases. The data show that masking peaks at the mask onset and offset—generating "ears" in the masking function. That is, the target spot was most difficult to detect when presented either at the onset or the offset of the mask. The temporal-locking of masking to the mask onset and offset is exactly what would be expected if masking were due to inhibition from transient responses produced by the mask.

Green (1981) extended Crawford's result by asking subjects to adjust the contrast of a test grating until it was just visible, and masking the grating with a light-flash mask. The grating varied in its spatial-frequency profile (1.0 or 7.8 cycles/degree). The data are shown in Figs 4.12B and C. "Ears" on the masking function were found only with the low spatial-frequency grating (1 cycle/degree). This result shows that transient responses produced by the light flash have their main effect by inhibiting transient responses generated by the target—hence their greater effect on

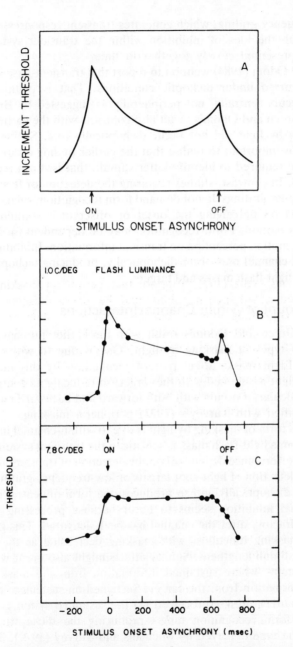

FIG. 4.12. Functions for masking by light flashes. Panel A schematically represents light detection increment thresholds reported by Crawford (1947). Panels B and C show increment thresholds for detecting gratings from Green (1981). Note the "ears" on the masking functions in Panels A and B but not in Panel C. (Reproduced from Green, 1981, with permission.)

the low-frequency grating, which generates transient responses. The data fit nicely with the idea of inhibition within the transient system when stimuli are presented closely together in time.

Green and Odom (1984) went on to report that transient-based masking by light occurred under dichoptic conditions. That is, within-channel inhibition occurs centrally, not peripherally as suggested by Breitmeyer and Ganz. Green and Odom's result also contrasts with the earlier finding that masking by light did not occur dichoptically (e.g. Schiller, 1965). However, it is important to realise that the earlier finding occurred when subjects were required to identify letter stimuli; that is, form recognition was required. In contrast, studies requiring the detection of flashed spots or low-frequency gratings do not demand form recognition; such responses can be based on perceiving the onset or offset of a stimulus, or on perceiving its motion. Form recognition may be dependent on sustained information, motion perception on transient information. Inhibition within the transient channel may occur dichoptically, producing dichoptic masking between light-flash masks and targets.

A New Account of Within-Channel Interactions

Comparing Green and Odom's result with the earlier findings, we can separate two types of masking by light. One is due to within-channel summation. Light masks affect pattern recognition by this mechanism because the light is summed with the target, so reducing its contrast. The effect is monocular, it occurs with both forward and backward masks, and can be identified with Turvey's (1973) peripheral masking.

The second form of masking by light is due to within-channel inhibition. Inhibition from a light-flash mask is specific to the transient system, and so only affects performance dependent on the detection of transient responses (such as the detection of light-spot targets or low-frequency gratings). This effect occurs dichoptically and so produces one form of central masking. Within-channel inhibition seems to occur because processing within a channel is refractory after the channel has been activated. This generates monotonic masking functions, with masking decreasing as the interval between the stimuli lengthens. Similar effects might also occur within the sustained system—where sustained information from the mask inhibits sustained information from the target. Sustained-on-sustained inhibition occurs with pattern masks (processed via the sustained system), and it is observed in form recognition tasks—producing the dichoptic forward masking of the type observed by Michaels and Turvey (1979). Thus our suggestion is that there are two types of within-channel masking: peripheral within-channel summation and central within-channel inhibition.

This two-component account also meshes with data reported by Georgeson and Georgeson (1987; Georgeson, 1988). They used a "grating detection" task, in which subjects were presented with two masks (vertical gratings) separated in time. Following just one of the masks, a target grating was shown. Subjects had to judge whether the target appeared with the first or the second mask. The amount of contrast needed to detect the target was measured.

With a very short interval between the target and the mask (under 50msec), detection of the target was improved by the mask—when the mask itself was dim, near-threshold, and identical with the target (i.e. same spatial frequency and phase). Target detection may be facilitated because responses in the same processing channels are summed, with the target then appearing bright relative to the other dim mask. Interestingly, the effect was abolished when the target and mask were out of phase so that the dark sections of the target fell on the light sections of the mask grating. This indicates that summation is closely tied to the location of the stimulus in the field.

With longer intervals between targets and masks, target detection was impaired by the mask. This would be expected if activation in a channel were followed by a refractory period. The impairment on target detection remained even when the stimuli were out of phase, indicating that the effect is less closely tied to absolute stimulus location. Georgeson also showed that only the inhibitory masking effect occurred under dichoptic conditions.

From Georgeson and Georgeson's work we can infer that peripheral summation occurs within a processing channel when there are very short intervals between masks and targets, and it is tied to retinal location. Central within-channel inhibition occurs with slightly longer intervals between the stimuli and it is not tied to retinal location. Interestingly, central within-channel inhibition displays many of the characteristics of perception that are revealed in adaptation studies—such as orientation and spatial-frequency specificity, transference between the eyes and indifference to spatial phase (see Chapter 2). This suggests that adaptation and this form of masking provide convergent means for studying properties of early vision.

Masking and Movement Perception

At the beginning of the chapter we discussed some of the different processes that seem to be involved in perceiving motion in continuously transforming images, and between static frames in motion perception. We have now reviewed in detail the problems and possible mechanisms involved in the visual masking of one image by a different image following in close temporal succession. What is the relationship between our perception of single forms in motion and the masking of one different visual form by another? One possibility is that the processes determining masking with very short interstimulus intervals are normally involved in some aspects of motion perception. For instance, consider Georgeson and Georgeson's finding that peripheral masking is sensitive to spatial phase. We can think of this result in the following way. The visual system sums activity within a channel over time, and compares the outputs at different times from neighbouring locations in the field—perhaps using directionally sensitive filters ("local movement detectors"). If a stimulus moves there will be a difference in the sum computed relative to when the stimulus is stationary, so providing a means of detecting local movement in the field. Such signals may be conveyed most strongly by transient cells, which have fast onset and offset times and so can respond to rapidly moving stimuli. Precisely these signals may be involved in our detecting short-range apparent motion (Braddick, 1980).

We suggest then that at least one type of visual masking taps aspects of motion detection. Consistent with this, short-range apparent motion does not occur if a light-flash is presented in the interval between stimulus frames (Braddick, 1973). In this case, transient information from the light flash interferes with the transient responses used to signal short-range motion.

What of other types of masking? In the next section we consider how masking affects other time consuming processes in vision, such as object and word recognition, and we consider how masking informs us of the processes involved in these tasks.

HIGHER-LEVEL PROCESSES IN VISUAL MASKING

The accounts of masking we have discussed so far have stressed that masking is a relatively "low-level" phenomenon—reflecting interactions at early stages of visual processing. The evidence indicates that masking can involve such "early" interactions, but can such interactions provide a complete explanation of masking? What role might our stored knowledge of stimuli have on their masking, and can masking directly affect apparently "later" stages of processing concerned with the retrieval of this knowledge?

Most of the studies we have discussed have not allowed stored knowledge to play much of a role in masking because they have used stimuli to which little meaning can be attached—light flashes, gratings or nonsense trigrams. When meaningful, familiar targets are used, clear effects of stored knowledge emerge. For instance, Michaels and Turvey (1979, Experiment E1) compared the effects of dichoptic backward pattern

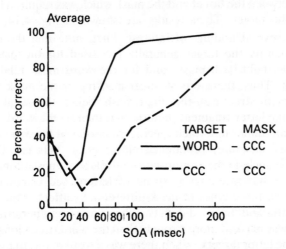

FIG. 4.13.   Masking functions for words and consonant trigram targets. (Reproduced from Michaels & Turvey, 1979, with permission.)

masking on the identification of words and nonsense trigrams. They used dichoptic backward pattern masking to ensure that they incorporated central interruption-type effects. Their data are shown in Fig. 4.13. Note that U-shaped masking functions occurred for both the words and the nonsense targets, indicating the involvement late-on of interruption-type effects. Words were less affected by masking than the nonsense trigrams, but this benefit was confined to the later portions of the masking function. Thus, it is not simply that words are easier to identify than nonsense trigrams—as performance was equivalent on the two types of target when there was a short interval between the target and the mask. Rather, words seem better able to escape the interrupting effect of the mask. This suggests that interruption-type masking can reflect competition for processing mechanisms sensitive to the properties separating words from nonsense trigrams—such as their meaning, their pronounceability or simply their visual familiarity (see Chapter 7 for further discussion of the relative roles of such factors in visual word recognition).

Masking and Word Recognition

Other investigators have studied the role of higher-order processes in masking by varying the nature of the mask. For instance, Taylor and Chabot (1978) had subjects identify either a single briefly presented letter or a whole word. The letter or word was followed by one of three types of mask: a light flash, a mask composed of randomly oriented fragments of letters (a pattern mask), or an unrelated word. Similarly to Turvey (1973), Taylor and Chabot varied the duration of the target and measured the critical ISI between the target and the mask which was required by subjects to identify the target. Their results are shown in Fig. 4.14.

There are several findings of interest. First, note that the critical ISI needed to identify the target generally increased for the pattern mask relative to the light-flash mask, and for the word mask relative to the pattern mask. Thus, there was stronger masking as the mask acquired a more patterned structure—the light flash being the weakest mask, followed by the letter-fragment pattern, and then by the word. Unfortunately, we again cannot tell which specific properties of the word mask were important (its meaning, pronounceability, etc.), because Taylor and Chabot did not include the appropriate controls (e.g. masks composed of a pronounceable but meaningless string of letters, see Chapter 7).

Secondly, the three types of mask differentially affected the identification of the letter and the word targets. When there was a pattern mask, the letter target was masked more strongly than the word (i.e. a longer ISI was needed for the letter target). When there was a word mask, there remained an advantage for the word target over the letter target, but the size of this advantage was reduced. When there was a light-flash mask, there was no difference between the identification of the letter and the word target.

The finding that a word can be identified more accurately than a single letter has been known since the work of Cattell (1886). In some respects the result is counter-intuitive, as one might expect that the letters in the word would have to be identified before the word, and therefore that the whole word could not be identified more efficiently than its constituent letters. However, there are many ways in which identification processes might benefit following the presentation of a word. For instance, words can be more redundant than letters, in the sense that identification of part of the word (e.g. its first three letters) can be more constraining than identification of part of a letter (say, the curve on the left). Thus, guessing might be more accurate for words than for letters. Alternatively, our stored knowledge about the word might in some way facilitate the processing of its parts (i.e. its letters). We discuss in more detail the mechanisms for this word advantage, known as the word-superiority effect (WSE) in Chapter 7. Taylor and Chabot's result is interesting because it indicates that, whatever the source(s) of the WSE, they can be selectively affected by a word mask. Thus the word mask must directly affect a relatively "high-level" process (e.g. access to stored knowledge about words). It also follows that the light-flash mask affects an earlier process common to both letters and words—as it eliminated the WSE. For instance, the light-flash mask may reduce the strength of the pattern information provided by the target letters (due to its summation with the target letters there will be some contrast reduction)—affecting both single letter and word targets equally.

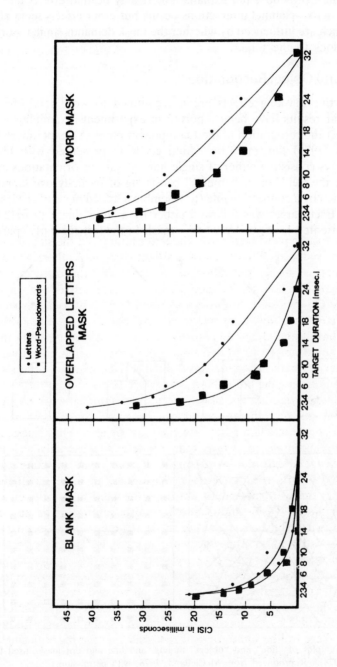

FIG. 4.14. Examples of masking functions for word and letter targets followed by light-flash (blank) masks, overlapping letter masks and word masks. The longer the critical interstimulus interval needed, the stronger the masking effect. (Reproduced from Taylor & Chabot, 1978, with permission.)

Such high-level effects in masking suggest that the spatial frequency account cannot provide a full explanation. It may be that effects due to within- and across-channel interactions occur, but other effects seem also to occur which are influenced by whether the mask demands similar stored representations to the target.

Masking and Object Recognition

These selective masking effects are not confined to word recognition. Quite similar results have been reported in experiments examining how objects affect the recognition of their component parts. An experiment by McClelland (1978) illustrates this. Subjects were presented with brief target displays consisting either of single lines at various orientations and positions in the field, or of "objects" consisting of partially overlapping squares joined by a connecting line (to resemble a folded piece of card; see Fig. 4.15). Each target was followed either by a "line" mask (a field of randomly oriented lines) or by a "dot" mask (a field of regularly spaced

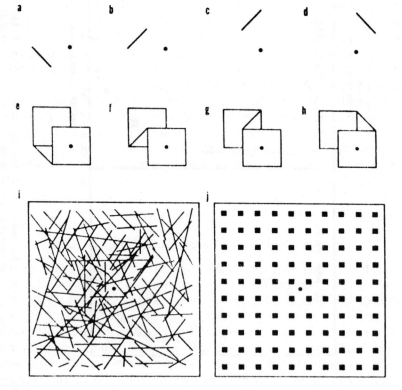

FIG. 4.15.   Examples of "line" and "object" targets, and line and dot masks used by McClelland (1978). (Reproduced from McClelland, 1978, with permission.)

dots). Subjects had to identify which of four possible line or object targets was present on each trial. Note here that the four target objects are differentiated only by single lines, which have exactly the same orientations and positions in the field as the single line targets. This means that—unlike Taylor and Chabot's (1978) experiment on word recognition—guessing is equated in the "line" and the "object" target conditions, and the experiment examines the role that the object context has on the processing of the distinguishing line (rather than the guessing of the line's identity from partial information).

McClelland found that, when a dot mask was used, single line targets were identified more accurately than object targets. Presumably, the dot mask reduced the contrast of the target, and so lowered its discriminability. Under this circumstance, the single line seems more discriminable than the equivalent line in the object. This may reflect some lateral (metacontrast type) masking on the target line from the other lines present in the object. When a line mask was used, the effects reversed. Now the object targets were reported more accurately than the line targets. This can be termed an object-superiority effect (OSE; see Weisstein & Harris, 1974; and see also the discussion of the face superiority effect in Chapter 3). McClelland's result shows that the line mask selectively disrupts identification of the single line targets—so much so that these targets lose any initial advantage in discriminability over the lines in the object. The lines in the object are somehow protected from this masking effect.

By varying the properties of the "object" in studies such as this we can learn something about the relations between objects and their parts. For instance, objects may be relatively immune from masking by random lines because they have a coherent three-dimensional structure (e.g. Lanze, Weisstein, & Harris, 1982), or because they contain configural properties that facilitate their identification (e.g. Enns & Printzmetal, 1984). Further work of this nature on visual masking may thus be revealing about the process of building object descriptions over time.

MASKING AND CONSCIOUS PERCEPTION

The above evidence indicates that masking is modulated by relatively "high levels" of form recognition (including possibly our stored knowledge about words). One question that has not been asked concerns what happens to the target information that is masked in such instances. Recently, there has been some controversy surrounding this issue, particularly over whether "high-level" information from a target (e.g. its meaning) is extracted even under masking conditions so severe as to prevent the target being detected (e.g. Merikle, 1982; Purcell, Stewart & Stanovich, 1983). The issue is of interest because, if positive evidence is found, it would indicate that we do not have conscious access to all the information currently being processed at any given time. This leads to the generation of information processing models in which perceptual identification is a relatively "late" process, possibly subsequent to the retrieval of some meaning about a stimulus.

Some of the most provocative evidence on this issue was reported by Marcel (1983). One experiment (Experiment 2) was based on a modified version of the Stroop task (1935). In the standard Stroop task, subjects have to name the hue of a word which can denote a colour name. Naming times are slowed when the colour name and the hue are incongruent relative to when they are congruent. In the modified version of this task used by Marcel, subjects had to name a colour patch which had a colour word superimposed in the centre. When the word is clearly visible, Stroop interference occurs (Dyer, 1973). Marcel conducted this experiment with the word pattern masked so that subjects apparently could not detect its presence. This was done via a two-stage experiment. In the first stage, subjects undertook a threshold-setting session in which the SOA between a target word and a pattern mask was reduced until discrimination of the presence of the target was less than 60% accurate. Marcel then used the SOAs established for each subject to mask the words in the Stroop-type task. Despite the words being masked, Marcel found the same magnitude of Stroop interference as when the words were clearly visible.

Subsequently, Marcel (1983, Experiment 3) used an associative priming procedure (see also Chapter 2), in which subjects made lexical decisions to target words or nonwords, preceded by a priming word (in a lexical decision task, subjects make timed decisions about whether a given letter string is a real word or not). Primes were either associated or unassociated with the target (e.g. BREAD–BUTTER vs NURSE–BUTTER). When primes are not masked, lexical decisions to target words are facilitated if the prime is an associate (Meyer & Schvaneveldt, 1971). Marcel examined this associative priming effect when the primes were masked so that subjects could not detect their presence. In one condition, primes were masked by a random noise field presented to the same eye as the target (monoptic presentation). In a second condition, they were masked by a pattern mask presented to a different eye to the target (dichoptic presentation). These two forms of masking were used to contrast peripheral, integration-type masking with more central, interruption-type effects (cf. Turvey, 1973). As in the previous experiment (Marcel, 1983, Experiment 2), subjects undertook a series of threshold trials prior to the main experiment to determine the target:mask SOA where they failed to detect the presence of more than 60% of the masked words. These SOAs were then used in the main experiment. Marcel found no associative priming when primes were masked by a random noise field, along with strong associative priming when primes were dichoptically masked by the pattern mask. This result again supports the distinction between peripheral and central masking effects. It suggests that peripheral masking limits the uptake of information from the target, so that, under severe masking conditions, the mask prevents the target from accessing any stored knowledge. However, the central masking used by Marcel seemed to have quite a different effect. In particular, it appeared that the mask did not prevent the target accessing stored knowledge (and so it generated associative priming). Marcel therefore proposed that central masking did not affect the processes involved in accessing stored knowledge about a target, but rather the integration of the accessed information with a visual record of the target—perhaps because the mask interrupts the visual record of a stimulus. Without this perceptual integration, the target cannot be consciously perceived.

However, two problems with Marcel's (1983) study are that subjects only undertook a small number of threshold trials, so that stable levels of performance may not have been reached; and that present/absent discriminations on masked words were only lowered to a 60% level, when chance would be 50%. Cheesman and Merikle (1984; 1985) remedied both these problems. They used backward pattern masking and the modified Stroop task. They found that when threshold discrimination was lowered to the true chance level, there was no Stroop interference. Interference then increased proportionally as word discrimination in the threshold task was allowed to increase from chance to perfect performance.

Does this mean that words cannot access stored knowledge unless they are consciously discriminated? The answer to this question is given in a further study by Cheesman and Merikle. They noted that subjects could be above chance at making a discriminatory response to a word (e.g. at judging whether a masked word was one of four colour words) even when they reported that they were unaware of the word's presence due to severe backward pattern masking. Based on their objective performance subjects were above chance; whilst at the same time the subjective reports were that the word was below threshold. Cheesman and Merikle therefore argue for the existence of two thresholds: one objective and one subjective, with the objective being the lower of the two. When they re-ran the Stroop-type task with the words below the subjective threshold but above the objective threshold, they, like Marcel, found reliable Stroop-type interference.

We might conclude from Cheesman and Merikle's study that masking (or more specifically interruption masking) simply reduces the confidence of subjects that a target has occurred, so they claim that they do not see it; masking does not affect some form of perceptual integration process occurring after stored information about the word has been accessed. However, such a conclusion would not hold true. Cheesman and Merikle (1985, Experiments 3 and 4) manipulated the percentage of trials on which the word and the colour were congruent, using the Stroop-type procedure. When the words are clearly visible, there is greater Stroop interference when the word is likely to match the colour (e.g. Lowe & Mitterer, 1982;

Taylor, 1977)—presumably because subjects adopt a strategy to try and maximise performance by taking advantage of the high degree of matching between the word and the colour. Cheesman and Merikle masked the words so that they were below the subjective threshold. Under this circumstance, there was no probability effect (i.e. there was equal Stroop interference in the high and low probability conditions).

Cheesman and Merikle's work indicates that there are qualitative differences between the operations that can be performed on words masked below the subjective threshold and on words which are above threshold. It seems that words masked below the subjective threshold do not acquire the kind of stable representation necessary for subjects to base a conscious strategy upon, yet such words can also gain access to stored knowledge. This is consistent with (central interruption-type) masking having a direct effect on perceptual integration, which occurs after at least partial access to stored information about the stimulus. However, as the SOA between the target and the mask decreases (producing more severe masking), masking can prevent a masked word gaining any access to stored information (at the objective threshold). It appears that masking influences a number of stages in form recognition. At short SOAs it disrupts the information needed to gain access to stored knowledge (such as the pattern information conveyed by activating sustained processing channels). At longer SOAs it seems to affect processes operating after initial access to stored knowledge has taken place (perceptual integration).

Overview and Future Directions

Visual masking is clearly complex. Its complexity comes about because it affects several processes in vision. The phenomena of masking again illustrate how the "seamless" facility of vision hides a plethora of complex mechanisms.

The evidence we have discussed shows several things. To begin with, masking is not a unitary effect. We can distinguish several masking effects according to whether they occur peripherally or centrally, and according to whether they operate prior or subsequent to contact with stored knowledge about the stimuli. Our suggestions can be summarised as follows:

1. With short SOAs between the stimuli there are interactions within transient and sustained visual processing channels. Peripheral channels summate activity occurring within small time periods, causing masking to take place when targets and masks arrive within the critical period. Such summation processes may play an important role in the detection of local movement of stimuli.

2. At slightly longer SOAs, the first stimulus activates central transient and sustained channels in the cortex. Following this central activation, there can be a refractory period—producing within-channel inhibition of a target presented within the refractory period.

3. Higher-order masking effects, influenced by stored knowledge about the stimulus, can also occur as the interval between the target and the mask increases still further. Such effects seem to follow a pattern of interruption-type masking, and seem due to competition from the mask for the representations mediating target identification. This competition seems also to produce the selective loss of an integrated percept of a target, despite the target activating its stored representation.

The work we have considered suggests that masking may serve an important purpose in normal vision, to prevent the overwriting of stimuli in tasks such as reading. It also provides experimenters with a tool to study processing mechanisms in vision—such as short-range motion detection mechanisms, or the kinds of perceptual features and stored knowledge operating in object or word recognition.

It is also true that many phenomena in both masking and motion perception remain only partially understood. For instance, consider what happens when more than two stimuli are presented in close temporal succession—a situation we will commonly face if masking operates outside the laboratory. We have earlier discussed one finding by Breitmeyer (1978) in which a mask was itself masked by another stimulus. This kind of result indicates that the interactions between three or more stimuli will not be easily predicted from interactions between target and mask pairs. Future work will indicate whether any general rules govern interactions between successive stimuli, and how these rules relate to our ability to keep separate ongoing visual events. A full picture of vision will not emerge until we better understand visual dynamics. In Chapter 5 we move on to consider the role of these dynamic processes in controlling our attention to visual stimuli.

5 Visual Attention

VISUAL ATTENTION AS A SPOTLIGHT

Trying to find a face in a crowd is notoriously difficult. Intuitively this seems to be because the face you are looking for (the target face) is similar to the surrounding faces. The surrounding faces act to distract one's gaze from the target. It is also plain that it is relatively easy to find someone who has outstanding physical characteristics, someone who is unusually tall or has unusually coloured hair. In such cases, one's gaze seems drawn to the target face. It is as if we see the face out of the "corner of our eye", and this draws our attention to it. It may only be after a stimulus captures our attention in this way that we make an eye movement and re-direct our gaze to the target's location. This armchair example indicates that attention is not synonymous with fixation; we can attend to objects we are not fixating. Nevertheless, in most circumstances we will be attending to an object at fixation.

Our ability to attend away from fixation has been commented on many times. Helmholtz (1866) first published a series of experiments where he remarked that he could direct his attention to regions of field away from fixation to read letters there. William James (1890) further conceived of visual attention as having a focus, a margin, and a fringe. It is almost as if we have some "internal spotlight" that can be aligned with an object to enable us to see it.

The idea that visual attention acts as an internal spotlight, benefiting visual perception, has gained more recent support from the work of Posner and his colleagues (e.g. Posner, 1978, 1980; Posner, Nissen & Ogden, 1978; Posner, Snyder, & Davidson, 1980). Posner developed a simple experimental procedure to look at visual attention in detail. Subjects were asked to perform a simple reaction time (RT) task, in which they pressed a button as soon as they detected the onset of a light in their visual field. The target light might occur within any one of several boxes placed at different locations in the field. Prior to the target appearing, subjects were given a cue that provided information about the target's location. This cue might be a central arrow pointing right or left, indicating that the target would appear in either the left or the right visual field; or it might be the brief illumination of the box where the target would then appear. We refer to these two different signals as *central* and *peripheral* cues (at least where the target box appears in the peripheral visual field). On a majority of the trials in an experiment this cue would be correct or *valid* (i.e. the target appeared where the cue had indicated); on a minority of trials, the cue would be incorrect or *invalid* (e.g. the target might appear to the right of fixation even though the subject was cued to the left). In addition, a third condition might be added where the cue is a central cross. Like the location cue, the cross can signal *when* the target will appear; unlike the location cue, the cross conveys no information about *where* the target will appear. The cross provides a *neutral baseline*, against which the effects of locational cueing can be measured.

Subjects are faster to detect the target when the spatial cue is valid than in the neutral cue condition, and they are slower than the neutral baseline when the spatial cue is invalid. This result is illustrated in Fig. 5.1.

This benefit from the pre-cue occurs even when subjects do not move their eyes to the cued location. For instance, experimenters may either

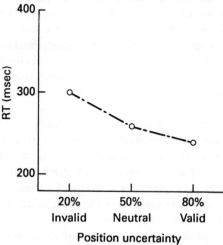

FIG. 5.1. RTs to targets as a function of whether a location cue is valid, neutral or invalid. The cue is valid on 80% of the trials when it appears, and invalid on the remaining 20% of the trials. In the neutral condition, the target appears to the right of fixation on 50% of the trials, and to the left on the other 50%. (Reproduced from Posner et al., 1980, with permission.)

reject trials where eye movements are made (Posner et al., 1978) or use intervals between the cue and the target that are simply too short for eye movements to occur (Eriksen & Hoffman, 1973). Posner (Posner et al., 1980, p.172) has suggested that:

> Attention can be likened to a spotlight that enhances the efficiency of detection of events within its beam.

THE SPREAD AND DIVISION OF THE SPOTLIGHT

There are several results that fit quite well with the spotlight metaphor. For instance, Eriksen and Eriksen (1974) proposed that attention was limited, in the sense that all stimuli close to a cued location seemed to gain from cueing—as though the spotlight has a fixed size, and cannot be reduced to focus on one item within a closely packed group. In Eriksen and Eriksen's experiments subjects had to determine which of four target letters was present on a trial. Subjects pressed one button to two of the targets (e.g. S and C), and another button to the other two targets (e.g. H and K). The target on any trial could be flanked by identical distractors (CCC), by distractors from the same response category (i.e. SCS) or by distractors from the opposite response category (KCK). Subjects knew that the target would be in the central location. Even so, the flanking letters slowed down responses to the target when they fell less than about 1 degree of visual angle from the target. This effect was most pronounced when the stimuli belonged to opposite response categories, suggesting that all the letters were identified and so generated response competition when they called for different responses. (Consistent with this response competition account is evidence that partial visual information can lead directly to motor response preparation; see Miller, 1987; 1988.) When the stimuli were separated by more than 1 degree, interference was minimised, and did not decrease further as the separation increased. Eriksen and Eriksen's conclusion was that the spotlight has a fixed size of about 1 degree.

It also seems difficult to pay attention to more than one spatial location at a time. Eriksen and Yeh (1985) had subjects search a display of letters arranged around a "clockface". The target was either the letter "S" or "Y", and it appeared at either 12, 3, 6 or 9 o'clock. Other positions around the clockface were filled with distractor letters. At 150msec prior to the displays, a time too short for accurate re-fixation, a bar marker appeared to indicate the location of the target. The "validity" of the cue was varied (i.e. the probability that it was correct). In the *40%* condition, the target appeared in the cued position on 40% of the trials and in the *opposite* location on another 40% of the trials (and in the remaining two locations on 10% of the trials each). In the *70%* condition, the target appeared in the cued location on 70% of the trials, and in the opposite location on only

10% of the trials. In the *100%* condition the target *always* appeared in the cued location. In a control condition, no pre-cue was given. The data are shown in Fig. 5.2.

Relative to the control condition, RTs were faster to letters at the location where the cue appeared (*the primary cue location*), and this benefit increased as it became more likely that the target would appear in that location (i.e. as the cue validity increased). RTs were slowed to targets in the non-cued locations, even when the target appeared in the secondary location (opposite the cued location), and when it had a high probability of appearing there (in the 40% condition). This shows that subjects could not attend as easily to the opposite location as they could to the cued location. They could not "split" the spotlight. Note, however, that RTs were faster to targets in the secondary location than to targets elsewhere. Eriksen and Yeh suggest that this is because, after attending first to the cued location, subjects attend to the secondary location. The effect is due to the spotlight being moved rather than being split.

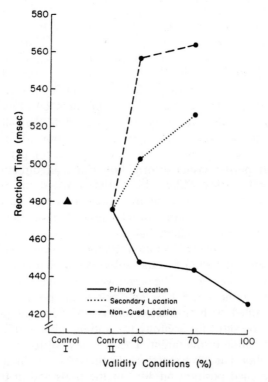

FIG. 5.2.   RTs to primary (cued), secondary (opposite), and non-cued locations as a function of the validity of the cue. Note that times to the primary (cued) location are always faster than to the other locations. (Reproduced from Eriksen & Yeh, 1985, with permission.)

GRADIENTS OF ATTENTION

Other investigators have examined how performance varies as a function of where the target falls on the retina. Downing and Pinker (1985) presented a target at one of 5 increasingly peripheral locations, either to the left or right of fixation. We can think of these locations as being numbered from 1 (far left) to 10 (far right). The cue was a number from 0 (neutral) to 10, that indicated the box that subjects should attend to. Performance was measured in terms of the *benefits* and *costs* in RT when the cue was correct or incorrect, relative to the neutral cue condition. The data are presented in Fig. 5.3, in terms of the costs to performance as a function of the location of both the target and the cue. Note that when performance benefits from the cue (when the cue is correct), the costs will be *negative*.

Figure 5.3 seems complex initially, but can be explained without too much difficulty. Consider performance when the cue was the number 5 or 6 (when subjects attended to locations close to fixation). Figure 5.3 shows that RTs to targets at positions 5 and 6 are fast (and facilitated relative to the neutral cue). As the target falls further away from the cued location, the costs increase rapidly.

Now, consider performance when the cue was the number 1 or 10. RTs at locations 1 and 10 were again facilitated, but this time the decrease in performance for targets at non-cued locations was much more gradual. It seems that we can "narrow" the focus of our attentional spotlight at the

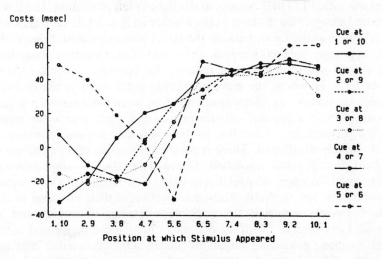

FIG. 5.3.   Costs in RT (i.e. the slowing in performance relative to the baseline condition) as a function of the relative locations of the cue and the target. (Reproduced from Downing & Pinker, 1985, with permission.)

fovea much more than in the periphery. Indeed, Humphreys (1981) showed that subjects could attend to a target and successfully ignore distractors falling only 0.5 of a degree away when they had foreknowledge and could fixate the target location. This suggests that the attentional spotlight may be a fixed size for particular regions of the visual field, but it is not of a fixed constant size.

ATTENTIONAL ZOOM LENS OR SPOTLIGHT?

So far, we have referred to visual attention as a spotlight that: (1) has a diameter that may be determined by the region of field that is attended; and (2) cannot be divided.

However, other data suggest that a spotlight metaphor is not wholly appropriate, and that an analogy of a "zoom lens" may be more fitting. The point about a zoom lens is that it can cover a wide range of field, but the resolution of detail within the wide field is poor. Resolution is improved when the field of view is constricted. This contrasts with the spotlight idea in a number of ways. For instance, attentional enhancement can occur across wide spatial areas (although it will then be weak). Also, attention may initially be set across a wide spatial scale, and then "focus in" over time. There may be specific time constraints on attentional processing.

Data supporting the "zoom lens" account come from Murphy and Eriksen (1987). Their task was similar to that of Eriksen and Yeh (1985). Subjects had to decide whether a target was the letter "A" or "U". The target was either 1, 2 or 3 degrees to the right or left of fixation, and it was presented along with a distractor (again either an A or a U). Subjects knew which letter was the target because the target was underlined. Prior to the target appearing, subjects were also pre-cued to target location. Responses were slowed when the distractor required the opposite response (AU vs AA or UU). However, the more interesting result was that the distance between the letters was relatively unimportant when there was no pre-cue. In contrast, with a pre-cue, only distractors that were close to the target affected performance. According to the zoom lens account, attention is initially widely distributed. There is parallel processing of all elements in the field, but at a low resolution. Because the discrimination between targets and distractors was relatively easy, high resolution (via focused attention) was not required. Thus, irrespective of their positions in the field, distractors activated the opposite responses to targets and so generated interference. With the pre-cue, attention can be focused at the target location, enhancing target processing. Only distractors that fall within this reduced area of enhancement then cause interference. It is as if target processing receives a boost that ensures that target responses win their race with responses activated by more distant distractors.

The effects of distributing attention across the field may also be to enhance the detectability of relatively coarse stimulus information at the expense of local stimulus properties; the converse may be true of focused attention. For instance, Shulman and Wilson (1987a;b) report that responses to low spatial frequency gratings are enhanced when subjects are performing a "global" discrimination task (such as identifying a large, global letter made from smaller, local ones, where subjects presumably attend to the global properties of the pattern). Similarly, responses to low spatial frequency gratings are enhanced when subjects discriminate stimuli presented to the visual periphery. Conversely, responses to high spatial frequency gratings are enhanced when subjects perform "local" discrimination tasks (identifying a local element in a compound letter) or when they discriminate foveally presented stimuli. Broad distribution of attention may be important for initial scene processing and segmentation, whilst still allowing gross discriminations to occur (see Chapter 3). Narrow distribution of attention may be important for fine discriminations and the identification of individual objects. The world we view is naturally composed of structures at different spatial scales. At a coarse level we may see a forest near a lake, at a somewhat finer level we see the trees that make up the forest, and more finely still we may see the individual leaves of a tree. The zoom lens metaphor for visual attention would capture the way we can choose to see either a forest or leaves at different times.

In Chapter 2 we introduced the idea that independent channels may initially be involved in the detection of intensity changes at different spatial scales, and in Chapter 3 we saw that for object recognition there seems to be a priority for the coarser ones over the finer ones. The MIRAGE algorithm (Watt, 1988; Watt & Morgan, 1985; see Chapter 2) makes some sense of such phenomena. Recall that the $\nabla^2 G^*I$ channels produce outputs whose positive $(S+)$ and negative $(S-)$ products are independently summed. The result of this is a *grouping* of the elements in the image and detection but not localisation of texture elements. However, because of the *error* due to noise in the system and errors introduced by sampling and filtering, the *positions* of the elements can only be accurately determined by an extensive process of comparison of each element's location with that of each other element present. Clearly, such pairwise comparisons will take a good deal of time, even in a parallel system, and the time will increase the more elements there are. For this reason Watt suggests that grouping elements into clusters and solving for position at successively finer spatial scales can be highly economical. If 12 dots are grouped into two equal clusters, the positions of each of the 6 dots within each cluster need to be related only to each of the other 5. In fact, Watt suggests that an optimally efficient system will work with progressively more finely resolved clusters, as illustrated in Fig. 5.4.

So, according to Watt, in order to do more than detect the finer scale structures, in order to *measure* the location of each of the texture elements

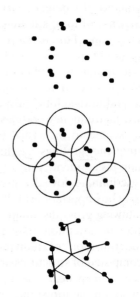

FIG. 5.4. An example of grouping produced by the MIRAGE algorithm. The positions of the five groups of dots can be computed more rapidly than the positions of the 16 dots. Representations for clusters are thus produced faster than those for individual items, producing a "zoom" effect. (Reproduced from Watt, 1988, with permission.)

(to eventually compute the positions of features within a structural description), there is a progressive switching out of the coarser $\nabla^2 G^*I$ channels' contribution to the summed $S+$ and $S-$ products. Each time a coarser channel is switched out, a slightly finer description is obtained whose own intrinsic spatial details may be economically measured. Progressing from the coarsest to finest detail of localisation, however, will take time, and may not always be necessary. For many purposes a statistical description of texture may suffice and therefore there may not be a need to compute the full spatial analysis. For instance, if we wish to bypass a forest, it is sufficient to represent the trees as part of the texture of the main object to which we direct our behaviour, namely the forest.

Watt's theory may explain why there is a priority for global form over local features in visual recognition, as detailed positional information will be revealed earlier for coarser scales of the image. To the extent that object recognition requires spatial localisation (which it certainly does—locating parallel edges or arrangements of component axes, for example, requires this kind of measurement), then we might expect larger scaled object descriptions to be constructed first.

SEPARATING THE ZOOM LENS AND THE SPOTLIGHT ACCOUNTS: MOVING ATTENTION

One way to separate the zoom lens and the spotlight accounts of visual attention is to consider the way in which attention may be moved across space. According to the zoom lens account, there is a narrowing of attention over time. According to the spotlight account, attention has a fixed aperture that "lights up" space as though a torch was moved across a scene.

In studies of attentional cueing, RTs to the target are typically faster as the interval between the cue and the target increases, up to some asymptote when no further benefits in RT accrue. Illustrative data come from an experiment by Tsal (1983), and are shown in Fig. 5.5. In this experiment, subjects had to decide whether the target was the letter "O" or "X". A pre-cue (a small dot) appeared slightly peripheral to the target location, and the interval between the onset of the cue and that of the target (the SOA, see Chapter 4) was varied. Figure 5.5 shows RTs for targets located 4, 8 or 12° of visual angle away from fixation. Tsal computed that the point of no further benefit (the asymptote of the RT-SOA function) for the 4, 8, and 12° targets was 83, 116, and 150msec respectively. If we assume that attention starts at fixation, then the different asymptotes can be taken to indicate the time necessary to move

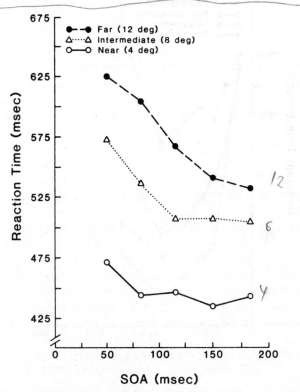

FIG. 5.5.   RTs to far, intermediate, and near targets at different cue-target intervals. (Reproduced from Tsal, 1983, with permission.)

attention accurately on to the target. It follows that attention is moved at a constant velocity of about 8msec per degree of visual angle (the difference in the asymptotes being 33 and 34msec as the target was moved by 4° intervals into the periphery).

Shulman, Remington, and McLean (1979) also argued that attention moves through intermediary positions in space when shifting from one location to the next. Their experiment was similar to Tsal's, except that subjects made a simple RT response to a target light that could appear 8 or 18° to the right or left of fixation. The pre-cue was a central arrow that indicated whether the target was in the left or right field, and when the pre-cue appeared the target was likely to be at the "far" (18°) location (on 70% of the trials). Shulman et al. were interested in responses to targets at the near location when subjects were trying to attend to the far location. When there was a short interval between the cue and the target, RTs were 9msec faster to the near than to the far location (on the expected side). This may

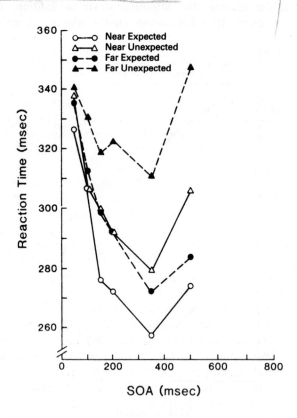

FIG. 5.6.   RTs to near expected, near unexpected, far expected, and far unexpected targets at different cue-target intervals. (Reproduced from Shulman et al., 1979, with permission.)

be because subjects were attending to fixation, and so the near target was closer to the "focus" of the spotlight. As the interval increased, the advantage for the near location increased (to a maximum of 23msec) and then decreased (back to 12msec). These data can be given the following account. After the cue is presented, subjects shift attention away from fixation to the far location. When the interval is short, attention has shifted only as far as the near location, producing a greater benefit for that location. When the interval is longer, attention shifts to the far location, producing a relatively larger benefit at that position. These data are shown in Fig. 5.6.

The idea of attention shifting at a constant velocity from one location to another fits well with the concept of attention as some form of internal spotlight. However, the account is not without its problems. Interpretation of Tsal's (1983) data depends on a number of assumptions, any of which may be questioned (Eriksen & Murphy, 1987). We mention just one. This is that attention has a fixed focus that does not vary according to whether we attend to stimuli in central or peripheral vision. However, we have seen that this is probably not true. Another interpretation of the data can therefore be given. Let us assume that attention is initially broadly distributed, and that different degrees of "focus" are required for discriminations on different parts of the retina. For any given discrimination, peripheral presentation will produce lower performance because acuity is lower; thus peripheral discriminations may require more focused attention than foveal discriminations (even though subjects may be able to produce finer "spatial tuning" of attention in central vision). The time differences found by Tsal as the target was presented more peripherally may thus reflect the extra focusing time needed, and not the time taken to shift a fixed attentional spotlight.

There are also difficulties in interpreting the results of Shulman et al. (1979), on moving attention through space like a spotlight. For instance, consider performance shown in Fig. 5.6 when the SOA was 200msec. At this point there are fast RTs to the near target on the cued side, equal RTs to the far cued target and to the near target on the uncued side, and slow RTs to the far uncued target. Shulman et al.'s argument was that, at this juncture, subjects are attending to the near cued location (on route to attending to the far cued location). But it is then difficult to explain the equal RTs to the far cued and to the near uncued locations. Subjects had not had time to move their eyes. The far location should therefore suffer due to its peripheral retinal position. That this did not occur suggests that cueing produced effects at the far location even at the short SOAs. The data are in fact *inconsistent* with the idea of a fixed attentional spotlight moving through space; they are more consistent with attention having a more broadly based effect at short SOAs, and with there being additional benefits for targets presented near to fixation (presumably due to retinal acuity).

We discuss these results in some detail to illustrate current controversies concerning movements of attention. At present, the data seems to be at least as consistent with the zoom lens account as with the spotlight proposal.

ATTENTION AND EYE MOVEMENTS

We have discussed how visual attention can be shifted *covertly*, without moving our eyes. Nevertheless, in real life, attentional shifts may facilitate eye movements to the locations of salient stimuli. If we detect a brief peripheral signal (such as a pre-cue), it may be useful to make an eye movement to the location of the signal so that any object there falls on high acuity regions of the retina, allowing it to be recognised. Visual attention can operate covertly, but it may be linked to the eye movement system.

Various claims have been made concerning the relations between attention and eye movements, ranging from claims that they are unrelated to claims that attentional effects are due to feedback produced when subjects prepare to make an eye movement to signals (see Klein, 1980, for discussion of these accounts). We believe that the data suggest that at least some inter-dependencies exist between attention and eye movements. For instance, consider the study by Rizzolatti, Riggio, Dascola, and Umiltà (1987). They had subjects fixate a central box, and presented four other boxes, two to the left and two to the right of fixation (boxes 1–4, going from left to right). The boxes were each 4° of visual angle away from each other. Subjects were cued with a digit in the central box (1 to 4, or 0 on neutral trials). Rizzolatti et al. were interested in RTs when subjects were cued to the more central boxes (2 and 3), and the target appeared elsewhere. For instance, when cued to box 2, the target might appear at box 1 (4° away but on the cued side of fixation), box 3 (4° away but on the opposite side of fixation), or box 4 (8° away on the opposite side of fixation). In such a case, RTs were faster to targets in box 1 than box 3, and faster to targets in box 3 than box 4. That is, even when two locations are equally distant from fixation, RTs are quicker to a location on the cued side than to a location on the opposite side. Rizzolatti et al. propose that this is due to the relations between attention and eye movements. When cued to attend to a particular location, subjects program an eye movement to that location. When the target appears at another location, the eye movement must be modified. At the very least, the extent of movement must be changed; and, when the target is on the opposite side of fixation, the direction of the eye movement must also be altered. Modifying the direction of movement is more disruptive than modifying its extent, hence the effect of shifting attention across fixation.

Zimba and Hughes (1987) have also shown that under some conditions there is *only* an effect of the attentional field on fixation, and not the distance of the target from the attended location. Subjects made a simple RT response to a light that either appeared within a box (as in the majority of studies on visual attention) or in an uncluttered field. When the cue was incorrect, there were strong effects of whether the target was on the cued or the uncued side of fixation. This was true both when the field contained boxes and when it was uncluttered. However, when the field was

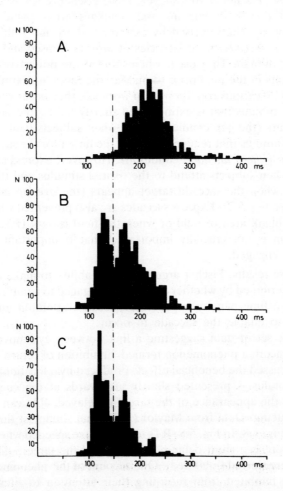

FIG. 5.7.   An example of express saccades (within 150msec). Each panel shows the number of saccades produced at different time intervals. Panel A shows the overlap and attention condition, Panel B the gap conditions, and Panel C the overlap without attention condition. Express saccades may occur in the gap and overlap without attention conditions. (Reproduced from Fischer, 1986, with permission.)

uncluttered, there was no effect of the distance of the uncued target from the attended location. The effect of distance was apparent only with a cluttered field (as in Downing and Pinker's study, 1985). Zimba and Hughes propose that distance effects occur because targets are masked by the other items in the cluttered field. Masking becomes more severe the further the target is from the attended location.

An even more direct link between attention and eye movements comes from investigations of *express saccades*. Fischer and his colleagues (Fischer, 1986; Fischer & Breitmeyer, 1987; Fischer & Ramsperger, 1984) have shown that both humans and monkeys are capable of making saccades that are characterised by extremely short and stable latencies. These *express saccades* have latencies of around 75msec and 100msec in monkey and in man. They occur when subjects are not actively attending to other points in the field prior to making the saccade. Express saccades are released by various conditions. For instance, they occur when subjects attend to a stimulus that is extinguished shortly before the target for the saccade occurs (the *gap* condition), and when subjects fixate but do not attend to a stimulus that remains on when the target for the saccade occurs (the *overlap without attention* condition). However, express saccades are prevented when subjects attend to the fixated stimulus and that stimulus remains on when the saccade target appears (the *overlap and attention* condition; see Fig. 5.7). Express saccades are also prevented when subjects attend to a blank area of field or when the field is dark (Fischer, 1986). Thus fixation is not crucially important; what is important is whether attention is engaged.

From these results, Fischer argues that the ability to make a saccade is crucially determined by whether attention is engaged to stimuli in the field. When it is, a time penalty is generated because attention must then be disengaged to enable the saccade to occur.

One other set of data suggesting a link between eye movements and attention concern a phenomenon termed "inhibition of return". Hitherto, we have discussed the beneficial effects produced by a locational cue when a target stimulus is presented shortly afterwards at the cued location. However, if the appearance of the target is delayed, RTs can actually be slowed by cueing. Data from Maylor (1985) that show just this result are provided in Fig. 5.8. In Fig. 5.8, RTs to targets are speeded when the cue is valid and there is a short delay between it and the target; with a longer delay, RTs are slowed (inhibited). One account of this phenomenon is that subjects are inhibited from returning their attention to sites that have already been attended. Presumably this provides a mechanism to prevent subjects re-fixating on areas of the field already fixated. Interestingly, this inhibition is not based on retinal coordinates. For instance, inhibition is not affected by subjects moving their eyes so long as the target falls in the same relative position in space as the cue (Maylor & Hockey, 1985). This is in

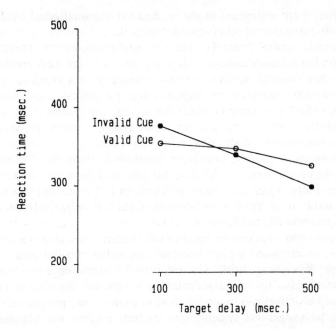

FIG. 5.8.   An example of "inhibition of return". Reaction times to targets preceded by valid or invalid peripheral cues at different cue-target delays. (Reproduced from Maylor, 1985, with permission.)

keeping with subjects using a non-retinotopic spatial representation to represent information across eye movements (see Chapter 6).

Overall, the data indicate quite close relations between visual attention and eye movements. However, we also doubt that the *sole* effect of attending to regions of space is to program an eye movement to it. For instance, there seems little reason to think that stimulus detection should be improved because an eye movement is programed to its location. Perhaps it is more plausible that attending to visual stimuli has two separate consequences, one on visual processing and one on motor preparation.

ATTENTION TO CENTRAL AND PERIPHERAL STIMULI

So far we have made no distinction between cues that are centrally presented and cues presented to peripheral vision. Yet there are empirical reasons to distinguish between the attentional mechanisms affected by peripheral and central cues. Peripheral cues: (1) produce rapid cueing effects, with asymptotes within 100msec; (2) produce the same effects irrespective of whether they are informative; (3) cannot be ignored even when subjects are instructed to do so; and (4) are unaffected by asking subjects to carry out another concurrent task.

In contrast, central cues: (1) have generally slower effects; (2) are affected by the informativeness of the cue; (3) can be ignored; and (4) are affected when subjects perform another concurrent task (Jonides, 1981).

These results converge to suggest that peripheral cues generate *automatic* shifts of attention, whilst the effects on central cues can be controlled by the subject. Posner (1980) distinguishes between an *exogenous* attentional system, driven by the properties of external stimuli, and an *endogenous* system, that can be controlled voluntarily. Clearly, we need to take care to separate the different effects of peripheral and central cues when discussing visual attention. Properties of visual attention, such as its resistance to being divided between objects, may be true of one but not both attentional mechanisms.

Exogenous and endogenous attentional systems may also interact. In Chapter 4 we discussed a phenomenon termed the "far-out jerk" effect (Breitmeyer & Valberg, 1979). This refers to the interference produced on the detection of a foveal target when a peripheral stimulus is briefly presented. This effect can be understood in terms of the peripheral signal engaging the exogenous system, that in turn inhibits the endogenous system, thus making detection of the central target difficult. Inhibitory interactions between these systems may also be important in everyday life. For instance, by inhibiting the endogenous system, external signals are able to produce switches of attention to the locations of salient stimuli in the field. Conversely, inhibition of the exogenous system by the endogenous system may enable us to ignore irrelevant variation taking place in the background when we fixate particular stimuli. Indeed, just this sort of inhibition seems to be involved in the suppression of express saccades when subjects attend to a point in space (Fischer & Breitmeyer, 1987). When endogenous attention is engaged, the exogenous system may be "damped down", and so produces a retarded response to the signal for the eye movement relative to when endogenous attention is not so engaged.

DISORDERS OF VISUAL ATTENTION: UNILATERAL VISUAL NEGLECT

Other evidence suggesting the existence of separate components of visual attention comes from studies of patients with disorders of visual attention. Perhaps the most commonly occurring neurological deficit in visual attention is unilateral visual neglect. Sometimes following a lesion, a patient may fail to act upon, to identify, or even to acknowledge the presence of stimuli on the side of space contralateral to the side of the lesion. For instance, the patient may fail to eat the food on one side of the plate, to address people standing on one side of them, to draw one side of

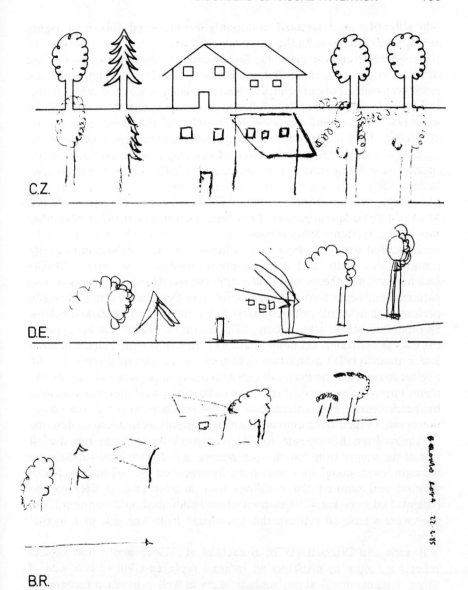

FIG. 5.9. An example of drawings produced by patients showing unilateral left-sided neglect. (Reproduced from Gainotti et al., 1986, with permission.)

an object (see Fig. 5.9), to read words from one side of a page or letters from one end of a word, or even to acknowledge that a hemiplegic (paralysed) limb on the affected side of their body is their own (see Friedland & Weinstein, 1977). This gross neglect of one side of space is most commonly encountered following right-hemisphere damage (with the patients neglecting the left side of space). It also tends to be most severe in the first months post-lesion, and can resolve within a few weeks. Nevertheless, even following the resolution of the gross symptoms, patients can still manifest neglect when stimuli on the affected side compete for attention with those on the unaffected side. Thus when two visual stimuli are presented briefly and simultaneously, one in each visual field (a procedure termed *double simultaneous stimulation)*, patients can show "extinction" (lack of response) to the stimulus on the affected side for months, or even years, after the lesion occurred (De Renzi, 1982).

A simple account of neglect would be that the patients fail to see the affected side of space because they have a profound visual field defect. This can be discounted. For instance, it fails to explain why neglect tends to be associated with right-hemisphere damage, as field defects are equally common after right- and left-hemisphere damage. Also, many patients with losses of half their visual field (hemianopias) do not show neglect, and patients with neglect do not necessarily have field defects (e.g. they can perform well in simple tests requiring the detection of lights flashed against an otherwise blank field; Albert, 1973; Karnath, 1988). Finally, patients can also show neglect on non-visual tasks. In a now classic study, Bisiach and Luzzatti (1978) asked two right-hemisphere damaged patients with neglect to describe the Piazza del Duomo in Milan, a place very familiar to them. First, they were asked to describe the square as if they were standing by the cathedral. The patients omitted the buildings from the left side of the square in their descriptions. Then the patients were asked to describe the square from the opposite side. They omitted the buildings from the left side of the square from the new perspective and included the buildings on the right, even though they had originally described the buildings they now omitted and omitted the buildings they now described! Clearly, the patients had some knowledge about which buildings should be present, but they were unable to retrieve this knowledge from one side of a mental image.

Bisiach and Luzzatti (1978; Bisiach et al., 1981) argue that neglect reflects a failure to construct an internal representation of one side of space. Patients manifest neglect in imagery as well as in visual recognition tasks because internal representations of space need to be constructed in both instances.

One problem with this argument is that patients with neglect can improve their report of stimuli on the affected side when cued to attend in that direction. Bisiach et al. (1981) observed this in their imagery task, and Riddoch and Humphreys (1983) found similar effects in a line bisection task (where neglect patients typically neglect towards the unaffected side).

These cueing effects suggest that neglect may best be thought of as an attentional disorder.

The effects of cueing on neglect have been examined more systematically by Posner and his colleagues (Posner et al., 1982; 1984). Posner et al. (1984) tested 13 patients, all of whom suffered brain damage to the parietal region of the brain (7 with left-hemisphere damage, 6 with right). All the right hemisphere patients showed some classical signs of neglect (from extinction to double simultaneous stimulation to complete inattention to stimuli on the affected side). Similar symptoms were also present in 3 of the left-hemisphere damaged patients. The cue was the brightening of a box on the screen, and on 80% of the trials the target appeared in the cued box. When the cue was valid, there were few differences in RTs to targets presented ipsilateral and targets presented contralateral to the side of lesion. When the cue was invalid the target appeared on the opposite side of the screen to the cue. On these occasions large differences emerged between responses to targets ipsilateral and targets contralateral to the side of lesion, with RTs to contralateral stimuli being extremely slow. Indeed, when there was a short interval between the cue and the target the patients often missed the contralateral targets altogether. Data from the patients with right parietal damage are shown in Fig. 5.10.

To account for these results Posner et al. (1984) distinguish three aspects of visual attention: (1) the ability to engage attention to a target; (2) the ability to disengage it; and (3) the ability to shift attention from one target to another. Posner et al. found that, with valid cues, the patients showed minimal differences between RTs to ipsilateral and to contralateral targets (Fig. 5.10). From this they conclude that the patients do not have problems in engaging their attention on stimuli presented contralateral to the side of lesion. Also, because the patients show similar RT patterns to cued contralateral and ipsilateral targets as the interval between the cue and the target varies, they conclude that the patients have no problems in shifting their attention to the contralateral side. The problems with contralateral stimuli arose only when the patients were cued to the ipsilateral side (on invalid trials). According to Posner's framework, the patients have problems in *disengaging* attention from ipsilateral stimuli to detect targets on the contralateral side.

Posner's framework is further supported by work with patients with lesions to other brain areas. For instance, Posner, Rafal, Choate, and Vaughan (1985) conducted analogous experiments with patients suffering from progressive supranuclear palsy, who have lesions to parts of the midbrain, including a structure termed the superior colliculus. The patients were greatly impaired at making voluntary eye movements, with the deficit being worst for movements in the vertical direction. When cued to attend to the locations of forthcoming targets, these patients showed a clear

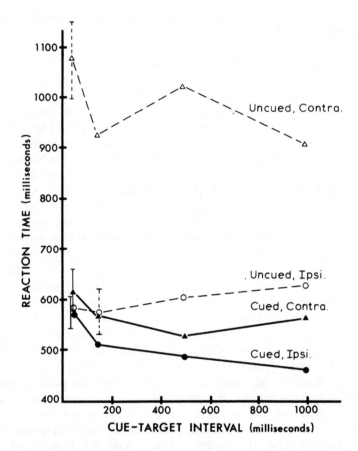

FIG. 5.10. RTs for 6 patients with right parietal lesions. Note the extremely slow times to uncued targets presented on the side of space contralateral to the lesion. (Reproduced from Posner et al., 1984, with permission.)

difference between their ability to use cues projected along the horizontal and vertical meridians. In the horizontal meridian the patients showed relatively normal cueing effects even with short intervals between the cue and the target. In the vertical meridian the patients only showed cueing effects when there were long intervals between primes and targets. Posner et al. propose that the patients have problems shifting their attention vertically. Illustrative data are presented in Fig. 5.11. Note that the lack of a cueing effect is due to a problem in the patients shifting their *attention* not their eyes, because they show a deficit with intervals between cues and targets that are too short to allow eye movements to occur.

In contrast, in studies with a third set of patients, this time with lesions to a forebrain structure, the thalamus (involving damage to various thalamic nuclei including the centro median, the ventral lateral, and

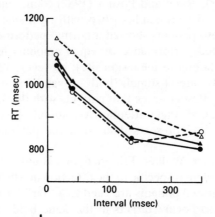

FIG. 5.11. RTs to spatially cued targets from a patient with progressive supranuclear palsy affecting vertical eye movements. Targets were presented in the vertical (circles) or the horizontal dimensions (triangles). Valid cue trials are given solid lines and symbols. Note that the effect of cueing for targets presented along the vertical dimension is present only at the long cue-target interval. (Reproduced from Posner et al., 1980, with permission.)

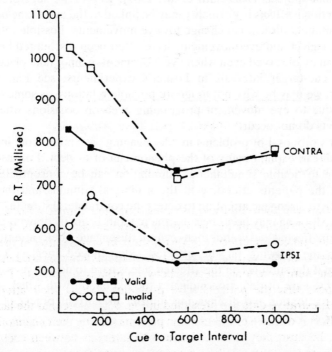

FIG. 5.12. Data from 3 patients with thalamic lesions showing RTs as a function of the cue-target interval, the cue validity, and the location of the target (contralateral or ipsilateral to the lesion site). Note the generally slow responses to contralateral targets. (Reproduced from Rafal & Posner, 1987, with permission.)

the lateral posterior), Rafal and Posner (1987) found another pattern of results. Three patients were studied, two with right-side and one with a left-side lesion. These patients showed a normal pattern of cueing effects (i.e. cueing facilitated performance by equal amounts for targets either ipsilateral or contralateral to the lesion site); however, all their responses were slower to contralateral stimuli (both on valid and on invalid trials). From this Rafal and Posner argue that patients with thalamic lesions have problems in "engaging" their attention on stimuli contralateral to the lesion side. Figure 5.12 presents data from the patients with thalamic lesions.

In other work Posner, Walker, Friedrich, and Rafal (1987) showed that the "disengage" problem is specific to the direction in which attention must be moved. When parietal patients are cued to a "far" location in the non-affected field, RTs to "near" targets in the same field are again grossly affected. The point here is that such "near" targets require an attentional shift in the contralateral direction, even though they are on the unaffected side of space relative to the patient's body. The effect of the *direction* of the attention shift here is reminiscent of the effects of directional cueing found with normal subjects (Rizzolatti et al., 1987). Earlier we suggested that such directional effects in normality may be linked to the extra time needed to programme a directional change for eye movements. Possible relations between neglect and eye movements have often been discounted because neglect can be observed even when eye movements cannot take place (e.g. at short cue-target intervals in Posner's experiments; see Fig. 5.10). However, we may be wise not to ignore possible relations, as some effects may be due to eye movement programing even on occasions when eye movements do not occur.

Posner's proposal of problems in "disengaging" attention from ipsilateral stimuli can explain many of the phenomena of neglect. For instance, extinction to double simultaneous stimulation can be conceptualised in terms of the patients attending to the ipsilateral stimulus and then not being able to disengage attention to detect the contralateral stimulus. Also, neglect in drawing may occur because the patients begin by drawing stimuli on the unaffected side and then cannot disengage their attention to complete the drawing on the affected side. Indeed, neglect can be magnified if the stimulus on the affected side is hard to detect, presumably because the ease of detection indicates the likelihood with which stimuli "capture" attention, so disengaging it from its current object of focus (Riddoch & Humphreys, 1987c).

None the less, it is also becoming increasingly clear that neglect is not a unitary syndrome. For instance, Gainotti et al. (1986) examined neglect in tasks requiring either scanning and visual search or the selection of items from a complex stimulus presented to central vision. The scanning task required the patients to detect a target animal in a cluttered display (see Fig 5.13a). The central selection task required the patients to detect various targets in a set of overlapping figures (Fig. 5.13b). Both left- and right-hemisphere damaged patients showed neglect of contralateral stimuli in the scanning task. Only right-hemisphere damaged patients omitted contralateral stimuli in the overlapping figures. This suggests a possible dissociation between the processes involved in detecting stimuli across the visual field and those involved in central selection. We can relate this to the distinction between exogenous and endogenous attentional mechanisms. Possibly deficits in scanning and search tasks reflect the breakdown in an exogenous attentional system that normally detects target stimuli in peripheral regions of the field, enabling attention to be disengaged and moved to the target. Problems in the central selection task may then reflect an impaired endogenous system which selects only stimuli from one side of space.

Possible dissociations within the neglect syndrome are also suggested by Posner's own data, as patients with either unilateral parietal or thalamic lesions show some neglect of stimuli on the affected side, but the nature of the attentional process impaired in these two cases differs. Further, Bisiach, Perani, Vallar, and Berti (1986) report various dissociations between clinical symptoms of neglect such as the denial of any hemiplegia and neglect in search tasks. Joanette, Brouchon, Gauthier, and Samson (1986) have shown that the magnitude of neglect can depend on the kind of motor response made (more neglect was shown for right- rather than for left-handed responses by patients with right-hemisphere lesions). Costello and Warrington (1987) even report one patient who misread the left sides of words but neglected the right sides of displays in search tasks! The interesting implication of these dissociations is that, in normality, there may exist various different attentional processes—some concerned with specific aspects of attending to, and selecting visual stimuli, others concerned with motor planning and/or coordination (see Goldberg & Segraves, 1987). And, within these broad areas, different attentional responses may be tuned to specific stimuli (e.g. words, faces, etc.). Much work needs to be conducted with normal subjects to assess this proposal arising from clinical work.

FIG. 5.13. Examples of stimuli used to separate "search" and "selection" problems in patients with unilateral neglect by Gainotti et al. (1986). (a) Stimuli from the search task. (b) Stimuli from an overlapping figures task. (Reproduced from Gainotti et al., 1986, with permission.)

166

SPATIAL OR OBJECT-BASED ATTENTION?

It is easy to conceptualise visual attention in terms of a spotlight or a zoom lens, that has definite *spatial* properties (e.g. it is a certain size, moves with a certain speed, etc.). This may be because *space* is intrinsic to visual processing; it is the medium in which vision operates (see Kubovy, 1981). However, there are occasions when we seem not to attend to a particular region of space, but to the objects that occupy those regions. For instance, when an animal moves through the undergrowth we wish to attend to the whole animal, even though the parts in view may be constantly changing. Common movement was one of the attributes proposed by the *Gestalt* psychologists as important for perceptual organisation, and we seem able to attend to a set of moving stimuli even when they cross a cluttered, stationary background—as when a group of birds fly in front of a tree. Our attention is often drawn to the moving group even when any two moving items are no closer than individual moving and stationary items. We shall return to discuss the effects of movement on performance later. For now, we use it only to illustrate that attentional processes cannot be rooted to particular spatial locations.

An alternative view is that we attend to *objects*, rather than to regions of space (Duncan, 1984). One piece of evidence for this object-based view is that subjects seem to find it easier to detect two attributes of the same object than to detect two attributes of different objects. In the study by Duncan (1984), the display contained an outline box with a gap on one side, plus a tilted line running through the box (Fig. 5.14). Both the box and the line had two attributes. The box could be short or long, or it could have a gap slightly to the left or right of its centre; the line could be dotted or dashed, or tilted clockwise or anticlockwise. The display was briefly presented and backward masked, and subjects had to make either one or two judgements (e.g. was the box long or short, was the line clockwise or anticlockwise?). Subjects were worse at making the second of the judgements, relative to when only one judgement was required, but only when the attributes belonged to different objects. That is, subjects were good at detecting both the length of the box and the position of the gap, or both the orientation and nature of the line. They were poor at detecting, say, box length and line orientation. Duncan argued that this is because subjects attend to single objects. Performance is impaired when attributes belong to different objects because subjects must then switch attention between objects. This impairs performance under the short exposure conditions used in the experiment.

It is also possible to think of Duncan's (1984) result in terms of the kinds of spatial filtering mechanisms proposed by Watt (1988). If Duncan's stimuli are passed through the MIRAGE algorithm, the information about the

Stimulus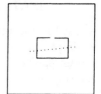

FIG. 5.14. "Box and line" stimuli used by Duncan
(1984) to examine object-based attention. (Reproduced from Duncan, 1984, with permission.)

box can be picked up even when outputs from all the filters are combined,
whilst information about the line is picked up only when the coarser filters
are switched out (see Fig. 5.15). Subjects may respond to the box on the
basis of the combined outputs, whilst responses to the line must await the
completion of the finer-scale analysis made possible by switching out the
coarser filters. "Box detection" will be less efficient when the lines are
reported first because subjects must then wait for the relatively slow finer-
scale analysis to be completed, relative to when report is based on the
faster coarse-scale analysis. Future work needs to tease these different
accounts apart. For now however, we stress the object-based account, as it
allows us more generality, in that it can be readily applied to moving
stimuli where spatial scale is not the only determining factor.

How does the object-based account fit with the data showing that our
ability to attend to objects can be spatially limited, so that responses to one
object are affected by neighbouring distractors (e.g. Eriksen & Eriksen,
1974; see earlier)? A fit could be achieved in various ways, given that early
visual processes "package together" neighbouring items into groups (Watt,
1988). We still attend to one object, but the object is the group. We may
then need to select a target from the group. This may be both time-
consuming and liable to interference from distractors. This idea of
attending to groups of objects as well as individual objects seems
attractive, as it allows for objects to be coded at different spatial scales. We
could attend to a building, a door in the building, or the handle on the door
(see Duncan, 1984). Each item is represented in most detail when it is the
focus of attention. When we attend to a building the door is represented as
a part of the building, and so its own parts may not be articulated. It is
represented in less detail than when it is the focus of attention. This fits
with ideas such as those of Marr (1982) concerning the hierarchical
representation of objects (Chapter 3).

One other point is that we may need to distinguish between the cues
used to summon attention and the nature of what is attended. Attention
may be summoned to regions of field where there are salient cues (such as
the onset of a bright light, or movement against a stationary background).
Such cues may be local and spatially based, and need not necessarily
involve whole-object information. When attention is captured by such
local cues, the processing of information at the attended spatial region may
be facilitated. However, we seem to *select* from the field *objects* that are

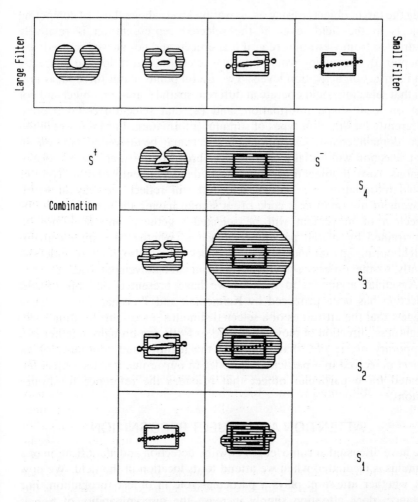

FIG. 5.15. An example of outputs produced by the MIRAGE algorithm to Duncan's (1984) box and line stimuli. S_4 indicates that 4 different-sized filters are engaged, S_3 indicates 3 filters are engaged, S_2 that 2 filters are engaged, and S_1 that 1 filter is engaged. Filters are switched out in the order largest to smallest. Note that, at S_4, the box but not the line is represented. (Reproduced from Watt, 1988, with permission.)

used as the targets for future actions (see Allport, 1987; Styles & Allport, 1986). Salient stimulus properties "capture" an exogenous attentional mechanism that feeds back to further activate the early visual representations involved. Similar processes may also operate when subjects are given a peripheral cue indicating the location of a forthcoming target: that is, there may be position- and viewpoint-specific feedback. Nevertheless, *selection* of stimulus information for report could be based on the currently most active *object* representations. Note that such feedback will benefit only the target object, raising its activation levels above those of competing objects in the field, even if the selected representation is relatively abstracted from viewpoint (e.g. if it is object- and not viewer-centred; see Chapter 3). Pre-cueing would improve selection, but it does so indirectly via its effect on activation levels. Two useful points about these ideas are: (1) that selection could operate at different spatial scales, on object and not just on local shape information; and (2) that selection could operate differently for different types of stimulus information. For instance, in the form domain, coarse descriptions of objects may be arrived at early on, so that selection will initially operate over broad rather than narrow spatial regions. Also, if object movement is coded independently of other types of visual information (see later), selection will reflect the way in which movement information is coded (e.g stimuli having the same velocity or direction of movement will be selected together), and need not be constrained by spatial parameters (such as whether the stimuli are in neighbouring spatial locations). Feedback could also operate independently to the processes involved in form and movement coding.

A similar argument to the one we have presented on object-based selection has been proposed by Kahneman and Treisman (1983). They suggest that the attributes of a selected stimulus, its colour, location, size, brightness, direction of movement, and so forth, are brought together in a temporary *object file,* that maintains the identity and continuity of an object perceived in a particular episode. In our terms, it is the object file created for a particular object that provides the reference for future actions.

ATTENTION AND OBJECT RECOGNITION

We have discussed at some length how the detection and identification of a stimulus is facilitated when we attend to its location in the field. We now ask whether attention plays a particular role in object recognition. For instance, does attention simply increase the discriminability of signals and/or the ease with which such signals are transmitted to subsequent processes? Or, would certain processes in object recognition simply not occur without our attending to the object concerned?

Some evidence for a particular role of visual attention in object recognition was reported in Chapter 3. There, we noted Humphreys's (1984) finding on shape matching. Subjects matched shapes using global shape information when they could not attend to the locations of the shapes in the field, whilst they matched shapes using local shape information when the locations of the shapes were predictable. This result suggests that, by attending to local parts of shapes, subjects are able to constrain the types of information used for shape representation. Similar conclusions can be made from studies using compound letters. In

Chapter 3 we mentioned Navon's (1977) work showing that responses to global compound letters were faster than to the constituent local elements, and the incongruent global letters interfered with responses to the local letters. This "global advantage" can be overcome when subjects can attend to, and fixate the local constituent letters (Grice, Canham, & Boroughs, 1983; Pomerantz, 1983).

However, there are limits to our ability to constrain shape processing. Some parts of objects are highly structured, in the sense that they have properties that make them *intrinsic* to the representation of the whole object (see Chapter 3). Take the example of a face. The position of the local parts, such as the eyes and nose, are intrinsic to the representation of the whole face, in that the representation of the face would change if these parts were moved or substituted. Studies have shown that the detection of such intrinsic local parts is facilitated when they are presented within the whole object (e.g. Purcell & Stewart, 1988). This suggests that attention is not easily narrowed to such intrinsic parts, or that the representation of the whole object (e.g. the face) is so salient as to affect performance even without attention. Hughes et al. (1984) have also shown that subjects cannot easily restrict their attention to the constituent parts of configurations of the type shown in Fig. 5.16. Unlike compound letters, the orientation of the global shape continues to affect performance even when subjects can attend to and fixate the local parts.

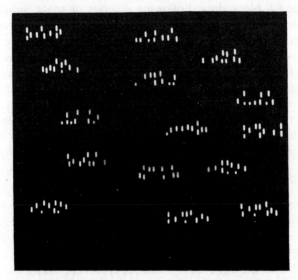

FIG. 5.16.   An example of the displays used by Hughes et al. (1984). The orientation of the global figures cannot easily be ignored when subjects respond to the orientation of the local figures, even when local and global discriminabilities are equated. (Reproduced from Hughes et al., 1984, with permission.)

From this we can suggest that there can be competition between stimulus properties that attract attention to the whole object, and voluntary control of attention to local parts of objects. By narrowing attention we can force processing to be based on the local parts of objects, but our degree of control depends on the characteristics of the objects involved. Control is limited when the parts form some type of spatial configuration. Possibly, spatial configurations produce high levels of activation across the group of elements, overriding local, attentionally based activation.

Other experiments indicate that paying attention to objects can also alter how they are represented. Rock and Gutman (1981) presented subjects with two overlapping shapes in different colours (Fig. 5.17). Subjects rated one of the shapes for "pleasantness". Subsequently, subjects were asked to recognise whether various shapes had appeared in the rating study. Recognition memory was good for the rated shape, but it was at chance for the non-rated (unattended) shape. Rock suggests that subjects do not form integrated representations of shapes without attending to the complete shape.

Epstein and his co-workers (e.g Epstein & Lovitts, 1985) have further argued that, without attention, we do not take depth information into account in our coding of objects. Epstein and Lovitts presented subjects with irregularly contoured shapes, each of which could appear at a number of depth rotations. On the vertical axis of each shape there was a line of between 5 and 8 black dots. Following a series of trials, subjects were presented with comparison shapes and asked to judge which shapes they had seen earlier. Some of the comparison stimuli were the same *objective shapes* as the original targets; some corresponded to the *projected shapes* of the targets (i.e. the shape of the targets on the retina, which of course would not correspond to the objective shape of a stimulus that has been depth-rotated); some were completely different shapes. Subjects were divided into two groups. One group was told the nature of the experiment (the *shape-directed group*). Another was told to judge whether there was an odd or an even number of dots on the initial shapes (the *dot-directed group*). The shape-directed group tended to choose comparison shapes

FIG. 5.17.   An example of overlapping figure stimuli used by Rock and Gutman (1981). In their experiment, the 2 stimuli were in different colours. (Reproduced with permission.)

matching the *objective* shape of the target. In contrast, the dot-directed group tended to choose items matching the *projected* shape. It is as if the dot-directed group only perceived the targets as being two-dimensional shapes, and did not integrate the shape description with depth information to produce the correct objective shape representation.

There are several interesting aspects of these results. Take the study of Rock and Gutman (1981). Subjects in that study apparently formed an integrated representation only for the object they attended. Remember, however, that the objects were overlapping. The target object could not be selected simply by subjects attending to a particular region of field. So, in this respect, the data favour "object-based" over "space-based" theories of attention. Subjects seemed to attend to the object defined by the designated target colour even though it occupied the same spatial region as the distractor.

Also, although both results suggest a role for attention in object perception, the interpretations offered are subtly different. Rock and Gutman suggest that shapes are not integrated without attention. Subjects may code that shapes have angles or lines of particular length, etc., but they do not code which angles go with which lines (cf. Treisman, 1986; see the next section). Epstein and Lovitts (1985) suggest that attention is needed to combine two-dimensional shape information with depth cues. Note, however, that the shape information itself is thought to be integrated.

The above distinction, although subtle, is critically important for understanding the role of attention in object perception, and in particular for understanding whether attention is crucial for combining various types of visual information. In Chapter 2 we discussed the proposition that certain stimulus properties are coded independently in the first stages of vision. Given this account, it becomes important to know how the properties are recombined so that we can see coherent objects in coherent scenes. From the evidence discussed so far, it seems possible that attention is central to this recombination process. However, is it essential for recombining the features of shapes, or for combining whole shapes with their surface properties such as colour and depth? We return to these questions after considering probably the most explicit account to date of the role of attention in object perception: that offered by Ann Treisman (e.g. Treisman, 1986, 1988; Treisman & Gelade, 1980; Treisman & Gormican, 1988; Treisman & Souther, 1985).

FEATURE INTEGRATION THEORY

According to Treisman's feature integration theory, early visual processing involves the parallel extraction of simple local properties of objects, such as lines of particular orientation, colour, size, and movement direction. We can think of these local properties as the features upon which all later coding processes operate. These early parallel processes are followed by a second stage in which the separate features are recombined to form *objects* that have a specific shape, colour, size, and movement. There are three ways in which the features of objects may be combined (Treisman & Schmidt, 1982). One is by attending to the location of the object. Attention acts to "glue" together the features for each of the dimensions. Feature combination can also be constrained by stored knowledge. For instance, if an object has a characteristic colour, then it is likely that the colour will be combined with the object shape when both are present in the display even when the object is not attended. A carrot is likely to be combined with the colour orange, a tomato with the colour red, etc. This provides a second means of feature combination. The third means is to combine features together randomly. This will sometimes produce the correct combinations of features, but, more often, incorrect combinations will be formed (so-called "illusory conjunctions").

Figure 5.18 provides an outline of the two major stages posited by feature integration theory. In this outline, separate "feature maps" are presented for two stimulus dimensions: colour and orientation. When a set of horizontal red lines is present on the retina, detectors in the appropriate "red" and "horizontal" feature maps are activated. However, the presence of the "red horizontal" lines is only coded by attending to the location occupied by those features in the "master map" of locations. Once this occurs, a temporary object representation (an object file) is created that can be used for object recognition (by matching it against stored representations).

There are several pieces of evidence consistent with feature integration theory. Perhaps the most striking comes from visual search tasks, where subjects have to detect a target item against a background of varying numbers of distractors. Search efficiency is measured in terms of the effects of the number of distractors (the *display size*) on performance. There seems to be a qualitative shift in search when the target is defined by a single feature relative to the distractors, compared with when the target is defined by a *conjunction* of features. For instance, search for a target defined by its colour or orientation is efficient (e.g. a blue or horizontal target relative to red vertical or green oblique distractors). RTs to detect such feature-defined targets typically show minimal effects of the display size, and when such effects do occur, RTs increase non-linearly as the number of distractors increases. In contrast, search for a target defined by a conjunction of colour and orientation is inefficient (e.g. a red horizontal target relative to blue horizontal or red vertical distractors). More particularly, RTs increase linearly with the display size, with the slope of the function for present responses about half that for absent responses

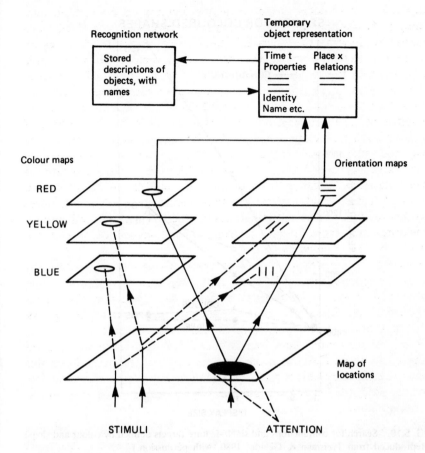

FIG. 5.18. A processing framework illustrating feature integration theory. (Reproduced from Treisman, 1988, with permission.)

(Quinlan & Humphreys, 1987; Treisman & Gelade, 1980). Figure 5.19 presents data from Treisman and Gelade (1980) illustrating this contrast between single- and combined-feature search. The joint search characteristics of conjunction search —linear search functions and the 1:2 slope ratio for present:absent responses—are important because they suggest that conjunction search is serial and self-terminating. That is, subjects seem to search through each item in the display in turn until they either find the target or check through all the items (when the target is absent). Because, on average, the target will be found after half the distractors have been checked, the slopes for present responses will be about half those for absent.

The serial self-terminating search found for conjunction targets fits with the idea that feature conjunctions are coded by means of an attentional

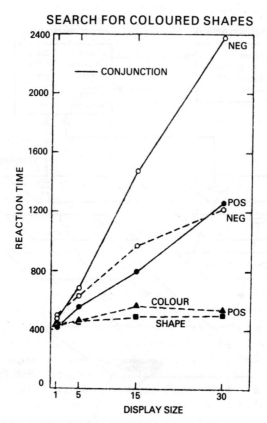

FIG. 5.19.   Search for conjunctions and single-feature targets defined by colour and shape.
(Reproduced from Treisman & Gelade, 1980, with permission.)

mechanism that is applied serially to all the items in a display. The non-linear or even flat search pattern for single feature targets fits more easily with their being detected via a parallel search process. According to feature integration theory, single features are detected in parallel because the maps for these features are "hardwired" in parallel in the system.

In the above example, the target was defined by a conjunction of colour and form. Using similar targets, Treisman and Gelade (1980) also showed that conjunction search remained serial even when subjects were given extensive practice. It seems as if subjects are forced to scan serially to detect such targets, as if this were a basic limitation of the system that is not overridden by practice. Also, the primary result is not confined to conjunctions of colour and form. Search can also be serial when targets are defined by a conjunction of line features (e.g. R vs P and Q distractors; Treisman & Gelade, 1980; or L vs T and I; Humphreys, Quinlan, &

Riddoch, 1989), and for targets defined by conjunctions of size and colour and size and shape (Quinlan & Humphreys, 1987).

Further evidence for feature integration theory comes from studies of "illusory conjunctions". Treisman and Schmidt (1982) conducted a study in which subjects were presented (for 300msec) with a row of coloured letters flanked by two digits. The main task for subjects was to report the flanking digits, and only after that were they to report letters and their colours. The exposure duration used was sufficient to produce good report of the digits, whilst being too brief to allow all the letters to be attended individually. Treisman and Schmidt found that subjects made errors to the letters. In particular, they would mix up the letters present with their colours— producing "illusory conjunctions" of colour and form. For instance, if the display contained blue X, red G, and green F, subjects may report that a red X and a blue G were present. These illusory conjunctions occur more often than would be expected by chance identification of two of the features present (i.e. a single form and a single colour). They therefore seem to reflect the joint occurrence of the features in the display, but with their being combined incorrectly. This is exactly as predicted by feature integration theory, which holds that arbitrary conjunctions of colour and form are combined at random unless they are attended individually.

We can also ask about the relation between feature integration and visual attention as manipulated by spatial cueing. Briand and Klein (1987) investigated this in the following way. Subjects were presented with pairs of letters, either about 4 degrees to the left or the right of fixation. The task was to decide if the letter R was present in each pair. In the *conjunction task,* the target (R) had to be discriminated from the distractor letters P and Q. To perform this task, subjects need to know about the particular combinations of the features in the letters. In the *feature task,* the distractors were the letters P and B. In this case, the target can be discriminated by the presence of a diagonal line (in R but not P or B). In both tasks, subjects were given a central arrow cue prior to the letters on each trial, that signalled where the pair of letters was likely to appear. On trials where the cue was valid, performance was facilitated, but it was facilitated to the same extent for the feature and conjunction tasks. Apparently, having subjects attend to the location of the letters did not differentially improve conjunction detection, as might be expected if attention were critical for forming feature conjunctions. However, in a further experiment Briand and Klein used a peripheral cue to the location of the letters. Now valid cues improved performance more for the conjunction than for the feature task (see also Treisman, 1985; Prinzmetal, Presti, & Posner, 1986). This is consistent with attention being important for conjunction detection. Briand and Klein suggest that these different results reflect the different properties of exogenous and endogenous attentional mechanisms. Exogenous attention provides the "glue" that ties features together, whilst endogenous attention influences later processes concerned with selecting a response to an integrated representation.

Feature integration theory can also be used to account for the results of experiments on "texture discrimination". In experiments in the 1960s and 1970s, Beck and his colleagues (Beck, 1966, 1967; Beck & Ambler, 1972, 1973) reported several important findings. We present just one for illustration. Using displays of simple letter-like forms, Beck (1967) showed that it was easier to detect a boundary between fields of Ts and *T*s than between fields of Ts and Ls (see Fig. 5.20). Yet, if subjects are asked to rate the similarity between these figures they rate T and *T* as being more similar that T and L, presumably because Ts and *T*s have the same name. Thus the easier perceptual separation of Ts and *T*s than Ts and Ls has nothing to do with their rated similarity. According to feature integration theory, the difference occurs because Ts and *T*s are distinguished by a salient single feature (line orientation). This feature can be detected in parallel across the display, producing easy perceptual segmentation. However, Ts and Ls contain the same features (horizontal and vertical line segments), and are distinguished only by the way the features are combined. The combination of features can only be detected by a serial search, producing poor perceptual segmentation. Textures are based on populations of local elements, so that texture discrimination requires that differences are computed across the populations, rather than being confined to single elements at a time; i.e. processing should be spatially parallel. Feature integration theory holds that texture discrimination occurs if regions of field differ in terms of some salient local feature.

Feature integration theory can thus account for the results from several experimental procedures. Besides this, the theory is important because it provides one answer to a basic question in vision research; namely, how do independently coded features come to be re-combined together correctly?

FIG. 5.20.   An example of texture segregation using orientation or line conjunction differences. (Reproduced from Beck, 1966, with permission.)

Feature integration theory answers this question in the following way. The visual system does not "hardwire in" information about all possible combinations of features. Instead, conjunction information is coded episodically by the application of serial attention to particular spatial locations.

SOME PROBLEMS FOR FEATURE INTEGRATION THEORY

Let us now consider again one of the basic propositions of feature integration theory: That attention is needed to correctly combine all the features of objects, including lines of different orientation, and shape with surface detail. We need to ask how feasible this proposition is. For instance, it seems plausible that the outline shape of an object needs to be computed before surface detail (brightness contrasts, texture, colour) can be integrated (otherwise there would be no boundaries to surfaces; see Grossberg & Mingolla, 1985). Feature integration theory does allow for some more complex types of shape information to be detected in parallel if the local features can be coded into a larger "emergent feature". For instance, two curved line elements can be coded as a single closed figure [()] or a single open figure [)(], depending on their local orientations (Pomerantz & Schwaitzberg, 1975). Emergent features such as these can be detected in much the same way as single line features (Treisman & Paterson, 1984). However, emergent features are still essentially local aspects of shape; they do not offer perceptual boundaries for integrating surface detail. We suggest that, because of the constraints involved in integrating surface detail, feature integration is unlikely to occur simultaneously for *all* the features of objects.

Letters and Words as Whole Units

There is also evidence that certain features do not require serial attention to be integrated correctly. In studies of word recognition, subjects seem able to attend to the complete string and not to the constituent letters (Johnston & McClelland, 1974; LaBerge, 1983; see Chapter 7). This seems difficult to reconcile with the notion that the features of letters must first be integrated prior to the integration of the letters in the word. Also, when words are simultaneously and briefly presented, subjects make "migration" errors where letters from particular positions in the words are transposed (e.g. RUST and VENT may be reported as RUNT and VEST; Allport, 1977; Duncan, 1987; Mozer, 1983; Treisman & Souther, 1986; see Chapter 7). Such errors maintain the positions of the letters in the words. Thus the transposed letters and letter clusters seem to act as single units, coded for their relative positions within the words. Indeed, at least some experimenters have found it difficult to produce equivalent migrations between putative features of letters (such as particular strokes; Duncan, 1987), even though feature integration theory predicts such migrations should occur in just the same way as the migrations producing illusory conjunctions of colour and form.

These pieces of evidence fit better with the idea that the features of letters do not require focal attention to be integrated correctly. Perhaps the fact that letters are encountered so commonly means that they behave like single features. But, if learning alone produces this result, why did it not change the serial nature of search for targets defined by conjunctions of colour and form (Treisman & Gelade, 1980; though see below)? There are also contradictions. For instance, why should search for letters sometimes be serial (e.g R vs P and Q; Treisman & Gelade, 1980)? Also, why should peripheral cueing affect the detection of letter conjunctions more than the detection of their features (Briand & Klein, 1987)? Differential effects of peripheral cueing could occur because exogenous attention refines position coding, because it feeds back to early visual processes that are position-specific. Accurate position coding is crucial to detecting conjunctions but not features (Quinlan & Humphreys, 1987). Such a result could occur even if the features in letters are conjoined correctly without attention. However, the serial search data are more problematic. We turn to these data in the next section.

Parallel Search with Combined Forms

Search for conjunctions of form elements can be serial. This result typically occurs when subjects have to discriminate a target from a set of mixed (heterogeneous) distractors (e.g. R vs P and Q; Treisman & Gelade, 1980). In these experiments the target tends to resemble one or other of the distractors at least as much as the distractors resemble one another (e.g. R resembles P more than P resembles Q). Experiments where subjects search for a combined-form target against *homogeneous* distractors produce quite different results. With homogeneous distractors, combined-form targets can be detected from a parallel search. For instance, Humphreys, Riddoch, and Quinlan (1985) found minimal effects of display size when subjects searched for a ⅃ target against homogeneous T distractors, even though targets and distractors contain the same elements (horizontal and vertical lines; cf. Beck, 1967). With displays plotted to form a regular shape (such as a square or a circle) absent responses tended also to be faster than present. These "fast absent" responses argue against subjects responding to some form of higher-order feature that "emerges" when the target is present. Rather, subjects seem to respond directly to a property of the whole display—such as the configuration of the regular shape or the consistency of the texture over the combined forms. (When there is a consistent texture, subjects respond "target absent", with the presence of the target being signalled by a "break" in the texture provided by the discrepant item.)

The above data indicate that conjunctions of form elements are represented in parallel across visual displays. The result is quite general and not confined to the use of letter stimuli (Humphreys et al., 1989). Nevertheless, there are some constraints. One is that search depends on the relation between the area of the display and the size of the figures. Parallel search occurs when the figures are quite large relative to the area of the display (so that the whole area is no bigger than about three times the size of the individual figures). Note that this factor probably explains the difference between these search results and the texture discrimination studies of Beck and his colleagues using similar stimuli. Remember that Beck found poor segmentation between stimuli distinguished by conjunctions of line elements. However, he used displays that covered large areas. Form conjunctions may only be coded accurately in parallel across fairly small areas, that increase to some degree when larger elements are used.

Parallel conjoining of shape information would be useful for the integration of surface details with object shape (see earlier). It would also be useful for other processes in object recognition, such as segmenting partially occluded figures (Fig. 5.21). For instance, if shape information is available in parallel across a display, it is possible to allow constraints between objects to influence segmentation in a crowded visual field. In Fig. 5.21, line ab cannot simultaneously be part of shape 1 and shape 2. Its assignment to either shape is facilitated if the objects are placed in competition with one another, so that evidence favouring the assignment of the line to one object acts as evidence against it being assigned to the other object. In our example, the fact that there is no boundary half way down the rear shape, perpendicular to line ab, supports the case for ab only being part of the front shape (because such a perpendicular line should exist if ab was also a boundary of the rear shape). This technique of pitting competing interpretations against one another to solve a problem is known as "mutual constraint satisfaction" (see Ballard et al., 1983). It is an extremely useful way of solving many visual problems, and one that depends on having the competing interpretations available in parallel.

Problems in processing pattern descriptions (and not just discrete features) in parallel may also underlie some object recognition impairments (agnosia) in patients. We have already discussed patient H.J.A.'s problems in object recognition in Chapter 3, where we argued that he is unable to gain normal access to stored structural descriptions of the appearance of objects, as he performs at chance level at an object decision task using line-drawings (Riddoch & Humphreys, 1987a). Yet, when the drawings were shaded in to form silhouettes H.J.A. did somewhat better (and now performed above chance level). Normal subjects find discriminations much harder with silhouettes, presumably because silhouettes only have outlines

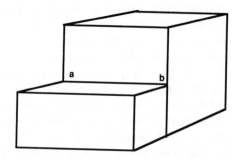

FIG. 5.21. An example of a set of overlapping figures, where segmentation may be facilitated by combining the form elements in parallel.

and show no internal details. Normally, the presence of the internal details enhances performance. In contrast, internal detail impairs H.J.A.'s performance. H.J.A.'s relatively good performance with silhouettes suggests that he can extract and use outline shape. His problems with line-drawings seem to be caused by the presence of internal detail. Why should internal detail disrupt performance? When identifying line-drawings, H.J.A., like many agnosic patients, adopts the strategy of articulating the major features of the objects and seems not to recognise the objects as perceptual wholes (see also Wapner, Judd, & Gardner, 1978). Possibly, internal details can give cues to segment objects into different parts, or even into separate "object descriptions", unless overridden by overall shape information. Clearly, this requires interplay between the visual descriptions derived from objects over different spatial scales, and segmentation might result if this interplay is disrupted. Of course, if segmentation takes place, object recognition will be impaired. Consistent with this, many of H.J.A.'s naming errors suggest the inappropriate segmentation of objects. For instance, he described a paint brush as "two things close together; a longish wooden stick and a shorter, darker object, though this can't be right or you would have told me it was two rather than one object". In this instance, he segmented the handle and the brush, and so failed to derive a description of a single object (see Humphreys & Riddoch, 1987a).

Other tests of H.J.A.'s pattern recognition abilities were conducted using visual search tasks of the type described earlier. H.J.A. could search quite normally for a target defined by a single salient feature, such as a 45 degree change in orientation. He could also conduct normal serial search for a target defined by a conjunction of features against a background of heterogeneous figures (e.g. ⌐ vs T and I distractors). However, relative to normal subjects he was impaired at searching for a conjunction target presented against homogeneous distractors (⌐ vs T distractors; Humphreys & Riddoch, 1987a; Humphreys et al., 1985). In particular, there was no sign of the "fast absent" responses that characterise normal performance with such displays. Earlier, we proposed that these fast absent responses are indicative of grouping processes that operate in parallel across visual displays. The absence of such responses in H.J.A.'s performance invites the conclusion that, for him, these grouping processes are impaired. This argument for impaired grouping processes also provides a good qualitative account of the types of recognition error H.J.A. typically made.

This leaves us with the following question: If shape information is conjoined in parallel, why does serial search ever occur for combined-form targets? One suggestion is that the detection of combined-form targets depends critically on grouping between the items in a display. With heterogeneous distractors (e.g. P and Q), the target will often group with one of the distractors (e.g. R with P). The display will then be segmented initially between one group of distractors plus the target (Ps and R) and another group of distractors (Qs). The target cannot be detected from this representation, and further segmentation is needed. In the limit, each item would need to be separated in turn, producing serial search. According to this argument, serial search for combined-form targets is *not* because form elements cannot be combined without attention; rather it is because of grouping between the items and the time then required to separate the grouped stimuli. Precisely this would occur if grouping initially operates quite coarsely, so that finer-grained information about the absolute locations of elements is not well specified (see Watt, 1988, for a similar argument). Note that this coarse initial grouping will often be sufficient to detect targets defined by a salient feature relative to the distractors, producing flat search functions in such cases. It will only be sufficient to detect combined-form targets when the resemblance between the distractors is higher than that between the target and the distractors, so that distractors group together (the limiting case being where the distractors are identical). In line with this argument for the importance of grouping and stimulus similarity, Wolfe, Cave, and Franzel (1989) have recently reported parallel search for conjunction targets based on three stimulus attributes (such as shape, colour, and size) when each distractor differed by two features from the target (lowering target-distractor similarity). A fuller account of such data in terms of the similarity relations between stimuli is provided by Duncan and Humphreys (1989).

Parallel Search with Cross-dimension Conjunctions

The initial work on feature integration was conducted primarily using stimuli defined on just two dimensions: colour and shape. More recent work suggests that the picture is not so simple (and, indeed, possibly more interesting) when other stimulus dimensions are also considered. Nakayama and Silverman (1986) presented displays with items at one of two stereoscopic disparities, so that half stood out in depth against the background. The "near" distractors were one colour (e.g. red) and the "far" distractors another colour (e.g. blue). The target, when present, was defined by a conjunction of depth and colour (e.g. it was a "near" blue item). They found that the detection of such conjunctions was not affected by the number of distractors present; that is, search was parallel. Such displays seem to segregate into two depth planes ("near" and "far" surfaces). Once this segmentation takes place the target can be discriminated because it differs in a salient single feature relative to the distractors in the same depth (in our example, the contrast is between "near" red distractors and a "near" blue target). Nakayama and Silverman (1986) found similar effects when motion and disparity were combined, and this has been extended to include combinations of colour and motion (Nakayama, quoted in Treisman, 1988), form and motion (McLeod, Driver, & Crisp, 1988), and combinations of colour, orientation, and size with disparity and with position-based properties of form. An example of a position-based property is whether lines are offset from each other (termed Vernier acuity; e.g. ||| vs ||| ; Steinman, 1987). The point about all these examples is that depth, motion, and position-offset all allow the visual field to be segregated, and they override grouping between neighbouring form elements. This may be because depth, motion, and position-offset are coded in systems that are functionally independent of those concerned with form identity. When segmentation takes place using the former cues, we witness the operation (and possibly also the characteristics) of the separate motion, depth, and position coding systems. Colour seems to be a less potent cue for "de-coupling" grouping between form elements, and so conjunctions of colour and form cannot be detected in the same way as conjunctions of form and motion (e.g. via segmentation into two colour "planes"). Perhaps motion, depth, and position override grouping based on form because these dimensions provide the spatial coordinates for any actions that must be made to stimuli. By coding that an object is moving in a particular direction or is at a particular depth, constraints can be imposed on any subsequent actions (e.g. the direction or extent of the action can be partially determined). This is not so for colour, which carries no information about where an object is in the field. It seems feasible that a basic limitation in human perfomance is that purposeful action can only be directed to one object at a time (see Allport, 1987). If so, then the limitation would be minimised by implementing grouping procedures sensitive to action-based constraints (so that grouping by depth overrides grouping by form). We make this point to illustrate how *computational constraints*, concerning, for instance, the evolutionary purpose of the system, can inform our thinking about visual performance (see Chapter 1).

From the above account we also expect there to be limitations to the selection of all "targets" for action, whether they are defined by a single feature or by a conjunction of features. Consistent with this is evidence that even single-feature defined targets can be selected serially, so that performance is impaired when subjects are asked to verify the presence of two rather than one such target in the field (Duncan, 1985; Quinlan & Humphreys, 1987).

Experiments such as those of Nakayama and Silverman (1986) illustrate some of the ways in which visual displays can be perceptually *segmented*. However, the experiments are not so diagnostic for understanding how different visual dimensions are *integrated*. It could still be true that features can only be integrated serially *across* stimulus dimensions. This would fit with the interpretation we originally offered for the work of Epstein and Lovitts (1985), concerning the integration of depth and two-dimensional shape. In this respect, a study by Pashler (1987) is of interest. Pashler examined search for targets defined by a conjunction of colour and form. Unlike most previous studies, he used only small displays of up to eight characters. He found that whilst RTs increased as the display size increased, they did so at the same rate for present and for absent responses (see Fig. 5.22). This result differs from that found with larger displays, where absent responses are on average about twice as slow as present responses (e.g. Treisman & Gelade, 1980; see Fig. 5.19). Pashler's data could reflect various search strategies on the part of subjects. For instance, subjects might search the display serially and continue searching until they have checked all the items present (even when they encounter the target half-way through the search); that is, search could be *serial and exhaustive*. However, Pashler also found that adding a *second* target to displays facilitated performance. This manipulation should not facilitate serial exhaustive search (as subjects should still search all the items even with two targets present). For this reason, Pashler argues that information about conjunctions of form and colour can be coded in parallel (otherwise absent responses would be slower than present). However, there are severe

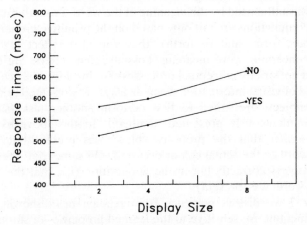

FIG. 5.22.   RTs to targets defined by conjunctions of colour and form when the display size is small. (Reproduced from Pashler, 1987, with permission.)

limitations on parallel processing in such cases. Essentially, parallel coding becomes markedly less efficient as the number of elements increases (even with up to eight items), producing linear effects of display size on search. Perhaps this is because the probability of incorrect integrations rises as the visual field becomes more crowded. Note, however, that the basic mechanism of feature integration operates in parallel. With displays of more than eight characters search becomes serial, producing the 1:2 difference in the slopes for present and absent responses. This suggests that parallel integration operates only over small numbers of items. In a search task with large numbers of items, the parallel integration process must be applied a number of times, introducing serial components to performance.

Illusory Conjunctions

One of the strengths of feature integration theory is that it draws on evidence from a number of experimental procedures. In addition to visual search, the theory draws on studies of illusory conjunctions. However, some problems in interpretation also arise here.

Consider a study by Virzi and Egeth (1984). They used a procedure very similar to that of Treisman and Schmidt (1982), who originally examined illusory conjunctions between letters and colours. Rather than using letters, Virzi and Egeth used words. A display might comprise the words BIG, BLUE, and WIDE, printed in red, green, and black. These words would be flanked by numbers. Subjects had to report the numbers and then any words and their colours. The interesting result was that subjects reported at a level greater than chance "illusory conjunctions" of a word in the colour of the colour name in the display (e.g. that the word BIG was written in blue). This is interesting because the colour blue was not present, only the corresponding word. So, in this instance, the illusory conjunction was influenced by the meaning of the word. From this it seems that illusory conjunctions are not only based on the primitive properties of objects (colour, form, and so forth); they can also reflect high-level information concerning word meaning. Possibly, some effects are due to memorial and not strictly perceptual processes. For instance, they could be due to the loss of visual information when displays are presented relatively briefly and subjects are asked to first perform another task (such as identifying simultaneously presented numbers). In the above example subjects remember that the property "blue" was present but forget whether the word or the actual colour occurred. On some trials they then report the property correctly but in the wrong form (i.e. that the colour and not the word was present).

In Chapter 7 we discuss evidence from reading tasks showing that illusory conjunctions are sensitive to the learned properties of stimuli. To anticipate this, note now that illusory conjunctions can be influenced by syllabic structure and/or by the frequency of letter clusters in words when the illusions involve the migration of colours between letters in words (Printzmetal, Treiman, & Rho, 1986; Seidenberg, 1987). These results could occur because letters and letter clusters come to be coded as single units in word recognition. However, this would contradict the proposal that only very primitive properties of shape are integrated together without attention.

The general lesson is that illusory conjunctions do not tap only early visual processes. Early visual processes could be responsible for some of the effects, but so also could "higher-order" processes concerning object or word meaning. In future, experimenters will need to take care to titrate out the contributions from these different sources.

The Fate of Unattended Objects: Negative Priming and Processing Delays

According to feature integration theory, there are two fates that await unattended stimuli (Treisman & Schmidt, 1982). If the stimuli are well known, their properties may be combined correctly because stored knowledge constrains feature integration. If the stimuli are not well known, and comprise arbitrary conjunctions of features (e.g. coloured letters), their features will be conjoined randomly with those of other objects in the field. Often, this will mean that features will be conjoined incorrectly. In the form domain, one might even expect that local features would not combine together to produce a representation of a complete shape. Precisely this argument can be made for Rock and Gutman's (1981) data, where subjects failed to remember the non-attended members of pairs of overlapping figures. Yet, how does this argument correspond with the evidence that form information can be integrated without attention?

Work by Tipper and his associates (Allport, Tipper, & Chmiel, 1985; Tipper, 1985; Tipper & Cranston, 1985; Tipper & Driver, 1988) is helpful in this respect. For instance, Tipper and Driver (1988) presented subjects with a series of overlapping red and green figures. Subjects might have to identify the red member of each pair and to ignore the green member. Sometimes, the ignored item on trial N became the target item on trial N + 1 (see Fig. 5.23). Tipper and Driver found that RTs were slowed on trial N + 1 on these occasions, relative to when the target had not appeared earlier in the experiment. They termed this the *negative priming effect*. Negative priming is interesting because it occurs even when subjects show poor memory for the ignored members of the overlapping figures, as Rock and Gutman observed. The important point is that poor memory (and perhaps even poor explicit report) for stimuli is no guarantee that the stimuli have not been processed to a high level. Indeed, Allport et al. (1985) and Tipper and Driver (1988) have further shown that negative priming extends to pairs of semantically related items. That is, target identification is inhibited even when the previously ignored item is non-identical but semantically related (Fig. 5.23). The data suggest that ignored members of overlapping figures are integrated, and can activate their stored representations (so generating semantic effects). However, when subjects do not attend to the figures, little about the figures is maintained. Paying attention to figures seems to provide more stable memories of them, but attention is not required for their perceptual integration.

One other interesting aspect of negative priming is the fact that it takes an inhibitory form. The identification of a stimulus is inhibited following its rejection as the unattended member of a pair of overlapping figures. This suggests that the act of selecting one item for identification has as its counterpart the inhibition of other competing items in the field. Such inhibition would be useful as a way of minimising competition between items, including minimising possible "cross-talk" during feature integration.

From negative priming we might conclude that the fate of unattended objects is simply the inhibition of their representations following the selection of other items in the field. This may reflect properties of the selection process. We have also argued earlier that attention can have separate, facilitatory effects on processing, due to the feedback of activation to the representations of stimuli at attended spatial locations. This feedback should in its own right create differences between the processing of attended and unattended objects. For instance, we might expect the processing of unattended objects to be retarded (relative to that of attended objects) even before selection takes place. This has been observed by Gathercole and Broadbent (1987). They were interested in the letter interference effects studied by Eriksen and his co-workers (Eriksen & Eriksen, 1974; Eriksen & Schultz, 1979). Remember that these interference effects involve the slowing of responses to a central letter when it is flanked by distractor letters requiring an incompatible response. A crucial aspect of this result is that it occurs primarily when the distractors fall within about 1 degree of visual angle of the target (Eriksen & Eriksen, 1974). This fits with the idea that all stimuli within a close spatial area are treated initially as a single perceptual object, or that they all benefit from falling within the "spotlight" of visual attention.

Gathercole and Broadbent found that interference effects could arise from stimuli outside the central 1 degree area, when the distractor letters were presented shortly before the target. That is, unattended distractors only interfere with the concurrent processing of target stimuli when they are given a "headstart" relative to the attended items, consistent with the processing of the unattended items being delayed. Note, however, that object processing does not seem to change qualitatively in the absence of attention; providing the headstart is given, the interference effects seem to mimic those found when the objects are attended.

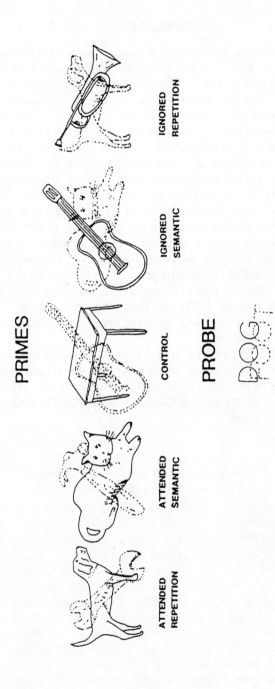

FIG. 5.23. Example stimuli used in studies of negative priming. Subjects respond only to the complete outlines and they ignore the dotted outlines. Primary interest is in responses to the target probe as a function of the different priming condition. (Reproduced from Tipper & Driver, 1988, with permission.)

SUMMARY

We have discussed the implications of feature integration theory at some length because this theory provides us with a computational role for serial, attentional processes in vision. The evidence we have reviewed has not been consistent with all aspects of the theory. In particular, we have suggested that form information can be integrated without attention, and that we attend to and select as targets for action *objects* in a scene. Because of the integration of form information, we seem able to attend to stimuli at various spatial scales, from the local parts of objects to whole shapes. It remains possible that our ability to integrate different dimensions of visual stimuli is severely limited, and, if not strictly serial, it is constrained to only a few objects at a time (Pashler, 1987). Feature integration theory may provide a relatively good account of integration across feature dimensions. Whether this conclusion is correct or not, the problem of how visual dimensions that are analysed independently come to be integrated remains central to understanding visual perception. It is also a problem that can be addressed using different research approaches, including computer vision (e.g. Feldman & Ballard, 1982) and neurophysiology (Crick, 1984). By considering evidence from these different approaches, future work may converge upon a solution.

From the evidence covered it is also clear that attending to objects, in the sense of selecting them from distractors in the visual field, is important for remembering them later. The act of selection results in explicit episodic representations or object files. In Chapter 6 we discuss the nature of visual memory in more detail.

6 Visual Memory and Imagery

INTRODUCTION

At several points in this book we have touched upon aspects of visual memory. In Chapter 4, for example, we mentioned a very transient form of visual memory—iconic memory—which seems to preserve visual information in a relatively raw form for fractions of a second. At the other end of the scale, the stored representations of objects (see Chapter 3) which allow us to recognise them as familiar entities can clearly be construed as "long-term memories" of object appearances. Such memories are much less tied to viewpoint than iconic memory, and are relatively stable and permanent—it is only following certain sorts of brain damage that we may forget what a dog looks like. Throughout our lives, however, we add to our store of visual appearances of things, whether through learning to recognise the faces of new aquaintances or learning new skills or hobbies which introduce us to novel categories of object.

In this chapter we will thus be mentioning some already familiar forms of visual memory, as well as introducing evidence relating to visual memories of intermediate duration ("short-term visual memory") and considering longer-term memories for particular pictures and events. We will consider the relationship between stores and representations needed to account for visual *remembering* and those needed to sustain visual imagery and visual perception. Towards the end of the chapter we will consider how visual memories may be used and modified in everyday life, by considering the task faced by the witness to crime.

ICONIC MEMORY

In Chapter 4 we reviewed research on memory for briefly glimpsed arrays of alphanumeric characters. Recall that subjects who are asked to try and write down all the letters they see from a briefly presented array of three rows of four letters can typically report only four or five correctly. Sperling's (1960) "partial report" studies showed that subjects who were cued after display offset to report just a single row of letters from such a display could, if cued immediately after display offset, recall about 75% of the letters from any one row, and so must have had available about 75% of the entire array, or 9 of the 12 letters. Sperling suggested that the letters were initially retained in a fast-decaying uninterpreted sensory memory: "Iconic memory". This "icon" was initially thought to be the same system which produces persistence for any brief visual event—such as when a "sparkler" firework or a glowing cigarette is moved in the dark and leaves a visual trail.

In Sperling's experiments, letters (or other items) must be identified from the icon—a process which takes time. Report of these letter identities then relies on their translation into verbal or written responses. In such accounts (e.g. Sperling, 1967; Coltheart, 1972), the limitation in reporting a whole array is attributed to the limited rate at which items can be identified from the icon before it has decayed. A partial report cue allows letters to be identified from the fading icon selectively, and thus, if presented immediately after display offset, can allow the majority of items from any particular row of the icon to be identified. In these terms, a partial report cue is seen to act directly upon the icon. It follows from this, given the *precategorical* nature of the icon, that partial report cues should only be effective (i.e. yield an advantage over a whole report condition) if they specify some subset of the display defined in sensory rather than categorical terms. Early experiments showing that selection from the icon was possible on the basis of such cues as the location (Sperling, 1960) or colour (Clark, 1969) of a subset of the items, but was not possible where subjects were cued to report only the letters from a mixed alphanumeric display (Sperling, 1960), provided support for such a theory.

This theory of how visual information is reported from very brief displays is not without its problems, however. Iconic memory is maskable but in Chapter 4 we raised some problems with an explanation of masking in terms of the integration of stimulus and mask within the icon. One particular problem was that information about the identities and locations of items in the icon seems to decay at different rates, and to be differentially susceptible to masking by noise. A second problem was that advantages of partial report cueing have occasionally been observed when report is cued categorically (e.g. when subjects are asked to report only the letters from a mixed display of letters and numbers—Merikle, 1980). It seems, then, that the system underlying partial report superiority, must be more complex than that we have equated with simple "visual persistence" (Coltheart, 1980; 1983).

Further distinctions between the system responsible for partial report superiority and visual persistence are revealed when effects of such variables as stimulus duration and luminance are examined. Studies of visual persistence have required subjects to perform tasks such as altering the temporal occurrence of an auditory tone until it aligns either with the apparent onset or offset of the display. The difference in time between the apparent onset and offset could then be taken to indicate the apparent duration of the display (e.g. Haber & Standing, 1970). Using this type of measure, it has been found that persistence is inversely related to the duration and luminance of the display (Haber & Standing, 1970). That is, persistence seems to decrease as a display is presented for longer durations and as it becomes brighter. On the other hand, studies have shown either no relationship between partial report superiority, and display duration and brightness (see Eriksen & Rohrbaugh, 1970, Scharf & Lefton, 1970, for studies of brightness effects; and DiLollo, 1978; Sperling, 1960, for studies of effects of display duration) or a positive relation with partial report superiority (partial report superiority is increased with bright displays providing the background is dim, see Adelson & Jonides, 1980; Long & Beaton, 1982). This suggests that visual persistence and partial report superiority are determined by quite different factors (although see Long & McCarthy, 1982).

It thus seems over-simple to attribute all the phenomena of very short-term visual *remembering* to the same kind of uninterpreted sensory buffer *store*. Although there are good grounds for proposing such a precategorical sensory icon, we must look elsewhere for an explanation of the partial report superiority effect. Coltheart (1983) suggests that partial report cues should be seen as operating on the *postcategorical* stage at which items have been identified, with the cue influencing transfer from this postcategorical stage to a response buffer. Coltheart (1983) identifies this postcategorical stage with the "object files" proposed by Kahneman and Treisman (1983) to which we referred in Chapter 5. Their proposal is that, when an object or event is first registered, a "file" specifying the location and time is opened, and as information about the sensory and semantic features of the object becomes available, so it is slotted into place within the file. On this view, the "icon" provides the sensory raw material from which object files can be constructed, but partial report cues are seen as allowing selectivity at the level of *object files* rather than at the level of the icon. This conception of the postcategorical stage is important, and we will return to consider it again in our discussion of "short-term visual memory" and "imagery" later. Whatever the ultimate explanation for the partial report superiority effect, however, it seems that phenomena at the level of visual sensory memory must be distinguished from those of some more durable, "post-iconic" visual memory that we discuss next.

POST-ICONIC, SHORT-TERM VISUAL MEMORY

The properties of what we will term a "short-term visual store" (STVS) were probably first explored by Posner and his associates, using verbal materials (e.g. Posner & Keele, 1967; Posner, Boies, Eichelman, & Taylor, 1969). Posner and Keele (1967) demonstrated the persistence of a visual code for at least 1.5sec after stimulus presentation, using a letter-matching task in which sequentially presented, letter pairs were to be judged as "same" or "different". "Same" pairs might be physically identical (*A* followed by *A*), or the same in name only (*A* followed by *a*). Posner and Keele found that reaction times (RTs) to respond "same" were made considerably more quickly to physically identical than nominally identical pairs, if the interval between first and second members was very small, but this advantage declined as interstimulus interval (ISI) was increased. At about 1.5sec ISI, name matches and physical matches took the same time to perform. They explained this by suggesting that there were two different codes which could be used to make the match: a "visual" code and a "name" code. The visual code declined over the first second or two following presentation, whereas the name code took some time to establish. Physically identical letters could be quickly matched on the basis of the visual code, whereas nominally identical letters could only be matched by means of the name code. As this took time to establish, name matches would be slower than physical matches. However, as the visual code decayed, later matches must be made on the basis of the name code alone, and thus would not be sensitive to the physical similarity of the to-be-matched items. As Phillips and Baddeley (1971) pointed out, however, the observation that matches made at ISIs of over 1.5sec are insensitive to physical form does not necessarily mean that the visual code has faded—merely that the name code has become the more efficient basis for the decision for whatever reason. Indeed, Posner and Keele (1967) demonstrated that if subjects were encouraged by the task demands to attend to the physical form of each letter, the visual code could persist for considerably longer.

Kroll and his associates (Kroll et al., 1970; Parks, Kroll, Salzberg, & Parkinson, 1972) have also demonstrated persistence of a code preserving the visual form of letters for up to 25sec. Kroll et al. (1970) found that visually presented letters were better recalled than auditorally presented ones, when the delay was filled with an auditory shadowing task which interferes with phonemic coding and rehearsal. For example, Kroll et al. (1970) presented a single letter to be remembered on each trial, and recall was tested after 1, 10, or 25sec. In the auditory target condition, the letter was heard in a male voice, whereas in the visual target condition it was briefly flashed on to a screen. In both conditions, these presentations were superimposed upon a continuous shadowing task which involved shadowing letter names spoken by a female voice at a rate of two per second. When recall of the target letter was tested one second after presentation, there was no difference between the auditory and visual presentation, showing that both led to equally good *perception* of the target letter. At 25 seconds delay, however, an auditorally presented target letter was only recalled correctly on 40% of trials, whereas visual presentation led to 67% correct trials. The difference must be due to retention of the visual form of the letter in the visual presentation condition. Parks et al. (1972) confirmed this interpretation in a matching task rather like Posner and Keele's. With an 8sec delay between letter-pairs, which was filled with an auditory shadowing task, an advantage was observed for physical over name matches, demonstrating again the persistence of the visual code.

Phillips (Phillips & Baddeley, 1971; Phillips, 1974) has investigated the properties of short-term visual memory in more detail, using non-verbal materials which are not easily described in words to minimise the contribution played by verbal memory. In an elegant series of experiments, Phillips (1974) was able to distinguish clearly between the properties of STVS and of iconic memory. In these studies the task was to say whether two sequentially presented matrices of black and white squares were the

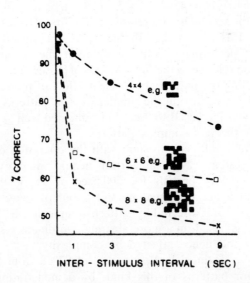

FIG. 6.1. The percentage of correct "same-different" responses as a function of inter-stimulus interval (ISI) and matrix size. (Reproduced with permission from Phillips, 1974; Experiment I.)

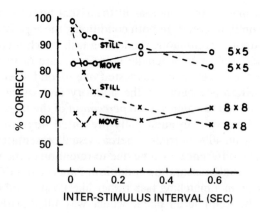

FIG. 6.2. The percentage of correct "same-different" responses as a function of ISI, matrix size, and movement. (Reproduced with permission from Phillips, 1974; Experiment II.)

same, or differed. Where there was a difference, this was in just one of the squares, making the task quite a difficult one when the matrices used were large. Phillips varied matrix complexity (from 4 × 4 to 8 × 8 matrices), and examined how accurately subjects could perform this task at different ISIs. Although performance dropped to chance quite rapidly with the most complex (8 × 8) matrices, performance on the simpler matrices was well above chance even at delays of 9sec (see Fig. 6.1). In a second experiment, Phillips varied matrix complexity (5 × 5 and 8 × 8 patterns were used), ISI, and location of the second matrix relative to the first. His results are shown in Fig. 6.2. At ISIs of less than 0.5sec, there was no effect of pattern complexity, but performance was disrupted if the second matrix was shifted in location relative to the first. At ISIs of 0.5sec and over, there was no effect of shifting the pattern, but a clear effect of pattern complexity, with much higher accuracy on the simpler (4 × 4) patterns. Performance declined as ISI was increased to 9sec, but remained well above chance at this interval for the less complex patterns.

This pattern of results is consistent with the operation of two distinct visual memory systems, a precategorical "iconic" memory system, and STVS. Iconic memory persists for 500msec or so, is tied to retinal coordinates (and hence disrupted by shift), but of relatively unlimited capacity, and hence not affected by pattern complexity. STVS is of much longer duration, is based on a more abstract coordinate system, but is of limited capacity and hence affected by complexity.

Phillips has also distinguished properties of STVS from those of long-term memory for patterns of this kind, by demonstrating a one item "recency effect" when a list of matrices is presented for retention (Phillips & Christie, 1977; Phillips, 1983). In verbal memory, the recency effect in free recall (Murdock, 1962) is the advantage in recall accuracy for the last few words of a list, which has usually been attributed to the temporary residence of these items in some kind of "short-term" memory store. Consistent with this, the recency effect is removed if subjects are prevented from rehearsing by performing a mental arithmetic task, although performance on earlier list items is unaffected by this rehearsal. Conversely, speeding up presentation of the list reduces recall probability for the majority of list items but has no effect on the recency portion of the serial recall curve (see Baddeley, 1976, for a review).

In visual memory, Phillips and Christie (1977) showed that if subjects were asked whether a particular matrix was the same as, or differed in one square from, one of the matrices in a sequence they had seen, performance was greatly superior for the last matrix in the series, whereas all earlier ones produced roughly similar, but considerably lower, accuracy. This advantage to the last item was removed if the subject was distracted by performance of a mental arithmetic task, but such distraction had no effect on performance on non-final items. Conversely, speeding up the overall presentation rate of the list reduced performance on other list members, but had no effect on the final item. These results are consistent with the retention of the most recent matrix in a short-term visual memory store, whose contents are disrupted by tasks involving some kind of visuo-spatial component (see Phillips, 1983), with other list members retained in some longer-term visual memory which is not susceptible to such interference. We will return to consider the nature of this long-term memory later in the chapter.

The STVS studied by Phillips appears to be a memory in which recent visual events are actively *visualised,* just as the short-term store (STS) of the traditional "modal" model of verbal memory was a store in which verbal information was maintained through rehearsal. Indeed, the properties of STVS which we have here described mesh well with those which might be attributed to the "visuo-spatial scratch pad" in Baddeley and Hitch's (1974) "Working Memory" model of short-term retention. Baddeley and Hitch (see also Baddeley, 1986) have proposed that performance in a variety of short-term memory and comprehension tasks can be accounted for by the action and storage capacity of a general purpose *central executive* combined with one or more modality specific "slave" storage systems. The *articulatory loop* provides additional storage for phonemic material, whereas the *visuo-spatial scratch pad* (VSSP) is proposed as the equivalent "shelf" on which visual information can be temporarily stored.

Such a distinction between a short-term store for phonemic material and one for visuo-spatial information is supported by the results of an experiment by Brooks (1968). In one condition of Brooks' experiment, subjects had to make a series of decisions about the parts of speech represented by each word in a memorised sentence such as: "A bird in the hand is not in the bush" (e.g. say "yes" if each word is a noun, otherwise say "no"). In another condition, they made decisions about the nature of corners of a memorised block letter (e.g. say "yes" if each corner touches the top or bottom of a box imagined to enclose the block letter, otherwise say "no"). Subjects signalled their responses either by speaking ("yes" or "no") or by pointing to a Y or an N. Brooks found that responding to the imagined block letters was seriously disrupted by pointing, and responding to the sentences was disrupted (although less dramatically) by speaking. Both these effects were shown relative to a control condition where responses were tapped. The pattern of interference suggested that the memorised sentences were being held in a store which was used in the planning and execution of speech (as the articulatory loop is held to do), whereas the imagined letters were held in a store sharing something with processes involved in visual search.

A similar dissocation between the processes underlying visual and verbal memory has more recently been demonstrated by Logie (1986). He found that concurrent presentation of irrelevant visual patterns disrupted the recall of words using an imagery mnemonic, but not their recall using rote rehearsal, whereas concurrent presentation of irrelevant words affected the rote recall task but not the use of imagery. This suggests that presentation of irrelevant visual patterns has a similar effect on the VSSP as articulation of irrelevant words ("the the the") has on the articulatory loop component of working memory. The generation and rehearsal of the images used in the pegword mnemonic technique is thought to make use of the VSSP which irrelevant patterns may selectively disrupt.

The VSSP appears to be more *spatial* than *visual*, as demonstrated by Baddeley and Lieberman (1980). They asked subjects to learn verbal material which could be organised into a spatial matrix—a task devised by Brooks (1967) (e.g. "In the starting square put a 1, in the next square up put a 2, in the next square to the right put a 3 . . ." etc.). Subjects are asked to repeat back this material, and their performance is used as an index of visuo-spatial memory. Baddeley and Lieberman found that performance was not disrupted by a concurrent brightness judgement task (a pure "visual" task) but was disrupted by a concurrent auditory tracking task (a pure "spatial" task), where the blindfolded subject was required to track with a torch a pendulum bob which emitted a steady tone.

Thus, there is strong evidence from a number of different experimental paradigms for the short-term retention of the physical appearance of a display, which is apparently distinct from short-term verbal memory, and from iconic and long-term visual memory. The short-term visual store apparently requires active attention for its maintenance, and seems to play an important role in active visualisation and imagery. It is tempting to attribute all manifestations of visual memory in the short term to a common store—most plausibly that labelled STVS (which we have in turn identified with Baddeley's VSSP). However, there is now a good deal of evidence which shows that short-term visual memory effects may be obtained more passively, without involving active visualisation, and may not always be subject to interference. Using a serial classification task, in which subjects respond positively if each item is, say, an A or an R, and negatively if an E or an N, Walker and Marshall (1982), and Kroll and Ramskov (1984) have found that there is greater short-term facilitation when successive letters are identical in case than when they agree in name alone. Such an effect, reminiscent of that shown by Posner and Keele, is found even if there is a predictable, but irrelevant, visual item between the repetitions, and in a situation where active matching and rehearsal strategies are unlikely to be employed. From the subjects' point of view, they are responding to a series of independent visual events, so that the task demands are quite unlike those of a same-different matching task. In this case, the facilitation seems more likely to be due to the recent activation of the durable structural descriptions used to recognise particular letters, than to active visualisation in STVS. We will return to elaborate upon this distinction later in this section and again in our discussion of imagery.

So far we have discussed the short-term retention, whether active or passive, of letter shapes or meaningless two-dimensional patterns. These are materials that we may need to recognise (as readers, for example), but with which we do not usually interact. Neither kind of material is typical of the kind of visual object we deal with in everyday life, which we must know how to approach or to avoid, to grasp or to throw. As we discussed in earlier chapters of this book, different kinds of activities may require the construction of different kinds of representation (for example, viewer-centred for guiding action, but, perhaps, object-centred for recognition), and these different representations might be expected to be remembered differently too. In order to explore the breadth of potential visual "memories" in the short term, we need to investigate short-term retention of the appearances of *objects,* not letters and patterns.

Bartram (1976) asked subjects to judge the sameness or difference of pairs of pictured objects. "Same" pairs could show identical viewpoints, different views of the same object, or two different objects sharing the same name. When photographs of common objects were used, Bartram found that there was virtually no difference in matching latency between identical and changed viewpoints, but both were faster than matching different objects with the same name. This effect was found at interstimulus intervals of 2sec and 25sec. (Uncommon objects gave a different pattern, showing a big advantage for identical viewpoints, but Bartram attributes this to visual confusability between the particular uncommon objects he selected.) When line-drawings of objects were used, with an interval of 1.5sec between the first and second members of each pair,

Bartram found a reliable advantage for identical pictures compared with different views. He suggested that his results could be explained in terms of the availability of three different types of code—a "pictorial" or literal description of a particular picture (which we might equate with a viewer-centred visual description), which Bartram suggests is generated for line-drawn but not photographed objects, an "object" level code (which we might equate with an object-centred visual description), and a non-visual semantic level code, at which two different objects sharing the same name would be equivalent.

More recently, Ellis and Allport (1985) have used a same-different matching task to demonstrate apparently differential decay rates for viewer-centred and object-centred representations of photographs of common objects. As in Bartram's task, subjects had to match successively presented items if these had the same name, but here the items to be matched were all photographed objects. As in Bartram's study, "same" trials could result from two identical photographs, from two photographs of the object taken from different angles, or from two photographs of objects which share the same name (e.g. two clocks). At short ISIs (100msec), the task was performed quickest in the identical photographs condition, with object matches in turn faster than name matches. However, with an ISI of 2sec, the advantage of identical over object-match pairs almost disappeared, while that of object-match over name-match persisted. The pattern at 2sec ISI matches that found by Bartram (1976) for common objects. Taken together, the results of these two separate studies provide quite strong evidence for the independence of viewer-centred from object-centred visual codes. Additionally, Ellis and Allport (1985) found in a second experiment that although the identical view benefit was eliminated by a pattern mask intervening between a pair of pictures, the object-match benefit was unaffected by the presence of the mask, providing even stronger evidence for the independence of these codes.

Whereas the kind of task used by Bartram and by Ellis and Allport might encourage the active retention of different visual codes, Marshall and Walker (1987) have shown repetition effects in serial classification tasks, which should minimise explicit matching strategies, using pictures of easily nameable objects. Subjects pressed one key if each object was a doll or a shoe, and another if each was a rabbit or a chair. Successive items could show the same object, a different object sharing the same name (i.e. a different rabbit), or a different object sharing the same response. Their results showed greatest facilitation if identical pictures were repeated, less if different views of the same object were repeated, and less still if different objects sharing the same name were repeated (compared with response repetition alone), suggesting distinct influences at the level of "visual" (viewer-centred), "object" (object-centred), and "name" codes. As in effects gained in similar tasks with letters, these effects appeared not to be disrupted by the presentation of a predictable, but irrelevant visual object, although the facilitation by identical pictures appeared to be reduced if an unpredictable visual event intervened.

How should we interpret such apparently passive short-term visual memory effects? One possibility would be to suggest (cf. Phillips, 1983) that there are two kinds of short-term visual memory effect: one due to active visualisation, the other due to effects of the restitution of letter or object identification procedures. Thus, just as it became clear in the study of verbal memory that studies of short-term verbal memory tapped both "STS" and "LTS" components, so we must distinguish different possible sources of effects in short-term visual memory tasks.

Of what use are these short-term visual memories in our everyday activities? One possibility is that STVS plays a role very like a "scratch pad"—used for constructing, maintaining, and manipulating images of things present as well as things remembered. We will return to consider this in more detail later, where we examine different theories of mental imagery. An additional possible role is suggested by the work of Thomson (1983) on the visual guidance of locomotion. He found that subjects who were shown a target that they had to walk, or run to, without vision, could get there accurately if the target could be reached within 8sec. If it could not—either because it was too far, or because a delay was introduced between viewing the target and setting out to reach it—the subjects got lost. These results are compatible with the storage of the target's location in a short-term visual memory which can be maintained for 8sec or so. Such a system may be an essential component in our everyday navigation, allowing us to remember the layouts of parts of the world that we are not currently looking at. In this respect, active visualisation may involve a representational system *beyond* that of the 2½D sketch and 3D models suggested by Marr (1982) (see Chapters 2 and 3). Marr suggested in his book that, once recognised via object-centred models, object descriptions would need to be appended to a current model of the scene, centred on the viewer. Such a scene model would be viewer-centred but, unlike the 2½D sketch, non-retinotopic and *interpreted*, and it may be that some of the experiments on STVS demonstrate the maintenance of a representation such as this.

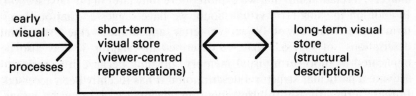

FIG. 6.3.   The short-term visual store can be seen as a buffer within which viewer-centred representations are constructed of scene features and object identities.

We can summarise these ideas in a simple model (Fig. 6.3) in which we identify "STVS" with a viewer-centred buffer in which representations are constructed of current surface layout and into which representations of recognised objects can be written from the store of structural descriptions. Such a suggestion is very consistent with proposals elsewhere in the literature. For example, at the end of the section on iconic memory we raised the possibility that the partial report superiority advantage arose because of an effect at the level of a post-iconic stage which Coltheart likened to Kahneman and Treisman's "object files". Our STVS system could be thought of in these terms. In the early stages of constructing an object file it will contain representations of what "features" are where in the world—where features may include intrinsic surface properties. However, once enough features are assembled, structural descriptions in long-term memory can be accessed and the objects at different locations identified. At that point, their semantic descriptions can be added to the object files to produce a representation of *what* objects are *where* in the world. We are suggesting, then, that viewer-centred representations of the current visual scene be regarded as the locus of STVS effects, that they require attention for active maintenance, and that they may contain either categorised or uncategorised information. The apparently *spatial* rather than *visual* nature of the store may be due to the primary role played by spatial location in integrating representations for each "object file". In the later section on imagery we will introduce further evidence suggesting that imagery results from activation within such a spatially organised visual buffer, consistent with this interpretation. Such an account still leaves some loose ends, however. For example, Ellis and Allport found the identical view benefit in object-matching was removed by a pattern mask whereas Phillips (1974) has shown that masking affects iconic storage but not STVS. Further elaboration of the model will be needed to explain such discrepancies.

The above paragraph has suggested that STVS is involved in active visualisation, which may be useful for imagining things which are not present in the visual scene, and for integrating and retaining a representation of things which are currently present in the visual scene. Such a position hints at a close relationship between visual *perception* and visual *imagery*, a relationship that we explore more fully later in the next section. In addition to short-term visualisation, we have suggested that our long-term representations of object or letter appearances (the "structural descriptions" of Fig. 6.3 that we described in Chapter 3) may also be implicated in short-term visual memory, possibly because it is easier to activate a particular structural description if it has recently been accessed. In these terms, the short-term repetition advantages observed by researchers such as Marshall and Walker (1987) in tasks where there is no explicit memory component are similar to longer-term repetition priming effects mentioned in Chapter 3 (where, for example, repetition effects are greater if the same view of an object is repeated than if a different view reappears). The limited, short-lived nature of the effects found in the serial choice reaction time tasks mentioned in this chapter may be a consequence of the restricted range of different items appearing in these tasks, rather than reflecting any fundamentally different mechanism to that revealed in longer-term repetition priming (see Roberts & Bruce, 1989, for further evidence and discussion). It remains to be seen whether the repetition effects observed in more "active" matching tasks, such as those of Ellis and Allport, are better understood in terms of re-activation of structural descriptions or active visualisation at the level of the visual buffer we have termed STVS.

VISUAL IMAGERY

It has been implicit in our discussion so far in this book that representations, whether of spatial structures, or of semantic states, are all comprised of symbolic propositions. A representation of an object's appearance might contain the proposition that one part *is next to* another part of the object, and so, in this sense, *represents* its spatial arrangement, but we have not at any point proposed that elements of the representation which describe adjacent regions are physically closer to one another than are elements which describe distant regions. It is not in the nature of propositional representations to mirror spatial arrangements in such a way.

The recent resurgence of interest in the properties of visual imagery has, however, given rise to a furious debate between those who claim that all knowledge is ultimately represented in propositional format (e.g. Pylyshyn, 1973; 1981), and those who claim that the recent study of images reveals that visual information may be represented in a fundamentally different format from that used for linguistic information (e.g. Paivio, 1971; Shepard, 1978; Kosslyn, 1981). Writers such as Paivio have argued that images are represented quite differently from words, and that mental images are *analogue* or "picture-like" representations. Such a position would maintain that in an image of a horse, for example, sizes and distances are preserved, so the image of the horse's tail is further from the image of its muzzle than is the image of its ears. The "mind's eye" can inspect an image just as the real eye can inspect a real picture, and, for example, will take longer to scan a larger distance across such an image, than a shorter distance.

The "imagery" position is based on more than the introspective quality of imagery. Recent years have seen a number of demonstrations of imagery phenomena which seem to demand an explanation in terms of analogue representations. Perhaps the most famous demonstrations are those of Shepard and his colleagues on "mental rotation". The now classic

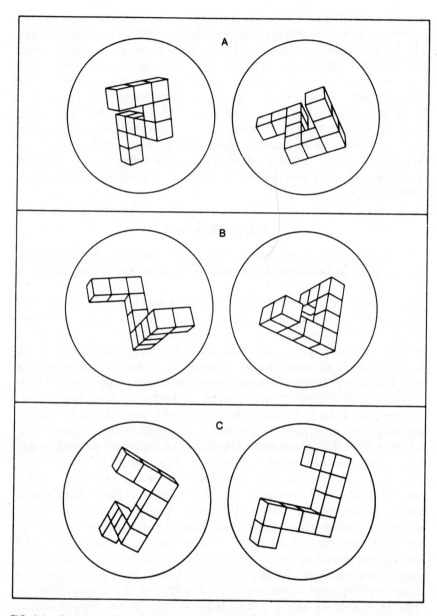

FIG. 6.4. Examples of the 3D stimulus pairs used by Shepard and Metzler (1971). Panel A shows a "same" pair differing by an 80° rotation in the picture plane. Panel B shows a "same" pair differing by an 80° rotation in the depth plane. Panel C shows a "different" pair where the objects drawn have different "handedness". They differ by a reflection as well as a rotation. (Reproduced from Shepard & Metzler, 1971, with permission.)

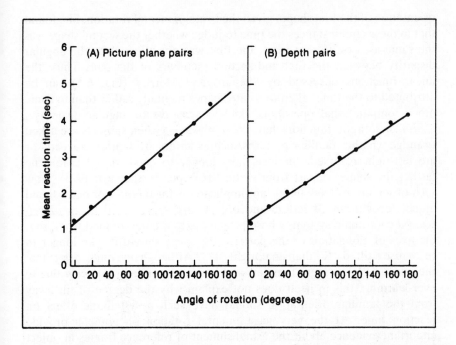

FIG. 6.5.   The mean RTs to respond "same" to pairs of objects as a function of the angle of rotation between the pair. Panel A shows the results for rotations within the picture plane (cf. Fig. 6.4A) and panel B shows the results for depth rotations (cf. Fig. 6.4B). (Reproduced from Shepard & Metzler, 1971, with permission.)

experiments of Shepard and Metzler (1971) involved asking subjects to decide as quickly as possible whether two complex block structures (e.g. see Fig. 6.4) were the same or different. Where the structures were different, their "handedness" differed, so that one member of the pair could not be superimposed on the other. Shepard and Metzler varied the orientation in which one member of the pair was presented relative to the other—and found that subjects' decision times were a simple linear function of the orientation difference between the two shapes (see Fig. 6.5). It was as if subjects were "mentally" rotating one shape to bring it into alignment with the other. Like physical rotation, mental rotation takes longer the further the distance involved, suggesting an internal imagery space with analogical properties.

To check this interpretation of the data, Metzler (1973) conducted an experiment in which she first determined each subject's rate of mental rotation (Fig. 6.5, for example, shows the average rate of rotation to be around 55 degrees per second). In the next part of the experiment, she showed subjects one shape of a pair and instructed them to begin rotating it in a particular direction. She then presented a test shape in a different orientation, at the time that the subjects should have "arrived" at the same orientation of the first shape, given their rate of mental rotation. She found that in these circumstances the time to judge whether the second shape was the same as, or different from, the first was not affected by the angular disparity between the first and second members of the pair. Thus, the linear functions observed by Shepard and Metzler (Fig. 6.5) can be attributed to the time taken to rotate shapes mentally rather than to some other computational operation which is sensitive to angular disparity.

Similar rotation functions have been observed when subjects are asked to judge whether familiar patterns such as letters are written correctly or are left-right reversed. Subjects take longer to make this decision the farther the shapes depart from vertical (Cooper & Shepard, 1973). Now such observations have important implications for theories of pattern and object recognition. If letters and objects are represented in an *object-centred* coordinate system, whose primary axes are determined from, say, the axes of elongation of the pattern, then why should it take longer to recognise a tilted "R" than an upright "R"? Although one might argue that the upright "R" is more familiar, and hence responded to quickly due to over-learning, this in itself does not explain why the degree of tilt away from the familiar orientation should have such a systematic effect on reaction time. At the very least, mental rotation phenomena provide important evidence about the establishment of reference frames in object perception (cf. Chapter 3).

Other experiments have suggested analogical representation of object shapes and sizes. Paivio (1975a) reported experiments in which subjects were asked which of two labelled or pictured objects was the larger in real life. He showed, first, that such questions could be answered more quickly if the items were pictured rather than labelled, and secondly, that answers were given more quickly the greater the physical difference between the objects in life, an effect called the "symbolic distance" effect. So subjects would be faster to decide that a car is bigger than an ant, than to decide that a car is bigger than a dog. Thirdly, he found that such decisions could be interfered with if the pictured objects were drawn in sizes which were incongruent with their real sizes. Thus, if the picture of the car was drawn smaller than the picture of the dog, this slowed up subjects' decisions. This was no mere Stroop-like effect, as it was not found if the words which labelled the objects were written in incongruently sized letters: Subjects were not slowed if "car" was written in tiny letters and "dog" in huge ones (see Fig. 6.6). It seems that the effects with pictures are due to interference between the literal form of the depicted object, and its stored appearance, suggesting to Paivio that the stored appearances shared pictorial properties.

These demonstrations by Paivio are compelling, but later results are more perplexing in terms of imaginal coding. Effects of presentation material, and/or of symbolic distance, reported earlier for size judgements have been repeated for more abstract qualities such as pleasantness and monetary value (Paivio, 1978), ferocity (Kerst & Howard, 1977), and intelligence (Banks & Flora, 1977). For all these examples, decisions can be made more quickly if the items are pictured, and Kerst and Howard (1977) additionally showed a symbolic distance effect in judgements of ferocity. If it were the case that every semantic judgement produced such a pattern, we could argue that the results reflect properties of an amodal semantic system which pictures contact more directly than words. However, te Linde (1982) has shown that whereas judgements of relative size are made more quickly from pairs of pictures, judgements of associative relatedness are not. Paivio and his colleagues (e.g. Paivio, 1978) thus argue that the results show how qualities such as size, intelligence, and ferocity are also encoded in the imaginal representations, in a manner quite distinct from the encoding of verbal meaning. [Paivio's position here strongly resembles that of researchers such as Warrington & Shallice (1984) (see Chapter 3) who have argued for a separation between "visual" and "verbal" semantic systems in order to account for patterns of impairment in some patients. In Chapter 3 we argued that the distinction should be made between a store of visual appearances of objects and an *amodal* semantic memory system. We should acknowledge at this point that the pattern of symbolic distance effects does not mesh well with the kinds of information which we would see as represented in "appearances" of visual objects, and thus provides a potential challenge to our theoretical position in this text.]

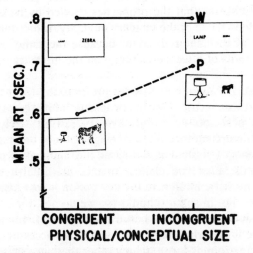

FIG. 6.6. RTs for deciding which of two presented objects is the larger in real life. The solid line shows the times to respond to word pairs, where it makes no difference whether the words are written in sizes which are congruent or incongruent with the decision. The dashed line shows the results with pictures. Decisions are made more quickly to pairs of pictures than pairs of words, but are slowed if the pictures of the objects are drawn in sizes incongruent with their real sizes. (Reproduced from Paivio, 1975b, with permission.)

Kosslyn and his colleagues have produced numerous further demonstrations that visual imagery shares properties with visual perception. Thus, as examples, subjects are slower to make judgements about images when they have been instructed to make the images small in size (Kosslyn, 1975), and they are slower to make judgements about items further from a specified focus point in an image (Kosslyn, 1973). For example, if instructed to image an elephant and focus on its tusks, subjects are faster to verify that an elephant has ears than that it has a tail—consistent with them having to scan to a more distant point in their image.

There is, then, a large amount of quite compelling evidence showing both that representations used in imagery share properties in common with pictures, and that inspecting mental images shares properties in common with visual scanning. Experiments already mentioned in this chapter which show apparent dissociations between processes of visual imagery and verbal short-term memory are clearly also of relevance here (e.g. Brooks, 1968; Logie, 1986). Indeed, Kosslyn (1976) was able to push this dissociation even further to show different properties emerging as a function of different instructions to his subjects, who were asked to decide whether certain statements were true or false (e.g. a bee has a sting; a cat has whiskers). If subjects were specifically instructed to form images as an aid to verifying the propositions, then subjects were faster to verify propositions containing larger (perceptually more salient) features (e.g. a cat has a head). But if no imagery instructions were given, subjects were faster to verify propositions with high associative strengths (e.g. a cat has whiskers). Thus, it seems that the properties studied by Kosslyn and his colleagues are indeed those of the imagery modality, rather than reflecting some peculiarity of the materials used, because the same materials can give different patterns of effects depending on the modality in which they are being tested.

Although Shepard, Paivio, and Kosslyn prefer to interpret these effects in terms of the intrinsic pictorial/spatial properties of images, this view has been challenged, most notably by Pylyshyn (1973; 1981). Pylyshyn claims that imagery is an epiphenomenon, and images cannot be in any way like "pictures in the head". Pylyshyn has criticised the dual-coding position on a number of grounds. First, he claims, images are interpreted wholes, whereas pictures must be interpreted. Information is lost from images in meaningful chunks, not in spatial chunks (so we do not, for example, lose the "corners" of images as in dog-eared photographs). Images must be interpreted symbolic descriptions if they are to be accessed and used—there must be some grounds for searching other than an exhaustive search through a library of photographs. Furthermore, if images were like pictures, then their storage would be unparsimonious. A catalogue of photographs, according to Pylyshyn, would use up the storage capacity of the brain. (This argument is one of Pylyshyn's least persuasive ones—the representation of even a simple picture in propositional terms is an immense and complex structure— it is not at all clear that propositions are any more parsimonious.)

How, however, can Pylyshyn account for the experimental evidence which seems so convincingly to point to some "analogue" medium? He argues (e.g. 1981) that imagery phenomena do not reflect properties of the medium but of tacit knowledge of the world. Imagery is "cognitively penetrable", it can be influenced by a subject's beliefs and desires. When subjects apparently rotate mental images, they are making use of their knowledge of the physical act of rotation in the performance of the task. It takes longer to rotate an image 180° than 45° because subjects believe that it should.

Pylyshyn thus argues that all information, whether verbal or pictorial, is represented in the same format: Modality free propositions. The representations which underlie our experience of mental images are symbolic *descriptions* of the structures which we imagine. Images can only *represent* qualities like distance, not have them as intrinsic qualities. Do we really want to explain Paivio's results by saying that our representation of an elephant is physically larger than our representation of a mouse? And how *can* an imaginal representation capture abstract values such as intelligence or ferocity?

Which position is correct? Anderson (1978) points out that it is not possible to explain any cognitive act by the nature of the representation alone. What provides an explanation is a specification of both the representation, and the processes which are held to act upon it. Once one realises that a theory comprises a representation-process pair, it becomes possible in principle, according to Anderson, to mimic any "propositional" theory with an "imagery" theory. Therefore, he suggests that the debate cannot be decided on the basis of behavioural data alone—we must await an argument in terms of brain physiology, or resort to principles of parsimony, in order to reveal the "truth".

Johnson-Laird (1983) also rejects the debate as meaningless. Although he acknowledges that at some (perhaps physiological) level, the code that the brain uses may be "truly" symbolic, he claims that such a level of description is not one which serves any useful role in cognition. What is important is not what the representations *really* are, but what functions they serve. He uses the analogy of an "array" in a computer program:

> an array is a structure in which elements can be accessed and updated by giving appropriate ordered sequences of integers corresponding to coordinate values...There is, of course, no corresponding physical array of locations in the computer. That would be wholly unnecessary. All that matters is that the physical embodiment should *function* as an array. Its elements can be accessed as an array, and its contents displayed or manipulated as an array. (1983, p.153)

At the level of useful description, he finds it sensible to distinguish representations which preserve spatial information (which he calls mental models) from those which do not, and claims that a mental image is a particular view of a mental model. Such a perspective makes it perfectly legitimate to investigate the functional properties of such representations, and how they are accessed and generated. Indeed, as we elaborate later, Kosslyn (1981) has produced a computational theory of image generation and use, which is implemented on a computer, whose machine code is undoubtedly discrete symbolic. His computational experiments are entirely justifiable within the framework suggested by Johnson-Laird.

In an excellent overview of the debate surrounding visual imagery, Pinker (1985) contrasts what he terms "structural description" theories of imagery (e.g. Pylyshyn) with "array" theories (e.g. Kosslyn). He lists a number of properties of imagery which the structural description position cannot readily account for. For example, he points out that imagery is subject to certain constraints—we cannot, for example, imagine two adjacent objects without imagining one to the left of the other, nor can we imagine the front and the back of an object simultaneously. This contrasts with our long-term memory for visual objects, where, as we shall see, it is quite possible to remember what was in a picture but not where it was.

It seems then that it is useful to consider images as a distinct form of representation in terms of their *functional* role in cognition as well as in terms of their *properties*. But can we go further, and understand in more detail how images are generated and used, and the relationship between visual imagery and visual perception? Recently, computer simulation and neuropsychological experiments have considerably advanced our theoretical understanding of imagery.

DISORDERS OF VISUAL IMAGERY

We noted in Chapter 5 that patients with visual neglect can have problems with imagery as well as with visual recognition tasks (as in the Piazza del Duomo example we described on p.160). Possibly visual imagery may tap many of the same processes as those mediating visual perception (e.g. Finke, 1980, 1985; Shepard, 1984). One way to examine this is to assess whether patients with visual recognition problems have coincident problems in visual imagery (e.g. Farah, 1984).

Interestingly, many patients with visual agnosia also seem to have problems in visual imagery. At an anecdotal level, patients sometimes report the loss of visual images in dreams (e.g. Nielsen, 1955). More formally, patients may be unable to draw, or describe from memory, objects that they fail to recognise. For instance, Beyn and Knyazeva (1962) report an agnosic patient who could recognise 13 out of 16 objects that he reported he could image, but of a further 16 objects that he said he could *not* image, he only recognised three.

This co-occurrence of visual recognition and imagery problems is most evident in patients who seem to have impaired visual knowledge about objects (see Chapter 3, p.57). Thus, these patients can have problems both identifying certain types of object, and defining them from memory. They also have problems answering visual, but not verbal, definitions (Silveri & Gainotti, 1988), consistent with the deficit being confined to the retrieval of stored visual knowledge.

Imagery and recognition problems can also co-occur in patients with apparently intact visual knowledge when the visual recognition system becomes "disconnected" from the semantic system. In Chapter 3 we suggested that J.B. (Riddoch & Humphreys, 1987b) had a problem accessing semantics from vision. He was also extremely poor at imagery tasks. Drawing from memory was practically impossible although he could copy adequately (see Fig. 6.7). Even when partially complete drawings were given to him and he was asked to draw in the missing part (see Fig. 6.8), he was very impaired (even if he could identify what the object was). On such occasions J.B. stated (with some accuracy):"I know what it is—I just can't picture it".

Because recognition deficits due to problems in the representation or access of stored visual knowledge co-occur with imagery problems, we can propose that visual recognition and imagery tap a *common* store of visual knowledge about object appearances. When we image "a horse" we are summoning up in the mind's eye the structural description that allows us to recognise a horse. One aspect of visual knowledge about objects—knowledge of their colours—can apparently be selectively impaired in visual imagery, and visual recognition. Patient H.J.A. (Humphreys & Riddoch, 1987a) whom we described in Chapters 3 and 5, has a visual object recognition problem that appears to be due to deficient visual grouping processes rather than any impairment to his store of visual appearances of objects. However, H.J.A. is also achromatopsic (see Chapter 2), and is relatively poor at retrieving and imaging colour information about objects. For instance, he stated that an elephant was green and a polar bear grey. It may be that H.J.A. has lost stored visual knowledge about colour, and that this jointly affects colour recognition and colour imagery in much the same way as disordered knowledge about the structural characteristics of objects jointly affects object recognition and imagery tasks (see earlier). Importantly, however, *spatial* aspects of imagery are intact in this patient. H.J.A. can recall routes from memory and mentally rotate letters.

Other patients may have impaired spatial imagery processes with apparently intact stores of visual knowledge about objects. Consistent with this, not all patients with imagery problems are agnosic. Levine, Wallach, and Farah (1985) describe a patient who, following parieto-occipital damage, was unable to perform many tasks requiring the coding of relative

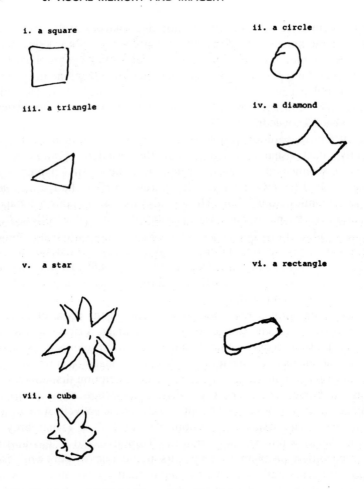

i. a square

ii. a circle

iii. a triangle

iv. a diamond

v. a star

vi. a rectangle

vii. a cube

FIG. 6.7. Examples of JB's drawings of familiar shapes from memory.

spatial locations in images. He could not describe the relative locations of cities in the U.S.A., of landmarks in his neighbourhood, or the furniture in his hospital room when blindfolded. However, he could give detailed descriptions of the appearances of objects. Apparently this patient had good long-term visual knowledge of objects, and may even have been able to image single objects (given his good descriptions of them). We may thus distinguish stored visual knowledge from the representation of visual images. Possibly stored visual knowledge takes the form of a structural description that is retrieved and then represented in some more explicitly *spatial* form in an image.

Kosslyn's (1981; 1983) model of imagery also suggests such a distinction. In this model, Kosslyn distinguishes short-term and long-term memory

FIG. 6.8. Examples of incomplete drawings given to J.B.

structures involved in imagery. The short-term structure is the *"visual buffer"*, the medium of mental imagery within which images are constructed and maintained. It is explicitly spatial, as it functions as a coordinate space or "array" of locations. Within long-term memory there are lists of *facts* about objects and stores of the *appearances* of objects. Kosslyn maintains that the appearances stored are "literal" and suggests that appearances are stored as lists of coordinates indicating where points should be placed in the visual buffer to depict the stored pattern. Kosslyn proposes a number of *processes* which act upon the long-term memory representations or the visual buffer. *Generation* processes create an image in the visual buffer from information in long-term memory. *Inspection* processes operate on the visual buffer to encode relationships and identify parts within the visual image. Finally, *transformation* processes can transform a visual image within the coordinate space (e.g. in mental rotation). According to this model, imagery shares many of the same representations and processes as visual perception. When an object is seen, its appearance is *encoded* from the retinal image into the visual buffer. It may then be *matched* to one of the appearances stored in long-term memory. When an object is imagined its appearance is *generated* from the long-term memory into the visual buffer. Whether seen or imagined, the contents of the visual buffer can be inspected or transformed in order to attempt a match or to answer a question (see Fig. 6.9).

Farah (1984) suggests that brain injury could lead to imagery deficits as a result of loss or impairment to any of the long-term memory structures or imagery processes. We have already distinguished imagery deficits which seem to result from loss of long-term memory for object appearances from those which seem to result from loss of ability to operate spatially. Farah's analysis allows us to make yet finer distinctions. She describes the abilities and deficits of a number of published case histories of patients reporting problems with visual imagery in terms of the component processes and representations needed to support each task on which the patient was tested. For example, where a patient can both *describe* and *recognise* visually presented objects she concludes that the processes of encoding information from the retinal image into the visual buffer are intact, and that inspection and matching processes must also be intact. To allow normal object recognition, stored visual appearances must also be intact. If the same patient cannot describe the appearances of visual objects from memory, it must be the image generation process which is deficient (see Fig. 6.10). She cites a number of cases of patients who appear to have selective deficits of image generation, and a different set who (following a similar task analytic approach to that illustrated in Fig. 6.10) seem to have impaired image inspection processes. A final set of patients she describes appear to have impairments at the level of long-term memory for visual object appearances, similar to those we have already described earlier in this section.

The account of visual imagery offered by Kosslyn and Farah (Fig. 6.9) bears some obvious similarities to the account of STVS which we gave in the last section, and we could consider both the "visual buffer" and "STVS" in turn synonymous with the "object files" proposed by Kahneman and Treisman (1983). However, we must not gloss over some fundamental differences between Kosslyn's model and that which we considered earlier (Fig. 6.3). The most important difference is that we have suggested that the long-term store of object appearances be construed as "structural descriptions", with the strong implication that these be considered to be *object-centred* rather than viewer-centred (cf. Chapter 3, particularly Marr and Nishihara's theory of object recognition). In contrast, research into imagery suggests that these stored visual appearances be better conceived as "canonical views" (see Chapter 3). For example, Pinker (1985) describes the results of his own research in which people found it difficult to visualise in a single step an arbitrary view of a familiar three-dimensional object. They seem instead to imagine an object in some "canonical" viewpoint first, and then mentally rotate it to the desired view. Pinker points out that these findings are not consistent with a view of image generation which takes an object-centred representation as input to a system which then specifies an arbitrary viewpoint of it. Instead, such data suggest that images are generated by activating stored *viewer-centred* representations. The implications of this may be far-reaching. Pinker suggests that his evidence from imagery implies that shape representations generally may be viewer- rather than object-centred:

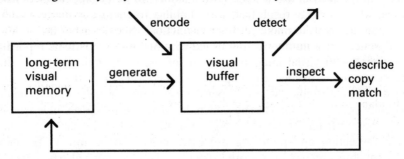

FIG. 6.9. Schematic diagram of the stores and processes involved in visual imagery and visual perception. (Adapted from Farah, 1984.)

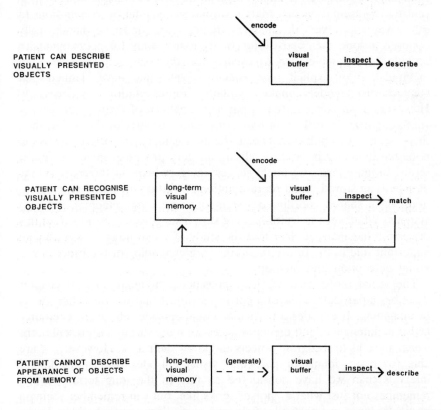

FIG. 6.10:   An example of how the model shown in Fig. 6.9 can be used to analyse patients' success and failure at different visual tasks, to infer a deficit in a particular store or process. In this case it is the image generation process which must be deficient. (Adapted from Farah, 1984.)

My experimental evidence suggests that long-term image representations are primarily viewer-centred. Both parsimony considerations and neurological evidence summarised by Farah (1984) suggest that the long-term representations of shape used in recognition are the same as those used in imagery. And Marr and Nishihara argue that shape representations used in recognition are primarily object-centred. One of these three claims has to give. (Pinker, 1985, p. 53)

It is interesting that Pinker sees visual imagery as evidence for a fundamental role for viewer-centred representations in object recognition. As we noted earlier and in Chapter 3, current connectionist accounts of visual pattern recognition are producing interesting demonstrations that recognition of novel views is possible following the storage of specific views. In this respect, the imagery theorists and the connectionists may be producing converging arguments against the kind of parsimonious object-centred representation that Marr regarded as essential for recognition. In other ways, however, the imagery theorists appear to be diametrically opposed to some members of the connectionist camp. Imagery appears to provide an example *par excellence* for the storage, retrieval, and manipulation of explicit *representations,* yet some have claimed that connectionist models make symbolic representations unnecessary. However, if we concede that a particular pattern of activity, or activity within a particular cell, itself *represents* some property of the world, then there seems no conflict between the two camps, and there seems no potential difficulty in conceptualising imagery processes in connectionist terms. In these terms we might suggest imagery involves the cross-linking of activity in stored visual representations with that in spatial representations via a shared coordinate system or some other mapping between systems. Whatever the fruitfulness of such a suggestion, we hope that this discussion has made it clear that the study of visual imagery will play an important role in the future theoretical understanding of the processes of visual perception and memory.

The visual buffer that we have considered at length in this chapter describes a particular view of a particular object that we are either seeing or imagining. It encodes a particular visual episode, although it requires active maintenance, and mediates access of more durable representations which allow us to recognise objects and know their uses. However, we are able to retain details of particular visual episodes over much longer intervals than we have considered so far. In the long term, we can remember not just what a "horse" looks like, but can remember seeing a particular horse in a particular field on a particular summer holiday. In the next section we turn to consider the nature and accuracy of such long-term visual memories.

LONG-TERM VISUAL MEMORY

For about 35 years between Bartlett's *Remembering* (1932) and the emergence of the new *Cognitive Psychology* (Neisser, 1967), the study of "memory" meant the study of verbal memory, and our ability to remember pictures, cars, and faces was ignored, if not apparently denied.

Interest in longer-term visual memory was revived by some demonstrations in the 1960s of apparently limitless capacity to remember pictures once viewed for a mere few seconds (e.g. Nickerson, 1965; Shepard, 1967; Standing, Conezio, & Haber, 1970). In all these studies, subjects were initially presented with several hundred pictures, usually culled from magazines and holiday snapshots, and hence forming a very varied set of items, each viewed individually for a few seconds. At some later time, subjects were required to discriminate "old" (originally shown) from "new" distractor pictures, either in a forced choice situation, in which one "old" and one "new" item was paired on each trial (e.g. Shepard, 1967), or in a series of single decisions to each of a random list of old and new distractor items (e.g. Nickerson, 1965). Performance in such studies was staggeringly high. Shepard, for example, found subjects were 98% correct on immediate testing of 68 old-new pairs following study of 600 pictures. Moreover, subjects were more accurate at remembering pictures than words (90%) or sentences (88%) tested by the same method. This superiority of pictorial over verbal memory is also found in tests of recall. If the task is to recall as many common nouns as possible from a particular list, accuracy is much higher if the nouns were originally pictured rather than merely labelled (see Paivio, 1971, for a review). Indeed, it is the superiority of pictorial over verbal representations in the recall of object labels which is usually referred to as the "pictorial superiority effect".

Initially, research on recognition memory for pictures seemed to concentrate on its apparent vastness and durability (Standing, 1973, showed that performance was remarkably high even following single presentation of each of 10,000 different pictures), rather than examining very critically the basis of such high performance levels. As argued by Goldstein and Chance (1974), the extreme heterogeneity of the items used in most of these experiments meant that subjects had a wealth of different cues available by which to distinguish new from old items. In a two-alternative forced choice procedure, subjects need only remember a single item or other aspect from a complex picture in order to distinguish target from distractor. Thus, the high performance levels do not necessarily imply that all, or even most, details of the presented pictures are stored away in memory.

Goldstein and Chance (1971) looked at memory for very homogeneous sets of pictorial materials, using a stringent test of recognition memory in which a small set of target items was intermixed with a large number of distractors. Pictures of snowflake crystal patterns led to above chance, but rather low overall recognition memory performance. Pictures of inkblot patterns were remembered with greater accuracy, and pictures of faces led to high levels of recognition memory, with no sign of forgetting over a 48-hour interval. Thus, there is a clear influence of "meaningfulness" on the storage of visual patterns. The most complex and abstract patterns (snowflakes) were least well remembered, although the fact that performance was still above chance is notable. Wiseman and Neisser (1972), and Freedman and Haber (1974) also showed how the meaning of a pattern can affect its retention. They showed their subjects the Mooney faces (Mooney, 1957)—a set of black and white high contrast patterns which all depict faces, but can be difficult to comprehend as such. They found that patterns which their subjects could "solve" (i.e. see as faces) were later recognised from distractors very well, whereas those which had not been solved were very poorly remembered. The fact that the same patterns could be well or poorly remembered depending upon their initial interpretation is important: It shows that long-term visual memory will have to be explained by some combination of pictorial (sensory) and interpretative (semantic) factors.

Paivio's (1971) dual coding theory (which we have already encountered in connection with visual imagery) was one framework which attempted to explain the pictorial superiority effect both in free recall of object labels, and in recognition memory. Paivio suggested that there were two, interlinked but distinct, long-term memory systems: the verbal and the imagery systems. A picture of an object or more complex scene would be represented in both systems, as most pictures can be labelled or described in words. A word or sentence, in contrast, would only find representation in the imagery system to the extent that it led to an image being generated. The more and stronger the representations in memory, the more likely it would be that the item would be recognised or recalled. Thus, pictures should lead to better memory performance than easily imageable words, which should, in turn, be better than very abstract words. This pattern has been observed for both recognition and recall (Paivio, 1971, reviews this literature). The theory also suggests that encouraging people to form images should aid recall—and certainly most of the effective mnemonic systems such as method of loci, and pegword techniques, involve imagery as an important component.

However, in its simplest form, the dual coding framework has some weaknesses. Its first, and major, weakness is the emphasis placed upon *verbal labelling* of pictures as a factor contributing to their retention. Dual coding in its simplest form predicts that pictures which are explicitly labelled or described in words at presentation should be better remembered than those which were not so labelled. Although there is quite a lot of evidence that explicit labelling of pictures leads to higher *recall* of the object labels, there is rather little evidence that labelling influences *recognition memory* for the pictures. For example, Bahrick and Boucher (1968) presented subjects with pictures of common objects that they were asked either to recall (as object labels) or to recognise by trying to select the actual picture originally learned from a selection of other pictures sharing the same name (e.g. to select the original cup from a set of 10 alternative cups). They found that recall performance was not correlated with recognition memory performance, and that subjects who were required to label the pictures overtly at presentation were no better (if anything, worse) at the later test of recognition memory. These results suggest that recall of object labels and recognition of pictorial detail rely on different components of memory, rather than both reflecting the combined strength of available imagery and verbal codes.

Another weakness of the dual coding framework is that it is not clear where in the system the semantics of items are to be found. Paivio's (1971) framework was developed in the aftermath of the American verbal associationist tradition, and is couched very much in terms stemming from that tradition—with "meaning" generally equated with verbal associative strength. This work predated the cognitive paradigm in which semantic representations play a major role in most accounts of object (and hence picture) processing. Paivio's original theory appeared to draw no distinction between *understanding* an object (knowing that it is a container, that its handle affords grasping, that one drinks from it, etc.) and *labelling* the object ("cup"). These distinctions are fundamental to many contemporary accounts of object recognition (see Chapter 3) and, as we have seen, become particularly crucial in the interpretation of patterns of visual deficit which sometimes result from brain damage. In later statements of the dual coding framework (e.g. Paivio, 1978), Paivio does consider semantic representation—and claims that in addition to the meaning captured by verbal association, the imagery system too captures certain semantic dimensions. Knowledge of an object's size, its pleasantness, value or intelligence are all claimed as properties contained within imaginal representations, as we discussed in the preceding section (where we also noted that this suggestion is at odds with most contemporary theories of semantic representation).

Nelson and his colleagues (e.g. Nelson & Brooks, 1973; Nelson & Reed, 1976; Nelson, Reed, & Walling, 1976) have produced a modified framework which explains the "dual coding" results in terms of sensory and semantic (rather than verbal) representations of pictures and their labels. Nelson and Brooks (1973), and Nelson and Reed (1976) obtained evidence from paired associate learning tests that pictorial meaning could be conveyed without any mediation from a verbal label (see also recent accounts of object recognition as discussed elsewhere in this book). For example, Nelson and Brooks (1973) used pictures (or their labels) as the stimuli in a paired-associate task, and unrelated words as the responses to be learned to these stimuli. The similarity between stimulus picture labels was manipulated, but found to have no effect in the picture-learning task unless subjects were explicitly instructed to label the pictures. On the basis of results such as these, Nelson and his colleagues suggested that both pictures and verbal labels could be represented in terms of sensory and semantic features, with the pictorial superiority effects resulting because the sensory features of pictures are generally more differentiating than those of words. Consistent with this framework, Nelson et al. (1976)

showed that increasing the schematic similarity between the pictures used in paired-associate learning tasks could eliminate or even reverse the normal superiority of pictorial representations in memory. Nelson et al. (1976) also suggest, unlike Paivio, that both pictures and their labels access a common, modality-free semantic system. Thus, the semantic code for a picture of a horse, or the label HORSE would be the same, though they acknowledge that pictures clearly access the semantic system more quickly.

The framework proposed by Nelson appears to provide a reasonable account of pictorial superiority effects, although Nelson et al.'s own tests of their framework have made use of a rather limited, paired-associate learning paradigm. Recent work which has been conducted broadly within the "levels of processing framework" (cf. Craik & Lockhart, 1972; Craik & Tulving, 1975), has revealed how the interpretation of any picture memory experiment requires a rather careful consideration of the nature of the sensory and semantic codes, and their deployment in the memory test. For example, Intraub and Nicklos (1985) found that encouraging subjects to attend to the physical characteristics of presented pictures by asking them to answer questions such as: "Is the object angular?" promoted better later recall of object labels than encouraging them to attend to the semantic properties of the objects (e.g. "Is the object edible?"). This result is in apparent contradiction to numerous demonstrations in the verbal memory literature of the better retention which follows "deeper" (semantic) encoding. It is even in apparent contradiction to other results obtained in visual memory, where a number of experiments have shown that making judgements about the apparent personality traits of presented faces promotes better later recognition memory performance than making judgements about physical features of the faces (e.g. Bower & Karlin, 1974; Patterson & Baddeley, 1977). However, it now seems clear that it is the relationship between encoding activities and the nature of the memory test which is important. Wells and Hryciw (1984), for example, showed that physical feature judgements led to better memory for faces than trait judgements if memory was tested using a task of reconstruction with Identikit, whereas trait judgements promoted better recognition memory. In Intraub and Nicklos' (1985) task the subjects must recall the names of the objects seen pictured in the study phase. If we assume that the kind of semantic coding induced in their incidental orienting conditions is an automatic aspect of picture perception then it could be argued that semantic orienting instructions are redundant. The physical judgement condition, on the other hand, will be providing an additional, distinctive sensory code which will increase the probability of recall of the associated name, just as encouraging subjects to form mental images at presentation improves verbal recall. Such work on picture memory thus provides a further challenge to the notion that simple "depth" of coding (where deep=semantic) is sufficient to account for memory performance.

The importance of semantic or "conceptual" coding of pictures in determining memory performance is given further support by work on *conceptual masking*. Intraub (1981) presented subjects with sequences of pictures in RSVP (rapid serial visual presentation, see Chapter 7) and asked them to spot when a particular target picture appeared. The target could be specified by name ("dog"), by category ("food") or by negative category ("the one that isn't food"). When each picture was exposed for 258msec, Intraub found that target detection rates were 89%, 69%, and 79% for the name, category, and negative category decisions respectively. Even when exposure duration was reduced to a mere 114msec per picture, these rates were 71%, 46%, and 35%. However, in an immediate recognition memory test only 58% of targets exposed for 258msec were recognised, and only 19% of those exposed for 114msec. It seems that in RSVP, pictures may be momentarily understood but then rapidly forgotten. One possible reason for the rapid forgetting may be that subsequent pictures *mask* preceding ones. Perhaps the later picture somehow "interrupts" the processing of an earlier one (cf. Chapter 4 where we dealt extensively with theories of visual masking). Intraub (1981; 1984) examined how recognition memory for briefly presented pictures was affected by filling the delay between each picture with more pictorial material. She found that when each briefly presented picture was followed by an unchanging pictorial "mask" in the delay, recognition memory was almost as good as when the delay period was blank. When the mask varied, however, performance was reduced, and the amount of reduction depended on the meaningfulness of the varying picture masks. When the changing mask was a nonsense picture, recognition memory was only marginally worse than when the mask was constant. When the changing pictures were meaningful, performance was substantially reduced, and when the masks were inverted meaningful pictures, performance was intermediate. These masking effects cannot be perceptual, as a constant mask should have a similar disruptive effect to a changing one. Rather, it seems that meaningful and varying pictures demand "conceptual" processing which disrupts the conceptual processing of the target items contributing to their memorability.

Loftus and Ginn (1984) produced further support for the conceptual masking hypothesis by showing that masking could be produced by pictures presented more than 300msec after target picture offset—at which point no perceptual masking of any sort should operate (see Chapter 4). Loftus, Hanna, and Lester (1988) have developed a model of conceptual masking which assumes that initiation of conceptual processing of the mask terminates the conceptual processing of the target, but that mask conceptual processing is itself initiated on a probabilistic basis.

Most of the research which bears on the sensory-semantic model of picture and verbal memory has emphasised memory for whole pictures of isolated objects or holiday snapshots. This is a task with rather little ecological validity, however. Normally, we will be trying to remember things like "where did I leave my glasses", or "how was the mugger dressed?"—i.e. we want to remember different kinds of detail from complex scenes containing many objects.

Jean Mandler has studied visual memory for line-drawings of complex scenes in order to investigate which kinds of information are well remembered and which forgotten. In particular, she has explored the role that "real world schemata" play in memory for visual scenes. A "real world schema" is a body of knowledge about the world which it is thought might play a role in the perception of the scene (cf. Minsky, Palmer, etc., see Chapter 3) by providing a background set of expectations against which the current scene may be compared. For example, if initial analysis led us to decide that we were looking at a "schoolroom" scene, then we might expect the scene to contain desks and chairs, books and maps, but not beds or cooking utensils. More generally, our knowledge of the world would lead us to expect to find certain objects in certain places—furniture on floors and pictures on walls. Mandler and Parker (1976) investigated the role of real-world schemata by comparing memory for the details of scenes organised coherently, as would be expected in the real world (clocks on walls, furniture on floors, etc.), with memory for unorganised scenes (furniture in the air or on walls) containing the same items. They compared memory for three different kinds of information—inventory (which items were present), appearance (what each item looked like), and arrangement (where items were located). They found that the presentation of items in organised or unorganised scenes had no effects on memory for inventory or the appearance of the items, but had a marked effect on memory for their spatial arrangement. When asked to reconstruct the originally presented scenes using pictures of the items remembered from them, subjects tended to place the items in locations in which they would normally occur (pictures on walls) rather than where they had actually occurred in the unorganised versions. Thus, subjects who had seen the organised versions were apparently more accurate in remembering the spatial arrangement of items within the scene.

Goodman (1980) looked at the influence of more specific "action" schemata on memory for visual details of scenes showing highly predictable activities such as "reading a book". She found that the occurrence of a schema-relevant object (e.g. the book) would be better remembered than the occurrence of a schema-irrelevant object (e.g. a plant), but that details of the appearance of the schema-relevant object would be *less* well recalled than those of the irrelevant object. This makes sense if we consider that the schema-relevant objects can be *inferred* rather than *remembered* from the scene, and in those cases where its presence was inferred, there would be no visual basis for its appearance to be remembered.

Our brief review of the literature on longer-term visual memory has outlined how research has shifted from mere demonstrations of picture memory capacity, towards some serious attempts to get to grips with *how* pictures are remembered. The demonstrated influence of general knowledge about the world on our visual memories of portrayed events will become important when we turn to consider applied aspects of visual memory, and the demands placed on the memory of a witness to a crime.

Our discussion of memory for pictured objects seems a long way removed from the kinds of long-term representations of visual appearance that we have considered might play a role in object recognition (see Chapter 3). Perhaps this is not surprising, as most cognitive psychologists would view the task of object recognition as involving the abstraction of the visually defining properties of an object from a specific instance of it, whereas our focus in this chapter has been on how we remember details of those specific instances. However, the recent revival of interest in massively parallel distributed memory models and other connectionist models could allow for an integrated treatment of picture "memory" and object "recognition". In Chapter 3, we mentioned that one of the attractions of distributed memory models, such as that of McClelland and Rumelhart, was their apparent sensitivity to the details of specific recent instances alongside their "abstraction" of a general object prototype. It will be interesting to see to what extent future developments of distributed memory models will allow a truly integrated treatment of visual recognition and visual memory.

EYEWITNESSING

For most practical purposes these theoretical concerns about the nature of visual memory matter rather little. What matters is its accuracy. At about the same time that psychology became impressed with the apparent powers of long-term picture memory, lawyers were becoming dismayed at the apparent fallibility of the eyewitness to a crime.

This concern about the inaccuracy of eyewitness testimony has led to increased research effort in two distinct, but related areas. The first is that of *identification* evidence. In the U.K. in 1976, the Devlin Committee produced a public report on the possible reasons behind a series of spectacular cases of mistaken identity, where witnesses had confidently but mistakenly identified innocent persons (as later established on other evidence) in police line-ups and/or files of photographs. The public concern provoked a good deal of research aimed at two things. First, psychologists began to examine the accuracy that could be expected in identifying a face glimpsed only briefly in circumstances that might be perceptually difficult, emotionally traumatic, and so forth. Secondly, possible improvements to the identification procedures used by the police which might minimise cases of mistaken identity were investigated. An excellent review of research in this area is provided by Shepherd, Ellis, and Davies (1982). At the same time, judges in the U.K. were advised that conviction should not usually be possible solely on the basis of identification evidence.

The second area of research was into possible causes of inaccuracy in *eyewitness testimony*. It became clear that the way in which witnesses are questioned about "what happened" can have quite dramatic effects on what they claim to remember. If we ask a witness: "What kind of weapon did you see?", this implies that a weapon was present, and may affect the way in which the witness "remembers" the incident. Just as Mandler, and Goodman (p.222) have shown that existing expectations about particular everyday scenarios can influence what is remembered from pictures, so Loftus and her colleagues (see Loftus, 1979 and 1983, for reviews) have shown the influence of general expectations and, in particular, misleading post-event information, on witness's memory.

The best known experiment is that of Loftus and Palmer (1974). Subjects were shown a film of a road traffic accident, and later questioned about the speed that the cars were going when they collided. Loftus and Palmer found that subjects who were asked: "About how fast were the cars going when they *smashed* into each other?" gave higher speed estimates than those who were asked: "About how fast were the cars going when they *hit* each other?". This in itself should urge caution in the manner in which witnesses are questioned. More worrying still, however, was Loftus and Palmer's subsequent finding that subjects who had been asked the "smashed" form of the question were more likely to answer positively when asked one week later if they saw any broken glass (in fact, none was present in the original film). Thus, the form of questions asked can have quite subtle effects on what people claim to remember.

If witness memories can be influenced by the form of the question used, perhaps also they can be influenced by downright inaccurate information. Loftus has supplied a number of demonstrations of the effects of misleading post-event information. One example is given by Loftus, Miller, and Burns (1978) who showed subjects an incident presented as a sequence of slide stills. In this incident, one car (a red Datsun) was shown knocking down a pedestrian. During the incident, a second car drives past the accident but does not stop. When questioned about the slide sequence, one question for half the subjects was: "Did another car pass the red Datsun while it was stopped at the *Yield* sign?", whereas the other half were asked: "Did another car pass the red Datsun while it was stopped at the *Stop* sign?" For half the subjects, the sign mentioned was consistent with what they had been shown in the original series, for the other half it was inconsistent. Later, when shown two identical signs, with one showing a Yield sign and one showing a Stop sign, 75% of those given the consistent information made the correct choice compared with only 41% of those given the inconsistent information.

Loftus' demonstrations are numerous, and they include examples which she claims indicate that the misleading information *modifies* the trace of the original event, rather than simply coexisting alongside it. For example, using the same slide sequence described earlier, Loftus (1977) suggested to half her subjects that the car which drove past the accident was blue rather than green. Subjects given this misleading suggestion tended to pick a bluish green when asked to pick the remembered colour of the car from a set of 30 different colours. The suggestion that misleading post-event information actually modifies that stored from the incident is important for both theoretical and practical reasons. Theoretically, it would be easier to accommodate effects in which stored visual memories were modified by subsequent verbal suggestions by proposing that all the information was stored in a common, modality free store. At a practical level, it suggests that the effects of misleading or biased questions, or even of misleading remarks overheard by a witness (cf. Loftus & Greene, 1980), will be unavoidable and irrevocable.

However, some ingenious experiments by Bekerian and Bowers (1983) suggest that Loftus may be wrong in her interpretation. Bekerian and Bowers repeated the Loftus et al. (1978) experiment, but compared the effects of the misleading information about the Stop/Yield sign in two different conditions. In the first, like Loftus et al., subjects had to make the forced choice between the critical pair of slides which were embedded in a slide sequence which did not mirror the order in which the original event occurred. In this condition, the Loftus results were replicated. In the second condition, however, the critical pair of slides was embedded in a sequence which reconstructed the original incident. In this situation, in which the context of the original event was reinstated, accuracy of choosing was not influenced by the misleading information. Such demonstrations suggest that the misleading information *coexists* with the original information. If contextual cues are presented, the original, accurate information is more likely to be retrieved, but in the absence of such contextual reinstatement, it is more likely that the most recent (i.e. post-event) information will be accessed. These findings have potentially important practical applications, because they suggest that the use of explicit contextual reinstatement, or implicit guided memory techniques, may act to neutralise any effects of post-event suggestion. Gibling and Davies (1988), for example, have shown how the biasing effect of a misleading composite image of a target face may be reduced if the original contextual cues are reinstated with a guided memory procedure.

Despite the numerous demonstrations of Loftus, Bekerian, and others on the effects of misleading post-event information, McCloskey and Zaragoza (1985) argued that there is no evidence that misleading information impairs memory for original events. They suggest that the reported effects arise from the demand characteristics of the tasks used. In the method used by Loftus and others to assess the impact of misleading information, subjects in the "misled" condition are given a question which mentions, in passing, an incorrect aspect of the original event. At test, they may be asked to select between the original and the incorrect detail. But in this case, memory for the original detail is confounded with memory for the misleading one. So, a subject with NO memory for the original information may choose the alternative simply because this, at least, yields some sense of familiarity. Also, some subjects may comply with the experimenter's authority and pick the information shown post-event, while knowing that there is a discrepancy with that shown originally. To look for effects of *impaired* memory for the original event, they argue, we must offer the original plus a completely new alternative as distractor (i.e. not the one used to mislead). Using this method, McCloskey and Zaragoza (1985) found no difference between memories of "misled" subjects and control subjects given no misleading information. Zaragoza (1987) extends this work to examine 3- to 6-year-olds' memories for pictures shown accompanying stories. As with adults, the "original" test procedure (i.e. that used by Loftus and others) shows an effect of misleading post-event information, but the "modified" test does not.

However, it seems that this issue is not quite as closed as these data suggest. For example, Ceci, Ross, and Toglia (1987), also using the modified test procedure, *do* find evidence of susceptibility to post-event information in children (ranging from 3 to 12 years old). They criticise the Zaragoza position for its all-or-none conception of memory, and consider possible outcomes of strong or weak traces of original and post-event occurrences. Issues of suggestibility and susceptibility to mis-information are far from dead, particularly in relation to child witness testimony.

The literature on witness identification and memory is now an extensive one, and our purpose here is mainly to stimulate interest rather than to attempt a comprehensive review. The interested reader should consult Clifford and Bull (1978), Shepherd et al. (1982), Loftus (1979) or Wells and Loftus (1984) for further details of the adult literature and Ceci, Toglia, and Ross (1987) for reviews of child eyewitness memory.

This chapter has provided a brief overview of the varieties of visual memory and the ways in which these have been investigated by psychologists. Besides its practical importance in the area of eyewitness testimony, the research is of theoretical interest in its indication of how some of the representations constructed in the process of visual perception may endure to affect our subsequent activities. In the next chapter, we will consider such issues again, in the context of repetition priming, as we turn to consider the nature of the processes of visual cognition which allow us to *read*.

7

Visual Processes
in Reading

INTRODUCTION

The previous chapters dealt with various component processes in object recognition, dynamic vision, visual attention, and visual memory. However,
vision does not only enable us to recognise objects; we can also learn to use
vision to interpret written symbols and to read. This adaptation of visual
processing to linguistic inputs is, in evolutionary terms, a very recent development. Because of this development we need to ask whether visual processes in reading reflect a new and independent processing module, or, if not
completely independent, to what extent the visual processes in reading and
object recognition overlap. This is the aim of the final chapter.

THE EVOLUTION OF WRITING SYSTEMS

In evolutionary terms, reading is a recent development, and the way in
which different writing systems have developed indicates some of the constraints governing visual processing in reading. It is, thus, worthwhile considering briefly the story of this evolution.

The earliest writing systems used pictographs, i.e. pictorial symbols (or
drawings), that directly represent the underlying concept. Examples of such
symbols remain commonplace today, especially where we wish to convey
meanings uncontaminated by language barriers (such as where drawings of
men and women are used to indicate different changing rooms). However,
pictographs are no longer used in writing systems. This is for various
reasons. For instance, people vary in drawing skills. Without stylisation of
the pictographs, it would be difficult to convey a constant meaning across
different transcribers, or even for a single transcriber to convey the same

meaning on different occasions. Thus, pictographs became stylised. With stylisation there came to be large numbers of pictographs to remember. Also, it is difficult to represent abstract concepts pictographically, and pictographic systems do not have a well-developed syntax (i.e. grammatical rules governing the ordering and relations between the symbols).

Because of these limitations, pictographic writing systems evolved. The first development involved using pictorial symbols to represent concepts to which the pictures themselves did not directly correspond. This development is documented at about the same time in a number of languages, including ancient Egyptian and Chinese (see Henderson, 1982). It can often involve a subtle change, such as when drawings of male and female clothing are used to signify different changing rooms. Here, the drawings represent the concepts of "male" and "female", and no longer stand for "clothing" *per se*. Similarly, pictographs for two different items were combined to stand for a new item. For instance, in the present-day Japanese script Kanji, the symbols for "speech" (言) and "tongue" (舌) are combined to form the word "story" (話). These developments allowed writers to express more abstract ideas. In this new, evolved role, the symbols are known as logographs.

A second change was that logographs were used to represent the sound of words. For instance, Chinese, which retains a logographic writing system, has a class of symbols ("phonetic compounds") composed of two components: A radical and a phonetic complement. The radical provides a cue to the semantic field of the concept, the phonetic complement cues the sound by reference to a similar sounding word. This is rather like being given clues in the game "charades", for instance that the item is a fruit whose name "sounds like" bear. This development made more explicit the relation between the written symbols and individual words in the *spoken* language.

In some languages little further evolution has taken place, perhaps because of the constraints of the spoken language. Spoken Chinese is monosyllabic. There was, therefore, perhaps little need to develop a writing system that expressed anything other than correspondences between symbols and whole words. However, in other languages other scripts evolved to represent the relations between the written symbol and sub-components of spoken words, such as their constituent syllables. This allowed for more flexibility, as new words could be created by varying the combination of the elements of the syllabic script; new words do not demand the creation of completely new symbols. Japanese maintained a logographic script, Kanji, borrowed directly from Chinese. In addition, syllabic scripts were developed. One syllabic script is used for foreign loan words (Katakana), another for grammatical forms (Hiragana). These two scripts are collectively known as Kana. There are 47 basic symbols in total in the two scripts, whilst adults know 1000 or so Kanji symbols, indicating the greater economy of speech-based writing systems in terms of the number of visual symbols that must be learnt.

Pictographs correspond closely to the objects they represent. We may, therefore, presume that they are recognised using processes similar to those used in object recognition (Chapter 3), at least insofar as pictures tap the same recognition processes as objects. The same may also be true, to some extent, of logographs. However, syllabic scripts have an explicit relation to speech. This makes it possible that their meanings are retrieved from speech-based (phonological) representations, and that these phonological representations are derived by processing each syllable in turn. We can contrast a direct recognition process, where meaning is associated with the written form of the word, with an indirect process, where the word's name is first retrieved, and then meaning is associated with the name. These two different processes are outlined in Fig. 7.1.

The syllabic script in Japanese can also be marked with extra detail, to indicate sub-syllabic parts of speech—such as which consonants must be "voiced" in pronunciation. In English, the use of sub-syllabic elements is taken even further. English uses an alphabetic writing system, in which a fixed set of letters or letter combinations (such as CH) correspond to the smallest unit in spoken language, the phoneme (where C,H, and CH each represent single phonemes, respectively /'k/, /'h/ and /tʃ/). Thus, it is possible that English words are understood only after they have been first translated into their names, with this translation operating between sub-word

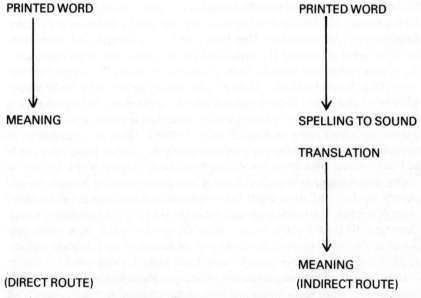

FIG. 7.1.   "Direct" and "indirect" routes to word meaning.

components, such as graphemes (the letters and letter clusters corresponding to phonemes) and phonemes.

PRELIMINARY ISSUES: PROCESSING "ROUTES" AND DIFFERENT TASKS

The distinction between "direct" and "indirect" routes to word meaning can
also be applied to the processes involved in pronouncing words. In this case a
direct route would comprise visual recognition of the word followed by a
process of addressing its phonology. An indirect route would bypass visual
recognition of the whole-word; instead, a phonological representation of the
word would be assembled by translating sub-word segments into their associated phonology (Patterson, 1982). Indeed, to complicate matters further,
we can distinguish two "branches" of the direct route. One involves retrieving the meaning of the word by association with its visual form, and then
addressing phonology from the word's meaning. The other branch involves
addressing phonology after recognition of the word's visual form, without
the intermediary retrieval of meaning (see Morton & Patterson, 1980). We
term these two branches the direct meaning-based route and the direct form-
based route.

The distinction we have drawn between "direct" and "indirect" routes to
word pronunciation can be contrasted with the argument presented in Chapter 3 concerning object recognition and naming. In Chapter 3 we suggested
that objects must first be visually recognised ("perceptually classified") and
then semantically classified before they can be named. Objects may not have
a direct route to their names. This difference between words and objects can
be understood in terms of the evolution of writing systems. Alphabetic writing systems allow associations to be generated between the components of
words (e.g. letters) and their sounds, and they allow the name of the whole
word to be assembled from the phonological components. In English such a
"phonological assembly" process works with regular words that follow the
spelling-to-sound rules of English (e.g. MINT). However, phonological
assembly is not appropriate for irregular words that violate these rules (such
as PINT, whose pronunciation differs from other English words ending in
-INT). Other languages, such as Serbo-Croatian or Japanese Kana are completely regular, and phonological assembly could in these cases be the dom-
inant procedure for reading aloud (although see later). In contrast to this,
there are no lawful relations between the phonological representations
associated with the parts of an object and the names of the complete object.
A phonological assembly process would not work for objects.

Recently, there has been considerable debate about whether the "routes"
suggested for word recognition and pronunciation operate independently of
one another (Carr & Pollatsek, 1985; Henderson, 1985; Humphreys &

Evett, 1985, and commentaries; Patterson & Coltheart, 1987; Patterson & Morton, 1985; Seidenberg, 1985). The point at issue here is whether a set of rules exists for translating letters (or sub-word segments) into sounds that are abstracted from, and operate without reference to, knowledge of particular words (Humphreys & Evett, 1985; Patterson & Coltheart, 1987). This debate is important for understanding how phonological information is retrieved in reading, and there continue to be advocates for and against the "independence" position (Patterson & Coltheart, 1987; Seidenberg & McClelland, 1989). However, our concern is with visual processing. In this context the debate is relevant because it impinges on questions concerning the types of visual information used in reading. In particular, different visual representations may be involved in the different "routes". Direct visual recognition might be based on a "holistic" coding of the word's visual pattern, or it might be based on parallel analysis of the constituent parts (in English, its letters). Similarly, the processes that translate print into sound could work at various "levels" of print, from single letters through to the whole word (Humphreys & Evett, 1985; Patterson & Morton, 1985; Shallice & McCarthy, 1985). These different possibilities each require different visual descriptions of the input. Descriptions at the sub-word level will also require some form of segmentation procedure (to treat one part of a word independently of the rest). This is also only to refer to single word recognition. Of course in most circumstances (except, perhaps, the psychology laboratory) we read text, consisting of words placed in meaningful sentences arranged across a page. Visual processing may then be constrained by information in the sentence. And, unless special conditions are applied (e.g. rapid serial visual presentation, RSVP, see later), we can only read text by making eye movements across the page. To understand visual processes in reading, we need to consider the role of eye movements, and the way in which words not at the centre of our current fixation, influence processing.

We begin by considering the reading of single words, and progress to discussing the reading of text. It is useful to make a preliminary point about the many different tasks used to investigate word recognition and identification. Some tasks clearly relate to normal reading situations, such as naming aloud or looking for a spelling error (proof-reading). The relation between other tasks and normal reading is more obscure. For instance, two common tasks are lexical decision, where subjects decide whether a stimulus is a real word or a nonword (a meaningless string of letters), and classification (e.g. does this word refer to an animal or not?). It is unclear whether we normally make such decisions as we read. Nevertheless, it can be argued that lexical decisions require subjects to recognise the visual forms of words, whereas classification requires access to word meaning. Thus, these tasks may respectively tap visual form recognition and semantic access (although, as we shall see, it is debatable just how selective such tasks are as tools for examining the word recognition system). Other tasks require subjects to match letter strings or words, or to report letters in briefly presented words and nonwords. These tasks do not demand word recognition at all, although performance often suggests that matching and letter recognition is sensitive to whether the letters involved form a word (as in the word superiority effect; Chapter 4). In general, it seems likely that each particular task could be performed in a number of ways, only some of which might be directly relevant to normal reading.

EFFECTS ON THE DERIVATION OF PHONOLOGY

Words versus Nonwords

We start with a task that seems more relevant to normal reading than most —speeded naming. Can access to meaning and pronunciation operate solely from sub-word segments, as it would if meaning is retrieved indirectly? If so, then nonwords should be processed as efficiently as words, as both words and nonwords can be translated into sound via the same set of sub-word translation rules. This turns out not to be the case. In simple naming tasks, subjects respond faster to words than to nonwords (see Patterson & Coltheart, 1987, for a review). This result still occurs if nonwords are constructed to have exactly the same pronunciation as words (when nonwords are "pseudohomophones", such as PRUVE; McCann & Besner, 1987), and when nonwords have common spelling patterns, matching those in words (e.g. BINK vs PINK) (Glushko, 1979; Stanhope & Parkin, 1987). The word advantage is thus not due to simple familiarity with phonological representations or spelling patterns, and instead the results show that word processing is not based solely on sub-word segments.

Now, English is a language with very irregular spelling-to-sound rules, often due to the incorporation of foreign words into the language. Words such as YACHT, GAUGE, and WHARF cannot be translated into sound from their component letters or letter clusters. For instance, the a and ch in YACHT would be pronounced /a/ and /tʃ/ if considered in isolation. It is therefore reasonable to think that sub-word based reading is not adopted by English readers. However, as we have already noted, Serbo-Croatian and Japanese Kana have highly regular spelling-to-sound correspondences (i.e. they have a phonologically "shallow" orthography), yet the word advantage in naming latency also occurs in these languages (Katz & Feldman, 1983, for Serbo-Croatian; Besner & Hildebrandt, 1987, for Kana). It seems that skilled readers cannot help but become sensitive to word-level information, even when reading could proceed perfectly satisfactorily at a sub-word level.

Spelling-to-Sound Regularity Effects

Are words always read using information represented at the word-level? One way to investigate this is to test the effects of spelling-to-sound regularity on the processing of words. If words are always read at the word-level, the spelling-to-sound regularity of the sub-word segments should be irrelevant.

In fact, there is an advantage for regular over irregular words in speeded naming tasks (Baron & Strawson, 1976; Gough & Cosky, 1977; Stanovich & Bauer, 1978) even when irregular words have familiar spelling patterns (i.e. when words such as PINT are used; Parkin, 1984; Seidenberg, Waters, Barnes, & Tanenhaus, 1984a). This finding alone indicates that word processing is not confined to the word-level, but that it proceeds at a sub-word level too, perhaps in parallel. For instance, whilst the name of a word is being addressed directly, a second process of phonological assembly may get underway. When the assembled and addressed names match, naming times are fast (see, for instance, Norris & Brown, 1985; Patterson & Morton, 1985, for details of this idea). For these processes to operate in parallel, words must be visually analysed jointly at a word, and a sub-word, level.

Unfortunately, the argument cannot stand there as the empirical evidence suggests a yet more complex picture. The difference between "orthographically familiar" regular and irregular words occurs in pronunciation tasks, but not in lexical decision (Coltheart, Besner, Jonasson, & Davelaar, 1979; Parkin, McMullen, & Graystone, 1986; Seidenberg et al., 1984a). Also, the regularity effect in pronunciation tasks is confined to words that occur relatively infrequently in the language. Frequent words are named equally fast irrespective of whether they have regular or irregular spelling-to-sound correspondences (Seidenberg et al., 1984a). To some extent, these results can be caught by one assumption: That speed of processing is a major determiner of the kinds of information used in reading. Pronunciation latencies are particularly long for low frequency words (e.g. Seidenberg et al., 1984a). Sub-word information, and its associated phonology, may be derived relatively slowly. Consequently it only influences tasks that are performed quite slowly (the naming of low frequency words). For instance, when low frequency words are named there may be sufficient time for a phonological representation to be assembled before responses are carried out. But what about lexical decision? Remember that lexical decisions tend not to show regularity effects. The "speed of processing" argument accounts for this as long as lexical decisions are faster than naming responses (Seidenberg et al., 1984a); but, this is not always so (Forster & Chambers, 1973; Frederiksen & Kroll, 1976). The data are more consistent with the idea that lexical decisions are based on visual descriptions coded at a whole-word level, and so show minimal effects of sub-word based spelling-to-sound regularity. Such descriptions may enable "familiarity" judgements to occur, discriminating words from nonwords. This account is also supported by data showing that word length does not affect lexical decisions to words (at least with words up to six letters long; Frederiksen & Kroll, 1976): If recognition were based on sub-word components then the number of such components should affect performance. In summary, the following case can be made. Words are visually processed at various "levels". Lexical decisions can be based on descriptions coded across the whole-word. More local descriptions of sub-word segments are also derived, but more slowly. Such segments can be transcribed into phonology, and primarily affect naming tasks.

Consistency Effects

One other result is also relevant. This is that words with regular spelling-to-sound correspondences can be named slowly if there exist other (irregular) words with similar endings but different pronunciations (i.e. if the letter pattern has an inconsistent spelling-to-sound correspondence). For instance, CAVE is a regular, inconsistent word because it has a regular spelling-to-sound correspondence (e.g. -AVE corresponding to /eiv/), but it is spelt similarly to HAVE, which has an irregular correspondence. Consistency effects were first reported by Glushko (1979), and they are strongest for words that have many inconsistent "neighbours" (e.g. PLOUGH, which has a regular correspondence for OU→/au/, although the majority of -OUGH words are pronounced differently; COUGH, BOUGHT, ROUGH, etc.; see Kay & Bishop, 1987). The result is interesting for several reasons. Primarily it shows that spelling-to-sound regularity is a continuous, and not a dichotomous, variable. Words vary in their regularity according to the number (and perhaps the frequency) of other words sharing the same spelling pattern (e.g. Brown, 1987). In terms of the "two route" framework we have sketched (Fig. 7.1), this can mean one of two things. One is that the indirect route is complex, containing more than simple all-or-none correspondences between graphemes and phonemes (e.g. such correspondences may be probabilistic, to produce a "continuum" of regularity). The second is that this route is not independent of the direct route, and so shows "word specific knowledge" in the way it operates (e.g. according to the number of words that are spelt similarly, but pronounced differently, to the word presented). For our purposes the result is interesting because it highlights the importance of the end or "body" (Patterson & Morton, 1985) sections of words. One important sub-word level component of analysis seems to be the "body" segment of a word.

However, it is unlikely that sub-word analysis is confined to body segments. Consider a nonword such as JOOV. There are no words in English that have -OOV as a body, yet we can pronounce such strings quite easily (Carr & Pollatsek, 1985; Coltheart, 1981). Also, a nonword such as JOOK tends to be pronounced regularly (as JUKE) even though the majority of words with the same body are pronounced irregularly (e.g. BOOK, TOOK, LOOK, etc.; Patterson & Morton, 1985). Clearly, such nonwords are not pronounced simply by reference to their body sections. Kay (1985) has also shown that the front-end segments of nonwords are important for their pro-nunciation. A nonword such as WOOK does tend to be pronounced irre-gularly (as in BOOK), presumably because words beginning WOO- are gen-erally pronounced that way. The data suggest that various sub-word seg-ments can be used for phonological assembly, beginning as well as end (body) segments.

EFFECTS IN SEARCH, LETTER RECOGNITION, AND MATCHING

Word-level Coding

We have discussed evidence for there being multiple levels of coding in visual word processing, from the whole word down to a single letter level, drawing on lexical decision and speeded naming tasks. However, to some extent, both tasks are divorced from the specifically visual aspects of word processing. Naming latencies may be determined primarily by the efficiency of translating between spelling and sound. Lexical decisions could reflect various processes addional to familiarity judgements, such as the time need-ed to determine a word's meaning (James, 1975). Effects of sub-word seg-ments on retrieving phonology or meaning might occur even if form recogni-tion is at a whole-word level. For instance, it is possible to recognise a com-plete word corresponding to the name of a character in a Russian novel, or the author of a research paper, but only to pronounce it by using sub-word segments (as word-level mappings from spelling-to-sound may not exist). The fact that sub-word segments are used for this task does not mean that they are involved when words are recognised as visual forms.

We therefore turn to other tasks to evaluate the multiple-levels argument. In *single word search* tasks subjects have to decide whether a display con-tains a predesignated target word (word-search task) or a predesignated target letter (letter-search task). Thus, in a word-search task subjects might be asked whether the word NEXT is present, and then be presented with either the correct word (respond yes) or a distractor sharing all but one letter (e.g. NEST; respond no). In a letter-search task they might be asked whether the letter "X" is present in either the word NEXT (yes) or the word NEST (no). Typically, subjects respond faster in the word search task than in the letter search task (e.g. Johnson, Turner-Lyga, & Pettegrew, 1986), despite the fact that the same letters distinguish targets and distractors in both cases. This suggests that a word can be identified as a single unit before the identities of its letters are verified.

Letter recognition studies have examined whether letter recognition is affected by being part of a word. In Chapter 4 we discussed the well-established result that letters are better identified when part of a word than when they are part of a nonword, or even relative to when they occur in isolation: The word superiority effect (WSE). The WSE occurs under conditions where subjects are given a forced-choice of letter alternatives, as well as when they are given free choice of report (as in Taylor & Chabot's 1978 experiment, discussed in Chapter 4). For example, subjects might be presented with the word NEXT and asked to choose whether an X or an S was in the third position. As both alternatives make a word, there is no advantage for guessing between the alternatives in words relative to when a nonword string is presented (EN_T). Nevertheless, performance remains better with words than with nonwords or even single letters (Reicher, 1969; Wheeler, 1970).

The general benefit for words over nonwords could be due to many factors. Words are pronounceable, they tend to have familiar component spelling patterns, they are familiar as whole letter strings, etc. Any of these factors could alone be responsible for the WSE. One important result, then, is that there is a WSE even when nonwords are chosen to have equally familiar spelling patterns (e.g. Manelis, 1974; Marmurek & Briscoe, 1982; McClelland, 1976). This suggests the involvement of word-specific knowledge in the effect; e.g., because words but not nonwords are stored as familiar forms in memory. This advantage for words over nonwords with similar component spelling patterns fits with the idea that access to stored knowledge operates using word-level information.

The WSE also occurs in other tasks, such as when subjects have to decide whether simultaneously presented letter strings are the same or different. Words are matched more quickly than nonwords (e.g. Eichelman, 1970; Pollatsek, Well, & Schindler, 1975). Eichelman (1970) showed that string length affects the matching of nonwords (e.g. responses to VIB-VIB are faster than to VIBRAD-VIBRAD), but not words (responses to CAR-CAR are no faster than to CARPET-CARPET). The null effect of string length supports the case for word-level representations being used in matching. Stored representations do not exist for whole nonword strings, and so they tend to be matched using smaller units. As string length increases so do the number of units that must be matched, slowing responses.

One other result to note here is that recognition is more accurate when letters are arranged in familiar acronyms (e.g. FBI, LSD) than when the same letters are presented in random order (BFI, DLS; Egeth & Blecker, 1971; Henderson, 1974; Noice & Hock, 1987). This "acronym advantage" occurs even when the acronym is neither orthographically regular nor pronounceable (Noice & Hock, 1987). Also, the position of the critical (probed) letter in the acronym is unimportant (identification of the first letter is as accurate as the last). In contrast, the position of the critical letter strongly affects report in random letter strings (identification of the first letter is by some margin better than the last; Noice & Hock, 1987). These results suggest familiarity with an acronym or word enables responses to be based on whole-string representations.

Intermediary Representations

If the case for word (or whole-string) level representations is supported, what about that for sub-word components? There is evidence for the coding of sub-word components in at least some of the tasks we have discussed. For instance, letter recognition is influenced by whether the letter is part of an orthographically regular and pronounceable (nonword) letter string (a "pseudoword"; Baron & Thurston, 1973; Carr, Davidson, & Hawkins, 1978; McClelland, 1976; Spoehr & Smith, 1975). If we presume that nonwords cannot be identified with reference to a word-level representation, then this "pseudoword advantage" implicates coding based on component letter clusters.

It is difficult to separate out whether these cluster effects occur because the letters are part of a familiar spelling pattern (an orthographic effect) or because pseudowords can be translated into a phonological representation that is useful for report. Relevant evidence here is that letter identification is impaired if, instead of being given single letter alternatives, subjects choose between word alternatives with the same name (i.e. homophones such as CITE and SITE), relative to alternative words with different pronunciations (SAME vs CAME; Hawkins, Reicher, Rogers, & Peterson, 1976). This suggests the involvement of phonological representations. Also, the pseudoword advantage is affected by whether subjects expect pseudowords to be presented; the same is not true of the WSE (Carr et al., 1978). This strategic effect does not fit easily with the idea of the spelling pattern being important, as this pattern ought to be encoded in all cases during the processing of the string (just as word-level representations appear to be). However, it does fit with the pseudoword advantage being due to phonological coding, with the products of this coding being subject to optional use.

Of course the "phonological" and "orthographic" interpretations of the pseudoword advantage are not mutually exclusive. Indeed, Rumelhart and McClelland (1982) showed that letter recognition can be facilitated in unpronounceable consonant strings when the strings share their spelling pattern with many words (e.g. SPNT, relative to, say, NTSP). This particular effect seems not to be due to the pronounceability of the strings, and suggests that there can be specific orthographic effects. What seems to "drive" these orthographic effects is whether the letter clusters in the string are shared with words. One way to think of this is that letter clusters "activate" stored representations for words, which then support letter identification (see later). For both phonological and orthographic effects to occur, visual information about letter clusters must be derived in parallel with whole-string representations, although these effects alone do not show that stored representations for the clusters exist separate from word-level representations.

Other evidence for sub-word unit coding comes from "priming" studies, that investigate the effect of a prior contextual item on responses to a subsequent target. Evett and Humphreys (1981; Humphreys, Evett, Quinlan, & Besner, 1987; Humphreys, Evett, & Taylor, 1982) had subjects identify letter strings presented briefly at the same location. These strings were preceded and followed by a pattern mask. Subjects found it extremely difficult to report the first string, yet were facilitated in reporting the second string if the first contained letters in the same positions. This effect occurred between lower case "primes" and upper case "targets", and so was not due to simple summation of visual information from the strings. Rather, it seemed due to some form of intermediary orthographic coding of the letters in the prime which facilitated the subsequent coding of the same letters in the target. It does not stem from the priming of single letter representations because performance improves non-linearly as the number of letters shared by the strings increases. There are larger effects when the strings share 3 out of 4 letters than would be expected from the effects when there are only 1 or 2 common letters. The effects also occur as long as letter clusters maintain their relative positions within the string (internal letters remain internal, end-letters remain at the ends of the string). For instance, o*lat* and *bl*ot prime BLACK, but *lato* and o*bli* do not (Humphreys, Evett, & Quinlan, in press).

Another set of experiments indicating position-coding of sub-word units also use briefly presented, masked displays. Subjects see displays containing two or more words (e.g. MALE and POST), and have to report the words present. Under these circumstances "migration" errors can occur, where subjects report words comprising mixtures of the letters presented (e.g. MAST and POLE; Allport, 1977; Duncan, 1987; McClelland & Mozer, 1986; Mozer, 1983; Shallice & McGill, 1978; Treisman & Souther, 1986). Such errors can also be encountered in more usual circumstances. For instance, Wilkins (cited in Woodworth, 1938, p. 744) presented the following examples:

Psychment

Departology

Woodson

Wilrow

If we glance quickly at these items we are likely to misread them as Psychology, Department, etc., interchanging sections from the different strings. Such migration errors preserve the relative positions of the letters in their parent words (in our first example, MA and PO are reported in the first positions, ST and LE in the final positions). Here, letter clusters seem to be coded for their relative positions within the words.

Are these letter cluster effects orthographic or phonological in nature? Most studies have not addressed this question. However, Humphreys et al. (1982) failed to find any extra priming between pseudohomophone primes and targets (e.g. nale-NAIL) over and above any effects due to their common spelling patterns (e.g. when contrasted against a control condition such as nalc-NAIL). The point here is that pseudohomophones had the same name as the target word they were paired with, and yet this produced no extra benefit. From this it seems that the orthographic relations are of primary importance.

WORD-LEVEL REPRESENTATION: WHOLE FORM OR PARALLEL LETTER ANALYSIS?

Earlier we reviewed evidence for words being analysed as whole units. However, we have been deliberately vague about the nature of word-level coding. It could consist of some form of global pattern analysis; for instance, a low spatial frequency description of a word. Alternatively, it could be based on the parallel analysis of the letters in the word, where the letters are not treated as an integrated single pattern. This issue can be examined by varying the visual characteristics of the words. If word-level coding involves global pattern analysis, then coding should be disrupted by distorting the pattern. Also, any effects should be greater on familiar words than on unfamiliar words or on nonwords, as global pattern information should be used mainly for the identification of high-frequency words.

The global pattern information most useful for word identification would comprise the pattern of ascending, descending, and neutral letters in lower case words (as these produce the most discriminable global shapes). This information will not be available when words are printed in upper case. Consequently, if the information is used, there should be an advantage for reading lower case print. This turns out to be generally true. Woodworth (1938) first reported that lower case texts are read faster than upper case, and this has been confirmed by Smith (1969) and Fisher (1975). However, a general problem confronts any direct contrast of reading across the different typescripts; this is that the discriminability of the individual letters may differ in addition to any differences in their global patterns. Individual lower case letters tend to be more discriminable than individual upper case letters.

The problem of letter discriminability besets other attempts to investigate the role of word shape in reading. For instance, studies of proof-reading have looked at the effect of making a spelling error that maintains a word's shape (e.g. tesf for test) relative to errors that change word shape (tesc for test). Spelling errors are harder to detect when word shape is maintained (Haber & Schindler, 1981; Monk & Hulme, 1983). However, letters that do not change the word's shape are also closer in shape to the target letters than

are letters that change the word's shape. The effects could be caused by discriminability at the letter level. A more controlled study by Paap, Newsome,
and Noel (1984) illustrates this. They introduced spelling errors into texts by
substituting letters that were or were not confusable with the substituted
letter. Also the "confusable" or "distinct" letters could either maintain or
change the word's shape. Thus the word "than" was replaced either by
"tban" or "tdan". Both substitutions maintain the word's general shape,
but h and b are more confusable at a letter level than are h and d. Similarly
"than" could be replaced by either "tnan" or "tman". In this instance the
word's shape is changed, though h and n are similar at a letter level (and
more so than h and m). Paap et al. (1984) found that the confusable letters
produced proof-reading errors irrespective of whether they changed the
word's shape. Interestingly, proof-reading errors were also more likely with
common function words (such as *the* or *and*). Function words are read as
single units, but the unit is not based on word shape.

   Another manipulation is to present words and nonwords in MiXeD case
(where the letters are alternating upper and lower case). Mixing case has a
large effect on a number of tasks: text reading speed (Smith, 1969); word
naming latency (Besner & McCann, 1987; Mason, 1978); lexical decision
(Besner & McCann, 1987); tachistoscopic identification (Adams, 1979;
McClelland, 1976); same-different matching (Pollatsek et al., 1975); and
category classification (Meyer & Gutschera, 1975). This could be for various
reasons. The number of letter shapes is increased in mixed relative to single
case stimuli, which could produce a general slowing of performance. The
distinctive pattern of ascenders and descenders in a lower case word may be
lost when the letters are flanked by upper case letters. Also, in some tasks an
unusual reading strategy may be induced, such as reading letter-by-letter.
For instance, Pollatsek et al. (1975) showed that the WSE in a matching task
is reduced with mixed case stimuli (RoAd-rOaD vs OaDr-oAdR). Mixed
case words also show strong effects of length on matching, unlike words in
single case (Bruder, 1978; Eichelman, 1970). Such length effects implicate a
change in reading strategy.

   What about the effects of mixing case in other tasks? A crucial result here
is that the WSE (over pseudowords) is not affected by whether the stimulus
is in single or mixed case (McClelland, 1976). Moreover, Besner and his
colleagues (Besner, Davelaar, Alcott, & Parry, 1984; Besner & Johnston,
1987; Besner & McCann, 1987) have shown that mixing case affects nonwords more than words in both naming and lexical decision. This is completely contrary to the idea that word shape is critical for word recognition,
as the effects should then be stronger on words. Also, in naming tasks, mixing case disrupts low-frequency words more than high-frequency words (Besner & McCann, 1987), again contrary to the "word shape" hypothesis. In
lexical decision the data are rather less clear, but the main conclusion may
still be supported—mixing cases tends to impair the least familiar stimuli

most (see Besner & Johnston, 1987; Besner & McCann, 1987, for discussion). This is at odds with recognition being based on word shape.

The above argument is also supported by studies of handwriting effects on reading. According to the word shape account, handwriting should be particularly disruptive to the reading of familiar words. This prediction is wrong. Manso de Zuniga (1988) has shown that low-frequency words are more disrupted by handwriting than high-frequency words.

The evidence we have marshalled points overwhelmingly against word shape being the predominant information for visual word recognition. Also, there is little evidence to indicate that word shape plays a more limited role, for instance in the identification of high-frequency "function" words, such as *the* or *and* (Paap et al., 1984), or in the identification of words preceded by an appropriate context (Paap et al., 1984). However, this conclusion does not mean that word processing is always insensitive to visual familiarity. For instance, Brooks (1977) had subjects search through a list of mixed case words for a particular target name. Subjects were then transferred to new lists using the same materials but with the case mixing reversed (e.g. HEnRy became heNrY). Case reversal disrupted transfer (see Jacoby & Hayman, 1987, for a more recent example). Word processing is sensitive to the visual familiarity of the words. However, it also seems likely that, in the long term, we forget details about the visual characteristics of words we encounter (see later), and our memories for the words may also be modified by all the other occurrences of the word when we read different texts. Instead of the word recognition system being highly tuned to particular visual patterns it will be more broadly tuned to general types of lower or upper case scripts. Recognition will be less affected by global shape than by the mere presence of all the letters in a word.

MODELLING WORD RECOGNITION

Interactive Activation

Word processing seems based on the parallel analysis of the letters in words. Information represented at the word level can then be used to facilitate various tasks which, in some respects, ought to precede word recognition (such as letter recognition, search, and matching). These findings provide important constraints on visual word recognition, which were first captured in detail in the interactive activation model of McClelland and Rumelhart (1981; Rumelhart & McClelland, 1982). This model has had a pervasive influence on subsequent work and modelling of word recognition, and so it provides the focus of our discussion.

McClelland and Rumelhart argued that word recognition is based on a set of hierarchical processes, involving the activation of visual features in letters, letter processing, and word processing. Representations of features

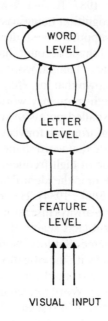

VISUAL INPUT

FIG. 7.2. The interactive activation model of word recognition. (Reproduced from McClelland & Rumelhart, 1981, with permission.)

and of letters are contacted prior to representations of words, but letter recognition is not completed before word representations are activated. This is because partial activation can be passed from one level in the hierarchy to the next (i.e. processing is not discrete; see McClelland, 1979). This means that word representations can be activated concurrently with letter representations, and can feed back to influence letter processing. The architecture of this system is shown in Fig. 7.2.

When a word is presented, the features making up its letters activate consistent features at the "feature level". Active features in turn activate the representations of letters that they are part of, and inhibit letters that they are not part of. Active letter representations similarly activate consistent word representations and inhibit inconsistent ones, whereas activated word representations feed back to activate consistent, and inhibit inconsistent, letter representations. In addition, there are also within-layer inhibitory links, so that an active representation at one level will inhibit all other representations at the same level. Figure 7.3 conveys something of the flavour of the interactions that can take place within such a system.

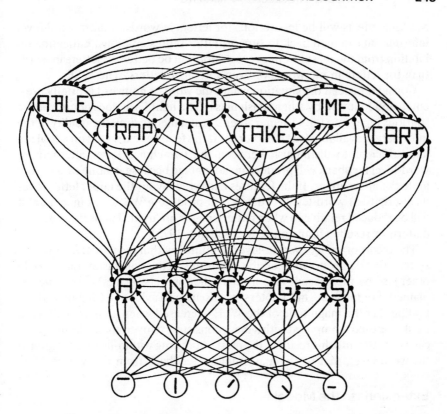

FIG. 7.3. The pattern of activation created within the interactive activation model when the letter T is presented at position 1 in a word. Note that feature and letter representations are position-specific. (Reproduced from McClelland & Rumelhart, 1981, with permission.)

It is assumed that the features in letters and words are extracted over time (Chapter 4). Thus, initially the representations for a number of letters and words will become active because the first features will not discriminate between different letter and word candidates. As more features are extracted so activation accumulates for letters and words consistent with the input, and the active representations inhibit "competing" representations. Gradually, the system comes to converge or "relax" upon a single interpretation of the input. Word "recognition" takes place.

In Chapter 4 we discussed how a WSE can be produced under pattern masking conditions. According to the interactive activation model, pattern masking disrupts performance by creating spurious activation at the feature level, that subsequently inhibits letter representations. When single letters or nonwords are presented, such spurious activation has serious consequences because target letters can be inhibited by the features in the mask.

Masking effects will be less serious for letters in words because word-level information can feed back to support letter representations, mitigating inhibition from the mask. Letter recognition will be better for letters in words than for letters in nonwords or even for single letters: The WSE.

Consider instead the situation where the word or nonword is briefly presented and followed by a light flash mask. The light flash does not introduce spurious input into the system; rather it is assumed to limit the quality of the information available (see Chapter 4). If the features extracted on a trial are not sufficient to distinguish between the two-choice letter alternatives, word-level feedback will produce no advantage because it alone cannot separate the alternatives. If the features extracted favour the target letter (over its alternative) word-level feedback will produce a WSE, but in general it will be reduced relative to when pattern masks are used. This is the observed pattern of results (Johnston & McClelland, 1973).

The incorporation of within-layer inhibition within the model enables the system to "damp down" (inhibit) spurious activation faster than would otherwise be the case. It also allows other aspects of the WSE to be explained. For instance, in Chapter 4 we discussed Taylor and Chabot's (1978) finding that the magnitude of the WSE decreased when an unrelated word mask was used (compared with a mask consisting of overlapping letters). We can now attribute this result to the mask producing within-layer inhibition at the word level; that is, the mask inhibits feedback from the word.

Extensions to the Model

The interactive activation model gives a good fit to much of the data collected on the WSE. The model is based on the idea that information processing is conducted using units that are computationally simple; essentially representations simply excite or inhibit other representations they connect to, depending on the nature of the connection. Computational complexity comes about because of the way that units are interconnected within a processing network. Processing is governed by the properties of the network rather than by those of single units within the network. Thus, the model is an example of a connectionist processing system (Chapter 2), applied to visual word recognition.

However, the original model does not cope happily with all effects, and here we mention some that require modification of the model.

Word Frequency

A long-established finding is that high-frequency words are recognised and identified more efficiently than low-frequency words. This is true in almost all tasks that have been used to examine word recognition (see Paap,

McDonald, Schvaneveldt, & Noel, 1987). According to the kind of connectionist model proposed by McClelland and Rumelhart, word frequency effects come about because stronger connections are established between letter representations and high-frequency words, and/or because high-frequency words retain a higher resting level of activation. This means that high-frequency words should activate their constituent letters more than low-frequency words, producing better letter report under tachistoscopic presentation conditions and a larger WSE for high-frequency words. However, it turns out that word frequency effects are often weak with tachistoscopic presentation (e.g. Manelis, 1977; Paap & Newsome, 1980), and that the WSE is no larger for high- than for low-frequency words (Gunther, Gfroerer, & Weiss, 1984). On face value the data do not mesh with the interactive activation account.

One solution is to abandon the model, and some theorists have presented alternative accounts. For instance, the verification model developed by Becker (1976) and Paap, Newsome, McDonald, and Schvaneveldt (1982) represents one such development that provides a better account of word frequency effects under degraded conditions. However, it should be realised that the operation of models such as the interactive activation model are complex, and will depend on how various processes are set to operate (e.g. the differences in resting levels of activation for high- and low-frequency words, etc.). Such models may only be fully tested by examining performance in detail across a range of conditions. For instance, we need a complete picture of how frequency affects word recognition by examining its effects over a wide range and under different degrees of masking.

Letter Clusters

The interactive activation model contains no representations for letter clusters. This is because there is little evidence that cluster information plays a large part in the WSE (e.g. Johnston, 1978; McClelland & Johnston, 1977). What seems to be more important is whether there are many words sharing the same letters in the same positions (as in the SPNT example earlier; Rumelhart & McClelland, 1982). According to the model, such effects are due to feedback from the word to the letter level.

Nevertheless, we have discussed other evidence favouring the involvement of letter clusters in word recognition, coming from bigram matching and priming experiments (Evett & Humphreys, 1981; see also Greenberg & Vellutino, 1988). It may simply be the case that letter clusters are themselves susceptible to pattern masking, and so do not generate the effects found with word-level feedback in the 2AFC procedure. More complete accounts of word recognition need to include a role for intermediary coding between letters and words (see later).

Letter Position

In the model, letter representations are activated when there are appropriate features in the input. Such features are position-specific. An "H" contains two vertical lines joined by a horizontal one. To identify the letter, the system must keep the two vertical lines separate by coding them in their specific positions. Now, what happens when a letter is repeated within a word? Essentially, this problem is solved in precisely the same way. Letter representations are position-specific. In a word such as NEED, the E in the second position will activate a completely different set of representations to the E at the third position (coding from left to right). This means that the set of letter representations is repeated for each of the positions for all lengths of word. This is a very uneconomical way of coding letter position. It is also contravened by some of the priming results we have discussed, which occur as long as letters retain their relative (not their specific) positions in words (Humphreys et al., in press).

More recent modifications of the model have taken steps to remedy this. One particular step has been to use what is termed "coarse coding". Instead of there being one representation for each letter, representations conform to letter clusters (McClelland, 1986; Mozer, 1987). A word such as NEED would activate units corresponding to *Ne, nEe, eEd, and eD*, where * denotes a space. The representations for the second and third "E" in the word now differ (being nEe and eEd respectively) because the letters are adjacent to different letters. However, the nEe and eEd representations are not tied to ordinal positions within a word, and they can be activated by appropriate letters at any internal position within a word (although end letters are assigned a special status because they need an adjacent space to become active). Thus the nEe representation would be activated by the "E" in the third position of SNEER, because it has the correct surrounding letters; similarly, the eEd representation would be activated by the "E" in the fourth position of GREEDY. The same recognition units are activated despite the fact that the particular letters are in different ordinal positions relative to when they are in the word NEED.

Early Coding

In this model, letter processing takes place in parallel across a word, and word-level representations are activated in this way and not by word shape. This conforms to the evidence we have discussed (e.g. McClelland, 1976). Nevertheless, letter and word processing are co-temporous because word-level representations are activated prior to the completion of processing at the letter level.

Letter recognition is also *deterministic*. That is, letter representations are activated whenever the appropriate features are present. A difficulty with this is that deterministic processes cannot deal easily with distorted input. A feature that is in the wrong orientation, as in the final letter of the word FAT, would cause a letter representation not to be activated. A more flexible approach may be to use a *probabilistic* rule, so that there is a certain probability of a particular feature activating a letter according to how close it is to the required orientation. At base, perceptual input for letter recognition must be defined as flexibly as that for object recognition (see Chapter 3). Note, however, that even within a deterministic system distortions can be overcome if the other letters in a word provide sufficient evidence to activate the representation of the distorted letter. Consistent with this kind of top-down effect, the perception of distorted letters is strongly affected by appropriate letter contexts (e.g. Massaro, 1979).

Extensions

We have presented the interactive activation model in some detail because it is probably the most complete account of word recognition to date, and because it has a number of interesting properties that hold for other connectionist models. The interactive activation framework can also be extended to cover other aspects of reading concerned with how various types of stored knowledge influence processing (McClelland, 1987). The general framework would propose that different types of knowledge comprise other levels of representation within the system. Processing at each level would be modulated by the activation in other, connecting levels (see Fig. 7.4). The main properties of such a system should conform to those of the interactive activation model. Performance should be weakly affected by context when the bottom-up input is strong. Performance should be strongly affected by context when bottom-up input is weak (think of the large WSE under pattern masking conditions). Later in the chapter we discuss how well such an account explains context effects on the visual processing in reading.

ACQUIRED DISORDERS OF READING

Our understanding of the types of visual information used in reading has also been aided by studies of patients with acquired reading disorders. Patients with impaired reading are classified as dyslexics. The term "acquired dyslexia" is used to refer to patients whose reading problems reflect damage to a previously normal reading system, so distinguishing such patients from developmental dyslexics who encounter problems in learning to read. Different types of acquired dyslexia have been classified according to the patterns of errors made by the patients and the types of word they have problems reading. Note, however, that each general type can subdivide according to the

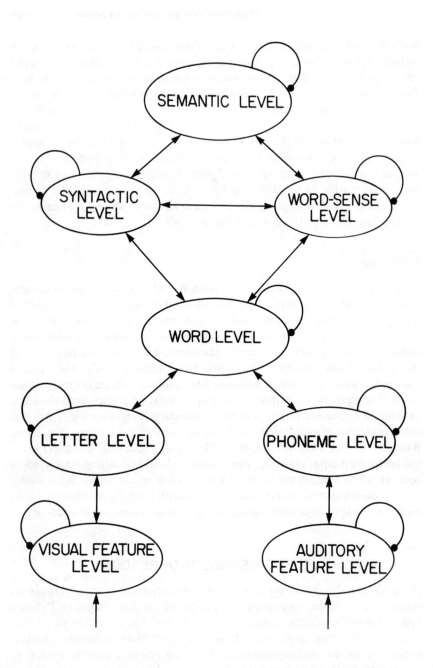

FIG. 7.4. An example of how the interactive activation approach could be extended to allow many types of representation to interact. (Reproduced from McClelland, 1987, with permission.)

way in which the reading process is impaired to produce the observed symptoms.

We consider four types of dyslexia briefly, paying particular attention to visual aspects of the disorders and their implications for understanding normal visual processes in reading.

Letter-by-Letter Reading

The label "letter-by-letter" reader is applied to patients whose reading is slow and laborious, so that their reading times increase markedly as a function of the length of words. In some cases, letter-by-letter readers name each letter aloud as they proceed, so that the classification is easy to apply. In those patients who do not do this, classification is based on reading times alone. One problem here is that reading rates vary quite dramatically amongst the different letter-by-letter readers reported in the literature (e.g. from around 2sec to upwards of 30sec to name a 6-letter word; compare patient R.A.V., Warrington & Shallice, 1980; with patient C.H., Patterson & Kay, 1982). Given such wide differences in reading rate, we may wonder whether quite different problems may underlie the reading impairments in such patients. Nevertheless, in all such cases reading is abnormally slow, hence the classification.

Early interpretations of this disorder suggested that it was due to problems in encoding multiple visual forms simultaneously (Wolpert, 1924; Kinsbourne & Warrington, 1962b). If a patient is only able to encode a few features simultaneously, individual letter recognition may be relatively well preserved. However, reading at the whole-word level will be seriously impaired. This would mean that the effects of word length on reading become magnified because the patients can no longer read words as single units. Note that this argument parallels one we have made about visual agnosia due to impaired encoding of multiple visual features, and indeed patients with this type of agnosia have been found to be letter-by-letter readers (e.g. Humphreys & Riddoch, 1987a). It also follows that letter-by-letter readers should be very impaired at reading stimuli for which global shape is normally very important. A plausible example here is handwriting, as handwritten words often have poorly formulated letters along with preserved overall shape. Consistent with this, handwriting can prove extremely difficult for some letter-by-letter readers to read (Humphreys & Riddoch, 1987a; Warrington & Shallice, 1980).

Despite the above arguments, some authors have doubted the relations between multiple feature coding and letter-by-letter reading. This is because patients can be impaired at reporting briefly presented multiple-letter displays and yet not fit the clinical description of letter-by-letter readers (Warrington & Rabin, 1971). However, given the variation in letter-by-letter reading rates (see earlier), clinical descriptions may not be sensitive to the reading problems of patients. Further work is needed to clarify the exact relations between letter-by-letter reading and deficits in multiple feature coding.

Alternative accounts of letter-by-letter reading also exist. These accounts differ from the aforementioned by emphasising that letter-by-letter reading reflects damage within the word recognition system, and so occurs independently of any deficits in visual processing (with objects). Warrington and Shallice (1980) proposed that letter-by-letter reading results from damage to the "word-form" system, that represents stored descriptions of words as whole visual forms. Because of this, words can only be read by bypassing the word-form system and using analysis based at the single letter level. In contrast, Patterson and Kay (1982) argue that such patients have intact stored recognition units for words. Instead, they suggest that the patients are impaired at mapping letter information on to the stored word-level descriptions. The problem is due to the transmission of information within the word recognition system.

There are various difficulties for both accounts. Howard (in press) notes that letter-by-letter readers can sometimes read words surprisingly quickly. The likelihood of this happening decreases linearly as word length increases. He suggests that this pattern is consistent with the idea that such patients process the letters in words in parallel, but that their parallel letter processing is noisy and error prone—becoming increasingly inefficient with longer words. The data do not fit with serial letter processing in the patients, or with the patients suffering a loss of word-level representations.

One line of work also suggesting partial parallel access to word-level representations comes from studies of "implicit" recognition in letter-by-letter readers. Shallice and Saffran (1986) and Coslett and Saffran (1989) have reported letter-by-letter readers who perform at better than chance levels on forced choice categorisation tasks with words briefly presented to prevent explicit identification. For instance, the patients could judge whether written names were appropriate for males or females when forced to guess, even though they were able to identify only the first letter when asked to name the word aloud. This can be explained in terms similar to those proposed with cases of implicit face recognition in prosopagnosia (Chapter 3). For instance, the word recognition system may be "disconnected" from the system(s) required for explicit identification, or the word recognition system itself may fail to reach threshold. Note, though, that the letter-by-letter readers documented so far have been far from perfect at forced choice categorisation. It remains plausible that such patients have impaired input coding of letter strings but produce above chance performance when constrained by the choices offered by the experimenter.

A final but telling point is that not all letter-by-letter readers manifest implicit word recognition on forced-choice tasks (see Patterson & Kay,

1982). Letter-by-letter reading, like many neurological disorders, is probably not a unitary phenomenon. Letter-by-letter reading could be forced on some patients who have problems assembling multiple visual features simultaneously, or it could be adopted as a strategy by patients who lack explicit access to outputs from word recognition units. Studies need to tease these different types of patient apart in order to relate the disorders to models of normal reading.

Surface Dyslexia

Another type of acquired dyslexia that seems to reflect problems in whole-word reading is surface dyslexia. The main characteristic of surface dyslexic reading is that patients find it difficult to name irregular words (such as PINT; see Patterson, Marshall, & Coltheart, 1985). At the same time, surface dyslexics find it relatively easy to read regular words (such as HINT) and nonwords (e.g. FINT). The relatively preserved reading of regular words and nonwords suggests that the processing of sub-word segments (single letters, letter clusters) is relatively intact, and that the difficulty primarily affects whole-word reading. Irregular words suffer because they are assigned the wrong (regular) pronunciation if their phonological representation is assembled in a piecemeal fashion, using the phonology associated with sub-word orthographic segments. Consistent with this idea, many of the naming errors of surface dyslexics comprise "regularisations".

However, we should again be wary of thinking that all patients who produce regularisation errors have the same underlying problem. For instance, some surface dyslexics comprehend words according to the pronunciation they assign to them. Having mispronounced the word BREAD as "BREED", the patient may state that the word refers to reproduction (cf. Coltheart et al., 1983). Other patients, though, have intact comprehension that is based upon the printed form of the word (e.g. BREAD→ "BREED", "you eat it"; cf. Deloche, Andreewsky, & Desi, 1981; Kay & Patterson, 1985; Kremin, 1985). In the first case, the patient does not gain access to correct semantic information about the word from vision. In the second case, visually based semantic access occurs, and the problem seems more one of naming. Apparently the latter patients fail to access phonology from the correctly accessed semantic description. The patients also fail at accessing phonology from any direct associations that may exist between whole-word visual recognition and the word's pronunciation. To name words, such patients seem to have to bypass whole-word phonology, and to rely on the retrieval and assembly of sub-word phonological segments. Perhaps not surprisingly, the latter type of surface dyslexia is associated with acute disturbances in naming stimuli presented via other modalities (visual or tactile objects, auditory definitions, etc.). Only the first type of surface dyslexics (Type I patients) seen to have a problem in *visual* word recognition.

We need to ask about the nature of the impairment in Type I surface dyslexics. Coltheart et al. (1983) reported that these patients can read out the
names of all the letters in the words they misread (e.g.
BREAD→"BREED", "B", "R", "E", "A", "D"). Thus, the problem is
not in visual letter recognition. Henderson (1981) proposes that such patients have difficulty maintaining a short-term representation of the whole-
word. Temporary maintenance of a visual or graphemic representation of a
word may be useful to support whole-word recognition. Shallice and
McCarthy (1985) propose that Type I surface dyslexics have impaired visual
recognition units for whole-words (as the same authors also argue to be true
of letter-by-letter readers). According to this approach, surface dyslexics
differ from letter-by-letter readers only in that their recognition is based on
letter *sounds* rather than letter *names*. These arguments are difficult to
evaluate from present evidence, as detailed investigations of visual processing have not been conducted with such patients. For instance, it would
be interesting to assess whether Type I surface dyslexics can read out letter
names at a normal rate (suggesting some distinction between them and letter-by-letter readers).

A further complication is that there is a third group of patients who also
have problems in reading irregular words. This third group can be distinguished from other surface dyslexics because they have poor comprehension for all printed words (not just irregular ones), they have
approximately normal word naming latencies, and they are sensitive to the
degree of spelling-to-sound irregularity (Shallice, Warrington, & McCarthy, 1983). One way to characterise this set of symptoms is to suggest that
the patients have lost semantic knowledge about the words, and also the
normal means of transcribing between the stored orthographic unit for the
whole-word and its corresponding phonological unit. Visual aspects of
reading may be presumed to be intact because of the normal reading speed
(Shallice et al., 1983), but mapping between orthography and phonology
operates only at sub-word levels.

More direct evidence for the above claim comes from a patient reported
by McCarthy and Warrington (1986b). This patient could name regular,
although not very irregular words, correctly, at a relatively normal reading
rate, but he could not then comprehend them. When presented with sets of
three words typed alongside each other with no spaces (e.g. OR-
ANGECHICKENRED), the patient (K.T.) was able to read each word
aloud and to copy the items as separate words (ORANGE CHICKEN
RED). This suggests that K.T. was able to segment letter strings using
whole-word orthographic knowledge, despite being quite unable to comprehend what each word meant.

From this we may conclude that surface dyslexia is not necessarily due to
impaired visual analysis of whole words; in at least some cases it could reflect

general problems in retrieving whole-word phonology or more specific problems in mapping from whole-word orthographic, to whole-word phonological units.

Deep Dyslexia

The syndrome that has come to be known as deep dyslexia has four main characteristics:

1. Patients have difficulty reading nonwords (Marshall & Newcombe, 1980).
2. There is a "part of speech" effect; content words are read more accurately than function words (e.g. patients may read BEE but not BE; Morton & Patterson, 1980; Saffran & Marin, 1977).
3. Patients make various types of reading errors, which can be classed as visually related (SHALLOW→SPARROW), semantically related (SWORD→DAGGER), or derived from the root morpheme of the target word (STRENGTH→STRONG) (Marshall & Newcombe, 1973).
4. There is an imageability effect, such that high imageability words are read more accurately than low imageability words (Marshall & Newcombe, 1973). The effect of imageability may underlie the part of speech effect (Allport & Funnell, 1981).

When deep dyslexics make semantic naming errors to words they are often aware that their response is incorrect (Patterson, 1978). The same is not true when visual naming errors occur. This suggests that deep dyslexia involves multiple deficits. Semantic errors occur on occasions when words gain visual access to semantics, with the errors reflecting impaired semantic knowledge or impaired output from the semantic system to phonology (see Coltheart, 1987). Visual errors seem to occur on occasions when visual access to semantics fails, so that the patient's comprehension reflects the error produced rather than the printed word. Thus, such patients have problems both in visual access to semantics and in retrieving phonology when semantic access does occur. In addition, deep dyslexics appear to have problems in mapping sub-word segments (letters, letter clusters) to their corresponding phonological representations, as witnessed by their impaired reading of nonwords.

Interestingly, deep dyslexics can show little or no effect of pattern distortion on reading. Saffran and Marin (1977) showed that their patient could read words when they were case alternated (dOg), written vertically (D

O

G),

vertically displaced (D   G), and when plus signs were inserted between the
O
letters (D+O+G). Also deep dyslexics can show good lexical decision performance, differentiating even low imageability words and function words
from nonwords (Patterson, 1979). This suggests that access to orthographic
representations for words is intact, and that it is disturbed output from these
representations that produces poor visual access to semantics. The lack of an
effect of pattern distortion for these patients also supports our earlier proposal that stored orthographic representations code letter identities and not
just descriptions of whole-word *patterns*.

However, intact access to stored orthographic units is not universal. Howard (1987) reports a deep dyslexic patient, T.M., who was impaired at lexical decision and who was disrupted by manipulations such as inserting plus
signs between the letters of words. T.M. also could not match upper and
lower case versions of letters. T.M.'s reading was poorer than most deep
dyslexics, in that he named only about 30% of concrete nouns correctly
(whereas other deep dyslexics score highly with such stimuli), but it was still
existent. Howard suggests that T.M. was reading using a global description
of words, and that he could not code individual letter identities. In this respect it is interesting that T.M. was not strongly affected by handwriting,
as we earlier noted that overall word shape may be more important for the
reading of handwriting than for the reading of print. However, the global
description apparently used by T.M. does not serve word recognition well,
given his overall poor level of reading. Although this may reflect a specific
disturbance in this patient, it is possible that global shape is normally of little
use unless supported by outputs from the letter identification process (cf.
our earlier discussion on the limited role played by word shape in normal
word identification).

Phonological Dyslexia

Phonological dyslexics have symptoms close to those of deep dyslexics, the
main difference being that phonological dyslexics do not make semantic
errors. Phonological dyslexics are poor at reading nonwords, they can make
visual or derivational errors, and they can have problems reading function
words (see Beauvois & Derouesné, 1979).

Although a number of phonological dyslexics have now been documented, there have been few systematic studies of visual processing in such patients. One study that looked at this a little was reported by Funnell (1983).
The patient concerned, W.B., showed few errors in reading words and his
problem was mainly confined to reading nonwords. Nonwords may require
different visual processes to words. Words can be read at the level of the
whole string, possibly using either overall word shape or parallel information about letter identities (or indeed both). Nonwords require segmenta-

tion and grouping of letters to form appropriate sub-word units (e.g. in the nonword CHIB, the C and the H must be grouped together to address the corresponding phonological representation /tʃ/). Funnell showed that W.B. could read aloud the embedded word (in this case FOR) in letter strings such as ALFORSUT, and suggests that W.B.'s ability to carry out orthographic segmentation was intact. Thus, in this case the problem in reading nonwords was probably not visual in nature, and more likely reflected difficulty in assigning phonology to sub-word orthographic segments. This is not to state that visual problems cannot lead to selective impairments in nonword reading, and on p.257 we discuss impairments of visual attention that may interact with reading processes to produce phonological dyslexia.

Summary

We have suggested that at least some disorders of reading are due to deficits in visual word recognition. Many of these deficits are selective to word recognition, reflecting problems in accessing stored orthographic representations or in mapping from these representations to semantic and phonological representations. The fact that many of these patients have no problem in object recognition shows that some visual processes are specific to reading.

The deficits can be thought of in terms of a "multiple level" account of visual word recognition. For instance, some patients may be impaired at accessing whole-word descriptions, forcing reading to operate at letter or letter cluster levels (e.g. in Type I surface dyslexia). Other patients seem impaired at single letter coding, forcing reading to operate using (imprecise) whole-word descriptions (e.g. Howard, 1987). The relative independence between such deficits also suggests that multiple visual descriptions of words are derived separately and in parallel. In normality, however, the different descriptions may interact co-operatively. Such co-operation may be needed to provide more accurate access to stored orthographic representations of complete words than is possible from word shape alone.

WORD PROCESSING AND VISUAL ATTENTION

Studies with Normal Subjects

So far we have argued that during word recognition, letter and word-level information can be activated together. The activation of word-level information has been treated as an inevitable consequence of presenting a word at fixation to skilled readers. However, there is also some evidence that readers can control such activation. For instance, Johnston and McClelland (1974) first showed that the WSE can be eliminated when subjects know the position of the critical letter in advance and are allowed to focus their atten-

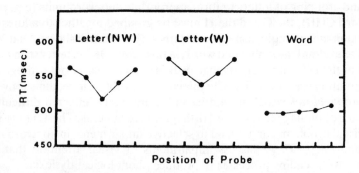

FIG. 7.5.   RTs to probes presented at different positions in 5-letter words or nonwords, according to whether subjects attend to the letters in the strings or the whole word. (Reproduced from LaBerge, 1983, with permission.)

tion on it. Paying attention to the critical letter position improves letter recognition in nonwords, but, paradoxically, it can impair letter recognition in words. Apparently, paying attention to the position of critical letters can limit activation at the word-level, decreasing top-down feedback when letters are in words (see also Holender, 1979; 1985).

We can think of this in terms of subjects having some control over the region of space that they attend to. Attending to the region of space where all the letters of a word fall allows the letters to be processed together, producing strong activation at the word-level. When only some of the letters are attended, processing of the non-attended letters may be delayed, limiting word-level activation.

The effect of paying attention to all the letters in a word seems to benefit the processing of the letters at the end positions. End letters will usually be further away from fixation (assuming we fixate centrally on a word), and so we would expect their processing to suffer. LaBerge (1983) has shown that when subjects process words as words their attention is distributed across the string so that RTs to probes are fast across all letter positions. When subjects search for letters in words RTs are fast only to probes at the central position (i.e. at fixation; see Fig. 7.5). This spread of attention found with word processing seems to boost the processing of end letters to overcome their disadvantage.

This end letter benefit also occurs in tasks where subjects report letters from briefly presented, masked displays. When subjects fixate the middle letter, the middle letter and the end letters are typically reported more accurately than letters in the other positions (e.g. Merikle, Coltheart, & Lowe, 1971). This is true only for letter and number stimuli. When the stimulus is a row of geometric shapes, there is good identification of the middle shape and increasingly poor identification out to the shapes at the ends of the string (i.e. there is an inverted U rather than a W-type function; Hammond & Green, 1982). The inverted U-shaped function is what might be expected if performance was determined solely by retinal acuity (acuity being highest at the centre of fixation). The result with letters and numbers indicates that subjects can use special, possibly material-specific processes, perhaps tied to attention being distributed across a string, rather than focused at the central position.

Attentional Disorders and Reading

Visual attentional problems can disturb reading in neurological patients. The term "neglect dyslexia" is applied to patients who misread the words just on one side of the page, or the letters at one end of a word (see A.W. Ellis, Flude, & Young, 1987). Interestingly, Patterson and Wilson (1988) have reported a patient whose problem was confined to single words, and who had no particular difficulty with words on one side of the page. Such a dissociation would follow if deficits in scanning the whole page are separate from those in the identification of stimuli in central vision: A separation consistent with the existence of independent scanning and selection mechanisms in visual attention (an argument we proposed in Chapter 5).

The most detailed studies of neglect dyslexia have been conducted on single word reading. Here the reading errors show several interesting characteristics. For instance, they tend to be words rather than nonwords (Kinsbourne & Warrington, 1962c). Also, they tend to involve the substitution of letters (e.g. PEAR→DEAR), rather than additions (PEAR→SPEAR) or deletions (PEAR→EAR), even when all error types would produce word responses (A.W. Ellis et al., 1987). Further, the patient's comprehension seems to be based on the error response. These characteristics suggest that neglect dyslexia can affect the process of mapping letters on to word representations, so that access to word representations (and correct comprehension) is impaired. Nevertheless, the preponderance of substitution errors also suggests that word length is being coded (as substitution errors preserve word length). Word length may represent one of the parameters of a global description of a word that is picked up independently of individual letter processing.

In an interesting manipulation, A. W. Ellis et al. (1987) presented their patient with inverted words. Whereas formerly the patient neglected the beginnings of words, she now neglected their ends; that is, she neglected the letters that fell at the left-hand end of the strings, irrespective of whether they were the first or last letters in the words. This shows that the patient's neglect is based on spatial coordinates, and not on the positions of the letters in the words (at the end or the beginning).

Sieroff, Pollatsek, and Posner (1988) have also shown that neglect dyslexia can be more severe for nonwords than for words. Under tachistoscopic presentation conditions, patients with right-parietal lesions made proportionately more errors to the left-hand letters of nonwords than words, whereas patients with left-parietal lesions made proportionately more errors to the right-hand ends of nonwords. These problems with nonwords are not due to abnormal forgetting of their letters, as the patients were instructed to report the left-hand letters first. Instead, Sieroff et al.'s results are consistent with the idea that words can be identified as single units. Nonwords require some form of sequential selection and identification of their letters. In Chapter 5 we proposed that visual neglect can be due to a problem in disengaging attention. Patients who have problems in disengaging attention from previously attended stimuli will have greater problems with nonwords than with words because nonwords require more "fixations" of attention. Also, in line with the argument that the patients have problems in identifying multiple targets, Sieroff et al. showed that patients do neglect words when two words are presented simultaneously (where words require two acts of selection).

These data indicate that attentional processes interact with recognition, in that the ease of visual selection is at least partly determined by the types of stimulus representation mediating recognition. Selection is made easier if there exist stored representations for stimuli, and this differentiates words from nonwords. Because of this interaction we need to be cautious in interpreting recognition problems just in terms of the "architecture" of the recognition system. For instance, a selection problem in reading nonwords but not words might be taken as evidence for the independence of word (lexical) and nonword (non-lexical) processing (e.g. Coltheart, 1985). However, as we have noted, the differences could arise because of the contrasting attentional demands of the stimuli. What we need here is converging evidence for the nature of the patient's problem. Selection problems with nonwords can be mimicked by simultaneously presenting patients with more than one word (Sieroff et al., 1988). This should not hold if the patient's problem is in non-lexical, but not lexical processing. The moral is that patterns of dissociation should only be the beginning of an investigation into a patient's problem.

One rather different impairment in the attentional processes involved in reading has been noted by Shallice and Warrington (1977). They report two patients who could read words quite well but were poor at naming the letters in the words. When asked to identify letters in a letter string, the patients would make localisation errors, so that when asked to report the middle letter in the string GTLKE, they would report "T" or "E" rather than L. This problem was not confined to the reading of single letters in words or letter strings. When reading text, or cards with more than one word on them, the patients made "migration errors" (see earlier). For instance, when shown a card with the words FED and WIN on them, one patient reported the words "FIN" and "WED", combining the letters from the two words and maintaining the relative letter positions. These errors seem analogous to the migration errors normal subjects make when briefly presented with more than one word at a time. One way to conceptualise these effects in normal subjects is to suggest that, with brief presentations, there is rather a broad "attentional window", allowing interchange between the letters of words. In Shallice and Warrington's (1977) patients, brain damage seems to have left them with a broad attentional window even under normal (not time-limited) presentation conditions.

LINGUISTIC CONSTRAINTS ON VISUAL PROCESSING

Words are not simply visual patterns, they also play a specific linguistic role within sentences. Some words are nouns, some verbs, some grammatical function words, and so forth. Further, the meanings of words can be lawfully related to their spelling patterns. Consider the following family of words: READ, READS, READER, READING. These words differ in terms of their *endings* or *suffixes*, but they all have the same *root morpheme*: READ. A morpheme is the smallest spelling unit that carries a unique meaning. In English, families of words conveying a similar meaning can be built around a common root morpheme, with different "inflections" used to specify different grammatical forms. Inflections are usually indicated by suffixes, but can be indicated by vowel change in "irregular" forms (MOUSE→MICE). In other cases, words can be derived from the same root morpheme to take on new meanings. The simplest example here would be where a *prefix* is added to the front of a word to change its meaning (CLEAR→UNCLEAR), although derivational changes are not confined to the addition or substitution of prefixes. A major question is whether the visual processing of words is sensitive to the underlying morphological composition of words. For instance, if word processing can involve various levels of coding between single letters and words, are these intermediary codes determined by morphological rules?

Another possibility is that such intermediary codes are affected by the relations between printed words and their *sounds*. We have already raised the possibility that word endings (their *bodies*) might be thus coded (p.234, earlier). When combined with an initial consonant or consonant cluster (the *onset*), the body plus onset unit becomes a *syllable* (i.e. onset + body = syllable). Is visual word processing determined by rules concerning syllabic structure?

These questions are important for understanding visual word processing. If the answer to either is yes, the implication is that non-visual information (meaning-based morphology, or syllable-based phonology) constrains visual processing, even determining the nature of the visual "unit" derived from print. We discuss the questions consecutively, taking morphology first.

Morphological Effects on Word Processing

The strongest proponents of the idea that visual coding is determined by morphological rules have been Taft and his colleagues (Taft, 1979a, b, 1985, 1987; Taft & Forster, 1976). Taft proposed that word processing was based on something termed a BOSS (for Basic Orthographic Syllabic Structure).

The BOSS is the first part of a word up to its root morpheme, including all consonants following the first vowel without creating an illegal consonant cluster in the final position. In this context, an illegal consonant cluster is one that cannot occupy the final letter positions in an English word. The BOSS of WALRUS is WAL, not WALR, because LR is an illegal final consonant cluster. In contrast, the BOSS of LANTERN is LANT, because NT is a legal final consonant cluster. The BOSS also cannot be larger than a single morpheme, so that the BOSS of TEAPOT is TEA (the first morpheme), even though TEAP would have an orthographically legal ending. The BOSS thus represents a complex combination of morphological and orthographic constraints.

Taft suggested that word recognition initially takes place using the BOSS of a word, which is matched with a stored "listing" of BOSSes. Once a match has occurred, full information about the set of words that are morphologically related to the BOSS is made available, as illustrated in Fig. 7.6. It remains unclear how recognition of the particular word then takes place (e.g. that the word is FINAL as opposed to INFINITE, see Fig. 7.6), but presumably this is via a further process that recombines the stem with its affixes (the prefixes and suffixes that are attached to the root morpheme).

For such a system to operate, the word must first be divided up into its affixes and BOSS segments, so that the BOSS can be matched against stored knowledge. That is, there must be some form of *pre-lexical morphological decomposition* ("affix stripping"). It is clear that morphological decomposition adds a good deal of complexity to the word recognition process, and has the added disadvantage of being intuitively implausible to many people (see Henderson, 1985). Nevertheless, intuitive implausibility alone is not a good reason to reject a theory. Also, the added complexity due to decomposition can be weighed against the benefit of economy of storage. There needs only to be one entry for the root morpheme FIN in the BOSS listing that serves for the recognition of morphologically related words such as FINISH, FINITE, FINAL, INFINITE, etc. (Fig. 7.6).

The idea of morphological decomposition has been examined in a variety of ways (see Henderson, 1985, and Taft, 1985, for detailed reviews). Among the most impressive experiments are those examining priming between morphologically related words. In a typical experiment of this sort subjects first see a set of words, and are some time later re-presented with those words plus a set of (unprimed) words that were not originally present. Responses to the second set of (target) words are measured as a function of whether the words were primed and the nature of the priming relationship. Reliable morpheme-based repetition effects have been reported, over and above any effects due to the number of letters in common between morphologically-related primes and targets (e.g. CAR primes CARS more than CARD; see Murrell & Morton, 1974). This effect is more pronounced with

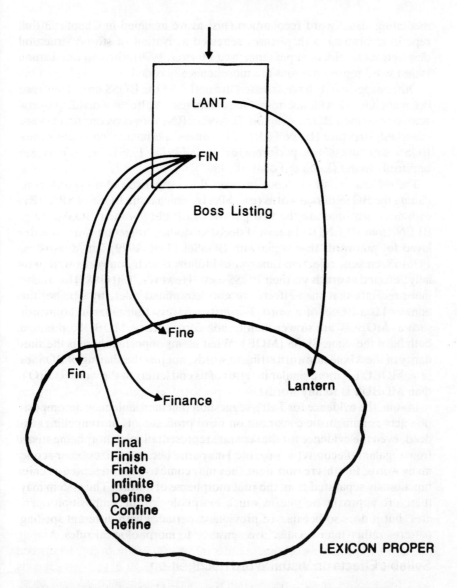

FIG. 7.6.   A processing framework for word recognition based on BOSSes. (Reproduced from Taft, 1987, with permission.)

regular inflections than with derivations (HOUSE primes HOUSES more then APPEAR primes its derivative APPEARANCE; Stanners, Neiser, & Painton, 1979). The interpretation of these priming effects obviously rests upon how one believes priming occurs (see later). However, if priming between primed words reflects activation of the stored representations mediating visual word recognition (just as we assumed in Chapter 3 that repetition priming with pictures reflected activation of stored structural descriptions of object appearance; see Morton, 1979), then an implication is that word representations are morphemically coded.

Other experiments have assessed the notion of the BOSS unit. There are two main lines of evidence here. One compares the effects of dividing words according to their BOSS structure (LANT/ERN) with divisions that violate the BOSS structure (LAN/TERN). In some experiments violations of the BOSS structure slows performance (Taft, 1979; 1987), but this is not uniformly found (Lima & Pollatsek, 1983).

The second line of evidence involves the comparison of nonwords containing the BOSS of real words (e.g. SPAD, which is the BOSS of SPADE), with nonwords that are the first part of words but *not* their BOSSes (e.g. BLEN from BLEND). In lexical decision studies, rejection times are delayed for nonwords that begin with BOSSes (Taft, 1979; Taft & Forster, 1976). Such slow rejection times would follow if such nonwords were initially detected as words via their BOSS code. However, Taft (1987) has found more recently that such effects are not determined solely by whether the nonword is a BOSS of a word. For instance, rejection times to nonwords such as MOBOT are slower than to nonwords such as MOBUS, although both have the same BOSS (MOB). What seems important here is the similarity of the whole nonword string to words, not just the sharing of BOSSes (e.g. MOBOT is more similar in terms of its end letters to the word ROBOT than MOBUS is to any words).

In sum, the evidence for Taft's suggestion that morphological decomposition acts as a linguistic constraint on word processing is uncompelling. Indeed, even the evidence for the separate representation of morpheme stems from regular inflections (-s, -ing, etc.) may arise because affixes occur across many words. For this reason alone they may come to be represented as units functionally separated from the root morpheme of a word. The system may therefore approximate one in which morphological decomposition operates, but it does so because of previous experience with different spelling patterns rather than because it is sensitive to morphological rules.

Syllabic Effects on Visual Word Recognition

We now consider whether the syllabic structure of English phonology affects visual word processing. Mewhort and Beal (1977) presented words as a series of segments from left to right across a display. Report of the words was little affected when the segments were syllables of the word (CAP-IT-AL), and drastically affected when the words were segmented non-syllabically (CA-PI-TAL). As the segments were presented at a fast rate (125msec per segment), it seems unlikely that they were named and that syllabic segmentation was important for naming. An alternative account is that spelling patterns conforming to syllabic segments serve as units in the visual coding of words (see Shallice & McCarthy, 1985, for this argument).

Other evidence pointing to the visual coding of syllabic spelling patterns comes from an experiment by Printzmetal, Treiman, and Rho (1986). These experimenters used the "illusory conjunction" phenomenon that we discussed in Chapter 5 (Treisman & Schmidt, 1982). In Printzmetal et al.'s study, words were printed in two colours. For instance, the word ANVIL had its first three letters printed in red and its final two letters in blue (we will represent this colour change by giving the different coloured letters different cases; e.g. ANVil for the above example). The subject's task was to detect the colour of a target letter (e.g. V). When such stimuli are briefly presented, subjects can make errors by reporting the colour of another letter in the display rather than the target's colour (e.g. that the V is blue and not red). Subjects seem to combine a letter from one location with a colour from another, to form an *illusory conjunction* of a coloured letter. Printzmetal et al. suggested that, if syllables are coded as single visual units, then illusory conjunctions should be less frequent when the target letter is coloured the same as the rest of its syllable (ANvil) than when it has a different colour (ANVil). This is what they found.

However, it turns out that the boundary between syllables in words is often marked by a pair of letters that otherwise occur infrequently together (such as the NV in ANVIL; see Adams, 1981). Instead of units being determined by syllabic rules they could be determined by the frequency of co-occurrence of particular letters. Seidenberg (1987) tested this by comparing pairs of words such as NAIVE and WAIVE. These words have similar spelling patterns, but only NAIVE is bisyllabic. Seidenberg found that NAIVE and WAIVE produced equal numbers of illusory conjunctions, even though WAIVE has no syllabic boundary. Presumably the end letters IVE are processed as a unit *even when they are not a syllable* and so minimise illusory conjunctions with adjacent letters.

There are thus grounds for similar conclusions concerning morphological and syllabic constraints on word processing. Effects can be found that are consistent with these constraints. Yet the constraints themselves seem less important than other properties of word structure, such as the frequency of occurrence of letter patterns. Visual processing may be more strongly determined by visual experience with letter patterns than with linguistic constraints *per se*—a result consistent with the kind of connectionist model of reading that we discussed earlier.

CONTEXT EFFECTS ON VISUAL PROCESSING

We have already considered the word superiority effect—where the context of a whole word facilitates the recognition of a letter within it. So far, however, we have considered only how single words are recognised. Yet in normal reading, words are incorporated into contexts, consisting of other related words and sentences (including repetition of the word itself). In this section we discuss how such contexts affect visual word processing. Many of the context effects that we discuss here are directly analogous to effects that we described in Chapter 3 on visual object recognition.

Repetition Effects

One of the most reliable effects in the word recognition literature is that word recognition is more efficient when a word is repeated within an experiment. This benefit from prior exposure occurs in a large number of tasks, from those clearly related to reading (such as word naming or lexical decision; Scarborough, Cortese, & Scarborough, 1977; Scarborough, Gerard, & Cortese, 1979) to those far removed from normal reading (such as word completion; e.g. what letters complete this word AIS_ _; Tulving, Schacter, & Stark, 1982). The benefit can occur when repetitions are separated by intervals of an hour (Morton, 1979), a day (Jacoby & Dallas, 1981) or even a year (Kolers, 1976; Salasoo, Shiffrin, & Feustel, 1985).

The Logogen Model

One influential account of repetition effects on word recognition is the logogen model (Morton, 1969; 1979). In some ways we can think of logogens as equivalent to word-level representations in the interactive activation model of word recognition that we considered earlier. When a logogen is activated to a critical threshold level, it "fires" and the word is "recognised". The logogen model accounts for repetition effects in the following way. Once a word has been recognised the activation in its logogen decays back to a resting level. However, provided the word is repeated before the representation is in its resting state, there will be a repetition effect because less activation will be needed to reach the threshold level. According to this model, repetition effects reflect changes in the activation states of word detectors. Consistent with this is evidence that repetition lessens the effects of stimulus degradation in lexical decision tasks (e.g. Besner & Swan, 1982).

Given this account, it becomes possible to use repetition effects as a tool to examine the nature of the recognition system. For instance, repetition effects are typically stronger for items re-presented within the same modality than for items re-presented in different modalities (see Chapter 3), suggesting the existence of modality specific recognition systems (Morton, 1979). In a similar vein, the fact that changing the case of words between re-presentations has little effect on repetition (Scarborough et al., 1977) can be taken to indicate that word detectors are "abstract", in that they respond to both lower and upper case letters.

However, not all repetition effects are long lasting. When words are repeated shortly after their initial presentation there is a large, but temporary, benefit followed by a smaller, but more persistent, benefit (Humphreys, Besner, & Quinlan, 1988; Ratcliff, Hockley, & McKoon, 1985). Thus, there are at least two components to the repetition effect. The short-term one may be linked to a temporary memory of the last few items; the long-term one may reflect activation within the word recognition system itself.

Proceduralism

Other accounts of repetition priming have also been offered. One is that performance benefits from repetition whenever subjects engage in the same *procedures* when processing stimuli (Kolers, 1979; Kolers & Smythe, 1979). For instance, subjects are faster at reading inverted text if they have seen the text previously in an inverted, rather than an upright, form (Kolers, 1975). As the same words are involved irrespective of whether the text is inverted, repetition based on logogen activation should be equivalent in the two cases. Instead, it can be argued that repetition of the same coding procedures was critically important.

However, other results are less consistent. Case change has only a minor (if any) affect on repetition, though different coding procedures may operate for lower and upper case words. It seems possible that the procedural account fares best when subjects engage in unusual or novel coding procedures (such as reading inverted text), that are maintained and re-enacted across long intervening intervals.

Episodic Memory

The essence of the logogen model is that word representations become abstracted from specific encounters with words, and so can be used to recognise words in different type faces, etc. The word recognition system is thus separated from an *episodic* memory system that holds information about specific episodes.

Another account of the word repetition effect is that it reflects aspects of episodic memory. According to this idea, previous encounters with words are stored as long-lasting episodic representations, that are re-activated when the words are subsequently recognised. The consequent benefit to performance is a function of the similarity of the re-presented word to the episodic trace (Jacoby, 1983). Also, the episodic system may initially be strongly activated, and then decay to a stable, but nevertheless activated level, to produce the two components of the repetition effect.

The episodic account can explain several findings that are problematic for the logogen model; for instance, that large changes in type font can influence repetition (Jacoby & Hayman, 1987; Kirsner, Dunn & Standen, 1987); that repetition effects increase as a function of the number of words that are repeated within a list (Jacoby, 1983); and that repetition effects decay over the period that recognition memory performance decays (Jacoby, 1983). By recognition memory performance we refer here to the ability of subjects to decide whether a word has been previously presented, a task that is taken as paradigmatic of episodic memory.

The episodic account has its own problems too. Most problematic is evidence showing that episodic memory, assessed by recognition memory performance, dissociates from the repetition effect. In word completion tasks, the ability of subjects to decide whether a word is a repeat (recognition memory success) is statistically independent of whether there is a repetition effect on completion time (Tulving et al., 1982). Also, encouraging subjects to engage in "deep" or semantic coding of words improves recognition memory relative to when words are given only "shallow" or surface coding; it has no influence on the size of the repetition effect (Jacoby & Dallas, 1981). These dissociations are consistent with the logogen account that separate systems mediate the repetition effect and recognition memory performance (namely, the logogen system and an episodic memory system). An alternative proposal is that the dissociations occur because the different tasks tap different processes. Repetition effects between printed words tap aspects of episodic memory concerned with representing the visual properties of words; recognition memory tasks tap more general context-bound retrieval cues (such as the relations between words in a list; Roediger & Blaxton, 1987). The fact that morpheme-based repetition can also occur remains problematic, however, if words are represented as complete episodic traces.

Distributed Memory

Earlier we discussed the interactive activation model of word recognition. Interactive activation is a connectionist model that has separate units for each letter and word in its "internal lexicon". McClelland and Rumelhart (1985) went on to develop a "distributed memory" model in which individual word units (logogens) were replaced by distributed representations. We have already discussed the distributed memory model as it applies to object recognition (Chapter 3). Here we discuss its relevance for understanding repetition effects in word recognition.

In the distributed memory model, stimuli are represented by patterns of connection and connection strengths between "processing units". Recognition takes place because of the characteristic different patterns of activation across the units in the system produced by different words, not because of activation in any single unit. The system can also learn. Learning involves changing the weights on the connections between units so that the system comes to produce the appropriate output to a given input (essentially the initial output from the system is compared with the correct output; where there is a discrepancy, connection weights are changed in a direction that will lessen it). Once the system has learned the correct response to one word, the pattern of activation produced when the word is re-presented constitutes an episodic trace. Following initial learning, connection strengths decay over time. As in the logogen model, a repetition effect is established if the stimulus is re-presented prior to decay being completed. For our purposes the interesting aspect of this model is that, as a word is re-presented across different occasions, the strengths of connections corresponding to variant information on the different occasions will decay. The connection strengths will thus come to reflect invariant aspects of words. That is, they will tend to reflect "abstracted" properties of the word. The model is able to incorporate results found difficult by both the logogen and the episodic memory accounts because it advocates that stimuli are not represented in single units; there can therefore be differential decay for the least reinforced aspects of words, and separate representation for sub-word components (such as stem morphemes and regular inflections, whose letters become "auto-associated", so that letters activate other letters that they tend to co-occur with). Note that the sub-word components generated will often correlate with "linguistic rules", where the rules reflect statistical regularities in the language—as we have suggested might be the case for syllabic effects in visual word perception. In this way connectionist models can operate very similarly to rule-based models without actually having any explicit rules (see Seidenberg & McClelland, 1989, who use a connectionist model to simulate the effects of spelling-to-sound regularity in naming words and nonwords aloud, and illustrate just this point). As far as repetition effects are concerned, the model accounts for associations between recognition memory performance and the word repetition effect provided specific episodic information has not decayed and is tapped by the task; dissociations occur when specific episodic information has decayed and/or when tasks tap visual aspects of performance (that are not assessed in recognition memory tasks).

The distributed memory account stresses the importance of *both* the initial episodic activation generated by stimuli *and* the creation of "abstract" long-term representations. This dual stress seems important because the achievement of an episodic representation seems important to generate long-term repetition effects in the first place. In Chapter 4 we discussed priming effects that occur even when primes are pattern masked so that they cannot be reported. Such masked priming effects last only for a few seconds (and are absent when targets are delayed longer than that; Forster & Davis, 1984; Humphreys et al., 1988). In the distributed memory model, connection strengths may only be adjusted when a word has been fully recognised and an episodic trace achieved. A word presented under sub-threshold conditions (e.g. due to masking) may partially activate its recognition units, and so facilitate subsequent recognition when it is repeated immediately. It will not generate long-term effects without consequent changes in the connection strengths between units. In some senses we can think of such sub-threshold effects as occurring when the prime and target are treated as a common perceptual event, when processes set into operation by the prime are "taken over" by the target (Humphreys et al., 1988).

A demonstration of such "within-event" priming comes from Treisman (1986). Subjects had to name a target letter. Prior to the target appearing, two "priming" letters were presented, each positioned within a box (see Fig. 7.7). The target letter was also positioned within a box. The interval between the prime and the target displays was set so that subjects saw apparent movement between the boxes in the two displays. There were three main conditions: (1) the prime display contained the target letter and it was in the box that moved to the location occupied by the box that contained the target; (2) the prime display contained the target letter but it was in the box that moved to a location not occupied by the target; and (3) the prime and target letters were different. Relative to the different-letter control (condition 3), performance was only facilitated when the prime letter was in the box that moved to the target's position (condition 1). Priming only occurred when primes and targets were perceived as the same episodic event.

In Treisman's study subjects could base their response on the single event they perceived on a trial. In contrast, if the task requires subjects to detect two events, repetition can actually be harmful. Humphreys et al. (1988) gave subjects relatively long (300msec) exposures of lower case prime words followed by briefly presented and masked upper case target words. By 300msec subjects achieve an episodic representation of the prime. Humphreys et al. found that target report was extremely poor when primes and targets had the same identity, so that repetition *impaired* performance. Essentially, repetition made it more likely that primes and targets were perceived as a single perceptual event so that subjects found it difficult to detect the presence of

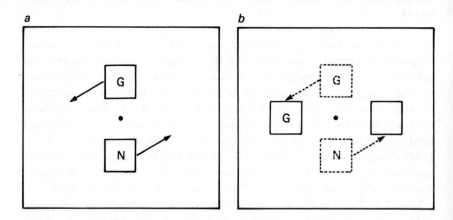

FIG. 7.7. Example displays used by Treisman (1986). Panel (a) shows prime displays which contain boxes that "move" into the locations of boxes in target displays (Panel b). (Reproduced with permission.)

repeated targets, despite their being different in case from primes. Indeed, we may encounter just that this phenomenon in proof-reading, when it is very difficult to notice that a word has been repeated incorrectly (as in "Paris in the the spring"). In the Humphreys et al. study, inserting a mask between the stimuli rendered them detectable as separate perceptual events and re-instated the repetition effect. Thus, "within-event" priming is helpful only when subjects respond to the primed event, otherwise targets must be trea-ted as a separate perceptual episode for priming to occur (priming across events). Various interpretations of these results can be offered, and research into the relations between priming and "event perception" is young enough to caution against over-firm conclusions. Nevertheless, one suggestion is that connection strengths within the word recognition system are re-set by signals that a new perceptual event has occurred (e.g. the activation of dif-ferent representations by a new word or a mask, or just a period of inactivity in the system when there is an interval between word presentations). When a word is repeated immediately it is less likely to be detec-ted as a separate perceptual event because it activates the same repre-sentations. The distinction between within-event and across-event priming fits with the distinction between unit activation and changes in connection strength between units made by the distributed memory model.

Associative Priming

In studies of word recognition, words benefit not only from prior repetitions but also from the prior presentation of associates (DOCTOR→NURSE). Unlike repetition effects, associative priming effects are relatively short last-ing (of the order of 4sec or so; Gough, Alford, & Holley-Wilcox, 1981; Meyer, Schvaneveldt, & Ruddy, 1975). There are various ways to con-ceptualise associative priming; for example, it may reflect feedback to the word recognition system from a semantic system where associative know-ledge is represented (Morton, 1969). One important point is that we need to distinguish associative and repetition priming effects, as repetition effects last for very much longer. For instance, long-term repetition may be due to altering connection strengths in the recognition system, associative priming to temporary fluctuation in activation levels in recognition units. Like the word repetition effect, associative priming is larger for degraded than for undegraded words (Becker, 1979; Meyer et al., 1975). This is consistent with associative priming having some direct effects on the word recognition system.

However, other evidence points to a rather greater difference between repetition and associative priming, because the two effects produce additive effects on performance (Den Heyer, Goring, & Dannenbring, 1985; Wild-ing, 1986). That is, the benefit for targets following associated primes remains the same even when targets are repeated from earlier trials. This additive relationship raises the possibility that repetition and associative priming influence different aspects of performance.

Of course, there is no guarantee that either repetition or associative priming is a unitary phenomenon. We have distinguished two separate short- and long-term components of the repetition effect. Different types of associative priming can also be distinguished. For instance, to achieve associative priming, primes and targets need to occur quite closely in time. In such cases subjects might "integrate" words together, to check whether they have consistent meanings (indeed, such integrative processes may normally play a critical role in text comprehension; Cairns, Cowart, & Jablon, 1981). Associated primes may exert their influence on integration processes operating *after* the words have been recognised.

The argument for *post-recognition* effects has been reinforced by studies contrasting word naming and lexical decision tasks. Several variables influence associative priming in lexical decision tasks but not in naming. One such variable is the proportion of related primes and targets in the experiment. In lexical decision, associative priming effects increase in size as the number of related primes and targets increase (Den Heyer, Briand, & Dannenbring, 1983; Tweedy, Lapinski, & Schvaneveldt, 1977). In naming, associative priming tends both to be smaller overall (although see Meyer et al., 1975) and to be unaffected by the proportion of related items (Seidenberg, Waters, Sanders, & Langer, 1984b). Also priming effects in lexical decision can occur between words that are syntactically but not semantically related (MEN→SWEAR, WHOSE→PLANET) (Goodman, McClelland, & Gibbs, 1981). Syntactic priming has not been found in naming tasks (Seidenberg et al., 1984b). The difference between lexical decision and naming tasks could reflect several factors. If only regular words are used, naming could be based on "assembled" phonology, and whole-word recognition need not be involved (see earlier). Alternatively, lexical decision may be more affected by post-recognition text-integration processes (it is often slower, it involves a binary yes-no decision that may encourage matching strategies, etc.; see Humphreys, 1985). The proportion of related items, and their syntactic relations, may affect post-recognition integration processes and not word recognition itself. Thus some effects of associative priming may occur after word recognition has been achieved. That being the case, the additive relations between repetition and associative priming could be due to their separate effects on pre- and post-recognition processes.

Automatic and Strategic Priming

Hitherto we have discussed context effects as if they were "automatic" consequences of word processing. However, it is possible to distinguish automatic effects from those that reflect strategies adopted by subjects in particular experiments. Consider an experiment by Neely (1977). He used superordinate category names as primes (e.g. fruit, body part, etc.), followed by word or nonword targets. The task was lexical decision. For some category names subjects were told to expect a target from a *different* category (the "shift" condition). For instance, given the prime BODY PART, they were told to expect the name of an item of furniture as the target (e.g. TABLE). The effects of such primes were compared against a "neutral" condition, where the prime was a row of Xs. In the "shift" condition, performance was facilitated (relative to the neutral baseline) when there was a long interval between primes and targets. Neely suggests that this is because subjects take a long time to generate the expectation of the target from the prime. On a small number of trials, the prime in the shift condition was followed by a target from its own (i.e. real) category (e.g. BODY PART→ARM). On these trials RTs were facilitated when there was a short prime-target interval, and inhibited at long prime-target intervals. The facilitation at the short interval can be attributed to the prime automatically activating the target's representation, due to their learned relationship. The inhibition effect at the long interval can be attributed to the disruption produced when subjects' expectation of the target (e.g. as an item of furniture) does not match the target presented. Indeed, inhibitory priming tends to occur when there are a high proportion of related primes and targets in an experiment (Posner & Snyder, 1975), when it is likely that subjects will generate expectations of targets from primes.

It can thus be argued that automatic and strategic priming can be separated by a set of converging factors. Automatic priming is fast acting, based on learned relationships between items, it occurs even when there are few related items in an experiment, and it facilitates performance when the prime and target are related. Strategic priming is slow acting, can involve task-specific relations between items, occurs when there is a high proportion of related items, facilitates performance when expectations are correct, and inhibits performance when expectations are incorrect (Posner & Snyder, 1975). Subsequent research has produced some difficulties for this argument, however. For instance, it is difficult to design a truly neutral prime (Jonides & Mack, 1984); also inhibitory priming can occur even when it is unlikely that priming operates strategically (de Groot, 1984). This makes it difficult to interpret any single result in terms of the automatic/strategic distinction (e.g. it need not follow that priming is strategic simply because an inhibition effect occurs). Nevertheless, converging evidence may still be used to separate automatic and strategic effects, but to do so requires that contrasting conditions be incorporated into experiments. For instance, if fast acting facilitatory priming occurs, and if it is unaffected by varying the proportion of related primes, one can be more confident that the effect is automatic. Methodological considerations aside, it is important to bear in mind whether priming is automatic or strategic when interpreting results. We may infer that priming tells us about the processes involved in normal reading if the effects are automatic, and not due to specific experimental strategies. This point is relevant to our discussion of priming and visual processing. Seidenberg et al.'s (1984b) data suggest that the proportion of related primes influences post- rather than pre-recognition processes. As the proportion of related primes also determines strategic priming, it follows that strategic priming is a post-recognition phenomenon. Only automatic priming may reflect changes within the word recognition system that inter-acts directly with visual processing.

Sentence Contexts

Early studies of the effects of sentence contexts on reading tended to be unanalytic, in that they failed to control *how* sentence context effects occurred (e.g. whether they are automatic or strategic). To be more analytic, neutral contexts are required, and both the time interval and the proportion of related contexts need to be varied. When such measures are taken, the evidence is equivocal on whether sentential information affects visual word processing. Fischler and Bloom (1979) asked subjects to perform a lexical decision task in which the target was preceded by an incomplete sentence or a row of Xs (the neutral context). The target was either predictable from the sentence, unpredictable but semantically and syntactically appropriate, or it was semantically anomalous with respect to the sentence. For instance, the sentence might be *"She sat down on the"*, and it might be followed by the word *chair* (predictable), *floor* (unpredictable but appropriate) or *favour* (anomalous). Relative to the neutral condition, there were no benefits from priming in the appropriate context conditions, and only inhibition in the anomalous condition. This inhibitory effect can be attributed to the difficulty in integrating anomalous words and contexts; a post-recognition effect. The only evidence for facilitatory priming was for words that were *very* predictable from the sentence contexts. It could well be that such words are associatively related to other words in the sentence (such as *sat* and *chair* in our example). Such effects may not reflect priming from a sentence context so much as associative priming between words.

Stanovich and West (1983) used sentences with words that were associated with target words. Their neutral condition comprised a sentence such as *"They said it was the"*, that could be completed by *any* target. Relative to this control, there was facilitatory priming when the sentence related to the target. This result held for naming as well as lexical decision, and it was unaffected by the proportion of related contexts in the experiment. From this it can be argued that priming is automatic and operates on word recognition processes (and is not, in this instance, a post-recognition effect).

Stanovich and West also found that context effects were larger for degraded than for undegraded target words. This result has not been found in other studies of sentence context effects (e.g. Schuberth, Spoehr, & Lane, 1981, report that sentence contexts and degradation combine additively). These differences can be resolved if we separate priming between associates and priming from sentences. We suggest that Stanovich and West's experiments assessed associative priming between words, and that only these effects influence visual aspects of reading. The main effects of sentence contexts are not on word recognition but on the ease with which words are integrated into some form of coherent interpretation of the sentence. The effect of degrading a target word is then to add a constant increment to response time, as degradation influences an earlier process removed from text integration mechanisms.

Context Effects: A Summary

We have discussed three main types of context effect on reading, due to: (1) repetition of a word; (2) prior associates of a word; and (3) appropriate sentence contexts. Each of these context effects could occur automatically or they could reflect task-specific strategies adopted by subjects. Automatic priming is most relevant to understanding normal reading.

We have argued that repetition and associative priming directly affect visual processing; for instance, by changing activation levels or connection strengths between units in the word recognition system. However, sentence contexts seem to affect post-recognition processes. This suggests that word recognition processes are relatively *modular*, and detached from the processes involved in interpreting coherent sentences. This is inconsistent with extensions of the interactive activation framework, that hold that both sentential meaning and syntactic constraints feed back to influence word recognition (Fig. 7.4). If such feedback exists, it seems only to have a weak effect on visual word processing.

EYE MOVEMENTS IN READING

Our ability to resolve patterns presented to different regions of the visual field is very limited. There is a region of high acuity, the fovea, at the centre of the retina. However, acuity reduces to about half when a pattern is only half a degree of visual angle off the fovea. For letters to be equally perceptible when we fixate one region of a text, they would need to increase markedly in size as they become more peripheral (see Fig. 7.8). There would be room for few words on a page if print were arranged in this way!

To overcome our limitations in acuity, we need to make fixations across a text as we read, bringing words on to the fovea so that they can be accurately resolved. Thus, reading typically involves us making a series of *saccades*,

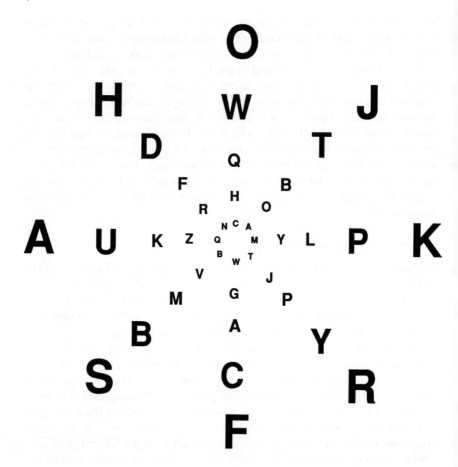

FIG. 7.8. Illustration of how letter size must be increased non-linearly as retinal eccentricity increases in order to maintain letter discriminability. (Reproduced from Anstis, 1974, with permission.)

separated by fixational pauses of 200–300msec. In this section we consider the kinds of information used to control eye movements and the role of peripheral visual information in reading.

Measuring Eye Movements

Eye movements during reading are typically measured using either the *moving window* or the *boundary* technique. In the moving window technique, eye movements are recorded as subjects read text. However, apart from a small window region, the rest of the text is mutilated (e.g. it consists of rows of Xs rather than words). Wherever readers look, the proper text is displayed, but as eye movements are made the previously displayed text is replaced by mutilated text and new text is displayed at the point of fixation. By altering the size of the window, experimenters can estimate the amount of information that is used on a given fixation (the *perceptual span*).

In the boundary technique, the full text is displayed, but a critical word or letter in a sentence is altered during a saccade. By varying the distance between the altered word or letter and the point of fixation, the perceptual span can again be measured. Illustrations of these techniques are given in Fig. 7.9.

Basic Characteristics of Eye Movements

Both fixation durations and saccade lengths alter as a function of the difficulty of the text, the experience of the reader, and so on (e.g. Just & Carpenter, 1980). Thus, measures of fixation duration and saccade length provide "on-line" measures of reading (as reading operates in real time).

```
The fluent processing of words during silent reading        Normal text


_____

                                                            13-character
XXXXXXXXXXprocessing ofXXXXXXXXXXXXXXXXXXXXXXXXXXXXXX        window (spaces
            .
                                                            filled)
XXXXXXXXXXXXXXXXssing of wordXXXXXXXXXXXXXXXXXXXXXXXXX
                        .

_____

                                                            13-character
XXX XXXXXX processing of XXXXX XXXXXX XXXXXX XXXXXXX         window (spaces
             .
                                                            preserved)
XXX XXXXXX XXXXXssing of wordX XXXXXX XXXXXX XXXXXXX
                     .

_____

XXX XXXXXX processing of XXXXX XXXXXX XXXXXX XXXXXXX         2-word
             .                                              window
XXX XXXXXX XXXXXXXXXX of words XXXXXX XXXXXX XXXXXXX
                        .

_____

The fluent processing of green during silent reading       Boundary
                 .                                          technique
The fluent processing of words during silent reading
```

FIG. 7.9.   An example of window and boundary techniques used to measure eye movements in reading. (Reproduced from Rayner & Pollatsek, 1987, with permission.)

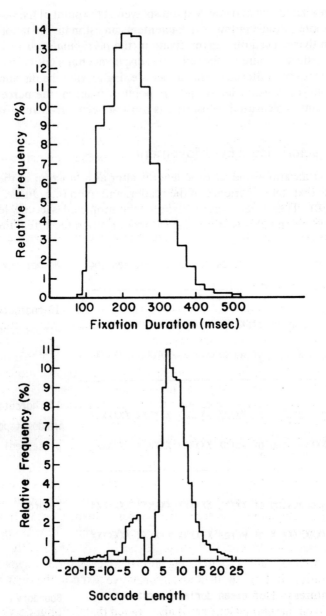

FIG. 7.10.   Typical range of fixation durations and saccade lengths found in reading text. (Reproduced from Rayner & Pollatsek, 1987, with permission.)

Data on the range of fixation durations and saccade lengths that can be observed in normal reading are shown in Fig. 7.10. Interestingly, saccade length is most accurately measured in terms of the number of characters between fixations, and not the visual angle (Morrison, 1983; O'Regan, 1983). This alone suggests that eye movements are affected by more than factors such as visual acuity, as the characters determining saccade length will differ greatly in their resolution at different visual angles.

Two other basic aspects of eye movements are: (1) that they can *regress* as well as moving forward through a text; and (2) that many words in a text are not fixated at all. Regressions tend to be determined by "high-level" factors, such as whether the currently fixated word fits with earlier interpretations of a sentence (Just & Carpenter, 1980). As we shall see, the skipping of words in text could be determined by many factors. For instance, function words tend to be skipped more often than other words; this might be because of their grammatical role, their high frequency in the language or because they are typically short words (or even some combination of these factors; see Carpenter & Just, 1983; Rayner & Pollatsek, 1987). By examining why skipping occurs, we can begin to understand how eye movements are controlled.

The Perceptual Span

Perhaps the simplest model of eye movement control in reading is one where subjects only process fixated words and then move their eyes to the next region of space. This simple model is clearly wrong. For instance, fixations would be highly inaccurate whenever the spacing between words in sentences varies. In fact, irregular spacing has little effect on eye movements (McConkie & Zola, 1987). Also, the model cannot explain why words are skipped, or a mass of data concerning the perceptual span in reading.

There are many studies showing that the perceptual span, although small, is larger than an average sized word at fixation (see Rayner & Pollatsek, 1987, for a review). The span is also asymmetric. It extends 3–4 letters to the left of fixation and up to 15 or so letters to the right of fixation (McConkie & Rayner, 1975, 1976; Rayner & Bertera, 1979). This asymmetry cannot be due to low-level visual processes. The asymmetry of the perceptual span is less marked for beginning than for skilled readers (Rayner, 1986). It is also reversed for readers of languages such as Hebrew, that are written from right to left (Pollatsek, Bolozky, Well, & Rayner, 1981). Apparently, visual processing becomes adapted to using informative material beyond the centre of fixation. In English, the most informative text is to the right of the current fixation; in Hebrew it is to the left.

Rayner, Well, and Pollatsek (1980) also argued that the boundary of the span to the left of fixation was determined by word rather than character information. The boundary could extend up to four characters, but it was less if the beginning of the word was fixated. In contrast, the boundary to the right of fixation seems determined by the number of characters. Rayner, Well, Pollatsek, and Bertera (1982) used the moving window technique.

Windows were defined either in terms of the number of words or the number of characters to the right of fixation. There was no difference between the conditions when the window size (in characters) was equal, though reading was faster in both cases than when only a one-word window was used (see also Lima & Inhoff, 1985; Lima, 1987).

Unfortunately there are complicating factors. Rayner and Pollatsek (1987) have pointed out that there may be different perceptual spans. The total perceptual span is the region of text from which any useful information can be acquired to facilitate eye movements. Experiments such as those by Rayner and his colleagues (Rayner et al., 1980; 1982), measuring saccade length and fixation durations, probably assess this. This span may differ from the letter or word identification span, referring to the region from which either letter- or word-specific information can be used. To illustrate this, consider a study by McConkie and Zola (1987). They used a boundary technique, where critical letters in a word were changed between fixations. Subjects were presented with sentences of the form: John does not store his tools in the shed any more because it (leaks/leans) so much. When subjects made a saccade to the target word from a fixation various character lengths away, the critical letter in the target word changed from a "k" to an "n" (or vice versa). Subjects were then asked which words were present. McConkie and Zola derived a measure termed the letter perception index, that refers to the probability that only one of the two critical words was reported when that word was the one present on the screen prior to the saccade. This measures the probability with which letter information in the periphery is used to determine word identity. The measure was calculated according to the distance of the prior fixation from the changing letter. The overall results are given in Fig. 7.11 (negative values on the x-axis indicate the number of character positions that subjects fixated to the left of the critical letter, positive values indicate the number of character positions to the right). These results show the normal asymmetric distribution of the perceptual span. There was a greater probability of a particular word being reported as its distance from fixation increased when subjects fixated to the left of the critical letter. However, note that the span is of the order of 7 rather than 15 characters. The region over which specific letter information is used for word identification is smaller than the total perceptual span. It seems likely that the total perceptual span involves the use of less detailed information about words, such as their length and boundaries, to guide fixations (Rayner & Pollatsek, 1987).

McConkie and Zola (1987) went on to derive separate measures for letters at different positions in five-letter target words. These results are shown in Fig. 7.12a (points where subjects fixate on the changed letter are indicated by an arrow). Figure 7.12a shows the same asymmetric distributions for each position occupied by the changing letter. The new result is that the curves are displaced along the x-axis. When the changing letter was at the end of the

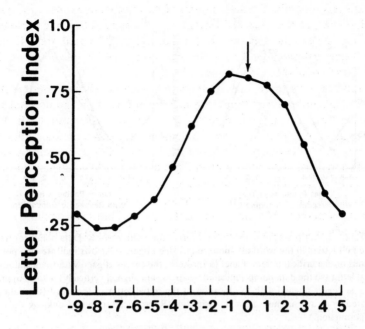

FIG. 7.11.   Letter perception distribution curve. The x-axis represents the location of eye fixations with respect to the critical letter (negative values are to the left, positive values to the right). The y-axis indicates the proportion of fixations on which the word displayed during the fixation was one the subject reported. The arrow indicates the data point for fixations on the critical letter. (Reproduced from McConkie & Zola, 1987, with permission.)

word, it exerted a wider influence on report (across a wider range of fixation positions) than when it was in the first or middle positions. Put simply, the span for the end letters extends to about 8 characters, whereas that for the first and middle letter positions extends to about 6. Also, the end letter in the word had a greater effect on report when subjects fixated one or two positions to its left than when it was directly fixated (note that in Fig. 7.12a, the arrow does not signify the maximum letter perception index). These results clearly cannot be due to differences in visual discriminability (the changing letter should be most discriminable when fixated). Instead, McConkie and Zola argue that the perception of peripheral letters in words is determined by an attentional process operating away from where subjects fixate. Interestingly, if performance is measured in terms of the number of characters between fixation and the critical *word* (rather than the changing letter), the curves for the first, middle, and last letter positions superimpose (Fig. 7.12b). This shows that subjects were using word, rather than letter, inform-

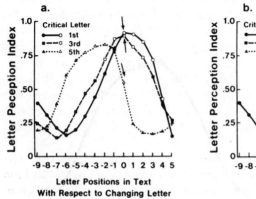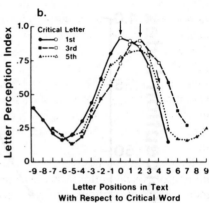

FIG. 7.12. Letter perception distribution curves for 5-letter words. Data points for fixations centred on letters in the word are indicated by open figures. Arrows indicate data points for fixations on the critical letters. Panel (a) presents the curves aligned with the location of the critical letter (so the data points indicated by arrows are aligned vertically). Panel (b) presents the same curves aligned with the location of the initial letter of the word (the data points indicated by arrows are now aligned vertically). (Reproduced from McConkie & Zola, 1987, with permission.)

ation. It matters little whether the changing letter is at the beginning, the middle or the end of the word, only how far subjects fixate from the word.

We have discussed McConkie and Zola's (1987) result in some detail because it suggests that the word or letter identification span is determined by word units. The total perceptual span and the word or letter identification span thus differ qualitatively (one based on the number of characters, one on the number of words), as well as quantitatively (in terms of the distance they cover). We can understand this if we separate two uses of parafoveal information in reading. One occurs when parafoveal information is identified, allowing the word to be skipped by the ensuing saccade. When this happens, subjects seem to attend to the whole word to the right of fixation (the word or letter identification span). The second occurs when information concerning word length and boundaries is used to guide eye movements (the total perceptual span).

The Integration of Information across Saccades

Other work has assessed whether partially identified letters from parafoveal words are integrated with information picked up when the word is subsequently fixated, so facilitating processing at fixation. Rayner (1975) gave subjects "parafoveal previews" of words that were later fixated. Fixation durations were measured. The preview could either maintain or alter the shape of the subsequently fixated word. For the target word *palace*, the preview might be: (1) *police* (a word with the same shape and terminal letters);

(2) *pcluce* (a nonword with the same shape and terminal letters); (3) *pyctce* (a nonword differing in shape but with the same terminal letters); or (4) *qcluec* (a nonword with different terminal letters but the same shape). Target fixations were longer if the preview was qcluec or pyctce than if pcluce was used. Fixations were shortest with the preview palace. Rayner suggested that preliminary visual information was extracted from the parafoveal word (e.g. concerning word shape and terminal letter identities), and integrated with the information picked up on the next fixation. Fixation times are lessened when the parafoveal and subsequently foveated information matches.

The integration of information across fixations could take place within an integrative visual buffer, a spatial representation that codes spatial position independent of fixations. We discussed the possibility of this type of representation in more detail in Chapter 6, where we dealt with different kinds of visual memory representation. However, despite the attractions of the idea, there is little other evidence for visual integration in reading. For instance, in Rayner's (1975) study, word shape is confounded with similarity between letters. The letters that change word shape are also likely to be less similar to the letters they replace than the letters that maintain word shape (see p.240 earlier). Further, McConkie and Zola (1979) conducted an experiment where subjects received mixed case words in which the letters alternated in case during each saccade (cHaNgE to ChAnGe). There was no effect of this alternation on either saccade length or fixation duration measures. Rayner, McConkie, and Zola (1980) also showed no effects of case alternation within a "parafoveal preview" experiment. These experiments indicate that integration operates using letter identities rather than letter shapes.

As well as evidence for integration based on letter identities, there is some evidence for morpheme-based effects. Inhoff (1987) found greater effects of a parafoveal preview if it was the first morpheme in a compound word (e.g. the cow in cowboy), relative to when it was the first part of a "pseudocompound" word (e.g. car in carpet). This may only hold for morphemes that are also words. Prefixes do not produce a larger parafoveal preview advantage than pseudoprefixes (replace vs rescue; Lima, 1987). There is also no positive evidence for semantic information from the parafoveal word influencing its subsequent fixation (Rayner, Balota, & Pollatsek, 1986).

In sum, the evidence points to integration based on partial information about the identities of upcoming letters, and there is little direct evidence for integration based on some form of visual buffer. Such effects can be conceptualised in terms of the parafoveal words partially activating their stored representations so that less information is then required when the words are fixated (McClelland, 1986). The involvement of stored representations also seems necessary to explain the morpheme-based preview effects, although the limitations on processing parafoveal words may be sufficient to minimise access to semantic information. Interestingly, the benefit from parafoveal previews can also be larger if the upcoming word is predictable from the prior sentential context (Balota, Pollatsek, & Rayner, 1985). This implicates some top-down effects on integration (perhaps parafoveal information is more effective if word representations are in an active state to begin with). Note, however, that similarly to the studies of sentential context we discussed earlier, these effects are limited to cases where the parafoveal words are highly predictable.

Eye Movement Control

We have discussed evidence showing that eye movements are affected by words and letters that fall on parafoveal regions of the retina. We have also suggested that parafoveal information can control subsequent fixations because: (1) it enables words to be skipped (when they are identified parafoveally); (2) it guides fixation on the basis of word boundary information; or (3) it reduces fixation time via integration across saccades. Eye movements must also be controlled by processes concerned with understanding the text, in order to produce regressions. Other arguments about cognitive control of eye movements stem from attempts to measure the durations of various processes as they occur "on-line" during reading. McConkie, Underwood, Zola, and Wolverton (1985) changed a word at fixation 100msec after fixation had begun. Fixation durations were affected by this change after about 200msec. This suggests that visual information from a word can be picked up and signalled to the eye movement system within as little as 100msec. This leaves considerable time during a typical fixation of 200–300msec for cognitive operations to determine where the next eye movement falls.

Yet not all eye movements can be open to cognitive control. For instance, fixations of 50–100msec duration sometimes occur during normal reading. Such fixations are simply too fast for many cognitive operations to direct subsequent eye movements (though the information picked up on such fixations may still be identified; the argument here is specific to whether this information can affect eye movements). Possibly some eye movements are pre-programmed on prior fixations. Morrison (1984) and Rayner and Pollatsek (1981) have conducted experiments where delays were introduced before the text was presented at each fixation. They found that anticipatory eye movements did occur before the text appeared. Morrison (1984) argued that two or more eye movements can be programmed at a time. As each word is processed, an attentional mechanism moves to the next word, and this triggers an instruction to make an eye movement. If the parafoveal word is identified, attention may be shifted again. The first eye movement can then be cancelled and only the second executed (producing skipping). There can also be intermediary effects. If attention is shifted too slowly there may be insufficient time to cancel the first movement. This produces two eye movements in rapid succession with only a brief fixation in between.

Other data showing that eye movements cannot be completely controlled come from studies examining where the eye tends to land in words. O'Regan, Levy-Schoen, Pynte, and Brugaillere (1984) reported that subjects tend to fixate at the centre of words. This occurs even though there are optimal locations for fixating words of different lengths. For longer words, the optimal viewing position is actually to the left of centre, and fixation durations increase if they fall in other locations. These effects are not influenced by word frequency (O'Regan & Levy-Schoen, 1987), and are not easily altered by telling subjects where to fixate in advance (see Fig. 7.13). One suggestion is that fixation location is governed by the perceived "centre of gravity" of the string, that is itself determined by low spatial frequency pattern information (see Findlay, 1982). Interestingly, if subjects delay their saccades, fixation is more accurate (Coëffé & O'Regan, 1987). Possibly finer local analysis of the target string can take place in those instances.

Eye movement control thus seems to involve interactions between fairly automatic mechanisms, governed perhaps by low spatial frequency informa-

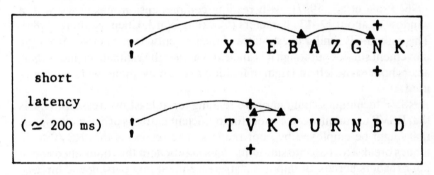

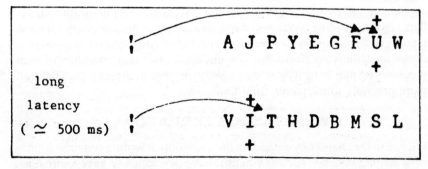

FIG. 7.13.   Example illustrations showing the positions where the eye tends to land in a 9-letter string when aiming for the positions indicated by crosses. (Reproduced from O'Regan & Levy-Schoen, 1987, with permission.)

tion in a string, and higher-level control mechanisms. These higher-level mechanisms may need to exert some inhibitory influence on the lower-level mechanisms to produce regressions and re-fixations of words (Rayner & Pollatsek, 1987): An idea we discussed in some detail in Chapter 5.

READING WITHOUT EYE MOVEMENTS: RAPID SERIAL VISUAL PRESENTATION

In computerised displays it is possible to present texts in such a way that the need for eye movements is eliminated. For instance, instead of spreading words across a page, words can be presented consecutively at the same spatial location, at rates similar to those found in normal reading (e.g. with new words presented every 250msec or so). This is termed rapid serial visual presentation (RSVP). Despite the apparent artificiality of RSVP procedures, subjects can adapt rapidly to them and show good comprehension for passages presented this way. RSVP reading is no worse, and can sometimes be better, than reading text on pages (Juola, 1988; Juola, Ward, & McNamara, 1982; Potter, Kroll, & Harris, 1980). The advantage for RSVP presented text can be larger for poor, relative to skilled, readers (Chen, 1986; Juola et al., 1987), with reading comprehension maximised with a window of about 12–13 characters (Cocklin, Ward, Chen, & Juola, 1984). This estimate is similar to estimates of the perceptual span derived from eye movement studies, although it is unclear whether the estimate includes characters both to the left and right of fixation as eye movements were not measured.

RSVP techniques could improve reading for at least two reasons. One is that RSVP techniques can correct for inefficient patterns of eye movements, that might be employed by poor readers. The second is that RSVP techniques break a text up into sub-units. This may benefit the comprehension of poor readers because it imposes a structure upon text parsing and integration (Juola, 1988). The findings indicate that although variations in eye movement patterns (changes in saccadic extent and fixation duration) reflect ongoing reading processes, these variations are not necessary for good reading comprehension. Text reading involves our adapting basic visual processes to optimise performance. By improving our understanding of such processes we may in turn be able to develop presentation techniques tailored more precisely to overcome their limitations.

WORDS AND OBJECTS: A CODA

We began the chapter by discussing the evolution of writing systems. Alphabetic writing systems, such as English, have developed to have a direct relationship between sub-components of words and their sounds. However, despite such direct relations, we have reviewed evidence showing that English words are read at a whole-word level, due to the spatially parallel processing of their letters. Processing can also take place at the sub-word level, but sub-word processing overlaps in time with that at the word-level. Visual processing thus seems to involve the processing of displays at multiple spatial levels. In reading, we can think of the processing of word units, letter cluster units, letter units, and so forth. This kind of hierarchical processing seems to apply to reading as much as to object recognition (Chapter 3). Similarly word recognition, like object recognition, seems constrained by stored knowledge, which feeds back to influence earlier processing.

We end by asking whether there are visual processes specific to reading, that are not encountered in object recognition. We highlight two. One concerns attentional processes and eye movements. During word recognition subjects seem able to attend to all the letters in words. This is useful because words often lack the redundancy of objects. Many words share the same spelling patterns, and so it may be difficult to recognise a word at a glance without paying attention to all its letters. This may be less true of objects. Often the parts of objects can be inferred even if they are unattended, because objects have more individual structures and because they have redundant properties, such as symmetry. Also, in reading, eye movements must be made systematically in a particular direction (left to right in English, regressions apart). Such eye movements also seem tied to shifting attention to the right during fixation. There is little evidence for eye movements being tied to a particular direction of movement in object recognition.

A second difference may occur due to the arbitrary relations between English words and their meanings (though obviously this is less true of languages that maintain ideographic writing systems, such as Kanji in Japanese). Words representing a particular class of objects will generally bear no greater resemblance to one another than words representing objects from different classes. This is not true for most objects (though there may be exceptions, such as faces). Objects from many natural classes resemble one another more closely than objects from other classes (e.g. many animals resemble one another, as do birds, insects, etc.). It may be that visual processing capitalises on these family resemblances to optimise recognition. As noted in Chapter 3, objects can be categorised more rapidly than words (Potter & Faulconer, 1975), particularly when object categorisation can be based on reliable physical differences between the categories. A different picture emerges when objects come from categories where there is high cross-category resemblance (e.g. distinguishing fruits from vegetables). In this case, categorisation can even be slower with objects than with words (presumably it is slower for objects because of the high levels of physical resemblance across the categories, so that objects from the two categories take a long time to distinguish visually; see Snodgrass & McCullough, 1986). Thus, at least part of the advantage for object categorisation over word categorisation seems to stem from sensitivity to visual characteristics that distinguish different classes of object. Additionally, categorisation times to objects from natural categories correlate minimally with categorisation times to their corresponding words, suggesting that the two tasks tap different types of information (e.g. physical resemblance vs semantic descriptions; Riddoch & Humphreys, 1987a). There are much stronger correlations between object and word categorisation for objects from man-made categories. These objects tend to have much lower levels of family resemblance, so that both objects and words are categorised using semantic descriptions. The different degrees of family resemblance between natural objects can have relatively profound effects on their processing; this holds for object, but not for word recognition.

Object and word recognition can thus diverge in various ways. These differences will need to be taken account of in any future attempts to model object and word recognition within a single system, and it may be because of these processing differences that we encounter selective disturbances in object and word processing following brain damage. This serves to emphasise the theme of this book—that a full understanding of visual cognition will only be achieved by a converging set of operations, where computational constraints are considered along with evidence from psychophysics, experimental psychology, and neuropsychology.

References

Adams, M.J. (1979). Models of word recognition. *Cognitive Psychology*, *11*, 133–176.

Adams, M.J. (1981). What good is orthographic redundancy? In H. Singer & O.J.L. Tzeng (Eds), *Perception of print*. Hillsdale, N.J.: Lawrence Erlbaum Associates Inc.

Adelson, J. & Jonides, J. (1980). The psychophysics of iconic storage. *Journal of Experimental Psychology: Human Perception and Performance*, *6*, 486–493.

Albert, M.L. (1973). A simple test of visual neglect. *Neurology*, *23*, 658–665.

Aleksander, I. (1983). Emergent intelligent properties of progressively structured pattern recognition nets. *Pattern Recognition Letters*, *1*, 375–384.

Allport, D.A. (1977). On knowing the meaning of words we are unable to report: The effects of visual masking. In S. Dornic (Ed.), *Attention and performance, VI*. Hillsdale, N.J.: Lawrence Erlbaum Associates Inc.

Allport, D.A. (1987). Selection for action: Some behavioral and neurophysiological considerations of attention and action. In H. Heuer & A.F. Saunders (Eds.), *Perspectives on perception and action*. Hillsdale, N.J.: Lawrence Erlbaum Associates Inc.

Allport, D.A. & Funnell, E. (1981). Components of the mental lexicon. *Philosophical Transactions of the Royal Society of London, B295*, 397–410.

Allport, D.A., Tipper, S.P., & Chmiel, N.R.J. (1985). Perceptual integration and post-categorical filtering. In M.I. Posner & O.S.M. Marin (Eds), *Attention and performance, XI*. Hillsdale, N.J.: Lawrence Erlbaum Associates Inc.

Anderson, J.R. (1978). Arguments concerning representations for mental imagery. *Psychological Review*, *85*, 249–277.

Anstis, S.M. (1974). A chart demonstrating variations in acuity with retinal position. *Vision Research*, *14*, 579–582.

Assal, G., Favre, C., & Anderes, J.P. (1984). Non-reconnaissance d'animaux familiers chez un paysan. *Revue Neurologie*, *140*, 580–584.

Averbach, E. & Coriell, A.S. (1961). Short-term memory in vision. *Bell System Technical Journal*, *40*, 309–328.

Baddeley, A.D. (1976). *The psychology of memory*. New York: Harper & Row.

Baddeley, A.D. (1986). *Working memory*. Oxford: Oxford University Press.

Baddeley, A.D. & Hitch, G. (1974). Working memory. In G. Bower (Ed.), *The psychology of learning and motivation, VIII*. New York: Academic Press, pp. 47–89.

Baddeley, A.D. & Lieberman, K. (1980). Spatial working memory. In R. Nickerson (Ed.), *Attention and performance, VIII*. Hillsdale, N.J.: Lawrence Erlbaum Associates Inc.

Bahrick, H.P. & Boucher, B. (1968). Retention of visual and verbal codes of the same stimuli. *Journal of Experimental Psychology, 78*, 417–422.

Ballard, D.H. & Brown, C.M. (1982). *Computer vision*. Englewood-Cliffs, New Jersey: Prentice-Hall.

Ballard, D.H., Hinton, G.E., & Sejnowski, T.K. (1983). Parallel visual computation. *Nature, 306*, 306–326.

Balota, D.A., Pollatsek, A., & Rayner, K. (1985). The interaction of contextual constraints and parafoveal visual information in reading. *Cognitive Psychology, 17*, 364–390.

Banks, W.P. & Flora, J. (1977). Semantic and perceptual processes in symbolic comparison. *Journal of Experimental Psychology: Human Perception and Performance, 3*, 278–290.

Barlow, H.B. & Levick, W.R. (1965). The mechanism of directionally selective units in rabbit's retina. *Journal of Physiology, 178*, 477–504.

Baron, J. & Strawson, C. (1976). Use of orthographic and word-specific knowledge in reading words aloud. *Journal of Experimental Psychology: Human Perception and Performance, 2*, 386–393.

Baron, J. & Thurston, I. (1973). An analysis of the word superiority effect. *Cognitive Psychology, 4*, 207–228.

Barrow, H.G. & Tenenbaum, J.M. (1981). Computational vision. *Proceedings of the IEEE, 69*, 592–595.

Bartlett, F.C. (1932). *Remembering*. Cambridge: Cambridge University Press.

Bartram, D.J. (1976). Levels of coding in picture-picture comparison tasks. *Memory and Cognition, 4*, 593–602.

Bauer, R.M. (1984). Recognition of names and faces in prosopagnosia: A neuropsychological application of the guilty knowledge test. *Neuropsychologia, 22*, 457–469.

Beauvois, M-F. (1982). Optic aphasia: A process of interaction between vision and language. *Philosophical Transactions of the Royal Society of London, B298*, 35–47.

Beauvois, M-F. & Derouesné, J. (1979). Phonological alexia: Three dissociations. *Journal of Neurology, Neurosurgery, and Psychiatry, 42*, 1115–1124.

Beck, J. (1966). Effect of orientation and of shape similarity on perceptual grouping. *Perception & Psychophysics, 1*, 300–302.

Beck, J. (1967). Perceptual grouping produced by line figures. *Perception & Psychophysics, 2*, 491–495.

Beck, J. & Ambler, B. (1972). Discriminability of differences in line slope and in line arrangements as a function of mask delay. *Perception & Psychophysics, 12*, 33–38.

Beck, J. & Ambler, B. (1973). The effects of concentrated and distributed attention on peripheral acuity. *Perception & Psychophysics, 14*, 225–230.

Becker, C.A. (1976). Allocation of attention during visual word recognition. *Journal of Experimental Psychology: Human Perception and Performance, 2*, 556–566.

Becker, C.A. (1979). Semantic context and word frequency effects in visual word recognition. *Journal of Experimental Psychology: Human Perception and Performance, 5*, 252–259.

Bekerian, D.A. & Bowers, J.M. (1983). Eyewitness testimony: Were we misled? *Journal of Experimental Psychology: Learning, Memory and Cognition, 9*, 139–145.

Benevento, L.A., Creutzfeldt, O.D., & Kuhnt, U. (1972). Significance on intracortical inhibition in the visual cortex. *Nature, 238*, 124–126.

Besner, D., Davelaar, E., Alcott, D., & Parry, P. (1984). Wholistic reading of alphabetic print: Evidence from the FDM and the FBI. In L. Henderson (Ed.), *Orthographies and reading*. London: Lawrence Erlbaum Associates Ltd.

Besner, D. & Hildebrandt, N. (1987). Orthographic and phonological codes in the oral reading of Japanese kana. *Journal of Experimental Psychology: Learning, Memory and Cognition, 13*, 335–343.

Besner, D. & Johnston, J.C. (1987). Reading and the mental lexicon: On the interaction of visual, orthographic, phonological, and lexical information. In W. Marslen-Wilson (Ed.), *Lexical processes and representation*. Cambridge, MA: MIT Press.

Besner, D. & McCann, R.S. (1987). Word frequency and pattern distortion in visual word identification and production: An examination of four classes of models. In M. Coltheart (Ed.), *Attention and performance, XII*. London: Lawrence Erlbaum Associates Ltd.

Besner, D. & Swan, M. (1982). Models of lexical access in visual word recognition. *Quarterly Journal of Experimental Psychology, 34A,* 313–325.

Beyn, E.S. & Knyaezeva, G.R. (1962). The problem of prosopagnosia. *Journal of Neurology, Neurosurgery, and Psychiatry, 25,* 154–158.

Biederman, I. (1972). Perceiving real-world scenes. *Science, 177,* 77–80.

Biederman, I. (1987). Recognition by components: A theory of human image understanding. *Psychological Review, 94,* 115–145.

Biederman, I., Mezzanotte, R.J., & Rabinowitz, J.C. (1982). Scene perception: Detecting and judging objects undergoing relational violations. *Cognitive Psychology, 14,* 143–177.

Bisiach, E. & Luzzatti, C. (1978). Unilateral neglect of representational space. *Cortex, 14,* 129–133.

Bisiach, E., Capitani, E., Luzzatti, C., & Perani, D. (1981). Brain and conscious representation of outside reality. *Neuropsychologia, 19,* 543–551.

Bisiach, E., Perani, D., Vallar, G., & Berti, A. (1986). Unilateral neglect: Personal and extrapersonal. *Neuropsychologia, 24,* 759–767.

Blakemore, C. & Campbell, F.W. (1969). On the existence of neurons in the human visual system selectively responsive to the orientation and size of retinal images. *Journal of Physiology, 203,* 237–260.

Bodamer, J. (1947). Die Prosop-Agnosie. *Archiv für Psychiatrie und Nervenkrankheiten, 179,* 6–53.

Bornstein, B. (1963). Prosopagnosia. In L. Halpern (Ed.), *Problems of dynamic neurology*. Jerusalem: Hadessah Medical School.

Bower, G.H. & Karlin, M.B. (1974). Depth of processing pictures of faces and recognition memory. *Journal of Experimental Psychology, 103,* 751–757.

Boynton, R.M. (1961). Some temporal factors in vision. In W.A. Rosenblith (Ed.), *Sensory communication*. New York: Wiley.

Braddick, O.J. (1973). The masking of apparent motion in random-dot patterns. *Vision Research, 13,* 355–369.

Braddick, O.J. (1980). Low-level and high-level processes in apparent motion. *Philosophical Transactions of the Royal Society of London, B209,* 137–151.

Braddick, O.J. (1982). Binocular vision. In H.B. Barlow & J.D. Mollon (Eds.), *The senses*. Cambridge: Cambridge University Press.

Braddick, O.J., Campbell, F.W., & Atkinson, J. (1978). Channels in vision: Basic aspects. In R. Held, H.W. Leibowitz, & H.L. Teuber (Eds.), *Handbook of sensory physiology, VII, perception*. Heidelberg: Springer.

Brainard, D.H. & Wandell, B.A. (1986). Analysis of the retinex theory of colour vision. *Journal of the Optical Society of America, 3,* 1651–1661.

Breitmeyer, B.G. (1978). Disinhibition in metacontrast masking of vernier acuity targets: Sustained channels inhibit transient channels. *Vision Research, 18,* 1401–1405.

Breitmeyer, B.G. (1980). Unmasking visual masking: A look at the "why" behind the veil of the "how". *Psychological Review, 87,* 52–69.

Breitmeyer, B.G. & Ganz, L. (1976). Implications of sustained and transient channels for theories of visual pattern masking, saccadic suppression, and information processing. *Psychological Review, 83,* 1–36.

Breitmeyer, B.G. & Valberg, A. (1979). Local, foveal inhibitory effects of global, peripheral excitation. *Science, 203,* 463–465.

Brennen, T., Baguley, T., Bright, J., & Bruce, V. (1990). Resolving semantically induced tip-of-the-tongue states for proper nouns. *Memory and Cognition, 18*, 339–347.

Briand, K.A. & Klein, R.M. (1987). Is Posner's "beam" the same as Treisman's "glue"? On the relationship between visual orienting and feature integration theory. *Journal of Experimental Psychology: Human Perception and Performance, 13*, 228–241.

Broadbent, D. (1985). A question of levels: Comment on McClelland and Rumelhart. *Journal of Experimental Psychology: General, 114*, 189–192.

Brooks, L.R. (1967). The suppression of visualization by reading. *Quarterly Journal of Experimental Psychology, 19*, 289–299.

Brooks, L.R. (1968). Spatial and verbal components in the act of recall. *Canadian Journal of Psychology, 22*, 349–368.

Brooks, L. (1977). Visual pattern in fluent word identification. In A.S. Reber & D.L. Scarborough (Eds.), *Towards a psychology of reading*. Hillsdale, N.J.: Lawrence Erlbaum Associates Inc.

Brown, G. (1987). Resolving inconsistency: A computational model of word naming. *Journal of Memory and Language, 26*, 1–23.

Bruce, V. (1983). Recognising faces. *Philosophical Transactions of the Royal Society of London, B302*, 423–436.

Bruce, V. (1988). *Recognising faces*. London: Lawrence Erlbaum Associates Ltd.

Bruce, V. & Green, P.R. (1985). *Visual perception*. London: Lawrence Erlbaum Associates Ltd.

Bruce, V. & Morgan, M.J. (1975). Violations of symmetry and repetition in visual patterns. *Perception, 4*, 239–249.

Bruce, V. & Valentine, T. (1985). Identity priming in the recognition of familiar faces. *British Journal of Psychology, 76*, 373–383.

Bruce, V. & Valentine, T. (1986). Semantic priming of familiar faces. *Quarterly Journal of Experimental Psychology, 38A*, 125–150.

Bruce, V. & Young, A. W. (1986). Understanding face recognition. *British Journal of Psychology, 77*, 305–327.

Bruder, G.A. (1978). Role of visual familiarity in the word-superiority effects obtained with the simultaneous-matching task. *Journal of Experimental Psychology: Human Perception and Performance, 4*, 88–100.

Bruyer, R., Laterre, C., Seron, X., Feyereisen, P., Strypstein, E., Pierrard, E., & Rectem, D. (1983). A case of prosopagnosia with some preserved remembrance of familiar faces. *Brain and Cognition, 2*, 257–284.

Burt, P. & Julesz, B. (1980). Modifications of the classical notion of Panum's fusional area. *Perception, 9*, 671–682.

Buxton, B.F. & Buxton, H. (1983). Monocular depth perception from optical flow by space-time signal processing. *Proceedings of the Royal Society of London, B218*, 27–47.

Cairns, H.S., Cowart, W., & Jablon, A.D. (1981). Effect of prior context upon the integration of lexical information during sentence processing. *Journal of Verbal Learning and Verbal Behaviour, 10*, 445–453.

Campbell, F.W.C. & Robson, J. (1968). Application of Fourier analysis to the visibility of gratings. *Journal of Physiology, 197*, 551–566.

Carpenter, P.A. & Just, M. (1983). What your eyes do while your mind is reading. In K. Rayner (Ed.), *Eye movements in reading: Perceptual and language processes*. New York: Academic Press.

Carr, T.H., Davidson, B.J., & Hawkins, H.L. (1978). Perceptual flexibility in word recognition: Strategies affect orthographic computation but not lexical access. *Journal of Experimental Psychology: Human Perception and Performance, 4*, 674–690.

Carr, T.H. & Pollatsek, A. (1985). Recognising printed words: A look at current models. In D. Besner, T.G. Waller, & G.E. MacKinnon (Eds.), *Reading research: Advances in theory and in practice, V*. New York: Academic Press.

Cattell, J.M. (1886). The time taken up by cerebral operations. *Mind, 11*, 220–242; 377–392; 524–538.

Ceci, S.J., Ross, D.F., & Toglia, M.P. (1987). Age differences in suggestibility: Narrowing the uncertainties. In S.J. Ceci, M.P. Toglia, & D.F. Ross (Eds.), *Children's eyewitness memory.* New York: Springer.

Ceci, S.J., Toglia, M.P., & Ross, D.F. (Eds.) (1987). *Children's eyewitness memory.* New York: Springer.

Cheesman, J. & Merikle, P.M. (1984). Priming with and without awareness. *Perception & Psychophysics, 36*, 387–395.

Cheesman, J. & Merikle, P.M. (1985). Word recognition and consciousness. In D. Besner, T.G. Waller, & G.E. MacKinnon (Eds.), *Reading research: Advances in theory and in practice.* New York: Academic Press.

Chen, H-C. (1986). Effects of reading span and textual coherence on rapid-sequential reading. *Memory and Cognition, 14*, 202–208.

Clark, S.E. (1969). Retrieval of colour information from preperceptual memory. *Journal of Experimental Psychology, 82*, 263–266.

Cleland, B.G., Levick, W.R., & Sanderson, K.J. (1973). Properties of sustained and transient cells in the cat retina. *Journal of Physiology, 228*, 649–680.

Clifford, B.R. & Bull, R. (1978). *The psychology of person identification.* London: Routledge & Kegan Paul.

Cocklin, T.G., Ward, N.J., Chen, H-C., & Juola, J.F. (1984). Factors influencing readability of rapidly presented text segments. *Memory and Cognition, 12*, 431–442.

Coëffé, C. & O'Regan, J.K. (1987). Reducing the influence of non-target stimuli on saccade accuracy: Predictability and latency effects. *Vision Research, 27*, 227–240.

Coltheart, M. (1972). Visual information processing. In P.C. Dodwell (Ed.), *New horizons in psychology.* Harmondsworth: Penguin.

Coltheart, M. (1980). The persistences of vision. *Philosophical Transactions of the Royal Society of London, B290*, 57–69.

Coltheart, M. (1981). Disorders of reading and their implication for models of normal reading. *Visible Language, 15*, 245–286.

Coltheart, M. (1983). Iconic memory. *Philosophical Transactions of the Royal Society of London, B302*, 283–294.

Coltheart, M. (1985). Cognitive neuropsychology and the study of reading. In M.I. Posner & O.S.M. Marin (Eds.), *Attention and performance, XI.* Hillsdale, N.J.: Lawrence Erlbaum Associates Inc.

Coltheart, M. (1987). Functional architecture of the language processing system. In M. Coltheart, G. Sartori, & R. Job (Eds.), *The cognitive neuropsychology of language.* London: Lawrence Erlbaum Associates Ltd.

Coltheart, M., Besner, D., Jonasson, J.T., & Davelaar, E. (1979). Phonological encoding in the lexical decision task. *Quarterly Journal of Experimental Psychology, 31*, 489–507.

Coltheart, M., Masterson, J., Byng, S., Prior, M., & Riddoch, M.J. (1983). Surface dyslexia. *Quarterly Journal of Experimental Psychology, 35A*, 469–496.

Cooper, L.A. & Shepard, R.N. (1973). Chronometric studies of the rotation of mental images. In W.G. Chase (Ed.), *Visual information processing.* New York: Academic Press.

Coslett, H.B. & Saffran, E. (1989). Evidence for preserved reading in "pure alexia". *Brain, 112*, 1091–1110.

Costello, A. de L. & Warrington, E.K. (1987). The dissociation of visuospatial neglect and neglect dyslexia. *Journal of Neurology, Neurosurgery and Psychiatry, 50*, 1110–1116.

Craik, F.I.M. & Lockhart, R.S. (1972). Levels of processing: A framework for memory research. *Journal of Verbal Learning and Verbal Behaviour, 11*, 671–684.

Craik, F.I.M. & Tulving, E. (1975). Depth of processing and the retention of words in episodic memory. *Journal of Experimental Psychology: General, 104*, 268–294.

Crawford, B. (1947). Visual adaptation relation to brief conditioning flashes. *Proceedings of the Royal Society of London, B134*, 283–302.

Crick, F.C. (1984). Function of the thalamic reticular complex: The searchlight hypothesis. *Proceedings of the National Academy of Sciences, 81*, 4586–4590.

Damasio, A.R., Damasio, H., & Van Hoesen, G.W. (1982). Prosopagnosia: Anatomic basis and behavioural mechanisms. *Neurology, 32*, 331–341.

Danta, G., Hilton, R.C., & O'Boyle, D.J. (1978). Hemisphere function and binocular depth perception. *Brain, 101*, 569–589.

Dartnell, H.J.A., Bowmaker, J.K., & Mollon, J.D. (1983). Human visual pigments: Micro-spectrophotometric results from the eyes of seven persons. *Proceedings of the Royal Society of London, B220*, 115–130.

Davy, E. (1952). The intensity-time relation for multiple flashes of light in the peripheral retina. *Journal of the Optical Society of America, 42*, 937–941.

de Groot, A.M.B. (1984). Primed lexical decision: Combined effects of the proportion of related prime-target pairs and the stimulus onset asynchrony of prime and target. *Quarterly Journal of Experimental Psychology, 36A*, 253–280.

de Haan, E.H.F., Young, A.W., & Newcombe, F. (1987). Face recognition without awareness. *Cognitive Neuropsychology, 4*, 385–415.

Den Heyer, K., Briand, K., & Dannenbring, G.L. (1983). Strategic factors in a lexical decision task: Evidence for automatic and attention-driven processes. *Memory and Cognition, 11*, 374–381.

Den Heyer, K., Goring, A., & Dannenbring, G.L. (1985). Semantic priming and word repetition: The two effects are additive. *Journal of Memory and Language, 24*, 699–716.

Deloche, G., Andreewsky, E., & Desi, M. (1981). Surface dyslexia: A case report and some implications to reading models. *Brain and Language, 15*, 12–31.

de Monasterio, F. (1978). Properties of concentrically organised X and Y ganglion cells of macaque retina. *Journal of Neurophysiology, 41*, 1394–1417.

De Renzi, E. (1982). *Disorders of space exploration and cognition*. Chichester: Wiley.

De Renzi, E. (1986). Current issues in prosopagnosia. In H.D. Ellis, M.A. Jeeves, F. Newcombe, & A.W. Young (Eds.), *Aspects of face processing*. Dordrecht: Martinis Nijhoff.

Derrington, A. & Henning, G. (1981). Pattern discrimination with flickering stimuli. *Vision Research, 21*, 597–602.

Devlin, Lord Patrick (1976). *Report to the secretary of State for the Home Department of the Departmental Committee on evidence of identification in criminal cases*. London: Her Majesty's Stationery Office.

Diamond, R. & Carey, S. (1986). Why faces are and are not special: An effect of expertise. *Journal of Experimental Psychology: General, 115*, 107–117.

Dick, A.O. (1974). Iconic memory and its relation to perceptual processing and other memory mechanisms. *Perception & Psychophysics, 16*, 575–596.

Di Lollo, V. (1978). On the spatio-temporal interactions of brief visual displays. In R.H. Day & G.V. Stanley (Eds.), *Studies in perception*. Perth: University of Western Australia.

Dow, B.M. (1974). Functional classes of cells and their laminar distribution in monkey visual cortex. *Journal of Neurophysiology, 37*, 927–946.

Downing, C.J. & Pinker, S. (1985). The spatial structure of visual attention. In M.I. Posner & O.S.M. Marin (Eds.), *Attention and performance, XI*. Hillsdale, N.J.: Lawrence Erlbaum Associates Inc.

Duncan, J. (1984). Selective attention and the organization of visual information. *Journal of Experimental Psychology: General, 113*, 501–517.

Duncan, J. (1985). Visual search and visual attention. In M.I. Posner & O.S.M. Marin (Eds.), *Attention and performance, XI*. Hillsdale, N.J.: Lawrence Erlbaum Associates Inc.

Duncan, J. (1987). Attention and reading: Wholes and parts in shape recognition. In M.

Coltheart (Ed.), *Attention and performance, XII*. London: Lawrence Erlbaum Associates Ltd.

Duncan, J. & Humphreys, G.W. (1989). Visual search and stimulus similarity. *Psychological Review*, *96*, 433–458.

Dyer, F.N. (1973). The Stroop phenomenon and its use in the study of perceptual, cognitive, and response processes. *Memory and Cognition*, *1*, 106–120.

Egeth, H. & Blecker, D. (1971). Differential effects of familiarity on judgements of sameness and difference. *Perception & Psychophysics*, *9*, 321–326.

Eichelman, W.H. (1970). Familiarity effects in the simultaneous matching task. *Journal of Experimental Psychology*, *86*, 275–282.

Ellis, A.W., Flude, B.M., & Young, A.W. (1987). "Neglect dyslexia" and the early visual processing of letters in words. *Cognitive Neuropsychology*, *4*, 439–464.

Ellis, A.W., Young, A.W., Flude, B.M., & Hay, D.C. (1987). Repetition priming of face recognition. *Quarterly Journal of Experimental Psychology*, *39A*, 193–210.

Ellis, R. & Allport, D.A. (1985). Multiple representations for visual objects: A behavioural study. *Paper presented at the Easter meeting of the Society for the Study of Artificial Intelligence and Simulation of Behaviour* (Warwick, 10–12 April, 1985).

Enns, J.T. & Prinzmetal, W. (1984). The role of redundancy in the object-line effect. *Perception & Psychophysics*, *35*, 22–32.

Enroth-Cugell, C. & Robson, J.G. (1966). The contrast sensitivity of retinal ganglion cells of the cat. *Journal of Physiology*, *187*, 517–552.

Epstein, W. & Lovitts, B.E. (1985). Automatic and attentional components in perception of shape-at-a-slant. *Journal of Experimental Psychology: Human Perception and Performance*, *11*, 355–366.

Eriksen, B.A. & Eriksen, C.W. (1974). Effects of noise letters upon the identification of a target letter in a nonsearch task. *Perception & Psychophysics*, *16*, 143–149.

Eriksen, C.W. & Hoffman, M. (1963). Form recognition at brief duration as a function of adapting field and interval between simulations. *Journal of Experimental Psychology*, *65*, 485–499.

Eriksen, C.W. & Hoffman, J.E. (1973). The extent of processing of noise elements during selective encoding from visual displays. *Perception & Psychophysics*, *14*, 155–160.

Eriksen, C.W. & Murphy, T.D. (1987). Movement of attentional focus across the visual field: A critical look at the evidence. *Perception & Psychophysics*, *42*, 299–305.

Eriksen, C.W. & Rohrbaugh, J.W. (1970). Some factors determining efficiency of selective attention. *American Journal of Psychology*, *83*, 330–342.

Eriksen, C.W. & Schultz, D. (1979). Information processing in visual search: A continuous flow conception and experimental results. *Perception & Psychophysics*, *25*, 249–263.

Eriksen, C.W. & Yeh, Y-Y. (1985). Allocation of attention in the visual field. *Journal of Experimental Psychology: Human Perception and Performance*, *11*, 583–597.

Evett, L.J. & Humphreys, G.W. (1981). The use of abstract graphemic information in lexical access. *Quarterly Journal of Experimental Psychology*, *33A*, 325–350.

Farah, M. (1984). The neurological basis of mental imagery: A componential analysis. *Cognition*, *18*, 241–269.

Feldman, J.A. & Ballard, D.H. (1982). Connectionist models and their properties. *Cognitive Science*, *6*, 205–254.

Findlay, J.M. (1982). Global visual processing for saccadic eye movements. *Vision Research*, *22*, 1033–1045.

Finke, R.A. (1980). Levels of equivalence in imagery and perception. *Psychological Review*, *87*, 113–132.

Finke, R.A. (1985). Theories relating mental imagery to perception. *Psychological Bulletin*, *98*, 236–259.

Fischer, B. (1986). The role of attention in the preparation of visually guided eye movements in monkey and man. *Psychological Research, 48,* 251–257.

Fischer, B. & Breitmeyer, B. (1987). Mechanisms of visual attention revealed by saccadic eye movements. *Neuropsychologia, 25,* 73–83.

Fischer, B. & Ramsperger, E. (1984). Human express-saccades: Extremely short reaction times of goal directed eye movements. *Experimental Brain Research, 57,* 191–195.

Fischler, I. & Bloom, P.A. (1979). Automatic and attentional processes in the effects of sentence contexts on word recognition. *Journal of Verbal Learning and Verbal Behaviour, 18,* 1–20.

Fisher, D.F. (1975). Reading and visual search. *Memory and Cognition, 3,* 188–196.

Forster, K.I. & Chambers, S.M. (1973). Lexical access and naming time. *Journal of Verbal Learning and Verbal Behaviour, 12,* 627–635.

Forster, K.I. & Davis, C. (1984). Repetition priming and frequency attenuation in lexical access. *Journal of Experimental Psychology: Learning, Memory and Cognition, 10,* 680–698.

Forster, P.M. (1982). A note on the masking of pictures. *Perception, 11,* 319–324.

Frederiksen, J.R. & Kroll, J.F. (1976). Spelling and sound: Approaches to the internal lexicon. *Journal of Experimental Psychology: Human Perception and Performance, 2,* 361–379.

Freedman, J. & Haber, R.N. (1974). One reason why we rarely forget a face. *Bulletin of the Psychonomic Society, 3,* 107–109.

Friedland, R. & Weinstein, E. (1977). Hemi-attention and hemisphere specialisation: Introduction and historical review. *Advances in Neurology, 18,* 1–31.

Frisby, J.P. (1979). *Seeing: Illusion, brain and mind.* Oxford: Oxford University Press.

Funnell, E. (1983). Phonological processes in reading: New evidence from acquired dyslexia. *British Journal of Psychology, 74,* 159–180.

Fukuda, Y. & Stone, J. (1974). Retinal distribution and central projections of Y-, X-, and W-cells of the cat's retina. *Journal of Neuropsychology, 37,* 749–772.

Gainotti, G., D'Erme, P., Monteleone, D., & Silveri, M.C. (1986). Mechanisms of unilateral spatial neglect in relation to laterality of cerebral lesions. *Brain, 109,* 599–612.

Garner, W.R. (1974). *The processing of information and structure.* Potomac, MD: Lawrence Erlbaum Associates Inc.

Garner, W.R. (1978). Aspects of stimulus: Features, dimensions and configurations. In E. Rosch & B.B. Lloyd (Eds.), *Cognition and categorization.* Hillsdale, N.J.: Lawrence Erlbaum Associates Inc.

Gathercole, S.E. & Broadbent, D.E. (1987). Spatial factors in visual attention: Some compensatory effects of location and the arrival of non-targets. *Perception, 16,* 433–443.

Georgeson, M.A. (1988). Spatial phase dependence and the role of motion detection in monocular and dichoptic forward masking. *Vision Research, 28,* 1193–1205.

Georgeson, M.A. & Georgeson, J.M. (1987). Facilitation and masking of briefly presented gratings: Time-course and contrast dependence. *Vision Research, 27,* 369–379.

Gibling, F. & Davies, G. (1988). Reinstatement of context following exposure to post event information. *British Journal of Psychology, 79,* 129–141.

Gibson, J.J. (1950). *The perception of the visual world.* Boston: Houghton Mifflin.

Gibson, J.J. (1966). *The senses considered as perceptual systems.* Boston: Houghton Mifflin.

Gibson, J.J. (1979). *The ecological approach to visual perception.* Boston: Houghton Mifflin.

Glaser, W.R. & Dungelhoff, F.J. (1984). The time-course of picture word interference. *Journal of Experimental Psychology: Human Perception and Performance, 10,* 640–654.

Glushko, R.J. (1979). The organisation and activation of orthographic knowledge in reading aloud. *Journal of Experimental Psychology: Human Perception and Performance, 5,* 674–691.

Goldberg, M.E. & Segraves, M.A. (1987). Visuospatial and motor attention in the monkey. *Neuropsychologia, 25,* 107–118.

Goldstein, A.G. & Chance, J.E. (1971). Visual recognition memory for complex configurations. *Perception & Psychophysics*, 9, 237–241.

Goldstein, A.G. & Chance, J.E. (1974). Some factors in picture recognition memory. *Journal of General Psychology*, 90, 69–85.

Goodman, G.O., McClelland, J.L., & Gibbs, R.W. Jr. (1981). The role of syntactic context in word recognition. *Memory and Cognition*, 9, 580–586.

Goodman, G.S. (1980). Picture memory: How the action schema affects retention. *Cognitive Psychology*, 12, 473–495.

Gough, P.B. & Cosky, M.J. (1977). One second of reading again. In N.J. Castellan, D.B. Pisoni, & G.R. Potts (Eds.), *Cognitive theory*, 2. Hillsdale, N.J.: Lawrence Erlbaum Associates Inc.

Gough, P.B., Alford, J.A., & Holley-Wilcox, P. (1981). Words and contexts. In O.J.L. Tzeng & H. Singer (Eds.), *Perception of print: Reading research in experimental psychology*. Hillsdale, N.J.: Lawrence Erlbaum Associates Inc.

Graham, N. & Nachmias, J. (1971). Detection of grating patterns containing two spatial frequencies: A comparison of single-channel and multiple-channel models. *Vision Research*, 11, 251–259.

Green, M. (1981). Spatial frequency effects in masking by light. *Vision Research*, 18, 861–866.

Green, M. (1984). Masking by light and the sustained-transient dichotomy. *Perception & Psychophysics*, 35, 519–535.

Green, M. & Odom, J.V. (1984). Interocular transfer of masking by light. *Perception & Psychophysics*, 35, 265–268.

Greenberg, S.N. & Vellutino, F.R. (1988). Evidence for processing of constituent single- and multi-letter codes: Support for multilevel coding in word perception. *Memory and Cognition*, 16, 54–63.

Gregory, R.L. (1973). The confounded eye. In R.L. Gregory & E.H. Gombrich (Eds.), *Illusion in nature and art*. London: Duckworth.

Gregory, R.L. (1980). Perceptions as hypotheses. *Philosophical Transactions of the Royal Society of London*, B290, 181–197.

Grice, G.R., Canham, L., & Boroughs, J.M. (1983). Forest before trees? It depends where you look. *Perception & Psychophysics*, 33, 121–128.

Grossberg, S. & Mingolla, E. (1985). Natural dynamics of perceptual grouping: Textures, boundaries and emergent segmentations. *Perception & Psychophysics*, 38, 141–161.

Gunther, H., Gfroerer, S., & Weiss, L. (1984). Inflection, frequency, and the word superiority effect. *Psychological Research*, 46, 261–281.

Haber, R.N. & Schindler, R.M. (1981). Errors in proofreading: Evidence of syntactic control of letter processing? *Journal of Experimental Psychology: Human Perception and Performance*, 7, 573–579.

Haber, R.N. & Standing, L. (1970). Direct estimates of the apparent duration of a flash. *Canadian Journal of Psychology*, 24, 216–281.

Hammond, E.J. & Green, D.W. (1982). Detecting targets in letter and non-letter arrays. *Canadian Journal of Psychology*, 36, 67–82.

Hawkins, H.L., Reicher, G.M., Rogers, M., & Peterson, L. (1976). Flexible coding in word recognition. *Journal of Experimental Psychology: Human Perception and Performance*, 2, 380–385.

Hay, D.C. & Young, A.W. (1982). The human face. In A.W. Ellis (Ed.), *Normality and pathology in cognitive functions*. London: Academic Press.

Heckenmuller, E.G. (1965). Stabilization of the retinal image: A review of method, effects and theory. *Psychological Bulletin*, 63, 157–169.

Helmholtz, H. von (1866/1925). *Physiological optics*. J.P.C. Sothall (Ed.), New York: Dover.

Henderson, L. (1974). A word superiority effect without orthographic assistance. *Quarterly Journal of Experimental Psychology, 26,* 301–311.

Henderson, L. (1981). Information processing approaches to acquired dyslexia. *Quarterly Journal of Experimental Psychology, 33A,* 507–522.

Henderson, L. (1982). *Orthography and word recognition in reading.* London: Academic Press.

Henderson, L. (1985). Towards a psychology of morphemes. In A.W. Ellis (Ed.), *Progress in the psychology of language, VI.* London: Lawrence Erlbaum Associates Ltd.

Hess, R., Negishi, K., & Creutzfeldt, O. (1975). The horizontal spread of intracortical inhibition in the visual cortex. *Experimental Brain Research, 22,* 415–419.

Heywood, C.A., Wilson, B., & Cowey, A. (1987). A case study of cortical colour "blindness" with relatively intact achromatopic discrimination. *Journal of Neurology, Neurosurgery and Psychiatry, 50,* 22–29.

Hinton, G.E. (1981). A parallel computation that assigns canonical object-based frames of reference. *Proceedings of the International Joint Conference on Artificial Intelligence,* Vancouver, Canada.

Hinton, G.E. & Anderson, J.A. (1981). *Parallel models of associative memory.* Hillsdale, N.J.: Lawrence Erlbaum Associates Inc.

Hoffman, D.D. & Richards, W.A. (1984). Parts of recognition. *Cognition, 18,* 65–96.

Hoffman, K.P., Stone, J., & Sherman, S.M. (1972). Relay of receptive-field properties in dorsal lateral geniculate nucleus of the cat. *Journal of Neurophysiology, 35,* 518–531.

Holender, D. (1979). Identification of words and of single letters with pre- and postknowledge vs. postknowledge of the alternatives. *Perception & Psychophysics, 25,* 313–318.

Holender, D. (1985). Disruptive effect of precueing on the identification of letters in masked words: An attentional interpretation. In M.I. Posner & O.S.M. Marin (Eds.), *Attention and performance, XI.* Hillsdale, N.J.: Lawrence Erlbaum Associates Inc.

Holmes, G. & Horrax, G. (1919). Disturbances of spatial orientation and visual attention with loss of stereoscopic vision. *Archives of Neurology and Psychiatry, 1,* 385–407.

Homa, D., Haver, B., & Schwartz, T. (1976). Perceptibility of schematic face stimuli: Evidence for a perceptual Gestalt. *Memory and Cognition, 4,* 176–185.

Horn, B.K.P. (1974). Determining lightness from an image. *Computer Graphics and Image Processing, 3,* 277–299.

Horn, B.K.P. (1975). Obtaining shape from shading information. In P.H. Winston (Ed.), *The psychology of computer vision.* New York: McGraw-Hill.

Horn, B.K.P. (1977). Understanding image intensities. *Artificial Intelligence, 8,* 201–231.

Howard, D. (1987). Reading without letters? In M. Coltheart, G. Sartori, & R. Job (Eds.), *The cognitive neuropsychology of language.* London: Lawrence Erlbaum Associates Ltd.

Howard, D. (in press). Letter-by-letter readers: Evidence for parallel processing. In D. Besner & G.W. Humphreys (Eds.), *Basic processes in reading: Visual word recognition.* Hillsdale, N.J.: Lawrence Erlbaum Associates Inc.

Hubel, D.H. & Wiesel, T.N. (1959). Receptive fields of single neurons in the cat's striate cortex. *Journal of Physiology, 148,* 574–591.

Hubel, D.H. & Wiesel, T.N. (1968). Receptive fields and functional architecture of monkey striate cortex. *Journal of Physiology, 195,* 215–243.

Hughes, H.C., Layton, W.M., Baird, J.C., & Lester, L.S. (1984). Global precedence in visual pattern recognition. *Perception & Psychophysics, 35,* 361–371.

Humphreys, G.W. (1981). On varying the span of visual attention: Evidence for two modes of spatial attention. *Quarterly Journal of Experimental Psychology, 33A,* 17–31.

Humphreys, G.W. (1983). Reference frames and shape perception. *Cognitive Psychology, 15,* 151–196.

Humphreys, G.W. (1984). Shape constancy: The effects of changing shape orientation and the effects of changing focal features. *Perception & Psychophysics, 36,* 50–64.

Humphreys, G.W. (1985). Attention, automaticity and autonomy in visual word processing.

In D. Besner, T.G. Waller, & G.E. MacKinnon (Eds.), *Reading research: Advances in theory and in practice, V.* New York: Academic Press.

Humphreys, G.W. (1987). Objects, words, brains and computers: Framing the correspondence problem in object and word recognition. *Bulletin of the British Psychological Society*, *40*, 207–210.

Humphreys, G.W. (1989). Parallel distributed processing and psychology. In R.G.M. Morris (Ed.), *Parallel distributed processing: Implications for psychology and neuroscience.* Oxford: Oxford University Press.

Humphreys, G.W., Besner, D., & Quinlan, P.T. (1988). Event perception and the word repetition effect. *Journal of Experimental Psychology: General*, *117*, 51–67.

Humphreys, G.W. & Evett, L.J. (1985). Are there independent lexical and nonlexical routes in word processing? An evaluation of the dual-route theory of reading. *The Behavioral and Brain Sciences*, *8*, 689–740.

Humphreys, G.W., Evett, L.J., & Quinlan, P.T. (in press). The orthographic description in visual word recognition. *Cognitive Psychology*.

Humphreys, G.W., Evett, L.J., Quinlan, P.T., & Besner, D. (1987). Orthographic priming: Qualitative differences between priming from identified and unidentified primes. In M. Coltheart (Ed.), *Attention and performance, XII.* London: Lawrence Erlbaum Associates Ltd.

Humphreys, G.W., Evett, L.J., & Taylor, D.E. (1982). Automatic phonological priming in visual word recognition. *Memory and Cognition*, *10*, 576–590.

Humphreys, G.W. & Quinlan, P.T. (1987). Normal and pathological processes in visual object constancy. In G.W. Humphreys & M.J. Riddoch (Eds), *Visual object processing: A cognitive neuropsychological approach.* London: Lawrence Erlbaum Associates Ltd.

Humphreys, G.W., Quinlan, P.T., & Riddoch, M.J. (1989). Grouping processes in visual search: Effect with single and combined-feature targets. *Journal of Experimental Psychology: General*, *118*, 258–279.

Humphreys, G.W. & Riddoch, M.J. (1984). Routes to object constancy: Implications from neurological impairments of object constancy. *Quarterly Journal of Experimental Psychology*, *36A*, 385–415.

Humphreys, G.W. & Riddoch, M.J. (1985). Authors' corrections to "Routes to object constancy". *Quarterly Journal of Experimental Psychology*, *37A*, 493–495.

Humphreys, G.W. & Riddoch, M.J. (1987a). *To see but not to see: A case study of visual agnosia.* London: Lawrence Erlbaum Associates Ltd.

Humphreys, G.W. & Riddoch, M.J. (1987b). *Visual object processing: A cognitive neuropsychological approach.* London: Lawrence Erlbaum Associates Ltd.

Humphreys, G.W., Riddoch, M.J., & Quinlan, P.T. (1985). Interactive processes in perceptual organization: Evidence from visual agnosia. In M.I. Posner & O.S.M. Marin (Eds.), *Attention and performance, XI*, Hillsdale, N.J.: Lawrence Erlbaum Associates Inc.

Humphreys, G.W., Riddoch, M.J., & Quinlan, P.T. (1988). Cascade processes in picture naming. *Cognitive Neuropsychology*, *5*, 67–104.

Ikeda, H. & Wright, M.J. (1972). Receptive field organization of "sustained" and "transient" retinal ganglion cells which subserve differential functional roles. *Journal of Physiology*, *227*, 769–800.

Inhoff, A.W. (1987). Parafoveal word perception during eye fixations in reading: Effects of visual salience and word structure. In M. Coltheart (Ed.), *Attention and Performance, XII.* London: Lawrence Erlbaum Associates Ltd.

Intraub, H. (1981). Rapid conceptual identification of sequentially presented pictures. *Journal of Experimental Psychology: Human Perception and Performance*, *7*, 604–610.

Intraub, H. (1984). Conceptual masking: The effects of subsequent visual events on memory for pictures. *Journal of Experimental Psychology: Learning, Memory and Cognition*, *10*, 115–125.

Intraub, H. & Nicklos, S. (1985). Levels of processing and picture memory: The physical superiority effect. *Journal of Experimental Psychology: Learning, Memory and Cognition*, *11*, 284–298.

Ittelson, W.H. (1952). *The Ames demonstrations in perception*. Princeton, N.J.: Princeton University Press.

Jacoby, L.L. (1983). Perceptual enhancement: Persistent effects of an experience. *Journal of Experimental Psychology: Learning, Memory and Cognition*, *9*, 21–38.

Jacoby, L.L. & Hayman, C.A.G. (1987). Specific visual transfer in word identification. *Journal of Experimental Psychology: Learning, Memory and Cognition*, *13*, 456–463.

Jacoby, L.L. & Dallas, M. (1981). On the relationship between autobiographical memory and perceptual learning. *Journal of Experimental Psychology: General*, *3*, 306–340.

James, C.T. (1975). The role of semantic information in lexical decisions. *Journal of Experimental Psychology: Human Perception and Performance*, *1*, 130–136.

James, W. (1890/1950). *The principles of psychology*, *1*. New York: Dover.

Joanette, Y., Brouchon, M., Gauthier, L., & Samson, M. (1986). Pointing with left vs. right hand in left visual field neglect. *Neuropsychologia*, *24*, 391–396.

Job, R. & Sartori, G. (1988). The oyster with four legs: A neuropsychological study on the interaction of visual and semantic information. *Cognitive Neuropsychology*, *5*, 105–132.

Johansson, G. (1973). Visual perception of biological motion and a model for its analysis. *Perception & Psychophysics*, *14*, 201–211.

Johnson, N.F., Turner-Lyga, M., & Pettegrew, B.S. (1986). Part-whole relationships in the processing of small visual patterns. *Memory and Cognition*, *14*, 5–16.

Johnson-Laird, P.N. (1983). *Mental models*. Cambridge: Cambridge University Press.

Johnston, J.C. (1978). A test of the sophisticated-guessing theory of word perception. *Cognitive Psychology*, *10*, 123–154.

Johnston, J.C. & McClelland, J.L. (1973). Visual factors in word perception. *Perception & Psychophysics*, *14*, 365–370.

Johnston, J.C. & McClelland, J.L. (1974). Perception of letters in words: Seek not and ye shall find. *Science*, *184*, 1192–1194.

Jolicoeur, P., Gluck, M.A., & Kosslyn, S.M. (1984). Pictures and names: Making the connection. *Cognitive Psychology*, *16*, 243–275.

Jonides, J. (1981). Voluntary versus automatic control over the mind's eye. In J. Long & A.D. Baddeley (Eds.), *Attention and performance, IX*. Hillsdale, N.J.: Lawrence Erlbaum Associates Inc.

Jonides, J. & Mack, R. (1984). On the cost and benefit of cost and benefit. *Psychological Bulletin*, *96*, 29–44.

Julesz, B. (1965, February). Texture and visual perception. *Scientific American*, *212*, 38–48.

Julesz, B. (1971). *Foundations of cyclopean perception*. Chicago: University of Chicago Press.

Julesz, B. & Miller, J. (1975). Independent spatial-frequency-tuned channels in binocular fusion and rivalry. *Perception*, *4*, 125–143.

Juola, J.F. (1988). The use of computer displays to improve reading comprehension. *Applied Cognitive Psychology*, *2*, 87–95.

Juola, J.F., Haugh, D., Trast, S., Ferraro, F.R., & Liebhaber, M. (1987). Reading with and without eye movements. In J.K. O'Regan & A. Levy-Schoen (Eds.), *Eye movements: From physiology to cognition*. Amsterdam: Elsevier.

Juola, J.F., Ward, N.J., & McNamara, T. (1982). Visual search and reading of rapid, serial presentations of letter strings, words, and text. *Journal of Experimental Psychology: General*, *111*, 208–227.

Just, M.A. & Carpenter, P.A. (1980). A theory of reading: From eye fixations to comprehension. *Psychological Review*, *87*, 329–354.

Kahneman, D. & Treisman, A. (1983). Changing views of attention and automaticity. In R. Parasuraman, R. Davies, & J. Beatty (Eds.), *Varieties of attention*. New York: Academic Press.

Kanade, T. (1981). Recovery of the three-dimensional shape of an object from a single view. *Artificial Intelligence*, *17*, 409–460.

Karnath, H-O. (1988). Deficits of attention in acute and recovered visual hemi-neglect. *Neuropsychologia*, *26*, 27–43.

Katz, L. & Feldman, L.B. (1983). Relation between pronunciation and recognition of printed words in deep and shallow orthographies. *Journal of Experimental Psychology: Learning, Memory and Cognition*, *9*, 157–166.

Kay, J. (1985). Mechanisms of oral reading: A critical appraisal of cognitive models. In A.W. Ellis (Ed.), *Progress in the psychology of language*, *2*. London: Lawrence Erlbaum Associates Ltd.

Kay, J. & Bishop, D. (1987). Anatomical differences between nose, palm, and foot, or, the body in question: Further dissection of the processes of sub-lexical spelling-sound translation. In M. Coltheart (Ed.), *Attention and performance, XII*. London: Lawrence Erlbaum Associates Ltd.

Kay, J. & Ellis, A.W. (1987). A cognitive neuropsychological case study of anomia: Implications for psychological models of word retrieval. *Brain*, *110*, 613–629.

Kay, J. & Patterson, K.E. (1985). Routes to meaning in surface dyslexia. In K.E. Patterson, J.C. Marshall, & M. Coltheart (Eds), *Surface dyslexia: Neuropsychological and cognitive studies of phonological reading*. London: Lawrence Erlbaum Associates Ltd.

Kerst, S.M. & Howard, J.H. Jr. (1977). Mental comparisons for ordered information on abstract and concrete dimensions. *Memory and Cognition*, *5*, 227–234.

Kinchla, R.A. & Wolfe, J.M. (1979). The order of visual processing: "Top-down," "bottom-up" or "middle-out". *Perception & Psychophysics*, *25*, 225–231.

Kinsbourne, M. & Warrington, E.K. (1962a). The effect of an aftercoming random pattern on the perception of brief visual stimuli. *Quarterly Journal of Experimental Psychology*, *14*, 223–224.

Kinsbourne, M. & Warrington, E.K. (1962b). A disorder of simultaneous form perception. *Brain*, *85*, 461–486.

Kinsbourne, M. & Warrington, E.K. (1962c). A variety of reading disability associated with right hemisphere lesions. *Journal of Neurology, Neurosurgery and Psychiatry*, *25*, 339–344.

Kirsner, K., Dunn, J., & Standen, P. (1987). Record-based word recognition. In M. Coltheart (Ed.), *Attention and performance, XII*. London: Lawrence Erlbaum Associates Ltd.

Klein, R. (1980). Does oculomotor readiness mediate cognitive control of visual attention? In R.S. Nickerson (Ed.), *Attention and performance, VIII*. Hillsdale, N.J.: Lawrence Erlbaum Associates Inc.

Kohonen, T., Oja, E., & Lehtio, P. (1981). Storage and processing of information in distributed associative memory systems. In G.E. Hinton & J.A. Anderson (Eds.), *Parallel models of associative memory*. Hillsdale, N.J.: Lawrence Erlbaum Associates Inc.

Kolers, P.A. (1968). Some psychological aspects of pattern recognition. In P.A. Kolers & N. Eden (Eds.), *Recognizing patterns*. Cambridge, MA: MIT Press.

Kolers, P.A. (1975). Memorial consequences of automatized encoding. *Journal of Experimental Psychology: Human Learning and Memory*, *1*, 689–701.

Kolers, P.A. (1976). Reading a year later. *Journal of Experimental Psychology: Human Perception and Performance*, *2*, 554–565.

Kolers, P.A. (1979). Reading and knowing. *Canadian Journal of Psychology*, *33*, 106–117.

Kolers, P.A. & Rosner, B.S. (1960). On visual masking (metacontrast): Dichoptic observation. *American Journal of Psychology*, *73*, 2–21.

Kolers, P.A. & Smythe, W.E. (1979). Images, symbols and skills. *Canadian Journal of Psychology*, *33*, 158–184.

Kosslyn, S.M. (1973). Scanning visual images: Some structural implications. *Perception & Psychophysics*, *14*, 90–94.

Kosslyn, S.M. (1975). Information representation in visual images. *Cognitive Psychology, 1*, 341–370.

Kosslyn, S.M. (1976). Can imagery be distinguished from other forms of internal representation? Evidence from studies of information retrieval times. *Memory and Cognition, 4*, 291–297.

Kosslyn, S.M. (1981). The medium and the message in mental imagery. *Psychological Review, 88*, 46–66.

Kosslyn, S.M. (1983). *Image and mind*. Cambridge, MA: Harvard University Press.

Kremin, H. (1985). Routes and strategies in surface dyslexia and dysgraphia. In K.E. Patterson, J.C. Marshall, & M. Coltheart (Eds.), *Surface dyslexia: Neuropsychological and cognitive studies of phonological reading*. London: Lawrence Erlbaum Associates Ltd.

Kroll, J.F. & Potter, M.C. (1984). Recognizing words, pictures and concepts: A comparison of lexical, object and reality decisions. *Journal of Verbal Learning and Verbal Behaviour, 23*, 39–66.

Kroll, N.E. & Ramskov, C.B. (1984). Visual memory as measured by classification and comparison tasks. *Journal of Experimental Psychology: Learning, Memory and Cognition, 10*, 395–420.

Kroll, N.E., Parks, T., Parkinson, S.R., Bieber, S.L., & Johnson, A.L. (1970). Short-term memory while shadowing: Recall of visually and aurally presented letters. *Journal of Experimental Psychology, 85*, 220–224.

Kubovy, M. (1981). Concurrent-pitch segregation and the theory of indispensible attributes. In M. Kubovy & J.R. Pomerantz (Eds.), *Perceptual organization*. Hillsdale, N.J.: Lawrence Erlbaum Associates Inc.

Kuffler, S.W. (1953). Discharge patterns and functional organization of mammalian retina. *Journal of Neurophysiology, 16*, 37–68.

Kulikowski, J.J. & Tolhurst, D.J. (1973). Psychophysical evidence for sustained and transient detectors in human vision. *Journal of Physiology, 232*, 149–162.

LaBerge, D. (1983). Spatial extent of attention to letters and words. *Journal of Experimental Psychology: Human Perception and Performance, 9*, 371–379.

Land, E.H. (1959, May). Experiments in color vision. *Scientific American, 200*, 84–99.

Land, E.H. (1986). Recent advances in retinex theory. *Vision Research, 26*, 7–21.

Land, E.H. & McCann, J.J. (1971). Lightness and retinex theory. *Journal of the Optical Society of America, 61*, 1–11.

Lawler, K.A. (1981). *Aspects of spatial vision after brain injury*. Unpublished Ph.D thesis, Oxford University.

Lanze, M., Weisstein, N., & Harris, J.R. (1982). Perceived depth vs. structural relevance in the object-superiority effect. *Perception & Psychophysics, 31*, 376–382.

Lee, D.N. (1980). The optic flow field: The foundation of vision. *Philosophical Transactions of the Royal Society of London, B290*, 169–179.

Levine, D., Wallach, J., & Farah, M. (1985). Two visual systems in mental imagery: Dissociation of "what" and "where" in imagery disorders due to bilateral posterior cerebral lesions. *Neurology, 35*, 1010–1018.

Lima, S.D. (1987). Morphological analysis in sentence reading. *Journal of Memory and Language, 26*, 84–99.

Lima, S.D. & Inhoff, A.W. (1985). Lexical access during eye fixations in reading: Effects of word-initial letter sequence. *Journal of Experimental Psychology: Human Perception and Performance, 11*, 272–285.

Lima, S.D. & Pollatsek, A. (1983). Lexical access via an orthographic code? The Basic Orthographic Syllabic Structure (BOSS) reconsidered. *Journal of Verbal Learning and Verbal Behaviour, 22*, 310–332.

Lindsay, P.H. & Norman, D.A. (1976). *Human information processing*. New York: Academic Press.

Loftus, E.F. (1977). Shifting human colour memory. *Memory and Cognition*, 5, 696–699.

Loftus, E.F. (1979). *Eyewitness testimony*. Cambridge, MA: Harvard University Press.

Loftus, E.F. (1983). Misfortunes of memory. *Philosophical Transactions of the Royal Society of London*, *B302*, 413–421.

Loftus, E.F. & Greene, E. (1980). Warning: Even memory for faces may be contagious. *Law and Human Behaviour*, 4, 323–334.

Loftus, E.F. & Palmer, J.C. (1974). Reconstruction of automobile destruction: An example of the interaction between language and memory. *Journal of Verbal Learning and Verbal Behaviour*, 13, 585–589.

Loftus, E.F., Miller, D., & Burns, H. (1978). Semantic integration of verbal information into a visual memory. *Journal of Experimental Psychology: Human Learning and Memory*, 4, 19–31.

Loftus, G.R. & Ginn, M. (1984). Perceptual and conceptual processing of pictures. *Journal of Experimental Psychology: Learning, Memory and Cognition*, 10, 435–441.

Loftus, G.R., Hanna, A.M., & Lester, L. (1988). Conceptual masking: How one picture captures attention from another picture. *Cognitive Psychology*, 20, 237–282.

Logie, R.H. (1986). Visuo-spatial processing in working memory. *Quarterly Journal of Experimental Psychology*, *38A*, 229–247.

Long, G.M. & Beaton, R.J. (1982). The case for peripheral persistence: Effects of target and background luminance on a partial-report task. *Journal of Experimental Psychology: Human Perception and Performance*, 8, 383–391.

Long, G.M. & McCarthy, P.R. (1982). Target energy effects on Type 1 and Type 2 visual persistence. *Bulletin of the Psychonomic Society*, 19, 219–221.

Longuet-Higgins, H.C. & Prazdny, K. (1980). The interpretation of moving retinal images. *Proceedings of the Royal Society of London*, *B208*, 385–397.

Lovegrove, W.J. & Evans, P. (1980). Colour selective adaptation in contrast thresholds for detecting the form but not the motion in moving gratings. *Perception & Psychophysics*, 27, 585–587.

Lovegrove, W.J., Martin, F., & Slaghuis, W. (1986). A theoretical and experimental case for a visual deficit in specific reading disability. *Cognitive Neuropsychology*, 3, 225–268.

Lowe, D.G. & Mitterer, J.O. (1982). Selective divided attention in a Stroop task. *Canadian Journal of Psychology*, 36, 684–700.

Mandler, J.M. & Parker, R.E. (1976). Memory for descriptive and spatial information in complex pictures. *Journal of Experimental Psychology: Human Learning and Memory*, 2, 38–48.

Manelis, L. (1974). The effect of meaningfulness in tachistoscopic word perception. *Perception & Psychophysics*, 16, 182–192.

Manelis, L. (1977). Frequency and meaningfulness in tachistoscopic word perception. *American Journal of Psychology*, 90, 269–280.

Manso de Zuniga, C.M. (1988). *The effects of handwriting and repetition on visual word recognition*. Unpublished Ph.D. thesis, London University.

Marcel, A.J. (1983). Conscious and unconscious perception: Experiments on visual masking. *Cognitive Psychology*, 15, 197–237.

Marin, O.S.M. (1987). Dementia and visual agnosia. In G.W. Humphreys & M.J. Riddoch (Eds.), *Visual object processing: A cognitive neuropsychological approach*. London: Lawrence Erlbaum Associates Ltd.

Marmurek, H.H.C. & Briscoe, G. (1982). Orthographic and lexical processing of visual letter strings. *Canadian Journal of Psychology*, 36, 368–387.

Marr, D. (1976). Early processing of visual information. *Philosophical Transactions of the Royal Society of London*, *B275*, 483–524.

Marr, D. (1977). Analysis of occluding contour. *Proceedings of the Royal Society of London*, *B197*, 441–475.

Marr, D. (1982). *Vision*. San Francisco: W.H. Freeman.

Marr, D. & Hildreth, E. (1980). Theory of edge detection. *Proceedings of the Royal Society of London, B200*, 269–294.

Marr, D. & Nishihara, H.K. (1978). Representation and recognition of the spatial organisation of three-dimensional shapes. *Proceedings of the Royal Society of London, B200*, 269–294.

Marr, D. & Poggio, T. (1976). Cooperative computation of stereo disparity. *Science, 194*, 283–287.

Marr, D. & Poggio, T. (1979). A computational theory of human stereo vision. *Proceedings of the Royal Society of London, B204*, 301–328.

Marr, D. & Ullman, S. (1981). Directional selectivity and its use in early processing. *Proceedings of the Royal Society of London, B211*, 151–180.

Marshall, E. & Walker, P. (1987). Visual memory for pictorial stimuli in a serial choice reaction time task. *British Journal of Psychology, 78*, 213–231.

Marshall, J.C. & Newcombe, F. (1973). Patterns of paralexia. A psycholinguistic approach. *Journal of Psycholinguistic Research, 2*, 175–199.

Marshall, J.C. & Newcombe, F. (1980). The conceptual status of deep dyslexia. In M. Coltheart, K.E. Patterson, & J.C. Marshall (Eds.), *Deep dyslexia*. London: Routledge & Kegan Paul.

Mason, M. (1978). From print to sound in mature readers as a function of reader ability and two forms of orthographic regularity. *Memory and Cognition, 6*, 568–581.

Massaro, D.W. (1979). Letter information and orthographic context in word perception. *Journal of Experimental Psychology: Human Perception and Performance, 5*, 595–609.

Mayhew, J.E.W. & Frisby, J.P. (1981). Psychophysical and computational studies towards a theory of human stereopsis. *Artificial Intelligence, 17*, 349–385.

Mayhew, J.E.W. & Frisby, J.P. (1984). Computer vision. In T. O'Shea & M. Eisenstadt (Eds.), *Artificial Intelligence*. New York: Harper & Row.

Maylor, E. (1985). Facilitatory and inhibitory components of orienting in visual space. In M.I. Posner & O.S.M. Marin (Eds), *Attention and performance, XI*. Hillsdale, N.J.: Lawrence Erlbaum Associates Inc.

Maylor, E.A. & Hockey, R. (1985). Inhibitory components of externally controlled covert orienting in visual space. *Journal of Experimental Psychology: Human Perception and Performance, 11*, 777–787.

McCann, R.S. & Besner, D. (1987). Reading pseudohomophones: Implications for models of pronunciation assembly and the locus of word frequency effects in naming. *Journal of Experimental Psychology: Human Perception and Performance, 13*, 14–24.

McCarthy, R. & Warrington, E.K. (1986). Phonological reading: Phenomena and paradoxes. *Cortex, 22*, 359–380.

McClelland, J.L. (1976). Preliminary letter recognition in the perception of words and nonwords. *Journal of Experimental Psychology: Human Perception and Performance, 2*, 80–91.

McClelland, J.L. (1978). Perception and masking of wholes and parts. *Journal of Experimental Psychology: Human Perception and Performance, 4*, 210–223.

McClelland, J.L. (1979). On the time relations of mental processes: An examination of systems of processes in cascade. *Psychological Review, 86*, 287–300.

McClelland, J.L. (1986). The programmable blackboard model of reading. In J.L. McClelland & D.E. Rumelhart (Eds.), *Parallel distributed processing: Explorations in the microstructure of cognition, II*. Cambridge, MA: MIT Press.

McClelland, J.L. (1987). The case for interactionism in language processing. In M. Coltheart (Ed.), *Attention and performance, XII*. London: Lawrence Erlbaum Associates Ltd.

McClelland, J.L. & Johnston, J.C. (1977). The role of familiar units in perception of words and nonwords. *Perception & Psychophysics, 22*, 249–261.

McClelland, J.L. & Mozer, M. (1986). Perceptual interactions in two-word displays: Familiarity and similarity effects. *Journal of Experimental Psychology: Human Perception and Performance, 12*, 18–35.

McClelland, J.L. & Rumelhart, D.E. (1981). An interactive activation model of context effects in letter perception. 1. An account of basic findings. *Psychological Review, 88*, 375–407.

McClelland, J.L. & Rumelhart, D.E. (1985). Distributed memory and the representation of general and specific information. *Journal of Experimental Psychology: General, 114*, 159–188.

McClelland, J.L. & Rumelhart, D.E. (1986). *Parallel distributed processing: Explorations in the microstructure of cognition. II. Psychological and biological models.* Cambridge, MA: MIT Press.

McCloskey, M. & Zaragoza, M. (1985). Misleading postevent information and memory for events: Arguments and evidence against memory impairment hypotheses. *Journal of Experimental Psychology: General, 114*, 1–16.

McConkie, G.W. & Rayner, K. (1975). The span of the effective stimulus during a fixation in reading. *Perception & Psychophysics, 17*, 578–586.

McConkie, G.W. & Rayner, K. (1976). Asymmetry of the perceptual span in reading. *Bulletin of the Psychonomic Society, 8*, 365–368.

McConkie, G.W., Underwood, N.R., Zola, D., & Wolverton, G.S. (1985). Some temporal characteristics of processing during reading. *Journal of Experimental Psychology: Human Perception and Performance, 11*, 168–186.

McConkie, G.W. & Zola, D. (1979). Is visual information integrated across successive fixations in reading? *Perception & Psychophysics, 25*, 221–224.

McConkie, G.W. & Zola, D. (1987). Visual attention during eye fixations while reading. In M. Coltheart (Ed.), *Attention and performance, XII*. London: Lawrence Erlbaum Associates Ltd.

McLeod, P., Driver, J., & Crisp, J. (1988). Visual search for a conjunction of movement and form is parallel. *Nature, 332*, 154–155.

Meadows, J.C. (1974). Disturbed perception of colours associated with localized cerebral lesions. *Brain, 97*, 615–632.

Merikle, P.M. (1980). Selection from visual persistence by perceptual groups and category membership. *Journal of Experimental Psychology: General, 109*, 279–295.

Merikle, P.M. (1982). Unconscious perception revisited. *Perception & Psychophysics, 31*, 298–301.

Merikle, P.M., Coltheart, M., & Lowe, D.G. (1971). On the selective effects of a pattern masking stimulus. *Canadian Journal of Psychology, 25*, 264–279.

Metzler, J. (1973). *Cognitive analogues of the rotation of three-dimensional objects.* Unpublished doctoral dissertation, Stanford University.

Mewhort, D.J.K. & Beal, A.L. (1977). Mechanisms of word identification. *Journal of Experimental Psychology: Human Perception and Performance, 3*, 629–640.

Mewhort, D.J.K. & Campbell, A.J. (1978). Processing spatial information and the selective-masking effect. *Perception & Psychophysics, 24*, 93–101.

Mewhort, D.J.K., Campbell, A.J., Marchetti, F.M., & Campbell, J.I.D. (1981). Identification, localisation and "iconic memory": An evaluation of the bar-probe task. *Memory and Cognition, 9*, 50–67.

Meyer, D.E. & Gutschera, K.D. (1975). *Orthographic vs. phonemic processing of printed words.* Paper presented to the Psychonomic Society, Colorado.

Meyer, D.E. & Schvaneveldt, R.W. (1971). Facilitation in recognizing pairs of words: Evidence of a dependence between retrieval operations. *Journal of Experimental Psychology, 90*, 227–234.

Meyer, D.E., Schvaneveldt, R.W., & Ruddy, M.G. (1975). Loci of contextual effects in visual word recognition. In P.M.A. Rabbitt & S. Dornic (Eds.), *Attention and performance, V.* London: Academic Press.

Michaels, C.F. & Carello, C. (1981). *Direction perception.* Englewood Cliffs, New Jersey: Prentice-Hall.

Michaels, C.F. & Turvey, M.T. (1979). Central sources of masking: Indexing structures supporting seeing at a single, brief glance. *Psychological Research, 41,* 1–61.

Miller, J.O. (1987). Evidence of preliminary response preparation from a divided attention task. *Journal of Experimental Psychology: Human Perception and Performance, 13,* 425–434.

Miller, J.O. (1988). Discrete and continuous models of human information processing: Theoretical distinctions and empirical results. *Acta Psychologica, 67,* 191–257.

Minsky, M. (1977). Frame system theory. In P.N. Johnson-Laird & P.C. Wason (Eds.), *Thinking: Readings in cognitive science.* Cambridge: Cambridge University Press.

Mollon, J.D. (1982). Colour vision. In H.B. Barlow & J.D. Mollon (Eds.), *The senses.* Cambridge: Cambridge University Press.

Mollon, J.D., Newcombe, F., Polden, P.G., & Ratcliff, G. (1980). On the presence of three cone mechanisms in a case of total achromatopsia. In G. Verriest (Ed.), *Colour vision deficiencies, V.* Bristol: Hilger.

Monk, A.F. & Hulme, C. (1983). Errors in proofreading: Evidence for the use of word shape in word recognition. *Memory and Cognition, 11,* 16–23.

Mooney, C.M. (1957). Closure time as affected by viewing time and multiple visual fixation. *Canadian Journal of Psychology, 11,* 21–28.

Morgan, M.J. (1984). Computational theories of vision. (A critical notice of "Vision", by D. Marr.) *Quarterly Journal of Experimental Psychology, 36A,* 157–165.

Morris, R.G.M. (Ed.) (1989). *Parallel distributed processing: Implications for psychology and neuroscience.* Oxford: Oxford University Press.

Morrison, R.E. (1983). Retinal image size and the perceptual span in reading. In K. Rayner (Ed.), *Eye movements in reading: Perceptual and language processes.* New York: Academic Press.

Morrison, R.E. (1984). Manipulation of stimulus onset delay in reading: Evidence for parallel programming of saccades. *Journal of Experimental Psychology: Human Perception and Performance, 10,* 667–682.

Morton, J. (1969). Interaction of information in word recognition. *Psychological Review, 76,* 165–178.

Morton, J. (1979). Some experiments on facilitation in word and picture recognition and their relevance for the evolution of a theoretical position. In P.A. Kolers, M.E. Wrolstad, & H. Bouma (Eds.), *Processing of visible language, 1.* New York: Plenum.

Morton, J. & Patterson, K.E. (1980). A new attempt at an interpretation, or an attempt at a new interpretation. In M. Coltheart, K.E. Patterson, & J.C. Marshall (Eds.), *Deep dyslexia.* London: Routledge & Kegan Paul.

Mowbray, G.H. & Durr, L.B. (1964). Visual masking. *Nature, 201,* 277–278.

Mozer, M.C. (1983). Letter migration in word perception. *Journal of Experimental Psychology: Human Perception and Performance, 9,* 531–546.

Mozer, M.C. (1987). Early parallel processing in reading: A connectionist approach. In M. Coltheart (Ed.), *Attention and performance, XII.* London: Lawrence Erlbaum Associates Ltd.

Murdock, B.J. Jr. (1962). The serial position effect in free recall. *Journal of Experimental Psychology, 64,* 482–488.

Murphy, T.D. & Eriksen, C.W. (1987). Temporal changes in the distribution of attention in the visual field in response to precues. *Perception & Psychophysics, 42,* 576–586.

Murrell, G.A. & Morton, J. (1974). Word recognition and morphemic structure. *Journal of Experimental Psychology, 102,* 963–968.

Nakayama, K. & Silverman, G.H. (1986). Serial and parallel processing of visual feature conjunctions. *Nature*, *320*, 264–265.

Navon, D. (1977). Forest before trees: The precedence of global features in visual perception. *Cognitive Psychology*, *9*, 353–383.

Neely, J.H. (1977). Semantic priming and retrieval from lexical memory: The roles of inhibitionless spreading activation and limited-capacity attention. *Journal of Experimental Psychology: General*, *106*, 226–254.

Neisser, U. (1967). *Cognitive psychology*. New York: Appleton-Century-Crofts.

Nelson, D.L. & Brooks, D.H. (1973). Functional independence of pictures and their verbal memory codes. *Journal of Experimental Psychology*, *98*, 44–48.

Nelson, D.L. & Reed, V.S. (1976). On the nature of pictorial encoding: A levels-of-processing analysis. *Journal of Experimental Psychology: Human Learning and Memory*, *2*, 49–57.

Nelson, D.L., Reed, V.S., & Walling, J.R. (1976). Pictorial superiority effect. *Journal of Experimental Psychology: Human Learning and Memory*, *2*, 523–528.

Neuhaus, W. (1930). Experimentalle Untersuchung der Scheinbewegung. *Archiv für die Psychologie*, *75*, 315–458.

Newcombe, F., Young, A. W., & de Haan, E. (1989). Prosopagnosia and object agnosia without covert recognition. *Neuropsychologia*, *27*, 179–191.

Nickerson, R.S. (1965). Short term memory for complex meaningful configurations: A demonstration of capacity. *Canadian Journal of Psychology*, *19*, 155–160.

Nielsen, J.M. (1955). Occipital lobes, dreams and psychosis. *Journal of Nervous and Mental Diseases*, *121*, 30–32.

Noice, H. & Hock, H.S. (1987). A word superiority effect with nonorthographic acronyms: Testing for unitized visual codes. *Perception & Psychophysics*, *42*, 485–490.

Norris, D. & Brown, G. (1985). Race models and analogy theories: A dead heat? A reply to Seidenberg. *Cognition*, *20*, 155–168.

O'Regan, J.K. (1983). Elementary perceptual and eye-movement control processes in reading. In K. Rayner (Ed.), *Eye movements in reading: Perceptual and language processes*. New York: Academic Press.

O'Regan, J.K. & Levy-Schoen, A. (1987). Eye-movement strategy and tactics in word recognition and reading. In M. Coltheart (Ed.), *Attention and performance, XII*. London: Lawrence Erlbaum Associates Ltd.

O'Regan, J.K., Levy-Schoen, A., Pynte, J., & Brugaillere, B. (1984). Convenient fixation location within isolated words of different length and structures. *Journal of Experimental Psychology: Human Perception and Performance*, *10*, 250–257.

Paap, K.R. & Newsome, S.L. (1980). A perceptual-confusion account of the WSE in the target search paradigm. *Perception & Psychophysics*, *27*, 444–456.

Paap, K.R., Newsome, S.L., McDonald, J.E., & Schvaneveldt, R.W. (1982). An activation-verification model for letter and word recognition: The word superiority effect. *Psychological Review*, *89*, 573–594.

Paap, K.R., Newsome, S.L., & Noel, R.W. (1984). Word shapes in poor shape for the race to the lexicon. *Journal of Experimental Psychology: Human Perception and Performance*, *10*, 413–428.

Paap, K.R., McDonald, J.E., Schvaneveldt, R.W., & Noel, R.W. (1987). Frequency and pronounceability in visually presented naming and lexical decision tasks. In M. Coltheart (Ed.), *Attention and performance, XII*. London: Lawrence Erlbaum Associates Ltd.

Paivio, A. (1971). *Imagery and verbal processes*. New York: Holt, Rinehart & Winston.

Paivio, A. (1975a). Perceptual comparisons through the mind's eye. *Memory and Cognition*, *3*, 635–637.

Paivio, A. (1975b). Neomentalism. *Canadian Journal of Psychology*, *29*, 263–291.

Paivio, A. (1978). Dual coding: Theoretical issues and empirical evidence. In J.M. Scandura

& C.J. Brainerd (Eds.), *Structural/process models of complex human behaviour.* The Netherlands: Sijthoff & Noordhoff.

Palmer, S.E. (1975a). Visual perception and world knowledge. Notes on a model of sensory-cognitive interaction. In D.A. Norman, D.E. Rumelhart, & the LNR Research Group (Eds.), *Explorations in cognition.* San Francisco: W.H. Freeman.

Palmer, S.E. (1975b). The effects of contextual scenes on the identification of objects. *Memory and Cognition, 3,* 519–526.

Palmer, S.E. (1980). What makes triangles point: Local and global effects in configurations of ambiguous triangles. *Cognitive Psychology, 12,* 285–305.

Palmer, S.E. (1985). The role of symmetry in shape perception. *Acta Psychologica, 59,* 67–90.

Palmer, S.E. & Bucher, N.M. (1981). Configural effects in perceived pointing of ambiguous triangles. *Journal of Experimental Psychology: Human Perception and Performance, 7,* 88–114.

Palmer, S.E., Rosch, E., & Chase, P. (1981). Canonical perspective and the perception of objects. In J. Long & A.D. Baddeley (Eds), *Attention and performance, IX.* Hillsdale, N.J.: Lawrence Erlbaum Associates Inc.

Palmer, S.E., Simone, E., & Kube, P. (1988). Reference frame effects on shape perception in two versus three dimensions. *Perception, 17,* 147–163.

Parkin, A.J. (1984). Redefining the regularity effect. *Memory and Cognition, 12,* 287–292.

Parkin, A.J., McMullen, M., & Graystone, D. (1986). Spelling-to-sound irregularity affects pronunciation latency but not lexical decision. *Psychological Research, 48,* 87–92.

Parks, T.E., Kroll, N.E., Salzberg, P.M., & Parkinson, S.R. (1972). Persistence of visual memory as indicated by decision time in a matching task. *Journal of Experimental Psychology, 92,* 437–438.

Pashler, H. (1987). Detecting conjunctions of colour and form: Re-assessing the serial search hypothesis. *Perception & Psychophysics, 41,* 191–201.

Patterson, K.E. (1978). Phonemic dyslexia: Errors of meaning and the meaning of errors. *Quarterly Journal of Experimental Psychology, 30,* 587–601.

Patterson, K.E. (1979). What's right with "deep" dyslexics? *Brain and Language, 8,* 111–129.

Patterson, K.E. (1982). The relation between reading and phonological coding: Further neuropsychological observations. In A.W. Ellis (Ed.), *Normality and pathology in cognitive functions.* London: Academic Press.

Patterson, K.E. & Baddeley, A.D. (1977). When face recognition fails. *Journal of Experimental Psychology: Human Learning and Memory, 3,* 406–417.

Patterson, K.E. & Coltheart, V. (1987). Phonological processes in reading: A tutorial review. In M. Coltheart (Ed.), *Attention and performance, XII.* London: Lawrence Erlbaum Associates Ltd.

Patterson, K.E. & Kay, J. (1982). Letter-by-letter reading: Psychological descriptions of a neurological syndrome. *Quarterly Journal of Experimental Psychology, 34A,* 411–441.

Patterson, K.E., Marshall, J.C., & Coltheart, M. (1985). *Surface dyslexia: Neuropsychological and cognitive studies of phonological reading.* London: Lawrence Erlbaum Associates Ltd.

Patterson, K.E. & Morton, J. (1985). From orthography to phonology: An attempt at an old interpretation. In K.E. Patterson, J.C. Marshall, & M. Coltheart (Eds.), *Surface dyslexia: Neuropsychological and cognitive studies of phonological reading.* London: Lawrence Erlbaum Associates Ltd.

Patterson, K.E. & Wilson, B. (1988, January). *A rose is a nose: A deficit in initial letter identification.* Paper presented to the Experimental Psychology Society, London.

Pentland, A. (1986a). Perceptual organisation and the representation of natural form. *Artificial Intelligence, 28,* 293–331.

Pentland, A. (1986b). Local shading analysis. In A.P. Pentland (Ed.), *From pixels to predicates*. Norwood, N.J.: Ablex.

Perrett, D.I., Mistlin, A.J., Chitty, A.J., Harries, M.H., Newcombe, F., & De Haan, E. (1988). Neuronal mechanisms of face perception and their pathology. In C. Kennard & F. Clifford Rose (Eds.), *Physiological aspects of clinical neuro-ophthalmology*. London: Chapman Hall.

Phillips, W.A. (1974). On the distinction between sensory storage and short term visual memory. *Perception & Psychophysics, 16*, 283–290.

Phillips, W.A. (1983). Short-term visual memory. *Philosophical Transactions of the Royal Society of London, B302*, 295–309.

Phillips, W.A. & Baddeley, A.D. (1971). Reaction time and short-term memory. *Psychonomic Science, 22*, 73–74.

Phillips, W.A. & Christie, D.F.M. (1977). Components of visual memory. *Quarterly Journal of Experimental Psychology, 29*, 117–133.

Pinker, S. (1985). Visual cognition: An introduction. In S. Pinker (Ed.), *Visual cognition*. Cambridge, MA.: MIT Press.

Pollard, S.B., Mayhew, J.E.W., & Frisby, J.P. (1985). PMF: A stereo correspondence algorithm using a disparity gradient limit. *Perception, 14*, 449–470.

Pollatsek, A., Bolozky, S., Well, A.D., & Rayner, K. (1981). Asymmetries in the perceptual span for Israeli readers. *Brain and Language, 14*, 174–180.

Pollatsek, A., Well, A.D., & Schindler, R.M. (1975). Familiarity affects visual processing of words. *Journal of Experimental Psychology: Human Perception and Performance, 1*, 328–338.

Pomerantz, J.R. (1983). Global and local precedence: Selective attention in form and motion perception. *Journal of Experimental Psychology: General, 112*, 516–540.

Pomerantz, J.R. & Schwaitzberg, S.D. (1975). Grouping by proximity: Selective attention measures. *Perception & Psychophysics, 18*, 355–361.

Posner, M.I. (1978). *Chronometric explorations of mind*. Hillsdale, N.J.: Lawrence Erlbaum Associates Inc.

Posner, M.I. (1980). Orienting of attention. *Quarterly Journal of Experimental Psychology, 32*, 3–25.

Posner, M.I. & Keele, S.W. (1967). Decay of visual information from a single letter. *Science, 158*, 137–139.

Posner, M.I. & Snyder, C.R.R. (1975). Facilitation and inhibition in the processing of signals. In P.M.A. Rabbitt & S. Dornic (Eds.), *Attention and performance, V*. New York: Academic Press.

Posner, M.I., Boies, S.J., Eichelman, W.H., & Taylor, R.L. (1969). Retention of name and visual codes of single letters. *Journal of Experimental Psychology, 79*, 1–16.

Posner, M.I., Cohen, Y., & Rafal, R.D. (1982). Neural systems control of spatial orienting. *Philosophical Transactions of the Royal Society of London, B298*, 187–198.

Posner, M.I., Nissen, M.J., & Ogden, W.C. (1978). Attended and unattended processing nodes: The role of set for spatial locations. In H.L. Pick & B.J. Saltzman (Eds.), *Modes of perceiving and processing information*. Hillsdale, N.J.: Lawrence Erlbaum Associates Inc.

Posner, M.I., Rafal, R.D., Choate, L.S., & Vaughan, J. (1985). Inhibition of return: Neural basis and function. *Cognitive Neuropsychology, 2*, 211–228.

Posner, M.I., Snyder, C.R.R., & Davidson, B.J. (1980). Attention and the detection of signals. *Journal of Experimental Psychology: General, 109*, 160–174.

Posner, M.I., Walker, J.A., Friedrich, F.J., & Rafal, R.D. (1984). Effects of parietal injury on covert orienting of visual attention. *Journal of Neuroscience, 4*, 1863–1874.

Posner, M.I., Walker, J.A., Friedrich, F.J., & Rafal, R.D. (1987). How do the parietal lobes direct covert attention? *Neuropsychologia, 25*, 135–145.

Potter, M.C. & Faulconer, B.A. (1975). Time to understand pictures and words. *Nature, 253*, 437–438.

Potter, M.C., Kroll, J.F., & Harris, C. (1980). Comprehension and memory in rapid-sequential reading. In R. Nickerson (Ed.), *Attention and performance, VIII*. Hillsdale, N.J.: Lawrence Erlbaum Associates Inc.

Printzmetal, W., Presti, D.E., & Posner, M.I. (1986). Does attention affect visual feature integration? *Journal of Experimental Psychology: Human Perception and Performance, 12*, 361–370.

Printzmetal, W., Treiman, R., & Rho, S.H. (1986). How to see a reading unit. *Journal of Memory and Language, 25*, 461–475.

Purcell, D.G. & Stewart, A.L. (1988). The face-detection effect: Configuration enhances detection. *Perception & Psychophysics, 43*, 355–366.

Purcell, D.G., Stewart, A.L., & Stanovich, K.E. (1983). Another look at semantic priming without awareness. *Perception & Psychophysics, 34*, 65–71.

Pylyshyn, Z.W. (1973). What the mind's eye tells the mind's brain: A critique of mental imagery. *Psychological Bulletin, 80*, 1–24.

Pylyshyn, Z.W. (1981). The imagery debate: Analogue media versus tacit knowledge. *Psychological Review, 88*, 16–45.

Quinlan, P.T. & Humphreys, G.W. (1987). Visual search for targets defined by combinations of color, shape and size: An examination of the task constraints on feature and conjunction searches. *Perception & Psychophysics, 41*, 455–472.

Rafal, R. & Posner, M.I. (1987). Deficits in human visual spatial attention following thalamic lesions. *Proceedings of the National Academy of Science, 84*, 7349–7353.

Ramachandran, V.S. & Gregory, R.L. (1978). Does colour provide an input to human motion perception? *Nature, 275*, 55–56.

Ratcliff, G. & Newcombe, F. (1982). Object recognition: Some deductions from the clinical evidence. In A.W. Ellis (Ed.), *Normality and pathology in cognitive functions*. London: Academic Press.

Ratcliff, R., Hockley, W., & McKoon, G. (1985). Components of activation: Repetition and priming effects in lexical decision and recognition. *Journal of Experimental Psychology: General, 114*, 435–450.

Rayner, K. (1975). The perceptual span and peripheral cues in reading. *Cognitive Psychology, 7*, 65–81.

Rayner, K. (1986). Eye movements and the perceptual span in beginning and skilled readers. *Journal of Experimental Child Psychology, 41*, 211–236.

Rayner, K., Balota, D.A., & Pollatsek, A. (1986). Against parafoveal semantic preprocessing during eye fixations in reading. *Canadian Journal of Psychology, 40*, 473–483.

Rayner, K. & Bertera, J.H. (1979). Reading without a fovea. *Science, 206*, 468–469.

Rayner, K. & McConkie, G.W. (1976). What guides a reader's eye movements. *Vision Research, 16*, 829–837.

Rayner, K., McConkie, G.W., & Zola, D. (1980). Integrating information across eye movements. *Cognitive Psychology, 12*, 206–226.

Rayner, K. & Pollatsek, A. (1981). Eye movement control during reading: Evidence for direct control. *Quarterly Journal of Experimental Psychology, 33A*, 351–373.

Rayner, K. & Pollatsek, A. (1987). Eye movements in reading: A tutorial review. In M. Coltheart (Ed.), *Attention and performance, XII*. London: Lawrence Erlbaum Associates Ltd.

Rayner, K., Well, A.D., & Pollatsek, A. (1980). Asymmetry of the effective visual field in reading. *Perception & Psychophysics, 27*, 537–544.

Rayner, K., Well, A.D., Pollatsek, A., & Bertera, J.H. (1982). The availability of useful information to the right of fixation in reading. *Perception & Psychophysics, 31*, 537–550.

Reicher, G.M. (1969). Perceptual recognition as a function of meaningfulness of stimulus material. *Journal of Experimental Psychology, 81*, 274–280.

Riddoch, G. (1917). Dissociation of visual perceptions due to occipital injuries, with especial reference to appreciation of movement. *Brain, 40*, 15–57.

Riddoch, M.J. & Humphreys, G.W. (1983). The effects of cueing on unilateral neglect. *Neuropsychologia, 21*, 589–599.

Riddoch, M.J. & Humphreys, G.W. (1986). Neurological impairments of visual object constancy: The effects of orientation and size disparities. *Cognitive Neuropsychology, 3*, 207–224.

Riddoch, M.J. & Humphreys, G.W. (1987a). Picture naming. In G.W. Humphreys & M.J. Riddoch (Eds), *Visual object processing: A cognitive neuropsychological approach*. London: Lawrence Erlbaum Associates Ltd.

Riddoch, M.J. & Humphreys, G.W. (1987b). Visual object processing in optic aphasia: A case of semantic access agnosia. *Cognitive Neuropsychology, 4*, 131–185.

Riddoch, M.J. & Humphreys, G.W. (1987c). Perceptual and action systems in unilateral visual neglect. In M. Jeannerod (Ed.), *Neurophysiological and neuropsychological aspects of spatial neglect*. Amsterdam: North Holland.

Rizzolatti, G., Riggio, L., Dascola, I., & Umiltà, C. (1987). Reorienting attention across the horizontal and vertical meridians. *Neuropsychologia, 25*, 31–40.

Roberts, T. & Bruce, V. (1989). Repetition priming of face recognition in a serial choice reaction-time task. *British Journal of Psychology, 80*, 201–211.

Rock, I. (1973). *Orientation and form*. New York: Academic Press.

Rock, I. & Gutman, D. (1981). Effects of inattention on form perception. *Journal of Experimental Psychology: Human Perception and Performance, 7*, 275–285.

Rodieck, R.W. & Stone, J. (1965). Analysis of the receptive fields of cat retinal ganglion cells. *Journal of Neurophysiology, 28*, 833–849.

Roediger, H.L. & Blaxton, T.A. (1987). Retrieval modes produce dissociations in memory for surface information. In D.S. Gorfein & R.R. Hoffman (Eds.), *Memory and cognitive processes: The Ebbinghaus centenial conference*. Hillsdale, N.J.: Lawrence Erlbaum Associates Inc.

Rosch, E., Mervis, C.B., Gray, W.D., Johnson, D.M., & Boyes-Bream, P. (1976). Basic objects in natural categories. *Cognitive Psychology, 8*, 382–439.

Rumelhart, D.E. & McClelland, J.L. (1982). An interactive activation model of context effects in letter perception. 2. The contextual enhancement effect and some tests and extensions of the model. *Psychological Review, 89*, 60–94.

Rumelhart, D.E. & McClelland, J.L. (1985). Levels indeed! A response to Broadbent. *Journal of Experimental Psychology: General, 114*, 193–197.

Rumelhart, D.E. & McClelland, J.L. (1986). *Parallel distributed processing. Explorations in the microstructure of cognition, 1. Foundations*. Cambridge, MA: MIT Press.

Runeson, S. & Frykholm, G. (1983). Kinematic specifications of dynamics as an informational basis for person-and-action perception: Expectation, gender-recognition, and deceptive intention. *Journal of Experimental Psychology: General, 112*, 585–615.

Sacks, O. & Wasserman, R. (1987, November). The case of the colorblind painter. *The New York Review*, 25–34.

Saffran, E.M. & Marin, O.S.M. (1977). Reading without phonology: Evidence from aphasia. *Quarterly Journal of Experimental Psychology, 29*, 515–525.

Salasoo, A., Shiffrin, R.M., & Feustel, T.C. (1985). Building permanent memory codes: Codification and repetition effects in word identification. *Journal of Experimental Psychology: General, 114*, 50–77.

Saye, A. & Frisby, J.P. (1975). The role of monocularly conspicuous features in facilitating stereopsis from random-dot stereograms. *Perception, 4*, 159–171.

Scarborough, D.L., Cortese, C., & Scarborough, H.S. (1977). Frequency and repetition effects in lexical memory. *Journal of Experimental Psychology: Human Perception and Performance, 3*, 1–17.

Scarborough, D.L., Gerard, L., & Cortese, C. (1979). Accessing lexical memory: The transfer of word repetition effects across task and modality. *Memory and Cognition, 7*, 3–12.

Scharf, B. & Lefton, L.A. (1970). Backward and forward masking as a function of stimulus and task parameters. *Journal of Experimental Psychology*, *84*, 331–338.

Schiller, P.H. (1965). Monoptic and dichoptic visual masking by patterns and flashes. *Journal of Experimental Psychology*, *69*, 193–199.

Schiller, P.H. (1969). Behavioral and electrophysiological studies of visual masking. In K.N. Leibovic (Ed.), *Information processing in the nervous system*. New York: Springer-Verlag.

Schiller, P.H. & Smith, M.C. (1965). A comparison of forward and backward masking. *Psychonomic Science*, *3*, 77–78.

Schiller, P.H. & Smith, M.C. (1966). Detection in metacontrast. *Journal of Experimental Psychology*, *71*, 32–39.

Schuberth, R.E., Spoehr, K.T., & Lane, D.M. (1981). Effects of stimulus and contextual information on the lexical decision process. *Memory and Cognition*, *9*, 68–77.

Seidenberg, M.S. (1985). The time course of information activation and utilization in visual word recognition. In D. Besner, T.G. Waller, & G.E. MacKinnon (Eds.), *Reading research: Advances in theory and in practice, V*. New York: Academic Press.

Seidenberg, M.S. (1987). Sublexical structures in visual word recognition: Access units or orthographic redundancy? In M. Coltheart (Ed.), *Attention and performance, XII*. London: Academic Press.

Seidenberg, M.S. & McClelland, J.L. (1989). A distributed, developmental model of word recognition and naming. *Psychological Review*, *96*, 523–568.

Seidenberg, M.S., Waters, G.S., Barnes, M.A., & Tanenhaus, M.K. (1984a). When does irregular spelling or pronunciation influence word recognition? *Journal of Verbal Learning and Verbal Behaviour*, *23*, 383–404.

Seidenberg, M.S., Waters, G.S., Sanders, M., & Langer, P. (1984b). Pre- and postlexical loci of contextual effects on word recognition. *Memory and Cognition*, *12*, 315–328.

Selfridge, O.G. (1959). Pandemonium: A paradigm for learning. In *The mechanisation of thought processes*. London: Her Majesty's Stationery Office.

Sergent, J. (1989). Structural processing of faces. In A.W. Young & H.D. Ellis (Eds.), *Handbook of research on face processing*. Amsterdam: North Holland.

Seymour, P.H.K. (1979). *Human visual cognition*. London: Collier Macmillan.

Shallice, T. & McCarthy, R. (1985). Phonological reading: From patterns of impairment to possible procedures. In K.E. Patterson, J.C. Marshall, & M. Coltheart (Eds.), *Surface dyslexia: Neuropsychological and cognitive studies of phonological reading*. London: Lawrence Erlbaum Associates Ltd.

Shallice, T. & McGill, J. (1978). The origin of mixed errors. In J. Requin (Ed.), *Attention and performance, VII*. Hillsdale, N.J.: Lawrence Erlbaum Associates Inc.

Shallice, T. & Saffran, E. (1986). Lexical processing in the absence of explicit word identification: Evidence from a letter-by-letter reader. *Cognitive Neuropsychology*, *3*, 429–458.

Shallice, T. & Warrington, E.K. (1977). The possible role of selective attention in acquired dyslexia. *Neuropsychologia*, *15*, 31–41.

Shallice, T., Warrington, E.K., & McCarthy, R. (1983). Reading without semantics. *Quarterly Journal of Experimental Psychology*, *35A*, 111–138.

Shepard, R.N. (1967). Recognition memory for words, sentences and pictures. *Journal of Verbal Learning and Verbal Behaviour*, *6*, 156–163.

Shepard, R.N. (1978). The mental image. *American Psychologist*, *33*, 125–137.

Shepard, R.N. (1984). Ecological constraints on internal representation: Resonant kinematics of perceiving, imagining, thinking and dreaming. *Psychological Review*, *91*, 417–447.

Shepard, R.N. & Metzler, J. (1971). Mental rotation of three-dimensional objects. *Science*, *171*, 701–703.

Shepherd, J.W., Ellis, H.D., & Davies, G.M. (1982). *Identification evidence: A psychological evaluation*. Aberdeen: University of Aberdeen Press.

Sherrington, C.S. (1906). *Integrative action of the nervous system*. New Haven: Yale University Press. (Reset edition 1947)

Shipley, W.C., Kenney, F.A., & King, M.E. (1945). Beta movement under binocular, monocular and interocular stimulation. *American Journal of Psychology, 58*, 545–549.

Shulman, G.L., Remington, R.W., & McLean, J.P. (1979). Moving attention through visual space. *Journal of Experimental Psychology: Human Perception and Performance, 5*, 522–526.

Shulman, G.L. & Wilson, J. (1987a). Spatial frequency and selective attention to local and global information. *Perception, 16*, 89–101.

Shulman, G.L. & Wilson, J. (1987b). Spatial frequency and spatial attention. *Perception, 16*, 103–111.

Sieroff, E., Pollatsek, A., & Posner, M.I. (1988). Recognition of visual letter strings following injury to the posterior visual spatial attention system. *Cognitive Neuropsychology, 5*, 427–450.

Silveri, M.C. & Gainotti, G. (1988). Interaction between vision and language in category specific semantic impairment for living things. *Cognitive Neuropsychology, 5*, 677–710.

Singer, W. & Bedworth, N. (1973). Inhibitory interaction between X- and Y-units in the cat lateral geniculate nucleus. *Brain Research, 49*, 291–307.

Smith, F. (1969). Familiarity of configuration vs. discriminability or features in the visual identification of words. *Psychonomic Science, 14*, 261–262.

Smith, M.C. & Magee, L.E. (1980). Tracing the time course of picture-word processing. *Journal of Experimental Psychology: General, 109*, 373–392.

Smith, M.C. & Schiller, P.H. (1966). Forward and backward masking: A comparison. *Canadian Journal of Psychology, 20*, 337–342.

Snodgrass, J.G. & McCullough, B. (1986). The role of visual similarity in picture categorization. *Journal of Experimental Psychology: Learning, Memory and Cognition, 12*, 147–154.

Sperber, R.D., McCauley, C., Ragain, R., & Weil, C.M. (1979). Semantic priming effects on picture and word processing. *Memory and Cognition, 7*, 339–345.

Sperling, G. (1960). The information available in brief visual presentations. *Psychological Monographs, 74* (Whole no. 498).

Sperling, G. (1963). A model for visual memory tasks. *Human Factors, 5*, 19–31.

Sterling, G. (1967). Successive approximations to a model for short-term memory. *Acta Psychologica, 27*, 285–292.

Spoehr, K.T. & Smith, E.E. (1975). The role of orthographic and phonotactic rules in perceiving letter patterns. *Journal of Experimental Psychology: Human Perception and Performance, 104*, 21–34.

Standing, L. (1973). Learning 10,000 pictures. *Quarterly Journal of Experimental Psychology, 25*, 207–222.

Standing, L., Conezio, J., & Haber, R.N. (1970). Perception and memory for pictures: Single trial learning of 2560 visual stimuli. *Psychonomic Science, 19*, 73–74.

Stanhope, N. & Parkin, A.J. (1987). Further explorations of the consistency effect in word and nonword pronunciation. *Memory and Cognition, 15*, 169–179.

Stanners, R.F., Neiser, J.J., & Painton, S. (1979). Memory representation for prefixed words. *Journal of Verbal Learning and Verbal Behaviour, 18*, 733–743.

Stanovich, K.E. & Bauer, D.W. (1978). Experiments on the spelling-to-sound regularity effect in word recognition. *Memory and Cognition, 6*, 410–415.

Stanovich, K.E. & West, R.F. (1983). On priming by a sentence context. *Journal of Experimental Psychology: General, 112*, 1–37.

Steinman, S.B. (1987). Serial and parallel search in vision. *Perception, 16*, 389–398.

Stevens, K.A. (1981). The visual interpretation of surface contours. *Artificial Intelligence, 17*, 47–73.

Stevens, K.A. (1986). Inferring shape from contours across surfaces. In A.P. Pentland (Ed.), *From pixels to predicates*. Norwood, N.J.: Ablex.

Stewart, A.L. & Purcell, D.G. (1970). U-shaped masking functions in visual backward marking: Effects of target configuration and retinal position. *Perception & Psychophysics*, *7*, 253–256.

Stonham, J. (1986). Practical face recognition and verification with WISARD. In H.D. Ellis, M.A. Jeeves, F. Newcombe, & A.W. Young (Eds.), *Aspects of face processing*. Dordrecht: Martinus Nijhoff.

Stromeyer, C.F. III & Julesz, B. (1972). Spatial frequency masking in vision: Critical bands and spread of masking. *Journal of the Optical Society of America*, *61*, 1176–1186.

Stroop, J.R. (1935). Studies of interference in serial verbal reactions. *Journal of Experimental Psychology*, *18*, 643–662.

Styles, E.A. & Allport, D.A. (1986). Perceptual integration of identity, location and colour. *Psychological Research*, *48*, 189–200.

Taft, M. (1979a). Lexical access via an orthographic code: The Basic Orthographic Syllabic Structure (BOSS). *Journal of Verbal Learning and Verbal Behaviour*, *18*, 21–39.

Taft, M. (1979b). Recognition of affixed words and the word frequency effect. *Memory and Cognition*, *7*, 263–272.

Taft, M. (1985). The decoding of words in lexical access: A review of the morphological approach. In D. Besner, T.G. Waller, & G.E. MacKinnon (Eds.), *Reading research: Advances in theory and in practice*, *5*. New York: Academic Press.

Taft, M. (1987). Morphographic processing: The BOSS re-emerges. In M. Coltheart (Ed.), *Attention and performance, XII*. London: Lawrence Erlbaum Associates Ltd.

Taft, M. & Forster, K.I. (1976). Lexical storage and retrieval of polymorphemic and polysyllabic words. *Journal of Verbal Learning and Verbal Behaviour*, *15*, 607–620.

Taylor, D.A. (1977). Time course of context effects. *Journal of Experimental Psychology: General*, *106*, 404–426.

Taylor, D.A. & Chabot, R.J. (1978). Differential backward masking of words and letters by masks of varying orthographic structure. *Memory and Cognition*, *6*, 629–635.

te Linde, J. (1982). Picture-word differences in decision latency: A test of common coding assumptions. *Journal of Experimental Psychology: Learning, Memory and Cognition*, *8*, 584–598.

Ternus, J. (1926). The problem of phenomenal identity. Translated in W.D. Ellis (1955, Ed.), *A source book of Gestalt psychology*. London: Routledge & Kegan Paul.

Thomson, J.A. (1983). Is continuous visual monitoring necessary in visually guided locomotion? *Journal of Experimental Psychology: Human Perception and Performance*, *9*, 427–443.

Tinbergen, N. (1951). *The study of instinct*. Oxford: Clarendon Press.

Tipper, S.P. (1985). The negative priming effect: Inhibitory priming by ignored objects. *Quarterly Journal of Experimental Psychology*, *37A*, 571–590.

Tipper, S.P. & Cranston, M. (1985). Selective attention and priming: Inhibitory and facilitory effects of ignored primes. *Quarterly Journal of Experimental Psychology*, *37A*, 591–611.

Tipper, S.P. & Driver, J. (1988). Negative priming between pictures and words in a selective attention task: Evidence for semantic processing of ignored stimuli. *Memory and Cognition*, *16*, 64–70.

Tolhurst, D.J. (1973). Separate channels for the analysis of the shape and movement of a moving visual stimulus. *Journal of Physiology*, *231*, 385–402.

Townsend, V.M. (1973). Loss of spatial and identity information following a tachistoscopic exposure. *Journal of Experimental Psychology*, *98*, 113–118.

Tranel, D. & Damasio, A.R. (1985). Knowledge without awareness: An autonomic index of facial recognition by prosopagnosics. *Science*, *228*, 1443–1454.

Treisman, A. (1985). Preattentive processing in vision. *Computer Vision, Graphics, and Image Processing*, *31*, 156–177.

Treisman, A. (1986, November). Features and objects in visual processing. *Scientific American*, 106–115.

Treisman, A. (1988). Features and objects: The fourteenth Bartlett Memorial Lecture. *Quarterly Journal of Experimental Psychology, 40A*, 201–237.

Treisman, A. & Gelade, G. (1980). A feature-integration theory of attention. *Cognitive Psychology, 12*, 97–136.

Treisman, A. & Gormican, S. (1988). Feature analysis in early vision: Evidence from search asymmetries. *Psychological Review, 95*, 15–48.

Treisman, A. & Paterson, R. (1984). Emergent features, attention and object perception. *Journal of Experimental Psychology: Human Perception and Performance, 10*, 12–31.

Treisman, A. & Schmidt, H. (1982). Illusory conjunctions in the perception of objects. *Cognitive Psychology, 14*, 107–141.

Treisman, A. & Souther, J. (1985). Search asymmetry: A diagnostic for preattentive processing of separable features. *Journal of Experimental Psychology: General, 114*, 285–310.

Treisman, A. & Souther, J. (1986). Illusory words: The roles of attention and of top-down constraints in conjoining letters to form words. *Journal of Experimental Psychology: Human Perception and Performance, 12*, 3–17.

Tsal, Y. (1983). Movements of attention across the visual field. *Journal of Experimental Psychology: Human Perception and Performance, 9*, 523–530.

Tulving, E. & Gold, C. (1963). Stimulus information and contextual information as determinants of tachistoscopic recognition of words. *Journal of Experimental Psychology, 66*, 319–327.

Turvey, M.T. (1973). On peripheral and central processes in vision: Inferences from an information processing analysis of masking with patterned stimuli. *Psychological Review, 80*, 1–52.

Tulving, E., Schacter, D.L., & Stark, H.A. (1982). Priming effects in word-fragment completion are independent of recognition memory. *Journal of Experimental Psychology: Learning, Memory and Cognition, 8*, 336–342.

Tweedy, J.R., Lapinski, R.H., & Schvaneveldt, R.W. (1977). Semantic-context effects on word recognition: Influence of varying the proportion of items presented in an appropriate context. *Memory and Cognition, 5*, 84–89.

Ullman, S. (1979). *The interpretation of visual motion.* Cambridge, MA: MIT Press.

Vaina, L.M. (1983). From shapes and movements to objects and actions. *Synthese, 54*, 3–36.

Vaina, L.M. (1987). Visual texture for recognition. In L.M. Vaina (Ed.), *Matters of intelligence.* Dordrecht: D. Reidel.

Virzi, R.A. & Egeth, H.E. (1984). Is meaning implicated in illusory conjunctions? *Journal of Experimental Psychology: Human Perception and Performance, 10*, 573–580.

Von Grunau, M. (1978). Interaction between sustained and transient channels: Form inhibits motion in the human visual system. *Vision Research, 18*, 197–201.

Wallach, H. & O'Connell, D.N. (1953). The kinetic depth effect. *Journal of Experimental Psychology, 45*, 205–217.

Walker, P. & Marshall, E. (1982). Visual memory and stimulus repetition effects. *Journal of Experimental Psychology: General, 111*, 348–368.

Wapner, W., Judd, T., & Gardner, H. (1978). Visual agnosia in an artist. *Cortex, 14*, 343–364.

Warren, C.E.J. & Morton, J. (1982). The effects of priming on picture recognition. *British Journal of Psychology, 73*, 117–130.

Warrington, E.K. & Shallice, T. (1980). Word-form dyslexia. *Brain, 30*, 99–112.

Warrington, E.K. & Rabin, P. (1971). Visual span of apprehension in patients with unilateral cerebral lesions. *Quarterly Journal of Experimental Psychology, 23*, 423–431.

Warrington, E.K. & Shallice, T. (1984). Category specific semantic impairments. *Brain, 107*, 829–854.

Warrington, E.K. & Taylor, A.M. (1978). Two categorical stages of object recognition. *Perception*, *7*, 695–705.

Watt, R.J. (1988). *Visual processing: Computational, psychophysical and cognitive research*. London: Lawrence Erlbaum Associates Ltd.

Watt, R.J. & Morgan, M.J. (1983). The recognition and representation of edge blur: Evidence for spatial primitives in human vision. *Vision Research*, *23*, 1457–1477.

Watt, R.J. & Morgan, M.J. (1984). Spatial filters and the localisation of luminance changes in human vision. *Vision Research*, *24*, 1387–1397.

Watt, R.J. & Morgan, M.J. (1985). A theory of the primitive spatial code in human vision. *Vision Research*, *25*, 1661–1674.

Wells, G.L. & Hryciw, B. (1984). Memory for faces: Encoding and retrieval operations. *Memory and Cognition*, *12*, 338–344.

Wells, G.L. & Loftus, E.F. (Eds.) (1984). *Eyewitness testimony: Psychological perspectives*. Cambridge: Cambridge University Press.

Weisstein, N. & Harris, C.S. (1974). Visual detection of line segments: An object-superiority effect. *Science*, *186*, 752–755.

Wertheimer, M. (1912). Experimentalle Studien über das Sehen von Bewegung. *Zeitschrift für Psychologie*, *61*, 161–265. Translated in T. Shipley (1961, Ed.), *Classics in psychology*. New York: Philosophical Library.

Wheeler, D.D. (1970). Processes in word recognition. *Cognitive Psychology*, *1*, 59–85.

Wilding, J. (1986). Joint effects of semantic priming and repetition in a lexical decision task: Implications for a model of lexical access. *Quarterly Journal of Experimental Psychology*, *38A*, 213–228.

Winston, P.H. (1975). Learning structural descriptions from examples. In P.H. Winston (Ed.), *The psychology of computer vision*. New York: McGraw-Hill.

Wiseman, S. & Neisser, U. (1972). Perceptual organisation as a determinant of visual recognition memory. *Paper presented at the Eastern Psychological Association Convention, Boston, April*.

Wolfe, J.M., Cave, K.R., & Franzel, S.L. (1989). Guided search: An alternative to the feature integration model for visual search. *Journal of Experimental Psychology: Human Perception and Performance*, *15*, 419–433.

Wolpert, I. (1924). Die Simultanagnosie-Störung der Gesamtauffassung. *Zeitschift für die gesamte Neurologie und Psychiatrie*, *93*, 397–415.

Woodhouse, J.M. & Barlow, H.B. (1982). Spatial and temporal resolution and analysis. In H.B. Barlow & J.D. Mollon (Eds.), *The senses*. Cambridge: Cambridge University Press.

Woodworth, R.S. (1938). *Experimental psychology*. New York: Holt, Rinehart & Winston.

Wyszecki, G. & Stiles, W.S. (1967). *Color science*. New York: Wiley.

Yin, R.K. (1969). Looking at upside-down faces. *Journal of Experimental Psychology*, *81*, 141–145.

Yin, R.K. (1970). Face recognition by brain-injured patients: A dissociable ability? *Neuropsychologia*, *8*, 395–402.

Young, A.W. & de Haan, E.H.F. (1988). Boundaries of covert recognition in prosopagnosia. *Cognitive Neuropsychology*, *5*, 317–336.

Young, A.W., Ellis, A.W., & Flude, B.M. (1988). Accessing stored information about familiar people. *Psychological Research*, *50*, 111–115.

Young, A.W., Hay, D.C., & Ellis, A.W. (1986). Getting semantic information from familiar faces. In H.D. Ellis, M.A. Jeeves, F. Newcombe, & A.W. Young (Eds.), *Aspects of face processing*. Dordrecht: Martinus Nijhoff.

Young, A.W., Hellawell, D., & de Haan, E.H.F. (1988). Cross-domain semantic priming in normal subjects and a prosopagnosic patient. *Quarterly Journal of Experimental Psychology*, *40A*, 561–580.

Zaragoza, M.S. (1987). Memory, suggestibility and eyewitness testimony in children and adults. In S.J. Ceci, M.P. Toglia, & D.F. Ross (Eds), *Children's eyewitness memory.* New York: Springer.

Zeki, S.M. (1978). Uniformity and diversity of structure and function in rhesus monkey prestriate visual cortex. *Journal of Physiology, 277,* 273–290.

Zihl, J., Von Cramon, D., & Mai, N. (1983). Selective disturbance of movement vision after bilateral brain damage. *Brain, 106,* 313–340.

Zimba, L.D. & Hughes, H.C. (1987). Distractor-target interactions during directed visual attention. *Spatial Vision, 2,* 117–150.

REFERENCE NOTES

1. Chertkow, H., Bub, D., & Caplan, D. (1988). *Two stages in semantic memory processing: Evidence from dementia.* Paper presented at a meeting on semantic representation, Montreal Neurological Institute, April 1988.

Author Index

317

Subject Index

Achromatopsia, 36, 211
Acquired disorders of reading, see Dyslexia
Adaptation, 16, 105
Affixes, 260
Agnosia, 88
Algorithm, 2, 7, 25, 29, 63 (see also Mirage)
  in attention, 149, 167
    colour perception, 36
    depth perception, 41–42
    directional sensitivity, 106
    connectionism, 83
    stereopsis, 47, 49
Ambiguous figures, 73
Analogue representations, 203–210
Anomia, 57, 59
Apparent motion, 108, 109, 127
Articulatory loop, 197, 198
Attention, 97, 127, 143–190, 127, 199, 202, 257–259, 279, 282, 283, 285, 287
Axes, 76, 78, 80, 81, 82
  of elongation, 64–73, 78, 206

Bars, 21, 27, 31–32
Basic level, 71
Basic orthographic syllable structure (BOSS), 259–262
Blobs, 21, 27, 88
Blur, 14, 23, 31–32
Brightness, 108, 193
  as a variable in masking, 111–116
Buffer store
  eye movements, 281
  imagery, and spatial locations, 213, 214, 216
  response buffer in partial report, 193
  short-term visual memory, 193, 203
  2 1/2 D sketch, 46

Canonical views, 78–88, 214
Cascade processes, 53, 60
Catalogue, 70–73, 81, 82, 101
Categories (see also Semantics)
  categorical nature of memory, 192
  faces, 88–95
  object categories, 51, 52, 56, 64, 69–71, 86–88

FIGURE ACKNOWLEDGEMENTS

Page 13, Fig. 2.3. Reproduced by permission of the publisher and authors: Bruce, V. & Green, P.R. (1985). *Visual Perception*. London: Lawrence Erlbaum Associates Ltd.

Page 14, Fig. 2.4. Reproduced by permission of the publisher and authors: Bruce, V. & Green, P.R. (1985). *Visual Perception*. London: Lawrence Erlbaum Associates Ltd.

Page 15, Fig. 2.5. Reproduced by permission of the publisher and authors: Campbell, F.W.C. & Robson, J. (1968). Application of Fourier analysis to the visibility of gratings. *Journal of Physiology, 197*, 551-566. Cambridge University Press, Copyright 1968.

Page 16, Fig. 2.6. Reproduced by permission of the publisher: Graham, N. & Nachmias, J. (1971). Detection of grating patterns containing two spatial frequencies: A comparison of single-channel and multiple-channel models. *Vision Research, 11*, 251-259. Pergamon Press PLC, Copyright 1971.

Page 19, Fig. 2.7. Reproduced by permission of the author: Bruce, V. & Morgan, M.J. (1975). Violations of symmetry and repetitions in visual patterns. *Perception, 4*, 239-249. Pion Ltd., Copyright 1975.

Page 22, Fig. 2.8. Reproduced by permission of the publisher: Marr, D. (1982). *Vision*. W.H. Freeman and Company Publishers, Copyright 1982.

Page 26, Fig. 2.12. Reproduced by permission of the publisher and authors: Enroth-Cugell, C. & Robson, J.G. (1966). The contrast sensitivity of retinal ganglion cells of the cat. *Journal of Physiology, 187*, 517-552. Cambridge University Press, Copyright 1966.

Page 27, Fig. 2.13. Adapted, by permission of the publisher from Marr, D. & Hildreth, E. (1980). Theory of edge detection. *Proceedings of the Royal Society of London, B200*, 269-294. Copyright 1976, The Royal Society.

Page 28, Fig. 2.14. Reproduced by permission of the publisher: Marr, D. (1976). Early processing of visual information. *Philosophical Transactions of the Royal Society, Series B, 275*, 483-524. Copyright 1976, The Royal Society.

Page 30, Fig. 2.15. Reproduced by permission of the publisher and author: Watt, R. (1988). *Visual processing: Computational, psychophysical and cognitive research*. London: Lawrence Erlbaum Associates Ltd.

Page 31, Fig. 2.16. Reproduced by permission of the publisher: Watt, R.J. & Morgan, M.J. (1983). The recognition and representation of edge blur: Evidence for spatial primitives in human visions. *Vision Research, 23*, 1457-1477. Pergamon Press PLC, Copyright 1983.

Page 33, Fig. 2.17. Reproduced by permission of the publisher: Watt, R.J. & Morgan, M.J. (1984). Spatial filters and the localisation of luminance changes in human vision. *Vision Research, 24*, 1387-1397. Pergamon Press PLC, Copyright 1984.

Page 34, Fig. 2.18. Reproduced by permission of the publisher: Barlow, H.B. & Mollon, J.D. (1982). *The senses*. Cambridge University Press, Copyright 1982.

Page 39, Fig. 2.20. Adapted, by permission of the author and publisher, from Julesz, B. (1965). Texture and visual perception. *Scientific American, 212, (February)*, 38-48. Copyright 1965, Scientific American, Inc.

Page 41, Fig. 2.21. Reproduced by permission of the publisher: Marr, D. & Poggio, T. (1976). Cooperative computation of stereo disparity. *Science, 194*, 283-287. Copyright 1976 by the AAAS.

Page 47, Fig. 2.26. Reproduced by permission of the publisher: Marr, D. (1976). Early processing of visual information. *Philosophical Transactions of the Royal Society, Series B, 275*, 483-524. Copyright 1976, The Royal Society.

Page 67, Fig. 3.8. Reproduced by permission of the publisher and authors: Palmer, S.E., Rosch, E., & Chase, P. (1981). In G.M. Long and A.D. Baddeley (Eds.), *Attention and Performance IX* Hillsdale, N.J.: Lawrence Erlbaum Associates Inc.

Page 69, Fig. 3.9. Reproduced by permission of the publisher and authors: Bruce, V. & Green, P.R. (1985). *Visual Perception*. London: Lawrence Erlbaum Associates Ltd.

Pages 70, 71, and 72, Figs. 3.11, 3.12 and 3.13. Reproduced by permission of the publisher: Marr, D. & Nishihara, H.K. (1978). Representation and recognition of the spatial organisation of three-dimensional shapes. *Proceedings of the Royal Society, B200,* 269-294. Copyright 1978, The Royal Society.

Pages 73 and 74, Figs. 3.14, 3.15, and 3.16. Reproduced by permission of the publisher: Hoffman, D.D. & Richards, W.A. (1984). Parts of recognition. *Cognition, 18,* 65-96. Copyright 1984, Elsevier Science Publishers.

Page 75, Fig. 3.17. Reproduced by permission of the publisher: Pentland, A. (1986). Perceptual organisation and the representation of natural form. *Artificial Intelligence, 28,* 293-331. Copyright 1986, Elsevier Science Publishers.

Page 76 and 79, Figs. 3.18 and 3.19, Reproduced by permission of the publisher: Biederman, I. (1987). Recognition by components: A theory of human image understanding. *Psychological Review, 94,* 115-145. Copyright 1987 by The American Psychological Association.

Page 79, Fig 3.20. Adapted, by permission of the authors and publisher: Palmer, S.E., Rosch, E., & Chase, P. (1981). In G.M. Long and A.D. Baddeley (Eds.), *Attention and Performance IX.* Hillsdale, N.J.: Lawrence Erlbaum Associates Inc.

Page 81, Fig. 3.21. Reproduced by permission of the publisher and authors: Humphreys, G.W. & Riddoch, M.J. (1984). Routes to object constancy: Implications from neurological impairments of object constancy. *The Quarterly Journal of Experimental Psychology, 36A,* 385-415. Copyright 1984 by The Experimental Psychology Society.

Page 84, Fig. 3.22. Reproduced from: Hinton, G.E. (1981). A parallel computation that assigns canonical object-based frames of reference. *Proceedings of the Seventh International Joint Conference on Artificial Intelligence.* Palo Alto, Cal.: Morgan Kaufmann.

Page 91, Fig. 3.24. Reproduced by permission of the publisher and authors: Bruce, V. & Young, A.W. (1986). Understanding face recognition. *British Journal of Psychology, 77,* 305-327. Copyright 1986, The British Psychological Society.

Page 93, Fig. 3.25. Reproduced by permission of the author and publisher: de Haan, E.H.F., Young, A.W., & Newcombe, F. (1987). Face recognition without awareness. *Cognitive Neuropsychology, 4,* 385-415. Original photographs copyright The Press Association.

Page 95 and 96, Figs. 3.26 and 3.27, Adapted, by permission of the publisher: Norman, D.A., Rumelhart, D.E., & LNR Research Group (Eds.) (1975). *Explorations in Cognition.* Copyright 1975, W.H. Freeman and Company.

Page 97, Fig. 3.28. Adapted from: Navon, D. (1977). Forest before trees: The precedence of global features in visual perception. *Cognitive Psychology, 9,* 353-383.

Page 98, Fig. 3.29. Adapted, by permission of the publisher and author: Palmer, S.E. (1980). What makes triangles point: Local and global effects in configurations of ambiguous triangles. *Cognitive Psychology, 12,* 285-305. Copyright 1980, Academic Press Inc.

Page 98, Fig. 3.30. Adapted, by permission of the publisher: Palmer, S.E., Simone, E. & Kube, P. (1988). Reference frame effects on shape perception in two versus three dimensions. *Perception.* Copyright 1988, Pion Ltd.

Page 104, Fig. 4.1 Adapted from: Johansson, G. (1973). Visual perception of biological motion and a model for its analysis. *Perception and Psychophysics, 14,* 201-211.

Pages 111, 112, 114, 115, and 117, Figs. 4.2-4.6. Reproduced by permission of publisher and author: Turvey, M.T. (1973). On peripheral and central processes in vision: Inferences from an information processing analysis of masking with patterned stimuli. *Psychological Review, 80,* 1-52. Copyright 1973 by The American Psychological Association.

Pages 124-126, Figs. 4.9-4.11. Reproduced by permission of the publisher and author: Breitmeyer, B.G. (1980). Unmasking visual masking: A look at the "why" behind the veil of the "how". *Psychological Review, 82,* 52-69. Copyright 1980 by the American Psychological Association.

Page 129, Fig. 4.12. Adapted from: Green, M. (1981) Spatial frequency effects in masking by light. *Vision Research, 18,* 861-866.

Page 133, Fig. 4.13. Reproduced by permission of the author. Michaels, C.F. & Turvey, M.T. (1979). Central sources of masking: Indexing structures supporting seeing at a single, brief glance. *Psychological Research, 41,* 1-61.

Page 135, Fig. 4.14. Reprinted by permission of the publisher: Taylor, D.A. & Chabot, R.J. (1978). Differential backward masking of words and letters by masks of varying orthographic structure. *Memory and Cognition, 6,* 633. Copyright 1978, The Psychonomic Society Inc.

Page 136, Fig. 4.15. Reprinted by permission of the publisher and author: McClelland, J.L. (1978).

Perception and masking of wholes and parts. *Journal of Experimental Psychology: Human Perception and Performance, 4*, 211. Copyright 1978 by The American Psychological Association.

Page 144, Fig. 5.1. Reprinted by permission of the publisher: Posner, M.I., Snyder, C.R.R., & Davidson, B.J. (1980). Attention and the detection of signals. *Journal of Experimental Psychology: General, 109*, 164 Copyright 1980 by The American Psychological Association.

Page 146, Fig. 5.2. Eriksen,C.W. & Yeh, Y.Y. (1985). Allocation of attention in the visual field. *Journal of Experimental Psychology: Human Perception and Performance, 11*, 587. Copyright 1985 by The American Psychological Association.

Page 147, Fig. 5.3. Reproduced by permission of the publisher and author: Downing, C.J. & Pinker, S. (1985). In M.I. Posner & O.S.M. Marin (Eds), *Attention and Performance XI*. Hillsdale, N.J.: Lawrence Erlbaum Associates Inc.

Page 150, Fig. 5.4. Reproduced by permission of the publisher and author: Watt, R.J. (1988). *Visual processing*. London: Lawrence Erlbaum Associates Ltd.

Page 151, Fig. 5.5. Reproduced by permission of the publisher and author: Tsal, Y. (1983). Movements of attention across the visual field. *Journal of Experimental Psychology: Human Perception and Performance, 9*, 525. Copyright 1983 by The American Psychological Association.

Page 152, Fig. 5.6. Reproduced by permission of the publisher and author: Shulman, G.L., Remington, R.W., & McLean, J.P. (1979). Moving attention through visual space. *Journal of Experimental Psychology: Human Perception and Performance, 5*, 524. Copyright 1979 by The American Psychological Association.

Page 155, Fig. 5.7. Reproduced by permission of the author. Fischer, B. (1986). The role of attention in the preparation of visually guided eye movements in monkey and man. *Psychological Research, 48*, 251-257.

Page 157, Fig. 5.8. Reproduced by permission of the publisher and author: Maylor, E. (1985). Facilitatory and inhibitory components of orienting in visual space. In M.I. Posner and O.S.M. Marin (Eds.), *Attention and performance XI*. Hillsdale, N.J.: Lawrence Erlbaum Associates Inc.

Page 159, Fig. 5.9. Reprinted by permission of the publisher and author: Gainotti, G., D'Erme, P., Monteleone, D., & Silveri, M.C. (1986). Mechanisms of unilateral spatial neglect in relation to laterality of cerebral lesions. *Brain, 109*, 599-612. Copyright 1986, Oxford University Press.

Page 162, Fig. 5.10: Reproduced by permission of the publisher and author. Posner, M.I., Walker. J.A., Friedrich, F.J., & Rafal, R.D. (1984). Effects of parietal injury on covert orienting of visual attention. *Journal of Neuroscience, 4*, 1863-1874. Copyright 1984 the Society for Neuroscience.

Page 163, Fig. 5.11, Reproduced by permission of the publisher: Posner, M.I., Snyder, C.R.R., & Davidson, B.J. (1980). Attention and the detection of signals. *Journal of Experimental Psychology: General, 109*, 160-174 Copyright 1980 by The American Psychological Association.

Page 163, Fig. 5.12. Reproduced by permission of the publisher and author: Rafal, R. & Posner, M.I. (1987). Deficits in human visual spatial attention following thalamic lesions. *Proceedings of the National Academy of Science, 84*, 7349-7353. Copyright 1987, The National Academy of Science.

Page 166, Fig. 5.13. Reproduced by permission of the publisher and author: Gainotti, G., D'Erme, P., Monteleone, D., & Silveri, M.C. (1986). Mechanisms of unilateral spatial neglect in relation to laterality of cerebral lesions. *Brain, 109*, 599-612. Copyright 1986, Oxford University Press.

Page 168, Fig. 5.14. Reproduced by permission of the publisher and author: Duncan, J. (1984). Selective attention and the organisation of visual information. *Journal of Experimental Psychology: General, 113*, 501-517. Copyright 1984 by The American Psychological Association.

Page 169, Fig. 5.15. Reproduced by permission of the publisher and author: Watt, R.J. (1988). *Visual processing*. London: Lawrence Erlbaum Associates Ltd.

Page 171, Fig. 5.16. Reprinted by permission of the publisher and author: Hughes, H.C., Layton, W.M., Baird, J.C., & Lester, L.S. (1984). Global precedence in visual pattern recognition. *Perception and Psychophysics, 35*, 361-371. Copyright 1984 The Psychonomic Society Inc.

Page 172, Fig. 5.17. Reprinted by permission of the publisher and author: Rock, I. & Gutman, D. (1981). Effects of inattention on form perception. *Journal of Experimental Psychology: Human*

Perception and Performance, 7, 279. Copyright 1981 by The American Psychological Association.

Page 175, Fig. 5.18. Reproduced by permission of the publisher: Treisman, A. (1988). Features and objects: the fourteenth Bartlett Memorial Lecture. *The Quarterly Journal of Experimental Psychology, 40A,* 201-237. Copyright 1988, The Experimental Psychology Society.

Page 176, Fig. 5.19: Reproduced by permission of the publisher and author: Treisman, A. & Gelade, G. (1980). A feature-integration theory of attention. *Cognitive Psychology, 12,* 97-136.

Page 178, Fig. 5.20: Reproduced by permission of the publisher: Beck, J. (1966). Effect of orientation and of shape similarity on perceptual grouping. *Perception and Psychophysics, 1,* 300-302. Copyright 1966, The Psychonomic Society.

Page 185, Fig. 5.22. Reproduced by permission of the publisher and author: Pashler, H. Detecting conjunctions of colour and form: Re-assessing the serial search hypothesis. *Perception and Psychophysics, 41,* 191-201. Copyright 1987, The Psychonomic Society Inc.

Page 189, Fig. 5.23. Reproduced by permission of the publisher and author: Tipper, S.P. & Driver, J. (1988). Negative priming between pictures and words in a selective attention task: Evidence for semantic processing of ignored stimuli. *Memory and Cognition, 16,* 66. Copyright 1988, The Psychonomic Society Inc.

Pages 195 and 196, Figs. 6.1 and 6.2. Reproduced by permission of the publisher and author: Phillips, W.A. (1974). On the distinction between sensory storage and short term visual memory. *Perception and Psychophysics, 16,* 283-290. Copyright 1974, The Psychonomic Society Inc.

Pages 204 and 205, Figs. 6.4 and 6.5. Reproduced by permission of the publisher: Shepard, R.N. & Metzler, J. (1971). Mental rotation of three dimensional objects. *Science, 171,* 701-702. Copyright 1971 by the AAAS.

Page 207, Fig. 6.6. Reproduced from: Paivio, A. (1975). Neomentalism. *Canadian Journal of Psychology, 29,* 280.

Pages 214 and 215, Figs. 6.9 and 6.10. Adapted from: Farah, M. (1984). The neurological basis of mental imagery: A componential analysis. *Cognition, 18,* 241-269.

Pages 242 and 243, Figs. 7.2 and 7.3. Reproduced by permission of the publisher and author: McClelland, J.L. & Rumelhart, D.E. (1981). An interactive activation model of context effects in letter perception. 1. An account of basic findings. *Psychological Review, 88,* 375-407. Copyright 1981 by The American Psychological Association.

Page 248, Fig. 7.4. Reproduced by permission of the publisher and author: McClelland, J.L. (1987). In M. Coltheart (Ed.), *Attention and Performance XII,* p.7. London: Lawrence Erlbaum Associates Ltd.

Page 256, Fig. 7.5. Reproduced by permission of the publisher and author: LaBerge, D. (1983). Spatial extent of attention to letters and words. *Journal of Experimental Psychology: Human Perception and Performance, 9,* 373. Copyright 1983 by The American Psychological Association.

Page 261, Fig. 7.6. Reproduced by permission of the publisher and author: Taft, M. (1987). In M. Coltheart (Ed.), *Attention and Performance, XII,* p. 267. London: Lawrence Erlbaum Associates Ltd.

Page 268, Fig. 7.7. Reproduced by permission of the publisher and author: Treisman, A. (1986). Features and objects in visual processing. *Scientific American, November,* 114. Copyright 1986 Scientific American Inc.

Page 274, Fig. 7.8. Reproduced by permission of the publisher: Anstis, S.M. (1974). A chart demonstrating variations in acuity with retinal position. *Vision Research, 14,* 579-582. Copyright 1974, Pergamon Press, PLC.

Pages 275 and 276, Fig. 7.9 and 7.10. Reproduced by permission of the publisher and author: Rayner, K. & Pollatsek, A. (1987). In M. Coltheart (Ed.), *Attention and Performance, XII,* pp. 332; 334. London: Lawrence Erlbaum Associates Ltd.

Pages 279 and 280, Figs. 7.11 and 7.12. Reproduced by permission of the publisher and author: McConkie, G.W. & Zola, D. (1987). In M. Coltheart (Ed.), *Attention and Performance, XII,* 391-392. London: Lawrence Erlbaum Associates Ltd.

Page 283, Fig. 7.13. Reproduced by permission of the publisher and author: O'Regan, J.K. & Levy-Schoen, A. (1987). In M. Coltheart (Ed.), *Attention and Performance, XII,* p. 381. London: Lawrence Erlbaum Associates Ltd.